HOLY WARS & HOLY ALLIANCE

THE RETURN OF RELIGION TO THE GLOBAL POLITICAL STAGE

MANLIO GRAZIANO

Translated from the French by Brian Knowlton

Columbia University Press

New York

Columbia University Press
Publishers Since 1893
New York   Chichester, West Sussex
cup.columbia.edu

Library of Congress Cataloging-in-Publication Data
Names: Graziano, Manlio, 1958– author.
Title: Holy wars and holy alliance : the return of religion to the
global political stage / Manlio Graziano.
Other titles: Guerra santa e santa alleanza. English
Description: New York : Columbia University Press, 2017. | Series: Religion,
culture, and public life | Includes bibliographical references and index.
Identifiers: LCCN 2016044984 | ISBN 9780231174626 (cloth : alk. paper) |
ISBN 9780231543910 (e-book)
Subjects: LCSH: Religion and politics—History—20th century. |
Religion and politics—History—21st century. | World politics—20th century. |
World politics—21st century. | Islam and politics—History—20th century. |
Islam and politics—History—21st century. | Jihad.
Classification: LCC BL65.P7 G69313 2017 | DDC 201/.72709045—dc23
LC record available at https://lccn.loc.gov/2016044984

Columbia University Press books are printed on permanent
and durable acid-free paper.

Printed in the United States of America

Cover design: Lisa Hamm

On décrit pendant des siècles des voyages imaginaires, comme Platon décrit les îles des Bienheureux, on se croit autorisé à placer le paradis terrestre quelque part dans le monde: c'est une contrée qui a longitude et latitude, la route en est perdue mais une exploration heureuse peut faire retrouver ses coordonnées. Béatitude et joie relèvent de la géographie.

—Paul Nizan

If rationalism and secularism have taken us so far . . . then we are incapable of understanding—and consequently defending ourselves against—religious movements that reverse the Enlightenment and affect today's politics.

—Robert D. Kaplan

CONTENTS

PART III. THE HOLY WAR

PART IV. THE HOLY ALLIANCE

ACKNOWLEDGMENTS

I would like to thank all the people who contributed in some way to the work described in this book: first and foremost, the people who taught me how to make sense of political affairs, who taught me that it is possible to understand them, and to deal with them, only when we know their constraints. Furthermore, I am deeply grateful to the people who encouraged me to continue and to develop my research into the geopolitics of religions, in particular Lucio Caracciolo, Michel Korinman, Vera Negri Zamagni, and Sergio Romano. I owe a special and personal thanks to Paolo Rampini, Emmanuel Ratwitz, and Thomas van der Hallen, whose criticisms, suggestions, and corrections during the writing of these pages were extremely valuable. Last but not least, I want to express here my gratitude to all my students in Paris, Versailles, Évry, Sophia Antipolis, and Suzhou, who, with their questions, doubts, and objections, pushed me to dig even deeper into this fundamental issue of our times.

For this English version, I want first of all to thank Victoria de Grazia, who put me in contact with Columbia University Press, then Anne Routon, who enthusiastically supported my project, and all the staff of CUP, who helped me in transforming it into an actual book; then my translator and friend Brian Knowlton, who brilliantly dealt with such a complex matter and made it even more comprehensible for English speakers; Constance Cooper, whose excellent English and deep concentration made her an ideal first consumer of this book; and in particular Cullen Stewart, who did a monumental and thorough job of editing.

HOLY WARS AND
HOLY ALLIANCE

INTRODUCTION

The world today is experiencing a striking disruption of the international balance of power, perhaps as sweeping as the shift in the geopolitical axis that occurred with the arrival of the Age of Discovery in the sixteenth century. In examining these changes through the prism of international politics, this book is structured around a certainty and a hypothesis. The certainty: the forces and political forms we grew accustomed to in the twentieth century are undergoing an all-out metamorphosis. The hypothesis: some of the voids they have left are being filled by religion and religious groups.

The period from the seventeenth century to the twentieth century saw the formation and consolidation of nation-states; politics gradually abandoned its religious foundation, finding justification in itself and imbuing the state with an almost sacred character. It was the time of *secularization*.

Like all other political forms, the nation-state experienced a rise and climax and is now in decline. The principle of sovereignty, its very cornerstone, is crumbling. Many institutions that flourished along with it—a monopoly on legal violence, universal military draft, fiscal centralization, national currency, the welfare state, a monopoly on formal trade, and parliamentary democracy—are declining as well. So is secularization.

These are some of the effects of the global shift of power under way today. Disorder and uncertainty now prevail; therefore people, as well as governments, are looking for solid landmarks to help guide them through unpredictable times. For many people, religions, which existed long before the nation-state and seem uncannily able to survive it, constitute the most solid landmark.

Understandably, the more religions gain momentum and occupy space in society, the larger their role becomes on the political stage. This is why they are ever more exploited for nonreligious purposes: to win elections, mobilize people, promote disorder in a foe's camp, provide cover for legal or illegal business, find a lower-price workforce, gain influence internationally, and so on. The salient trend here is that religion serves as the passive instrument of interests that have little or no link to spirituality or religiosity.

Moreover, there is another important, albeit little-noticed, trend, to which this book devotes close attention: the case of religions that manage to escape this fate and instead promote their own goal, which is to become again a central actor in public life. Almost every religion would covet such a role. However, the centralization, global network, rooted global presence, and, above all, accumulated experience of the Roman Catholic Church make it the only religious body with the potential to achieve this goal—through the instrument of an alliance among all major world religions.

The idea that the Catholic Church might become the protagonist of a new relationship between religion and politics goes against the conventional impression of a Church in a state of crisis; one serious enough to substantially reduce its ability to influence the destiny of the world. The assumption of this book, however, is that the conventional wisdom might overlook an important feature of the evolution in international relations, leaving it helpless to anticipate future events, just as the prevailing opinion of the late 1970s was caught unprepared when faced with the drastic developments in Iran and Afghanistan.

Many scholars have written about geopolitics and many others about religion. Very few have written about the geopolitics *of* religions. This book has the ambition to do so. The events of recent decades have inspired a few texts about international politics and religion, touching on some of the concerns we discuss. However, the *geo*politics of religions deserves to be a specific and separate discipline, devoted entirely to analyzing the interplay of politics and religious trends, using a geopolitical approach.

Geopolitics provides a particular way to study international relations. As Nicholas Spykman explained in 1938, its task consists in finding, "in the enormous mass of historical material, correlations between conditioning factors and types of foreign policy."[1] Put another way, the aim of geopolitics is to study constraints that restrict, condition, and orient the will of political actors.

Some of these constraints can be measured through quantifiable factors: geography, economics, demography, military power, alliances, institutions, and leadership. However, other unmeasurable or "immaterial" factors can play a consistent, even decisive, role: history, tradition, habits, ideologies, prejudices, and, of course, religions. Any shift in the weight of each of these factors can affect the relative strength of the political actors themselves, at a national or an international level.

When a geopolitician wants to analyze the evolving relative power of contending actors, he or she has to focus on the variations in these constraints. The building of a tunnel or a dam, a shift in gross domestic product (GDP), a variation in interest rates, a notable change in fertility rates, the establishment of a new government, or a modification in military expenditure—any of these can alter the relative weight and influence of a country. The same happens, though it is far harder to discern, when ideologies and social psychologies change, and when religious feelings grow more or less prominent in a society. In this book, I try to apply the methods of geopolitics to the renewed importance of the religious factor in modern society.

Of course, changes in "immaterial" factors are less noticeable, not only because they are not scientifically quantifiable but because they usually are much slower to develop. The global financial crisis of 2008 almost immediately accelerated the shift of relative power from the older industrialized countries toward the newer emerging ones. Yet the comeback of religions to the public stage, which started in the 1970s, went almost completely unnoticed for decades. For many, it remained unnoticed until it could no longer be ignored—starting with the September 11, 2001, attacks.

From a geopolitical point of view, each constraint is a political factor. However, when religion is treated as a political factor, new problems arise. Like ideologies, but to a much greater extent, religions involve essential, and even existential, feelings and passions. Believers of whatever creed consider their faith as something "other," "different," and "above" any other aspect of their personal and social lives; for them, it is difficult to admit that religion can be studied as a political tool; some consider that disrespectful, even blasphemous.

Viewed from an exclusively political standpoint, though, certain religious and secular forms are so close as to be almost indistinguishable. Civil religions have their temples—parliaments, presidential houses, pantheons, heroes' memorials; their rites—oaths, hymns, anthems, elections, national holidays; their mass functions—parades, rallies, certain sporting events; their prophets—Founding Fathers; and their gods—Reason, Fatherland, Civilization, Race, Progress, Liberty, Democracy. Two of the most significant political parties of the twentieth century were organized, to a degree, following the model of the Catholic Church: the fascist and Stalinist. The latter sometimes explicitly admitted this imprint; its militants even had the faith, insofar they could see what nonblessed people could not, such as the Soviet Paradise, and they behaved with the same average intolerance to others as did believers of conventional religions. Another example: many of the political features of China's Cultural Revolution resembled those of Afghanistan under the sway of the Taliban. There was only one true god and one only holy text, and in both cases, male-female integration, public displays of feelings, music, songs, dance, and any other form of amusement were strictly forbidden and severely punished. The same sort of rigorous bigotry can be found in the Calvinist Republic of Geneva in the sixteenth century, as well as under France's Comité de Salut Public at the end of the eighteenth century.

In the course of history, traditional religions often acted as pure political actors and were treated accordingly; this is why any process of secularization tends to push religion into the private realm. Today, when religious bodies claim that they do not "do politics," they simply mean that they do not engage in *some* forms of politics. The Catholic Church, for example, forbids its priests, bishops, and cardinals to take part in elections; but at the same time, as Pope Francis wrote in the apostolic exhortation entitled *Evangelii Gaudium* (2013), the church "proposes in a clear way the fundamental values of human life and convictions which can then find expression in political activity."

Nevertheless, when a geopolitical scholar considers religions as political actors, he or she should give them special attention because of their uncommon political nature: their followers believe that their faith carries supernatural force, and this provides a confidence and an impetus that followers of secular political forces no longer possess. Thus the superior motivation of religious actors should not be ignored or underestimated.

Holy Wars and Holy Alliance: The Return of Religion to the Global Political Stage is organized in four parts. Part 1 is devoted to the complex and paradoxical relationship between "modernity" and secularization; in fact, the former has determined the latter but also its opposite: desecularization.

During the long period when nation-states were forming and consolidating, the trend to secularization seemed irreversible. When it reached its climax—from the late nineteenth century through the first two-thirds of the twentieth century—the large majority of intellectuals considered religion as anachronistic, an obstacle to progress, even a psychological disorder; some went so far as to assume its inevitable demise.

After World War II, the freshly decolonized countries seemed to prove them right. Their new ruling classes, anxious not to upset the social balance from which they originated, had no trouble persuading themselves that the superiority of the "advanced" countries lay in their ideas and institutions; they hoped to reach modernity by simply adopting both. Among their key measures were the confiscation of clerical properties and the relegation of religion to the private sphere. From Italy to Mexico and from Iran to Spain, examples of countries that had already followed this pattern are legion, the most famous and the most accomplished of all being Mustafa Kemal Ataturk's Republic of Turkey.

In the 1950s, and especially in the 1960s, the incompatibility of religion and politics was taken for granted. In these decades, the popularity of the state as a major economic player and provider of jobs, social services, and security reached its peak. It was now the state that seemed able to fulfill prayers that in previous generations had been addressed to gods.

Things began changing in the 1970s, when two different and opposite processes revealed the dark side of modernity: in the so-called Third World, the very rapid process of industrialization disrupted, in just a few years, a social balance that had prevailed for centuries; and in the advanced world, industrial society failed to keep its promises of continuous improvement of living standards. The "crisis of modernity"—although experienced very differently in the developed and developing world—restored to all religions the role of anchor of solace and consolation whenever exclusively human solutions reveal their limits.

Part 2 examines specific cases where religion and politics started to converge: Indonesia, Egypt, Israel, India, Pakistan, Sri Lanka, Myanmar, and the United States. However, since the conventional wisdom was that religion was vanishing as an overarching force in society, nobody recognized the common thread running through these very distinct societies. In two other cases—Iran and Afghanistan—the lack of theoretical tools would lead to especially weighty and long-lasting consequences.

In 1978 Iranian liberals, democrats and leftists played the ayatollahs' game until the end, under the illusion of being able to replace them when the time came. Underestimating the religious factor in the uprising against the shah of Iran also led the United States and the Soviet Union to make fatal miscalculations whose consequences still influence the dynamics of international relations as a whole in the present.

Another case of misinterpretation, but this time with a tint of imperial arrogance, was at the origin of the proxy war that the United States and the Soviet Union fought against each other in Afghanistan. In 1978 Moscow fomented a coup in Kabul without sufficiently considering the mullahs' capacity to respond and mobilize. Conversely, Washington unreservedly solicited and supported jihad against the Soviets and their Afghan allies, confident in its capability to direct and control this foreign policy instrument if and when necessary. The American government's enthusiastic promotion of jihad proved to be a fatal error of perspective reminiscent of Pakistan's support for the Taliban starting in 1994, or even of Israel's support of the Palestinian Muslim Brotherhood in an effort to weaken the Palestine Liberation Organization after the Six-Day War in 1967.

In 1978 another major event of a religious nature would have an impact that continues to the present: the election of Karol Wojtyła to head the Catholic Church as Pope John Paul II. Many observers would credit him a posteriori with having played a significant role in the fall of the Berlin Wall. In reality, the turnaround that the Polish pope imposed on the church after its post–Second Vatican Council crisis has left a far deeper mark on the global political landscape, with consequences that could reshape the relationship between politics and religion in the twenty-first century and beyond.

Part 3 is devoted to proving the main weakness of the theory most commonly associated with Samuel Huntington's central thesis in his tome *The Clash of Civilizations and the Remaking of World Order* (1996). Huntington's narrative, with the well-defined boundaries it posits between different civilizations, met a need for simple and direct ideas of the sort that are urgent in times of confusion or crisis. The weakness of this thesis, so clear and so easily recognizable in these civilizations with their well-defined boundaries, is that it simply does not correspond to reality, past or present.

Following the period that witnessed the collapse of the Soviet Union, the rise of Japan, and the birth of the European Union, the United States launched a series of military operations in an attempt to restore a favorable international balance of power. The September 11 attacks were seen as the opportunity to refine this option with the onset of the so-called Global War on Terror, which appeared, in the eyes of many, to be a global war against Islam.

This confrontational representation of the relationship between Islam and the "West"—each perceiving itself as victim of the other's aggression—found its intellectual basis in the theory of a possible "clash of civilizations." After the Cold War, the next global conflict was projected to be fought between an alliance of "Islamic civilization" and "Sinic [Chinese] civilization" against "Western civilization" or "Western Christianity"—which are presented as synonyms by Huntington and other prominent writers sympathetic to his thesis.

In the wake of the 9/11 attacks and the subsequent American-led occupations of Afghanistan and Iraq, this theory has become very popular, and the relationship between religion and politics has been seen almost exclusively in terms of the connection between Islam and politics. There has been a sudden eruption in the number of self-appointed experts on Islam, and previously little known words, such as *jihad* and *sharia*, have entered everyday language—even if they are given the most disparate meanings. A long series of alleged features of Islam have become almost axiomatic, for both Muslim fundamentalists and the fiercest opponents of Islam: its lack of distinction between faith and politics; its inherent violence and subjugation of women; its authoritarian inclinations; its reactionary and obscurantist character; its sly design to conquer and dominate the world—starting with the citadels of a declining Europe and concluding with its proliferation through use of the "demographic weapon."

These ideas are so tenacious because, in politics, it is easier to retain what is noisy, stunning, and fierce. This is what helps sell newspapers in normal times, what helps collect votes at election time, and what helps mobilize the masses in times of war. Ideologies eventually become an essential part of reality. In the years that followed the 9/11 attacks, Islam—or at least this particular representation of Islam—helped to sell newspapers, collect votes, and even fight wars. What it has not done is help the global comprehension of political relations; quite the contrary. Seen through this distorting lens, phenomena such as international migration; riotous ghettos; the wars in Iraq, in Syria, in Afghanistan, and throughout Africa; the failure of the "Arab Spring"; the new roles of Turkey and Qatar; the ayatollahs' Iran; as well as some forms of terrorism are all reduced to a common denominator of an Islam hostile—or resistant—to supposed "Western values."

These ideas have not helped us to see that among the followers of all religions in almost every country, it is possible to find advocates of bigotry and holy war, as well as a common aspiration to religious law. If, for most Muslims around the world, sharia means a craving for more justice, then every faith community, "from the Amish to the Zoroastrians, has equivalent ways of doing right by God."[2]

Part 4 focuses on the hypothesis of a "holy alliance" among the most important faiths in the world, with the aim of making them the next primary ethical broker of modern—supposedly, "postsecularized"—societies.[3] If the 9/11 attacks provided arguments for anyone seeking to take sides in an already declared *war* among civilizations, they also provided grist for those believing that the best way to counter this clash was through an *alliance* among civilizations. The supporters of the alliance think in positive terms, in terms of addition, whereas the supporters of the clash think in negative terms, in terms of subtraction. Yet both share the belief that the world is divided by civilizational fault lines, and also, more or less explicitly, the belief that religions ultimately form the very heart of every civilization and thus define the alleged fault lines.

Those who would assemble a "holy alliance" to oppose the "holy war" form a very heterogeneous group. In general terms, their stated goal is to prevent conflicts by focusing on the aspects that bring civilizations closer together and by leaving in the shadows aspects that separate and oppose them. Their initiatives have a defensive, or at least derivative, nature: if the hypothesis of a clash of civilizations had not been made, or if the 9/11 attacks had not occurred, these initiatives might well not exist.

From a geopolitical point of view, those taking the offensive in regard to this proposed alliance of civilizations are far more significant in spirit and in behavior than their defensive counterparts. For them, the conflicts of this world are the result not of an excess of religion but rather of a lack of it, and the more religion is able to guide important political choices, the more these choices will be oriented toward justice and peace. These people believe that religions have both the right and the duty to inspire and illuminate politics.

If, amid the supporters of the alliance among civilizations, there are exponents of all faiths, not all faiths have the same attitude vis-à-vis this goal. Religions without formal hierarchical structure—such as Islam, Judaism, or Hinduism—obviously do not have a sole position, either in this case or in others. Religions that have a plurality of hierarchical structures—such as Orthodox Christianity, Anglicanism, and Buddhism—have as many positions, or shades, as hierarchies. As to Protestantism, it is a quite indefinite and indefinable galaxy, in which one can find everything and its opposite, from the literalist fundamentalism to the radical liberalism.

The only religious body capable of promoting a joint action of all faiths worldwide is the Roman Catholic Church. Besides its specific and unique assets mentioned above—a hierarchical organization, which is both the oldest and the vastest in the world—the Church of Rome is the only religious body that is able to think globally, and therefore to have a global strategy for its expansion.

This does not mean that the church and its strategy do not face internal divergences and external interference. Nonetheless, if the difficulties that the church meets on its way are essentially the same as those facing any other human institution, its ability to overcome them, thanks to its deep experience and extensive organization, is incomparably superior.

The proposition of an alliance of world religions emerged very slowly within the church until the aftermath of World War II; it became topical only in the era of decolonization. The dismantling of colonial empires had in fact put an end forever to the traditional ways in which religions expanded, through conquest and conversion. A half-century ago, the

Second Vatican Council formalized this new way of reaching "the ends of the Earth" by way of a "holy alliance" with other religions: structures were put in place and contacts were made to implement this project.

—⊶⊷—

The church's wish to draw closer to other world religions, though, is only the *subjective* side of this alliance. The transformation of international relations that began in the 1970s has provided this strategy with its *objective* basis.

Beginning in the 1970s, religions again began to offer a sense of belonging, of collective strength. The insistence on the wearing of distinctive signs—the yarmulke, the veil, the jalabiya, the turban, and so on—is the exterior sign of this quest for identity. The hypothesis of an alliance among civilizations—or a "holy alliance" among the major religions under the de facto control of the church—provides to this quest for identity an institutional framework as well as a political prospect.

In the current era of historic epochal transition, the "Western model," to the extent it ever existed, is called into question, including its presumption of the excellence of parliamentary democracy. Its limits are increasingly obvious, especially in Europe, and other forms of representation of interests and social strata are challenging it on its own ground.

At the end of the eighteenth century, the Persian traveler Mirza Abu Taleb Khan, who had gone to London, was flabbergasted to see that the English, lacking a revealed divine law, were forced to submit their most important decisions to the whims of the majority.[4] The church has never renounced the claim of the superiority of divine law over human law, and international politics seems today to have rewarded its perseverance: the risks that a majority could be persuaded to choose the "evil" over the "good" may indeed be as similar today as they were in Germany in 1933—one need only consider the possible electoral consequences of a rupture of the "generational compromise" in any major country, or the emergence of xenophobic and nationalist majorities in Europe, the United States, China, and Japan.

—⊶⊷—

Religions already play a much broader role on the public stage than they did a decade ago. It is possible, even likely, that this role will increase in the future.

Whatever happens in the future, though, religions are not, and will not be, the focus of political relations. But they will certainly be used in conflicts, and the more organized of them will try to exploit the conflicts to increase their weight and influence. Therefore it will be increasingly important to distinguish between instigators and perpetrators, and avoid any confusion that might only exacerbate these conflicts.

PART I

MODERNITY AND RELIGION

The Church can in fact be modern by being anti-modern.

—Joseph Ratzinger

1
THE DEATH OF GOD

THE DISENCHANTMENT OF THE WORLD

Late in the last century, a world-renowned sociologist of religion did some-thing few intellectuals have had the courage to do: he admitted he had been mistaken. In the 1950s and 1960s, the sociologist in question, Peter Berger, had helped develop the so-called *secularization theory*, according to which "modernization necessarily leads to a decline of religion, both in society and in the minds of individuals."[1] But by the end of the 1990s, Berger himself was rethinking the absolute character of this thesis, and very significantly qualifying it: "To be sure modernization has had some secularizing effects, more in some places than in others. But it has also provoked powerful movements of counter-secularization."[2]

To better understand the importance of this modification, it might be useful to be aware of its terminology. For sociologists, "modernization" is the stage of development characterized by industrialization and urbaniza-tion. In the 1950s and 1960s, "modernization" seemed for most intellectu-als to point in a single direction: toward progress. After the miseries of war came reconstruction, then the "economic miracles," monetary stability, full employment, the beginning of mass consumption and education, free or partially free social services; in short, the conviction took root that the standard of living was going to continue improving, constantly and indefi-nitely, one generation after another.

Of course, things were not really so idyllic: the rapid accumulation of goods and capital created, as it always does, ever greater gaps in wealth; the rural flight gave rise to the phenomena of marginalization and hyper-exploitation in industrialized cities, and certain countries—notably the United States, France, and Britain—were still involved in armed conflicts in different regions of the world. Those factors notwithstanding, the optimists' depiction of a constant trend toward progress endured, for the newly produced wealth was so abundant that it seemed to absorb and erase any and all "flaws" in the system. For the conscript who was no longer sent to the front; for the peasant turned stable city dweller; for the poor wretch who had made the transition, in only a few years, from a battered pair of shoes to a bicycle, then a moped, and, finally, to an automobile; for all those people, the change in their own lot constituted added proof that all was for the best in the best of all possible worlds.

And reigning without challenge over this sense of well-being was the state. With its multiple prerogatives and responsibilities, it seemed all-powerful, able henceforth to guarantee its citizens' existence "from cradle to grave," to borrow the famous slogan of the European welfare state. The totality of the life cycle of individuals, once the domain of the gods, was now in the hands of the state.

This was the result of a process of social psychology that Max Weber, in the 1910s, had called the "disenchantment of the world": the mystical interpretation of a phenomenon is abandoned the moment that it can be explained scientifically.[3] Similarly, the attempt to resolve a problem, any problem, by resort to celestial assistance is abandoned the moment the problem can be resolved through earthly means.

Sociologists—and with them the majority of intellectuals—lived and wrote in the great modern cities, so it is understandable that they would be inclined to give a theoretical spin to this triumphant march toward progress, of which they had been the privileged witnesses. They knew, of course, that things were evolving differently outside the industrialized world, but a large number of them viewed progress in teleological terms, that is, as an inescapable destiny to which, eventually, all would submit.

Therefore, in their view, the disenchantment of the world seemed certain to follow the same fatal path. Destined to lose its social function, religion was bound to fade and finally die (or, possibly, survive but only in the form of a pathology). At the culminating moment of this period, and of this concept, *Time* magazine published one of its most famous cover stories, introduced by the provocative question, "Is God Dead?"[4]

RELIGIOUS CAPITALISM

To understand secularization in its historic context, one must examine the origins of the society that produced it, which is to say capitalist society. The history of secularization intersects with that of capitalism and is characterized by the hostility between the bourgeoisie and clerical institutions. In the beginning, religion itself was not in question. To the contrary, in societies profoundly imbued with piety and spirituality, the earliest manifestations of capitalism took on the aspect of religious revolutions.

Several specialists have noted that the Muslim revolution of the seventh century had "semicapitalist" or "protocapitalist" characteristics, "disproving the too facile belief that these were invented later by Italians."[5] As Marshall Hodgson put it, a "new ethical and historical God" appeared in the Hejaz region when the polytheistic merchants of Mecca, softened and corrupted by the enormous inflow of riches that suddenly fell into their hands following the Byzantine-Sassanid War of 602–628, risked compromising the activities of their colleagues throughout the peninsula. In the early days of Islam, Hodgson affirms, the market was as much a part of life as the desert.[6]

A monetary economy, systems of credit and payment, and mercantile associations were economic mechanisms with which the Arab traders of the seventh century were already familiar: Italy indeed did not invent them but adopted them to the point of becoming the hotbed from which commercial capitalism radiated outward. This evolution led to the organization and autonomous control of the "burgs"—the source of the word "bourgeois"—under the political form of communes, in opposition to both the Catholic Church and the Holy Roman Empire.

Everywhere that communes were established—in Italy, Provence, and Flanders—Christian reform movements rose up: the Patarini, Cathars, Waldensians, Humiliati, Beghards, or simply those individuals who, in the name of religion, took a stand against the church, such as Arnold of Brescia or Fra Dolcino. Only with the greatest political skill was Pope Innocent III able to transform one of these inspired reformers, Giovanni, the son of the rich Umbrian merchant Pietro Bernadone and of a noblewoman from Provence, into a formidable asset for the church, and finally into one of the most venerated saints in the Catholic world, Francis of Assisi.

The succeeding step is surely one of the best known, almost proverbially associated with the birth of capitalism: the Protestant Reformation. It was in the sixteenth century, a turning point during which the geopolitical axis of the world shifted from the Mediterranean Sea to the Atlantic and Indian Oceans. Those powers that remained confined in the Mediterranean—the Italian states and the Ottoman Empire—began their decline, and the two religions that had their territorial base in this region—Catholicism and Islam—were powerfully affected.

As with Islam in the seventh century, the movement launched by Martin Luther in 1517 encountered—and gained momentum from—a series of favorable historic developments, of which it also became the instrument: the struggle of the German princes among themselves and against the emperor; the encirclement of the Germanic empire by the French, to the west, and France's Turkish allies, to the southeast; and the disarray of the church itself in the face of a war in which the pope was no longer able to impose his will. If Luther—excommunicated and banned by the empire—had not benefited from the protection of certain German princes against Emperor Charles V and the rival princes, it is highly probable that he would have ended up like most "reformers" before him, and his movement would have died with him.

In sixteenth-century Europe, however, the German princes were not the only ones interested in profiting from this schism with the Church of Rome. There was also the new social class, which had gained in importance and ambition since the Middle Ages, and which would gain much more thanks to the new oceangoing trade routes: the bourgeoisie. The bourgeoisie wanted to save on paying "unproductive" taxes and to return to general circulation the "frozen" assets that were part of the nontransferable properties of the clergy. This placed the bourgeoisie in a state of open hostility vis-à-vis the church across the continent and beyond. Yet, in an era that was still profoundly religious, the bourgeoisie also needed a moral endorsement for the principles of profit and prosperity, denied by a church whose history was still entangled with that of feudalism.

These highly dynamic social groups needed a new political form to protect and support their interests, first by centralizing the armed militias and tax collection. Once again, the weight of tradition meant these new political forms—the modern states—had to draw their legitimacy from religious institutions. Those that remained formally under the auspices of the church—Spain, France, and later Austria—relied on a clergy that was more sensitive to the interests of the nation than to those of Rome. The other modern states—Sweden at first, then Denmark, Iceland, Norway, England, the city-state of Geneva, the Netherlands, as well as the reformed German principalities—simply gave birth to new established "state churches." Whether Catholic or Protestant in configuration, the trend was toward a nationalization of religion, and to a subordination of the interests of the religious authority to the interests of the political authority.

ANTIRELIGIOUS CAPITALISM

The formalization of the principle of national sovereignty, considered a cornerstone of the modern state, followed a violent upheaval in Europe's geopolitical balance during the period known as the "wars of religion." The Peace of Westphalia of 1648, which put an end to these conflicts, was based on a commitment undertaken earlier, in 1555, at the time of the Peace of Augsburg: *cuius regio eius religio* (whose realm, his religion). This principle recognizes the absolute right of each ruler to govern his own territory, and, reciprocally, the duty of noninterference in the affairs of other states: the ruler is allowed to impose his religion—and any other of his desires— on his subjects, and other states must not interfere.

As paradoxical as it might seem, this principle, which plainly drew its authority from religion, also marked the start of the decline in influence of organized religions over political life. Indeed, the growth of the sovereign prerogatives of the absolute state led to a political weakening of the clergy. There are two fundamental reasons for this. First, the religions in question—essentially, Catholicism, Lutheranism, and Calvinism—existed in several different states and were thus not clad in the distinctive character that each state needs to differentiate itself from others—a ruling dynasty, language, flag, national anthem, and so on. Second, a ruler is absolute only insofar as he does not share his authority with anyone else, and certainly not with the once-powerful clergy; this is even truer when the clergy maintains privileged links to a major foreign power, like the Papal States.

Thus the church is either pushed out of power or else associated with it but in a subordinate position, as with the established state churches in the Nordic countries and England, or Gallicanism in France, and later Josephinism in Austria.[7]

The Renaissance, Reformation, and wars of religion left fertile ground for a new conception of the world, the ancestor of the twentieth-century "secularization theory": certain avant-garde intellectuals no longer limited themselves to attacking the powers and roles of the various churches; they began to undermine the very foundations of the religious principle. This movement began by creating a philosophical framework for the scientific discoveries of the sixteenth and seventeenth centuries, notably those of Copernicus, Kepler, and Galileo. Descartes, Hobbes, and Bacon—and then Locke, Spinoza, Hume, Bayle, and Fontenelle—opened the way for a current of thought that, in the following century, undertook the most radical criticism yet of religion: the Enlightenment.

If the Peace of Westphalia eliminated religious issues from the confrontations between powers, the separation between politics and religion in the internal affairs of individual states proved more challenging. In the Middle Ages, the ruler's legitimacy was based on divine right, with the church as guarantor. Once the church had submitted to a ruler's absolute authority, he—paradoxically—needed an even more powerful god than before, since he now lacked support from outside and above. The survival of the absolute monarch and of his national religion thus became inextricably linked. This situation led to a merciless struggle between, on the one hand, the ruler and his religion, and, on the other, the emerging bourgeoisie, which directly contested absolute power, with all its trappings and justifications.[8] A long and turbulent transition was necessary before monarchs felt compelled to accept both the authority of the law (liberalism) and the "will of the nation" (democracy). This transition period would last roughly one hundred years—from the end of the eighteenth century to the beginning of the twentieth century—before the political model of the "nation-state" was finally fully realized. As a result of this transition, in the words of Joseph Ratzinger, "the sacred foundation for history and for the existence of the state was rejected . . . the divine guarantee and the divine ordering of the political sector is abandoned and set aside."[9]

From that point forward, the state had to find its own source of legitimacy within itself. To do this, it adopted a "civil religion," to which all its subjects were to submit, regardless of their tastes or inclinations. This new religion was given substance by sacralizing everything the state represents within its national territory: its borders became sacred and "intangible," its rulers or leaders became "untouchable" or even "not responsible," its laws were engraved in constitutions, and insults to its flag, its sacred symbols, or its military were severely punished. The state endowed itself with a national mythology, places of "worship," collective ceremonies, saints and prophets, as well as with veritable new, positive divinities with names like Fatherland, Reason, Progress, and so on.

Again, state prerogatives grew in direct proportion to the shrinking of the prerogatives of religions. From the beginning of the nineteenth century to the early twentieth century, the state steadily grew more confident in its role. For G. W. F. Hegel, writing in 1820, it was "ethical substance that is conscious of itself."[10] For the Rudolf Kjellén—who coined the term *geopolitics*—writing a century later, the state was a "living form," a "geographic organism or phenomenon in space."[11] Intellectuals were merely describing and offering a theoretical justification for a change that was taking place before their eyes: the formation of the almighty state.

The state, which had developed over the four centuries beginning with the Peace of Westphalia, reached the apogee of its omnipotence in the industrialized countries during the three decades following World War II. At that time, in addition to the external forms of religions—their laws, rites, mythologies, and celebrations—the state importantly took on their social function, watching over the well-being of individuals "from cradle to grave." It is no accident that, in French, welfare state was given the highly evocative name of the *État-providence*.

Yet this absolute power of the state did not flow from its own qualities or capacities: it was rather a sort of secondary power, an effect of the total economic domination of the world by a very small group of powers, and for a very short period of history.

2
THE RETURN OF GOD

AN ILLUSION WITHOUT A FUTURE

The modern state is sovereign to the extent that it has the exclusive right to exercise its political, judiciary, fiscal, and military authority within a given geographic area. According to Max Weber, its essential characteristic as a political entity is its *Gewaltmonopol*: its monopoly over the exercise of legitimate physical force within its territory.

The monopoly on the use of force, however, is but a single result of the process that rendered the state all-powerful, not its cause or its origin. Its origins are found elsewhere, in the unparalleled productivity of industrial capitalism, for which the nation-state provides the institutional framework. Cheaply produced goods became the lever that could be used to lift—and conquer—the world. As Fernand Braudel wrote in 1963, "There will soon be nowhere in the world that has not been 'contaminated' by the industrial civilization that originated in Europe."[1]

In the first decades after World War II, a small group of industrialized powers appeared all-powerful for two key reasons: the first—a structural factor—is that these countries enjoyed near exclusive domination over global markets; and the second—tied to circumstances—is that these states, in addition to their political and administrative functions, had directly assumed the role of first-order economic actors, and in some sectors the exclusive actors.

The Wall Street crash of 1929 sharply accelerated a trend toward direct involvement of the state in the management of the economy, a trend that had begun in the second half of the nineteenth century. After World War II, with the elimination of two strategic competitors as important as Germany and Japan, the industrialized capitalist states were free to display their "liberal" faces, in both senses of this word: in the economic sense, by relaxing the strict protectionist controls that had contributed to the conflict; and, in its common sense, by providing particularly generous benefits to their citizens through social services, massive state employment, leisure-time activities, and escalating salaries.

But the state as entrepreneur/protector/benefactor was only a *temporary* expression of the *temporary* economic dominance of this relatively small group of countries. The confusion between the economic domination of the world by these countries (cause) and the all-powerful nature of their states (effect) explains the nostalgia of the new Keynesians. They contend that the state today should commit a share of its resources to restimulating consumption and reenergizing the productive machine, as was widely done in the latter half of the Great Depression. However, this policy framework misses an important point. In 1933, when Franklin D. Roosevelt was first elected president, the U.S. federal government debt represented 20 percent of the country's GDP, rising to 40 percent by 1936.[2] Comparatively, in 2013 America's total federal debt as a percentage of GDP reached 96 percent.[3] In the present era the doubling of the national debt to stimulate economic growth during a recession is not nearly as feasible an undertaking as it was during Roosevelt's first term.

In 2013 Stephen D. King, the chief economist at banking giant HSBC, published a book whose title minces no words: *When the Money Runs Out: The End of Western Affluence*. In the book King wrote that "this sense of ever-rising income turns out to have been no more than an illusion humming with quasi-religious fervor."[4] Such "faith," he continued, is open to the same criticism that Sigmund Freud applied to religious belief: "We call a belief an illusion when wish-fulfillment is a prominent factor in its motivation, while disregarding its relations to reality, just as the illusion does."[5]

In his 1983 work on nations and nationalism, Ernest Gellner employed similar language to note how the affirmation of industrial capitalism came almost simultaneously with the invention of the "concept and the ideal of progress." This simultaneity stemmed from the fact that "industrial society is the only society ever to live by and rely on sustained and per-petual growth, on an expected and continuous improvement. Its greatest weakness is its inability to . . . weather the loss of legitimacy which befalls it if the cornucopia becomes temporarily jammed and the flow falters."[6] If the "wish fulfillment" proves manifestly and definitively impossible, illusion gives way to disillusion, belief fails, and faith becomes skepticism. If there is no way to concretely fulfill the wish, a new illusion—preferably more solid than the previous one—becomes necessary and urgent.

FROM A RELIGION OF PROGRESS TO THE PROGRESS OF RELIGION

Peter Berger, explaining why modernization also provokes "powerful movements of counter-secularization," wrote in 1999 that "modernity, for fully understandable reasons, undermines all the old certainties; uncer-tainty, in turn, is a condition that many people find very hard to bear; therefore, any movement (not only a religious one) that promises to pro-vide or to renew certainty has a ready market."[7]

In the 1990s the connection between social uncertainty and the return of religions was not yet widely understood. The difficulty in discerning this connection lay largely, in King's words, in "our attachment to the Enlightenment idea of ongoing progress," which has remained, despite everything, "a reflection of persistent post-war economic success." More-over, this attachment "has left us with little knowledge or understanding of worlds in which rising prosperity is no longer guaranteed."[8]

What happens regularly in industrial societies is that "the cornucopia becomes temporarily jammed and the flow falters" when a crisis strikes. This can be a cyclical crisis, such as those of 1929 and 2008, or it can be a lasting one, determined by a global shift in the balance of power, such as the old industrialized powers have been experiencing since the 1970s. Cyclical crises can graft themselves onto longer-lasting crises and thereby accelerate them. That is what has been happening since 2008, and it is what lies behind "the end of Western affluence."

During the post–World War II period of economic success, the pos-sibility that Western affluence might ever end was barely considered. Faith in progress, in the almighty state, and, more or less explicitly, in the superiority of "Western civilization" had led many intellectuals in the developed world to adopt the viewpoint of Pangloss, Candide's teacher in the celebrated story by Voltaire: evil, in the form of crises, exists, but its function is to provide a challenge on the road toward achieving an infinitely greater good, namely, well-being.

In 1843 Karl Marx wrote that "the wretchedness of religion is at once an expression of and a protest against real wretchedness."[9] During *Les Trente Glorieuses* the illusion that "real wretchedness" could be eliminated led to the illusion that the end of "wretchedness of religion" was near.[10] Marx lambasted the Young Hegelians' critique of religion, which in a way anticipated *secularization theory*. Marx argued that it was not philosophy that could weaken religion, for religion was the product of "this state, [and of] this society"; therefore, so long as this society and its state exist, religion will exist as well, for it represents "the sigh of the oppressed creature, the heart of a heartless world, and the soul of soulless conditions."[11]

Marx drew this conclusion from his observations of a society that, he said, "has left remaining no other nexus between man and man than naked self-interest" and "has resolved personal worth into exchange value."[12] Marx's views on religion were not especially Marxist: they were shared by other thinkers of differing sensibilities who, like him, cast a cold and unbiased eye on the society of their day. According to Benedetto Croce, for example, the liberal bourgeoisie, once it had come to power, gave up its opposition to religion, "in the renunciation it made of, and even in the repugnance it felt towards, the continuance of the warfare that had been waged during the preceding centuries" against it, and it renounced this course because "the old faith was still a way, a mythological one if you will, to soothe and calm suffering and sorrows."[13]

Croce identified another element that cannot be ignored if we are to understand the present-day return of religion into public affairs. He asserted that to pursue this war would have been a "not very politic" choice, because "those beliefs and the consolation derived from them and their teachings were the basis, for many men, of the formula and the authority of social duties, and gave rise to foundations and institutions of social welfare and charity, and motives of order and discipline."[14]

This notion of "motives of order and discipline" recalls a well-known Augustinian argument: that of religion as *tranquillitas ordinis* (tranquility of order). Interestingly, this concept received a backhanded endorsement from one of the most virulent enemies of positive religion, Voltaire, who clearly knew as a member of the bourgeois where his interest lay: "I want my lawyer, tailor, valets, even my wife, to believe in God. I think that if they do I shall be robbed less and cheated less."[15]

Croce's reference to "foundations and institutions of social welfare and charity" clearly alludes to the role of religious groups and institutions in organizing the direct management of social services—education, health, leisure, welcoming, care of the needy, and retirement—in part through charity work. This role has been drastically eroded by the growth of the public welfare state, but it has not been eliminated, because it constitutes a social life buoy of inestimable value in those moments when "the cornucopia becomes temporarily jammed and the flow falters." This role partly explains the success of religious movements in countries where the attempt to constitute a nation-state has failed miserably, and it also explains the growing specific gravity of religions and churches in countries struggling with crushing debt burdens and budgetary restrictions.

In short, the reflected glare of "persistent postwar economic success" long obscured the fact that *modernity carries elements of both secularization and desecularization* within it. For modernity is a concrete example of dialectical unity of opposites that Hegel so loved: it brings well-being, longer life expectancy, improved health care, and the education of the masses, but it also leads to a loss of traditional values, the dissolution of family bonds, colossal waste, economic crises, unemployment, and, finally, war. The illusions that modernity creates one day, it destroys the next.

THE ENFEEBLEMENT OF THE NATION-STATE

The process of the formation of the nation-state progressively pushed religion out of public life. Today, as the role and prerogatives of the Westphalian nation-state are called into question, religions are returning to the public space. This does not mean the two processes are inversely proportional, if only because their respective courses are neither linear nor exclusively unidirectional, but it is also difficult to believe that this represents a simple coincidence.

Many academics and analysts consider the fall of the Berlin Wall as marking the end of the Westphalian era of international relations.

The reality is more complex: in a world characterized by uneven economic and political development, phenomena of devolution of national sovereignty exist even as some new states aspire to sovereignty, and as others attempt to force a national homogenization in order to complete, in just a few years, the path that the old nation-states took centuries to cover.

The fall of the Berlin Wall is but one step in a process of the weakening of the nation-state that stretched out over at least a century, and which first manifested itself in the same years that the nation-state was finally coming fully into form at the end of the nineteenth century.

During that period, the developed world was transformed by a series of economic, social, political, and technological innovations, often referred to as the "first wave of globalization": the rise of industrialism, the globe-spanning spread of colonial enterprises, the reduction of tariff barriers, the increase of direct foreign investment and international capital flows, as well as a general shortening of geographic distances owing to the development of means of transcontinental communication and travel and the opening of the Suez and Panama canals.

All these phenomena, notably the expansion of international financial activities and foreign trade, created multiple opportunities for mutual interference and provided a severe test of the impermeability and autonomy of sovereign states. However, it was quite possibly another major event, in the early 1890s, that finally catalyzed all these transformations and put in place the conditions for a gradual exit from the Westphalian system: the United States—a country that, for obvious reasons, was a stranger to both the spirit and letter of the Westphalian Peace—became the world's leading industrial and economic power.

In a series of texts whose common thread is "the end of the era of the nation," Carl Schmitt argues that the United States, by imposing, in 1919, the creation of the League of Nations, had replaced the principle of equilibrium among sovereign states that emanated from the Peace of Westphalia with a cosmopolitanism based on *die Tyrannei der Werte* (the tyranny of values). This latter notion hid, under a cloak of hypocrisy, a desire for absolute power, he said: "Nobody can valuate without devaluating, revaluating, and serving one's interests. Whoever sets a value, takes position against a disvalue by that very action. The boundless tolerance and the neutrality of the standpoints and viewpoints turn themselves very quickly into their opposite, into enmity, as soon as the enforcement is carried out in earnest."[16] In the Westphalian order, Schmitt says, enemies fought one another, but on an equal basis under the laws of the system, each recognizing the right of the other to do so; in the new "moral" order, the goal of war becomes the total destruction of the enemy, who is denied "the quality of being human and [declared] an outlaw of humanity." For Schmitt, the purpose is clear: "The concept of humanity is an especially useful ideological instrument of imperialist expansion, and in its ethical-humanitarian form it is a specific vehicle of economic imperialism."[17]

After World War II, with the Nuremberg trials and the creation of the United Nations, this trend became ever more manifest, all the more so because it was accompanied by the birth of a sort of "world government" endowed with institutions—not just the UN, but also the International Monetary Fund, the World Bank, and the General Agreement on Tariffs and Trade (GATT)—and international laws and courts that countries were expected to respect. Moreover, the invention of missiles and other technological vectors capable of transporting weapons of mass destruction far beyond national borders reduced the strategic importance of those borders. All those factors weakened the principle of the inviolability of national sovereignty, wounding the sacred character of the state.

This new supranational order was organized in such a way as to perpetuate for as long as possible the absolute global supremacy that the United States had gained in the wake of the two world wars. But the notion of supranational order was not an American invention. The first initiative to attempt to lay the bases of it came from Russia, another power that was a stranger to the Westphalian system. In 1899, at the initiative of Czar Nicholas II, an international conference convened in The Hague led to the creation of the Permanent Court of Arbitration, thus opening the era of what would later be called "international humanitarian law."

The long collaboration between the United States and the Soviet Union after World War II provides yet another proof of the common Russian-American interest in replacing the *jus publicum europæum* with a foreign policy imbued with missionary and "internationalist" connotations.[18] The "Yalta system" is a sort of caricature of the Westphalian system, to the extent that Washington and Moscow mutually recognize the principle of *cuius regio eius religio* but apply it not only to their own countries but to their entire spheres of influence, and at the same time they exclude the rest of the world from it.

The Yalta system ended with the collapse of the Soviet Union in the early 1990s. However, the new era of international relations had in reality begun some fifteen years earlier, when the economic crisis of 1973–1975 brought to light the emergence of a group of newly industrialized countries and prompted the opening of a new cycle of global free trade.

To summarize the effects of this cycle, recall that, from the early 1980s to the beginning of the twenty-first century, global production rose by over one and a half times, trade by a factor of three, and foreign direct investments by nearly five times. Thus the combination of this new wave of globalization and the end of the postwar political-military order gave rise to a series of phenomena linked by two common traits: the weakening of state sovereignty and a parallel strengthening of suprastate and interstate institutions, in particular institutions of regulation and "governance" such as the IMF, the Group of 20, and, in the specific case of Europe, the European Central Bank.

Notably, after the fall of the Berlin Wall, the number of regional groupings multiplied—the European Union, the North American Free Trade Agreement, Mercosur, the Association of Southeast Asian Nations, and so on—and international peacekeeping proliferated—seventeen missions between 1956 and 1989 compared to fifty-one missions between 1989 and 2010. This period also witnessed the birth of "humanitarian wars," which sometimes led to certain regions becoming, effectively, protectorates. Humanitarian wars led to the creation of ad hoc international criminal courts—for the former Yugoslavia, Rwanda, Sierra Leone, Lebanon—as well as a standing International Criminal Court in 1992. Finally, nonstate actors took on an ever more important role beyond their stated missions: international nongovernmental organizations and humanitarian groups proliferated—the UN recognizes 3,400 of them, but in 2001 as many as 40,000 were counted—diasporas spread; criminal and terrorist networks gained prominence; and, naturally, religions saw a heightened profile.

The European case, with certain countries voluntarily ceding a degree of sovereignty to a superior entity, obviously constitutes a special case. On the one hand, this process represents the most advanced expression of the dissolution of the Westphalian sovereign state; on the other, it progressively gives birth to a political/juridical entity of original character, which has no place in the traditional taxonomy—the centralized state, federal state, confederal state, and so forth—and this means that religions could eventually be granted a role that was excluded in the Westphalian nation-state. This possibility might explain the insistence with which the Catholic Church attempted to have the recognition of the Christian roots of the Old Continent written into the European Constitution of 2004. Furthermore, some people believe that article 16-c of the Treaty of Lisbon of 2007, given its place in the institutional scheme, might open the doors to a formalization of the role of churches, associations, or religious communities, possibly even reserving for them a right to scrutinize proposed laws.

Yet laws and constitutions merely give recognition to realities that have already imposed themselves in society and integrate them into the legal system. In the present case, this means that it is not law that grants religions a public role, but, to the contrary, it is the place that religions have taken in the public space that leads to their formal recognition under law. Now, in the advanced countries—which almost exclusively dominated the world until 1973—the return of religions has taken place at a rate inversely proportional to the credibility of the state: the less effective states become at offering their citizens both meaning and social services—with the latter often the best guarantor of the former—the more religions tend to reoccupy the public stage.

In a novel published in 2002, a Frenchman named Hector travels to a developing country and notices that "the trucks were often painted in all sorts of colors, with the words in big letters: 'The Good Lord Protects Us,' and he understood that the people here still had faith in God, much more so than in Hector's country, because there, the people still counted on Social Security to protect them."[19] But as the world we once considered "advanced" loses ground relative to the emerging powers, people even in Hector's country will find themselves relying ever more on religious institutions and organizations to protect them, and ever less on Social Security.

3
GOD'S REVENGE

THE INVISIBLE RELIGION

The economic crisis of the mid-1970s represented the intersection of two unequal processes: the emergence of certain developing countries and the gradual decline of the developed countries. This was a relative decline, to be sure, but a decline nonetheless, at the end of which the supremacy of the old industrialized countries is doomed to disappear.

The return of religions to the public stage also began around that time, both in the developing countries and in the old industrial powers. The two evolved in differing contexts, but the global context was the same for both. The emergence of the former and the decline of the latter were not directly proportional, for the world economic system is not inherently a zero-sum game, but they are strictly interdependent. As to their religious implications, these trends had the same effect: in both developing countries and the old industrial powers they increased the levels of real wretchedness in society.

In the developed countries, another factor has been at work, aggravating this real wretchedness: as the role of the state has weakened, society has increasingly perceived religions as eternal, not because of any promise of eternal life but because they vastly predated the nation-state—a transient form in history—and seem destined to outlast it, retaking certain functions, just as the Latin Church did while the Western part of the

Roman Empire was decaying. Religions are perceived, in short, much as the roses in Bernard de Fontenelle's well-known fable perceived their gardener: "If roses, which last but a day, were to tell stories . . . they would say, 'we have always seen the same gardener, in our roseate memories we have seen but him, he has always looked like himself, surely he does not die like us, he simply does not change.'"[1]

We speak of the return of religions onto the *public* stage because they never left the *private* stage. This point is worth emphasizing, for *secularization theory* and many contemporary observers have confused the reduced public visibility of religions with the notion of their disappearance.

José Casanova explained that the secularization phenomenon is composed of three "different, uneven, and unintegrated" parts: separation between religious and secular institutions; decline in religious belief and practices; and marginalization of faith, confining it to the private sphere.[2] For Casanova, one component of secularization is the *decline* of beliefs and practices—the former declining much less than the latter—not their *disappearance*. What has taken place, in fact, is that secularization has brought a definitive end to what René Rémond describes as the "osmosis and interpenetration"[3] that existed between religion and society under the ancien régime: modern societies are no longer steeped in religiosity the way they were for millennia.

It should be noted that when one speaks of the "privatization of religions," one is making an abstract generalization, which may be useful for properly marking the border between the *before* and *after* of the secularization process. In reality, there are few cases in which religion has been entirely excluded from the public domain: nearly all lay leaders of secularized states have recognized the value of religion on the grounds of "order and discipline" and for the "foundations and institutions of social welfare and charity," as described by Benedetto Croce.

That said, beliefs that have purportedly been relegated to the private sphere have become not only less socially significant but also, necessarily, less visible. Secularization theory, an eminently empirical doctrine, limited itself to describing phenomena that were immediately visible in the cities of industrialized countries, at a time when their economic and political domination over the rest of the world was at its zenith. It dealt with statistics on numbers of practicing churchgoers, of religious marriages and baptisms, while what took place behind closed doors, in the cities of industrialized countries and, above all, in rural areas and in the Third World, passed almost unnoticed.

And yet it was in the rural world that, until only a few years ago, the enormous majority of humanity lived, before being jerked rudely into the hurricane of history by famine, disease, wars, revolutions, and, finally, industrialization. It is only in this final stage—that is, when peasants have ceased to be peasants—that these individuals have begun to enjoy a stable political existence. So long as rural dwellers failed to interact with history, they remained confined in a sort of political black hole. However, once they left the countryside, they became essential to any understanding of this powerful movement of religions back into the public sphere.

Because of the threats constantly weighing on their activities—and on their very existence—peasants have always been strongly inclined to look for protection from the celestial forces that are supposed to govern natural phenomena, which explains why the rural world is extremely conservative in matters of religion. When new religions have emerged, it has taken centuries before peasants embraced them. The Latin word *paganus*, source of the word "pagan," simply means "country dweller": a lexical clue reflecting the long hostility toward Christianity of peasants under the Roman Empire. Such hostility was not hard to understand: for centuries they had entrusted their harvests to the protection of Ceres and prayed to Jupiter to preserve them from storms or send rain in times of drought; to betray these deities was to risk provoking their wrath, with all the disastrous consequences imaginable.

There are many such examples in the global history of peasants. In Egypt, as René-Georges Coquin reminds us, the majority of the population, "especially in the countryside," was Christian until at least the eleventh century.[4] In Afghanistan, the peasants of the valleys at the foot of the Hindu Kush continued to practice animism and shamanism until 1896, when their region, known to outsiders as Kafiristan (land of the infidels), was converted by force. Also on the Indian subcontinent, but in present days, the case of Muslim peasants who scrupulously care for the upkeep of Hindu sanctuaries is not unknown; the fact that one has one's own God, they say, does not mean one must provoke the anger of the gods of others. The same phenomenon is seen on the Indonesian island of Java, where Muslim peasants venerate all gods, their rice production depending on the favors of Dewi Sri, Vishnu's wife.

When they entered definitively into history—that is, when they emigrated toward the big urban agglomerations—these peasants carried with them, in their humble bags, their religion.

THE VISIBLE RELIGION

In the present era, it is a widespread belief that religion is an integral part of public life in Muslim countries because Islam allegedly makes no distinction between the public sphere and the private sphere. This belief has taken root despite the hard facts of history. In the 1950s and 1960s, political events in most Muslim countries pointed to quite the opposite conclusion, providing support for secularization theory.

Let us turn to Ali Allawi, a former Iraqi minister (2003–2006), who in 2003 drew this sketch of the situation in Muslim big cities in the mid-twentieth century: "Islam was not a noticeable factor in daily life," he wrote; in Baghdad, respect for Ramadan was considered an eccentricity, women did not wear the veil, alcohol was sold freely, there were movie houses, theaters, night clubs, and more. "Modernity was flooding in everywhere," he continued, adding that the same thing was happening in "Casablanca, Cairo, Damascus, Istanbul, Tehran, Karachi and Jakarta."[5] At that time, Tariq Ali recounts, barely one quarter of the population of his hometown, Lahore, Pakistan, fasted during Ramadan, and when he visited Palestinian refugee camps after the Six-Day War in 1967, no one evoked religion and no woman wore a veil.[6] Mohammad Qayoumi described his younger days in Afghanistan this way: "A half-century ago, Afghan women pursued careers in medicine [and] men and women mingled casually at movie theaters and university campuses in Kabul."[7] A 2009 New York Times article on the Afghan capital in the 1970s completed the tableau: "Afghan women not only attended Kabul University, they did so in miniskirts."[8]

The principal reason for the powerful wave of desecularization that swept the cities mentioned by Allawi, as well as many others not on his list, is rather simple: in the 1950s and 1960s these cities were still relatively small and were dominated both politically and culturally by the urban minority of the state's population that believed that it was enough to merely imitate the West in order to modernize their countries. These cities had not yet become the megalopolises they are today, overrun by millions of rural immigrants. Baghdad had fewer than 600,000 inhabitants—a quarter of them Jewish—representing roughly 12.5 percent of the country's entire population. Whereas today Baghdad's seven million people account for 22.5 percent of Iraq's population—in 2008 only seven Jews were counted.[9] In the other large cities mentioned by Allawi, the rapid transformation was even more radical (see table 3.1).

These massive processes of rural exodus and urbanization in a short period of time have to be viewed as the principal cause for religion's return to the social and political forefront of many developing countries. One might say that the "rate of religiosity" of society has remained static since the 1950s or 1960s, the difference being that, by shifting from the countryside to cities, it has become *visible*. In reality, things are, as usual, much more complex: the flood of millions of peasants to the rapidly industrializing cities of the Third World has had greatly disruptive effects on urban structures—housing, hospitals, education, and other social services—and cannot help but impact the entirety of a population, including the city-dwellers already in place.

TABLE 3.1 Population Values (in Thousands)

	1950s			1970s			2011		
	Total population	Largest city	%	Total population	Largest city	%	Total population	Largest city	%
Iraq	4,800	600	12.5	12,000	1,750	14.6	32,000	7,200	22.5
Iran	17,000	1,200	7.1	33,500	4,500	13.4	75,000	13,500	18
Egypt	19,100	2,100	11	38,500	6,800	17.7	82,000	19,500	23.8
Turkey	18,500	1,200	6.5	45,200	3,350	7.4	75,000	13,500	18
Pakistan	28,200	360	1.3	83,800	5,100	6.1	177,000	13,000	7.3
Indonesia	76,400	2,500	3.3	147,000	6,500	4.4	237,500	28,000	11.8

Sources: Census figures: Iraq (Baghdad), 1948, 1977; Iran (Tehran), 1947, 1976; Egypt (Cairo), 1947, 1976; Turkey (Istanbul), 1945, 1980; Pakistan (Karachi), 1941, 1981; Indonesia (Jakarta), 1948, 1980. Data and official estimates, 2011.

The most immediate objection to this thesis—the idea that the return of religion to the public stage in developing countries is due largely to urbanization—is that similar processes have taken place in many European countries, notably France, Italy, and Spain, in roughly the same period without, however, provoking a rise in the religious phenomenon. There are two possible responses to this objection.

First, urbanization in Europe has taken place at different speeds compared to the developing countries. Joel Beinin, a specialist on the working classes of the Middle East, notes that 75 percent of the region's population still consisted of country-dwellers in the 1960s.[10] In France, where the rural flight came relatively late compared to other European countries, working in the agricultural sector in 1950 amounted to only 23 percent of the country's total population; in Italy, despite Fascist laws against urbanization that remained in effect until 1961, peasants represented 29.1 percent of the population at the beginning of the 1960s. In Spain, during the same period, they represented approximately 35 percent of the population.[11]

The second response is that urbanized peasants in Western European countries found an extremely favorable economic situation in the cities: close to full employment, and a large network of social structures and supports that went far beyond what the Catholic Church was offering. In Spain, the *desarrollo* (development) was even more intense than in France or Italy—and second in the world, behind only Japan in terms of its intensity—with the size of the Iberian economy having grown more than sixfold in the 1960s; conditions were also propitious to union activity, as shown by the great wave of strikes that began in April 1962, and the growing power of the Comisiones Obreras (labor unions), despite severe repression by the Franco regime. Conversely, rural residents in most developing countries found neither a favorable employment environment as they struggled to adapt to urban life nor networks of social protection and support, except those offered by religious organizations.

It is widely asserted, in any case, that even if one considers only the developing countries, desecularization was much more intense in Muslim countries than in non-Muslim countries. This is true in part; yet the reason lies not in any intrinsic, or theological, qualities of Islam but in the history of Muslim civilizations, in the religion's manipulation for eminently political ends, and in the absence of a leadership that all the faithful can recognize. The latter aspect is particularly important: in the absence of a single authority recognized as a guarantor of orthodoxy, the faithful find their footing by the fervent repetition of religious rites, to the point that their spiritual content sometimes is reduced to a pure formality. For twenty centuries the Jewish diaspora kept the flame of faith alight by following that same path.

In any event, the "return of God" has affected every country that began a cycle of industrial development in the 1960s and 1970s, regardless of their religious traditions. When the former Singaporean prime minister Lee Kuan Yew noted, in 1994, the relationship between economic development and the return of religion, he pointed to several non-Muslim countries, saying: "If you look at the fast-growing countries—South Korea, Thailand, Hong Kong and Singapore—there's been one remarkable phenomenon: the rise of religion."[12]

THE THEOLOGY OF PROSPERITY

Lee Kuan Yew emphasized two crucial aspects of this process: speed and intensity. In the developing countries, the return of religion was more clearly manifest than in the old powers, for it was a collateral effect of the rural flight and of the extremely rapid, and often dramatic, process of industrialization.

Millions of country folk were torn away from their familiar habits, their traditions, their support networks, and sometimes their families and thrown into the anonymous and fiercely individualistic caldron of the big industrial cities. They often passed from a barter economy to a monetary economy, which is to say from the concrete to the abstract—or, and even more complicated, to the symbolic—where, instead of relying on the sun to keep time, they suddenly found their lives regulated by the clock. If they arrived with relatives, their family was immediately threatened by a social overcrowding that was unthinkable in the isolation of rural life.

For them, the attachment to tradition was often—along with family members and fellow immigrants from the same village or hamlet—one of the rare points of support to help them survive with dignity in the new urban environment, particularly when other sources of social protection or cohesion were few. Everywhere the process of industrialization has occurred, urbanized peasants have fought to defend their only real possession of value: the link to tradition.

Therefore we should not be surprised if, as part of these processes, there was a period when rural morality—highly patriarchal and conservative—was held up as the last rampart against the corruption, overcrowding, and immorality of urban mores. The history of the twentieth century includes cases in which the political and religious authorities competed over notions of traditionalism and "ruralism" as, for example, in Italy between the 1920s and 1970s. In his encyclical *Casti Connubii* (1930), Pope Pius XI asserted, for example, that for women to work outside the house meant "the debasing of the womanly character and the dignity of motherhood, and indeed of the whole family, as a result of which the husband suffers the loss of his wife, the children of their mother, and the home and the whole family of an ever watchful guardian."[13]

As a general rule, the more difficult it is to integrate into the urban fabric, the more bitterly tradition and rural morality are defended, and the larger and more important the role of the clergy—of whatever religion—becomes. The opposite is also true: to the extent that, in arriving in a city, the former country-dweller finds a job, housing, helpful contacts, and even social services whose very existence he or she had ignored, that person is less likely to seek comfort and consolation in tradition, and in the clergy. This explains why in France, Italy, and even Spain, urbanization during the "economic miracle" years did not take on a particularly religious character. It is also partially why, today, the most rapid and intense urbanization process ever seen—that of China—has similarly not taken on a particularly religious character.

To be sure, other specific factors are at work in China. There is a longstanding spiritual tradition in which exercise, diet, and meditation are more important than transcendental and supernatural beliefs. There is a plurality of religious offerings that inevitably dims the visibility of any growth in religious practices. Above all, central political control is extremely rigorous, imposing regimentation on the propagation of faith and limiting its tendency to overflow into the public sphere—a tendency all the more dangerous in Tibet and in the western Xinjiang autonomous region, where, respectively, Buddhism and Islam are also the expressions of a severely repressed nationalism.

Nevertheless, according to two surveys conducted in 2006, religion holds an "important" role in the lives of nearly one-third of Chinese, respectively, 31 percent and 31.4 percent, percentages that exceed those of either France or Japan.[14] Some specialists—in particular David Aikman, author of *Jesus in Beijing: How Christianity Is Transforming China and Changing the Global Balance of Power*—hold that if these trends continued, China could, within a few years, become both the most populous Christian country *and* the most populous Muslim country in the world.[15]

Looking back over the past two centuries, we can conclude that attempts to replace traditional religions by civil religions have essentially failed. In China during the Cultural Revolution, the Maoist civil religion reached its peak, going so far as to attribute miraculous powers to Chairman Mao's Little Red Book of quotations. Today the book and its quotations are almost forgotten. Undeniably, rapid economic growth and the attainment of well-being arrived *after*, and *in the place of*, Maoist mythology. On a smaller scale, if Turkey were to remain on its current path of rapid growth in the twenty-first century, the Kemalist mythology would probably face the same risk; indeed, we are already seeing the early signs of this evolution.

As illustrated with Fontenelle's parable, the withering away of civil religions has brought traditional religions back to the surface nearly everywhere, in forms that vary depending on local traditions and economic situations. One can, however, identify certain commonalities: in countries that experienced significant economic growth over the past few decades, the return of religion took place under the auspices of a "theology of prosperity."

The "theology of prosperity" was born—where else?—in the United States of the 1950s, but it gained fame through its successes in Latin America, South Korea, and, more recently, some African countries. It is based on a very simple principle, summed up by two Brazilian researchers: "Jesus came to preach to the poor so that they might become rich";[16] individual success depends on a contract one seals with God, who keeps his promises so long as man is faithful to his own.

This "theology" was offered in the religious marketplaces of Latin America, South Korea, and Africa by certain Pentecostal movements just at the moment when ever-growing strata of their populations were beginning to experience the beneficial effects of economic development; hence its success. A seminal text of this movement, published in 1990 by Bishop

Edir Macedo Bezerra, the founder of the Igreja Universal do Reino de Deus, is entitled *Vida com Abundância* (*Life with Abundance*).

In 2009 two journalists from the *Economist* published a book entitled *God Is Back: How the Global Revival of Faith Is Changing the World*. The book opens with an encounter between the authors and the members of a community of Christian businessmen from Shanghai: "Countries with lots of Christians become more powerful," one Chinese man said; followed by "America grew strong because it was Christian. The more Christian China becomes, the mightier it will be."[17] In 2008 Olivier Roy noted that a number of those who sing the praises of the Protestant ethic, including certain Buddhists and some Islamists, have never read the Bible or Calvin but only Max Weber: "In short, the triumph here is less that of Protestantism than of . . . capitalism."[18]

So the "theology of prosperity" is not exclusively Pentecostalist by any means. Catholics came to it as well, if belatedly: for them, notions of money as *stercum diaboli* (the dung of the devil) had long dominated, contributing to the disconnect between the Catholic masses in countries like France, Italy, and Spain at the moment of their "economic miracles."

And yet it was in Spain, during the 1960s, that certain Catholic circles began to pull the church in the other direction. Opus Dei worked to rehabilitate the profit motive, both within the church and in government. To José Casanova, if the "Opus Dei model" had taken root in Latin America, the church could have contributed to the modernization of society instead of being shackled to its old anticapitalist demons, which in his eyes were embodied by the Jesuits.[19] Pope John Paul II, the first pontiff to recognize "the legitimate *role of profit* as an indication that a business is functioning well," in his encyclical *Centesimus Annus* (1991), was also the pope who took Opus Dei under his personal protection and put the Jesuits under temporary receivership.

Since then the church has become much more accepting of the thirst for prosperity by its faithful—a likely reason for the slowing of the expansion of evangelicalism in Latin America and South Korea. In 2007, during the opening the Fifth Latin-American Episcopal Conference in Brazil, Pope Benedict XVI affirmed that the peoples of this region "aspire, before all, to the fullness of life that Christ brought us," and, for good measure, he added a citation from the Gospel (John 10:10), which is often found as well in the texts of Macedo: "I am come that they might have life, and that they might have it more abundantly."

It is now Africa's turn to pass through the most intense and chaotic phases of industrialization and urbanization. And it is in Africa that the Pentecostalists have positioned themselves most effectively. Worldwide Evangelization for Christ International, an evangelical missionary agency, estimates that half the Kenyan population is part of that movement, as are 37 percent of Ugandans, about a third of Central Africans, Zimbabweans, and Nigerians, a fourth of South Africans, Rwandans, Burundians, Zambians, and Ghanaians, and so on.[20] The Catholic Church, too, is now well positioned to profit from the new wave of religiosity produced by today's social tsunamis: it can profit from it directly, as reflected in its growing rates of personnel recruitment, which far exceed the demographic growth of Catholic populations on the African continent; and it can profit indirectly, for the evangelicals are plowing a field whose fruits will be harvested, in part, by the Church of Rome.

The surveys underscoring the evangelists' growth, however, also reflect their near-total absence from Muslim Africa. There are several reasons for this, one of which is certainly that Islam has its own "theology of prosperity": as we have seen, some specialists even assert that Islam was born out of a prosperity theology. According to Tariq Ali, the spiritual motivation of the Prophet Mohammed, who was a merchant, was nourished partly by his "desire to strengthen the commercial standing of the Arabs and to impose a set of common rules."[21] This set of rules, Maxime Rodinson writes, "in all the passages of the oldest layer of the Koran is defined almost exclusively by the right use of wealth."[22] *Al kasib u habibullah* affirms a hadith that can be seen in Istanbul at one entrance to the Grand Bazaar, as well as in the Blue Mosque: "He who earns is a friend of God," or, according to another translation, "God loves the merchant."[23]

Vali Nasr, the dean of Johns Hopkins University and an adviser to the U.S. State Department, asserts in his book *The Rise of Islamic Capitalism* (2009) that "Islam is a powerful supporter of the drive to modernity. The great majority of Muslims think that Islam improves their lives."[24] When this conviction meets an economic situation allowing a tangible improvement of living conditions, it is immediately confirmed and reinforced.

We are not speaking here of an abstract eventuality: in the years following the economic crisis of 2008, Indonesia enjoyed the world's second-strongest rate of economic growth—trailing only China—and Turkey, by then under the Islamic-oriented Erdoğan government, was the most dynamic economy in the zone encompassing Europe and the Mediterranean Basin, with growth rates four times greater than the European Union average. Other Muslim countries, such as Malaysia, Lebanon, Albania, Azerbaijan, and Bangladesh—not to mention the oil sheikdoms of the Persian Gulf—have experienced particularly intense rates of economic growth. As Patrick Haenni writes, all these examples point to a " 'theology of prosperity' tied to the emergence of a new *Muslim pride* based not on armed confrontation or the affirmation of some ostentatious piety, but rather on economic performance and competitiveness."[25]

There are also Hindu, Buddhist, and Jewish versions of the "theology of prosperity." The ethnologist Djallal G. Heuzé has analyzed this phenomenon in the Indian state of Gujarat, which was then led by Narendra Modi, the current prime minister.[26] Additionally, *The God Market: How Globalization Is Making India More Hindu*—published in 2010 by historian Meera Nanda—scrutinizes the entire country. On this subject Nanda writes: "The local deities who were once considered guardians of the village, and who protected against scourges like smallpox and other illnesses, are now being beseeched for blessings for success and sanctity in an increasingly competitive urban environment. . . . Old and new god-men and gurus offer a theology of prosperity which combines fashionable new-age spirituality with discourses on the Bhagavad Gita and Vedanta."[27]

Indian gurus, much like Brazilian evangelical preachers, Anatolian mullahs, and post–John Paul II Catholics, are perfectly aware that "values gain currency when they serve the economic and social interests of people."[28] Thus the more promptly they are able to respond to society's changing needs, the greater will be the success of their theological offerings.

A TURNING POINT IN THE 1970S

Regarding religiosity in major developing countries, Nanda observes that "the newly emerging middle classes in fast-growing economies like India, China, Brazil or Russia are displaying more religiosity, not less . . . *if poverty makes people pray, so does prosperity*."[29] This observation brings us back to modernity as a force unifying opposites. Those countries in which "poverty makes people pray" are, after all, the same ones in which "so does prosperity"; but it does so in different periods and, above all, at different stages of development and in differing geopolitical contexts.

To summarize: when masses of peasants are uprooted from their plurisecular practices and thrown into the unknown and often hostile realities of city life, tradition—nearly always wrapped up in religion—becomes their lifeline, and often their only one. Peasants are no longer praying for relief from the material poverty of rural life but for relief from the material and moral poverty of urban life. A minister who can take in, channel, and organize these prayers will be able to offer continuity to this religious feeling—and perhaps one day exploit it for political ends.

This continuity gains significance when, at a later stage of development, the former peasants, now definitively urbanized—having gradually relegated their religion to one corner of their existence—see their living standards noticeably improve. At this point, the return to prayer is explained by their fear of losing the newly acquired prosperity, or by the fear of failing to succeed where other peasants have shown it is possible. Also at this point, the gods are "beseeched for blessings for success and sanctity in an increasingly competitive, urban environment."[30] Later, when economic crisis strikes the now-prosperous society, the call for social conservation and a return to spiritual values will reinforce this trend. The link connecting the spiritual devotion of the "poverty" phase to that of the "prosperity" phase is the feeling of uncertainty in the face of an unknown future.

It was during the 1970s that the material and moral poverty of urban life in a number of secularized Asian, Latin American, and North African countries brought religion back to center stage. In this setting, political factors could explosively accelerate what had long been a latent process.

Numerous observers have pointed to the failure of Arab nationalism as the starting point for political Islam in the forms we know it today. A key event here is the Six-Day War of 1967, in which the Israeli Defense Forces humiliated their Arab adversaries. The war put an end to the pan-Arabist ambitions cultivated by Gamal Abdel Nasser, the Egyptian president, "whose military defeat was immediately construed as a sign of overall failure," wrote Gilles Kepel, one of the first specialists anywhere to have studied the "reconquering of the world" by the major religions.[31]

Yet the political crisis in this period was not only that of Arab nationalism, even if the Nasserite rout may be seen as symbolizing a broader trend. Two years before the Six-Day War, Indonesia's General Suharto carried out one of the bloodiest coups in the history of humanity, wresting power from Sukarno, the architect of the country's independence and a leader of the Non-Aligned Movement.[32] In 1971 Pakistan lost its eastern province of Bangladesh following a local insurrection and a war against India. By the start of the following decade, the hopes raised by the great wave of decolonization had been dashed nearly everywhere. The same process happened later in other developing countries—Vietnam, Angola, Mozambique, Zimbabwe, but also Maoist China—and just as rapidly.

Those who have sought a common thread through all these failures have sometimes found it in what they call "the crisis of the Western model." Much has been said about this deceptive geopolitical concept, and we will return to it later. For the moment, let us simply state that this phrase makes sense only if it refers not to some imaginary "West" but to the nation-state model and the rejection of so many attempts to implant it where social and economic conditions are not yet mature.

Of course, abortive attempts to create nation-states are not unique to the 1970s: the history of the past 150 years has seen more states without nations than nation-states, in the proper sense of the term. I have devoted a separate discussion to one of these cases—that of Italy—and concluded that, when social and economic conditions are not mature, the attempt to create a nation-state by merely borrowing and imposing its external characteristics and legal structures is, in most cases, a formula for failure.[33]

I am speaking here not of ideological failure but of material failure. For unless a broad national coalition of interest groups is established, any country may find itself prey to permanent conflict—not necessarily armed—between different interest groups, divided by geographic region, ethnicity, religion, economic sector, destination markets, and so forth. Lacking internal cohesion, the country will also be extremely vulnerable to outside influences, coming from countries and economic groups that are also competing among themselves, necessarily producing a multiplier effect on the various internal guerrilla forces. In these conditions, any wealth or resources enjoyed by the country, rather than being a plus, becomes *the* problem: indeed, the more the country is blessed with natural riches—as are many developing countries—or industrial and even geostrategic advantages, the more it will be torn apart internally, and the greater will be the interference coming from the outside. The material foundations of the state will thus be eroded, and an unfavorable economic downturn will suffice to precipitate a crisis, which can quickly take on a political and military face.

In the second half of the nineteenth century, Italy and Germany both undertook the process of creating a nation-state. In Germany, the attempt succeeded; in Italy, it failed. In Italy, the only relatively homogeneous nation-state that existed before unification—the Kingdom of Sardinia—was unable to compromise with the interests of the other regions annexed between 1859 and 1870, in particular, with those of the most economically dynamic region, Lombardy. In Germany, in contrast, the coalition between the efficient political-military machine of Prussia and the economic dynamism of the Rhineland constituted the central core of German national interest—that is, of the nation-state.

Seen as a case of rejection of an operation to transplant a nation-state, Italy is not qualitatively different from other failures, whether Egypt, Pakistan, or the Democratic Republic of Congo. What changes are the historic, cultural, and geopolitical contexts, and, with them, the amplitude and intensity of the repercussions of these failures. Nevertheless, the most important transformation in the 1970s was the end of the economic cycle of state capitalism and the beginning of the new cycle of globalization and so-called free trade.

The countries that entered an industrialization phase in the 1960s all adopted the model of state capitalism because no investor, or group of private investors, had sufficient capital to launch the productive cycle. Here again, this pattern was not unique to the latter twentieth century. Indeed, many countries followed similar paths, beginning with Wilhelmine Germany in the late nineteenth century.

Moreover, in the 1960s the entire global economy was still based, in large measure, on dirigisme, a legacy of the Great Depression. This system was partially liberalized after World War II, but its underlying nature did not change until the 1970s. During that decade, not only were Germany and Japan again two of the major global economic players, but new actors, unknown or little known up until then, also demanded the attention of the markets. These trends remained latent until the 1973–74 crisis, when they were loudly announced by the resounding "oil shock."

This new situation left the developed countries facing a choice: either they could return to the protectionist formulas of the 1930s, thereby raising not just the possibility but the near-certitude of a new war at the end of the road, or they could recognize that the benefits flowing from the exclusive domination of the world were lost forever and attempt to compensate by betting on the enormous potential, in terms of investments and profits, offered by the emerging markets. It was, of course, the latter option that, as history shows, ultimately prevailed. Thus the cycle of state-directed capitalism had run its course and a new free trade cycle gradually took its place.

During this same period, the developing countries took a "liberalizing" turn. Joel Beinin explains that, at the end of the 1960s, the dirigiste and protectionist development model in Tunisia, Egypt, and Turkey faced a crisis because of their undersized domestic markets and a lack of capital liquidity. The respective regimes then imposed austerity measures and cut public spending, which led politically to "the end of authoritarian-populism and the emergence of anti-popular-bureaucratic-authoritarian regimes."[34] The same mechanisms affected several other countries, including India, Pakistan, Brazil, Argentina, Chile, numerous African countries, and others.

In these same countries, Beinin continues, "industrialization was overwhelmed by massive urban-rural migration. Industrial development could not provide enough employment opportunities for rapidly growing urban populations. Vast shanty-town districts overpowered states' distributive capacities, resulting in declining standards of education, housing, health and sanitation services."[35] It was at this point that religions began to regain some of their traditional social public functions: they at first complemented and then supplemented the services of these failing states.

It was as these conditions of economic and, often, moral wretchedness converged that political factors—national and international—accelerated what was still a latent trend of desecularization. Thus, beginning in the 1970s, religions again became an intrinsic and inescapable element in the world's geopolitical panorama.

PART II

THE RESACRALIZATION OF POLITICS IN THE 1970S

Before too long, the turn-of-the-millennium neglect of religious factors may come to be seen as comically myopic, on a par with a review of the eighteenth century that managed to miss the French Revolution.

—Philip Jenkins

The 1970s were a pivotal decade for relations between religion and politics.

—Gilles Kepel

4
RELIGION AND POWER IN THE 1970S

Power invariably attracts religion, and religion attracts power.
Theology is secondary.
—Graham Fuller, 2008

THE "GREAT AWAKENING" OF THE 1970S

During the Six-Day War in 1967, Gilles Kepel recounts, Egyptian soldiers stormed Israeli positions shouting "Land! Air! Sea!" During the Yom Kippur War in 1973, these same soldiers crossed the Suez Canal shouting cries of *Allahu akbar* (God is greatest).[1] In 1970 Polish workers went on strike singing the *Marseillaise* and the *Internationale*; ten years later they walked out of the naval yards in Gdansk singing hymns in honor of the Virgin Mary.

It was during this long decade that religions began to resurface from the private sphere, where secularization had sequestered them for centuries, and returned to the public stage, boosted by the masses who had been pulled from the isolation of the countryside and plunged into the collective life of urban society.

The Catholic Church hierarchy, part of the Iranian Shiite clergy and, for different reasons, Tibetan Buddhist authorities—as well as, perhaps, a few evangelical preachers—were the only religious leaders capable of facing the decade's rapid changes with ideas about what needed to be done. Other religions became active in the political struggles without any spiritual authority, when such existed, providing any direction in the matter. However, certain regimes and certain political forces, having grasped the social and psychological underpinnings of this new Great Awakening, decided to exploit it to their own ends—ends that were rarely of a spiritual nature.[2]

This could only happen in a context where religions were already occupying an important place in society: one cannot, after all, exploit something that does not exist. Even in the case of the Catholic Church, the *reconquista* plan that Pope John Paul II embodied and valiantly implemented would have hobbled along on a single subjective leg—Catholic leaders' will—if not for the objective leg: a public eager to be reconquered.

Let us go back to the case of Egypt. During a trip to Cairo in the mid-1970s, the editor of the *Middle East Journal*, Michael C. Dunn, was stunned by the transformations the country had undergone in a very few years: "People were wearing beards everywhere . . . the mosques were overflowing, with people spilling out into the streets."[3] What had happened? Anwar Sadat had come to power in 1970, at an economically and politically critical moment for both Egypt and the region. He was seen as a transitional figure, destined to remain on the scene only until the real power struggle was decided. As David E. Long, an Arab specialist with the United States Foreign Service from 1962 to 1993, wrote, "In the United States expectations of Sadat were zip."[4] Elliot L. Richardson, the American undersecretary of state at the time, in Cairo for Nasser's funeral, told President Nixon that the new Egyptian president "wouldn't survive in power for no more than four or six weeks."[5] Sadat took three crucial decisions that helped him rise above the unfavorable predictions: he set Egypt on a path to economic liberalization; he lifted the ban on the activities of the Muslim Brotherhood; and he pulled Egypt out of the Soviet Union's orbit in favor of the United States.

These three decisions were interlinked, for Sadat had to arm himself for the inevitable fallout from having upset the balances of Nasserian power. Against any threat from abroad or from within the Egyptian military, his protection was assured by the United States, at a time when Washington could still make or unmake governments in many parts of the world. At home, his protection was assured by the Muslim Brotherhood. As John Esposito wrote, "To escape living in Nasser's shadow, Sadat shifted gears and made strong appeals to Islam"; he presented himself as the "believer-president . . . an allusion to the Islamic caliphs titled Commander of the Faithful."[6] This opportunistic maneuver could succeed only if there were in fact a large number of faithful in search of a commander.

THE ISLAMIZATION OF EGYPT IN THE 1970S

Since its founding in 1928, the Society of the Muslim Brotherhood has always played a role in Egyptian political life. But given its rather vague strategy—"Islam is the solution" and "God is our goal"—this role has generally been more passive than active. Although the Muslim Brotherhood was the only significant nongovernmental organized political force in Egypt from the 1960s onward, its brief rendezvous with power post–Hosni Mubarak caught its members insufficiently prepared and lacking any great clarity of ideas about what to do next.

Notwithstanding all that, its influence on society has always been considerable. Indeed, while its political agenda was rather nebulous, its practical actions were very concrete. Hassan al-Banna, the Muslim Brotherhood's founder, maintained that religious preaching should always be accompanied by a wide range of charitable work in the fields of health, education, and social services. This combination of social popularity and political elusiveness made the Muslim Brothers the ideal raw material for those who wanted to exploit them to other ends.

King Farouk, Nasser, Sadat, and, finally, Mubarak used them, successively, as a stepping stone toward gaining or reinforcing their power.[7] According to Olivier Carré and Gérard Michaud, when Nasser decided, in 1954, to crack down on the Brotherhood, he had 61,000 of its members arrested, 1,450 of them sentenced to jail, and some 130 executed—numbers that testify to their weight within Egyptian society.[8] And yet, despite their constant influence on the masses, the country was far from being politically "Islamized." In fact, the reason for the divorce between the Brotherhood and Nasser was precisely the latter's refusal to accept the principles of sharia law—however exactly defined—as the juridical basis of the new regime. Under Nasser, Cairo essentially remained the "glamorous . . . cosmopolitan" city that Cynthia Myntti described in her book *Paris Along the Nile* (1999).[9]

In 1971 Anwar Sadat shifted gears: after allowing the return of the exiled Brothers, he called a vote on a new constitution—which was to remain in effect for forty years—of which article 2 made sharia "*a* main source of legislation." A constitutional amendment in 1980, passed after the peace accord with Israel and signed over the Islamists' bitter dissent, made sharia *the* main source of legislation. To be sure, Sadat had always been close to the Brotherhood; he represented it within the leadership of the "Free Officers" behind the putsch of 1952. But Nasser too had been close to the Brotherhood in his time, so personal links to the Muslim Brothers cannot alone explain the proliferation of "people wearing beards everywhere" and overflowing mosques in the 1970s. The reason lay elsewhere.

As Myntti writes, "Time, alas, has been unkind to Cairo. At the turn of the [20th] century the city's population was about 600,000; it now [1999] exceeds 13 million."[10] In other words, urbanization preceded and helps explain the bearded ones, just as they precede and help explain Sadat's policies. However, this was not a simple cause-and-effect relationship; rather, it involved multiple and reciprocal influences, in which what might seem to be a final stage was, in reality, not one: indeed, the political exploitation of religious sentiments tended to multiply their impact on all society.

Consider a few key political events, which marked the decade: Sadat had the Nasserist leaders arrested in May 1971, threw out the Soviet advisers in July 1972, eliminated communists from the leadership of the sole labor union in March 1973, adopted *infitah*—his policy of economic liberalization— just as the Yom Kippur War (called in Egypt "Operation Badr") was about to start in October 1973, and eliminated price controls on bread, sugar, and tea in the autumn of 1976.[11] To achieve these ambitious objectives, the Egyptian president counted, of course, on the support of the United States—and on the benign neglect of the Soviet Union—but also on the "motives of order and discipline" and the "foundations and institutions of social welfare and charity" that the dominant religion was able to offer.

Methods and results varied according to circumstances. During the great strikes of 1977, the Islamists attempted to turn the workers against the casinos on the road to the pyramids as symbols of "Western corruption," deepening the divide between them and the "unionized urban workers."[12] But starting in the 1990s, Egyptian labor circles felt the clear weight of immigrant workers returning from the countries of the Persian Gulf, who would arrive back in Egypt bearing the conviction that only submission to Allah, and not the union struggle, would improve their fortunes.

The Islamists' successes on Egyptian university campuses were of quite a different scope. During the 1970s, while the number of students doubled, campus structures remained unchanged, filling the universities with, as Kepel says, "an agitation reminiscent of that of European universities."[13] The *gama'at islamyya* (Islamic associations) offered not only prayer but an array of practical services, such as welcoming committees for freshmen, free photocopies, and tutoring help for those struggling with their courses; separate buses for female students who were often harassed on public transit; and modest outfits at subsidized prices instead of the otherwise costly fashionable clothes. Violent confrontations between Islamists and leftists were not rare, and, according to Kepel, certain summertime training camps organized under the auspices of a Sadat counselor, Muhammad 'Uthman Isma'il, helped assure that the Islamic students would often prevail.[14] Yet it was essentially in the contest between the "abstract ideas" of the left and the "practical solutions" of the *gama'at* that the latter had the upper hand. By the middle of the decade, Kepel concludes, "photos of Lenin [were] definitively covered by the slogan *Allah akbar*."[15]

The conquest of university campuses and the takeover of the Union of Egyptian Students had a lasting impact. The Muslim Brothers, from the 1980s on, gained majority control of every professional union or association representing doctors, pharmacists, engineers, scientists, and lawyers, basing their hegemony on the "pious middle classes" who formed the social backbone of the "theology of prosperity." It was from within this politically radicalized younger generation, experienced in violent confrontation, that the leaders and militants of the terrorist wing of the Brotherhood emerged, among them Ayman al-Zawahiri, the leader of al-Qaeda after the death of Osama bin Laden.

Elsewhere in society, and particularly in the slums where the "decountrified countryfolk"[16] lived, new mosques were built using the resources at hand, and around them arose a proliferation of charitable associations providing the dual advantage of helping compensate for deficiencies in local infrastructure while offering residents protected and controlled spaces.

Little by little, the government came to see these forms of "bottom-up" Islamization as both a solution for its inability to fulfill the people's basic needs and a safeguard against social and political unrest. In short, religion again became a key element of the *tranquillitas ordinis* (tranquility of order) of a society where nothing was tranquil and nothing was well ordered.

Egypt, to be sure, presents certain unique characteristics: notably the existence of a religiously inspired political party that is among the world's oldest and best organized outside of certain European Christian Democratic parties; a rate of urbanization that is low compared to neighboring countries or other large industrialized countries; and a significant Christian minority—around 10 percent of the population—whose economic weight and influence are disproportionately large.

These unique characteristics put aside, the evolution of the Egyptian example described here was, in a broad sense, reproduced in many parts of the world during the 1970s. In some cases the influence of religions was indirect, merely complementing political influence, while in others it had an immediate political impact, thus regaining some of the functions it had before the secularization process began.

A SNEAK PREVIEW: INDONESIA, 1965

In the twentieth century, the first great political event to occur along religious fault lines was the bloody partitioning of the Indian Raj after World War II. Yet this episode had more to do with the British past than with the long and troubled history of relations among Islam, Hinduism, Sikhism, and Buddhism on the subcontinent, though its explosive aftershocks are still felt today. In fact, it was the social and political transformations of the 1970s that reopened the old wounds and politicized the dominant religions in the countries that had emerged from the fragmentation of the British Indian Empire, whether India, Pakistan, Sri Lanka, Bangladesh, or even Myanmar.

The beginning of the modern use of religion as a tool in a political struggle can perhaps be found in Indonesia, two years before the Six-Day War. Geopolitical motives weighed heavily on the Indonesian events of 1965, in particular the shared American and Soviet fears that the archipelago might fall into the Japanese sphere of influence with the help of China.[17]

This was a time when the United States was in the midst of a major escalation in Vietnam, in part to prevent Japan "from reaching an accommodation with the Communist world which would combine the manpower and natural resources of Asia with the industrial potential of Japan," as Dwight Eisenhower wrote to Winston Churchill in April 1954.[18] In 1962, following the early difficulties in Indochina, President John F. Kennedy and Prime Minister Harold MacMillan "agreed to liquidate President Sukarno, depending upon the situation and available opportunities."[19]

The Thirtieth of September Movement's failed coup d'état in 1965 can be seen as a sort of preview of the exploitation of religion for political ends; indeed, the vast sweep of the pogroms against the pro–Chinese Communist Party of Indonesia—known in Indonesia as the PKI—required a mass mobilization. According to a CIA report of 1968, "In terms of numbers killed, the anti-PKI massacres in Indonesia rank as one of the worst mass murders of the 20th century, along with the Soviet purges of the 1930s, the Nazi mass murders during the Second World War, and the Maoist bloodbath of the early 1950s."[20]

The Indonesian military alone could never have accomplished this enormous task, which consisted quite simply of eradicating the world's largest Communist Party—measured by total membership—after those of the Soviet Union and China; it lacked the means to carry out a massacre on such a massive scale and in so short a time—up to one million dead and eighty thousand political prisoners jailed between October 1965 and February 1966.[21] The military turned to some seasoned criminal gangs, and especially to the two largest Muslim groups in the country: the Nahdatul Ulama, a traditionalist Sunni organization, and the Muhammadiyah, a "modernist" Sunni group. The two organizations, which had fought each other bitterly for decades, were able to come together to carry out a religious duty: "to cleanse Indonesia of atheism."[22] An unprecedented "holy alliance" emerged when Catholic students in the Yogyakarta region joined in the massacres, and the Hindu leader of Bali, Ida Bagus Oka, told his fellow believers that the "cruelest enemies of religion . . . must be eliminated and destroyed down to the roots."[23]

It should be noted that this "holy alliance" was not the product of any premeditated choice but rather the effect of a widely held anticommunist sentiment, encouraged and often organized by the military, as well as from the simple fear, among religious, ethnic, and political minorities, that they themselves could end up in the crosshairs. Indeed, if the Indonesian communists were massacred by the hundreds of thousands, many Chinese and Indians were killed as well, as were members of the Nationalist Party, Christians of the Sunda Islands, and even the Abangan, a syncretic Muslim people on Java.

After the coup d'état, Islam gained unprecedented public importance. The Muslim business community was placed under government protection and the anti-Chinese pogroms were tolerated; a military man had to be Muslim if he hoped to advance through the ranks—although the chief of staff named in 1983, General Benny Moerdani, was Catholic. At the same time, political Islam was subjected to discipline and was nationalized. The four Muslim parties were forced to merge into the government-controlled Partai Persatuan Pembangunan (Party for Unity and Development). In 1984 the military killed at least one hundred protesters who were demanding the application of sharia law, and from 1989 to 1992 a war against the Muslim separatists of Aceh Province claimed at least twenty thousand lives.

In 1998, after the fall of General Suharto and the beginnings of democratization and decentralization, it was also in Aceh that, in 2001, the local legal code began to incorporate supposedly Islamic laws concerning dress restrictions, the sale of alcohol, gambling, adultery, and homosexuality. Today some fifty local governments claim to apply sharia. Yet Indonesia, which remains the country with the largest number of Muslim followers in the world, appears to be less and less fascinated by political Islam: between the legislative elections of 2004 and those of 2009, the four largest Islamist parties lost a total of twelve million votes, or 8.7 percent.[24] That may mean that the "religious middle classes" are beginning to become secularized and are embracing different priorities: the first generation had to remain sober to achieve its goals; the second wants to be able to drink to its successes.

As Jusuf Wanandi of the West Java Center for Strategic and International Studies put it, in the face of the overly restrictive rules that the Islamists want to apply everywhere, "members of the middle class that supported them now have second thoughts."[25] It is too soon to say so with certainty, but perhaps one could apply to Indonesia the same rule of "first in, first out" that Ardavan Amir-Aslani applies to his birth country, Iran: the first country to make use of political Islam is also the first to reject it.[26]

DISCLOSING UNSPOKEN RELIGIOUS UNDERCURRENTS: ISRAEL AND INDIA IN 1977

Within a few weeks in the spring of 1977, two secular leftist parties—the Congress Party in India and the Labor Party in Israel, which had governed their respective countries almost without interruption since the nearly simultaneous births of the two countries—lost elections to center-right coalitions, within which religious parties were beginning to flex their muscles as decisive political actors.

Israel and the states born of the breakup of the British Indian Empire had an element in common: an unspoken religious undercurrent that was sometimes mixed up with their very raison d'être. Even if atheist politicians—David Ben-Gurion in Israel, Mohammed Ali Jinnah in Pakistan, and Jawaharlal Nehru in India—were their founding fathers, some of these countries' borders had been drawn along religious fault lines. In retrospect, these borders were problematic from the start: in the cases of Israel, India, Sri Lanka, and Myanmar, they failed to exclude important minorities— Arabs, Muslims, Tamils. In the case of Pakistan, they proved unhelpfully rigid, for most of the Muslims of the subcontinent live outside of Pakistan, primarily in Afghanistan, Kashmir, and India; others separated from it— Bangladesh—and still others—the Baluchis, and some of the Sindhis and Pashtuns—would gladly do so if they could.

Israel was born as the "country of the Jews" and not as a "Jewish country." In the beginning, Zionism was simply the particular form of nationalism of a people demanding a state but who—unlike the examples of the Poles, Italians, or Irish—had no national territorial base. As Shlomo Sand put it, partisans of the national idea who "were confirmed atheists resorted to traditional religious symbols in their self-definition."[27] Despite that, they encountered ferocious opposition from some ultra-Orthodox Jews, for whom Zionism was a "repudiation of the fundamental messianic belief and a violation of the promise given to God to never take over the Holy Land through human efforts."[28]

In 1948 the nonreligious Laborites and Zionists reached an agreement with religious Jews to avoid any chance of civil war. Notably, the ultra-Orthodox were excluded from military service, and the rabbinate was given responsibility—which it still holds—for certain civil-status questions, such as access to Israeli nationality, marriages, divorce, and parentage. After the Six-Day War, as in Egypt, religion took on an ever larger place in the public debate: the Laborites, allied with the largest religious organization, the Mafdal, backed the establishment of the first Jewish colonies in the West Bank. That, of course, was just the start of Jewish settlements in the Occupied Palestinian Territories: in late 1976 the religious parties deserted the government, leaving it in the minority, over an episode of a Sabbath violation on an air force base. In the election campaign that followed, the right-wing Likud leader, Menachem Begin—in spite of the past atrocities carried out under his leadership of the Irgun—presented himself as a deeply religious man and carried the elections.[29] At the same time, the two religious parties enjoyed a significantly larger share of the national vote and, not surprisingly, took their place in the new Begin government with the wind at their backs.

No other place in the world has seen a more tremendous diversity of religious experience than has India: It was the birthplace of Hinduism, Buddhism, Jainism, and Sikhism—some would add Ahmadiyya Islam to that list. Also, it has been, and still is, host to many Jews, Zoroastrians, and Baha'is. India reached the apogee of its splendor during a Muslim dynasty; was governed, directly or indirectly, by a Christian power for roughly two centuries; and today is the country with the world's highest rate of Catholic priest recruitment.

And yet the partition of 1947 was based on a religious breakup, and it gave birth to a country whose religious and political borders were in rough alignment. It is true that India has maintained a pluralism of faiths—home to the third-largest number of Muslims of any country in the world—and in terms of its geopolitical prospects, it is important that it continues that tradition.[30] Still, the *only* common element binding the more than two thousand ethnic groups in the Indian union, the only characteristic that one could describe as *national*, is the *Sanātanadharma* ("eternal law" in Sanskrit; "Hinduism" to the West), an eternal law that, just to be sure, was officially established by the Supreme Court of India in 1966 and again in 1995.

A part of the Indian nationalist movement of the nineteenth and twentieth centuries had very close ties with Vedic tradition.[31] This linkage was consolidated by Mohandas Gandhi, who made, according to Fernand Braudel, "religious use of political forces" to draw peasants into the national struggle.[32] Tariq Ali adds that Gandhi's use of "Hindu religious imagery" was one of the reasons Muslims quit the Indian Congress Party and founded their own party in 1906.[33]

Sumathi Ramaswamy, who devoted a book to the "yearning for form" of Indian nationalism, wrote that one result of this aspiration was the birth of a new divinity: Bharat Mata (Mother India), a personification and sacralization of Indian territory, its skeleton formed by the paths of Hindu pilgrims. Following the creation of the Union of India, Ramaswamy described this new divinity as "gathered together in common celebration and devotion large sections of the region's vast population fissured by caste, language, ethnicity and local and regional sentiments, *even as she came to be perceived as escalating the irrevocable rupture between its two dominant religious communities, Hindu and Muslim.*"[34] Of present-day India, writes Meera Nanda, "the worship of nation is becoming indistinct from the worship of Hindu gods and goddesses."[35]

This sacralization has been part of Indian history since independence, despite its explicitly secular constitution and the fact that an explicitly secular party led the country during its first thirty years following independence. The coalition that prevailed in the national elections of 1977 was bound together only by its common aversion to the dominant party, and particularly to its leader, Indira Gandhi, who had declared a national state of emergency in 1975. The Janata Party was the keystone of this colorful coalition, which included one of the two Indian Communist Parties, a dissident faction in Congress, the peasants' party, and other groups. However, even in the heart of Janata, secular socialists rubbed shoulders with the Bharatiya Jana Sangh, the political arm of the Rashtriya Swayamsevak Sangh (National Volunteer Organization), a radical Hindu nationalist group founded in 1925 and made infamous around the world in 1948, when one of its former members assassinated Mohandas Gandhi. In 1977 the spokesman and the information minister of the victorious coalition was the BJS leader Lal Krishna Advani, a protagonist during some of the most violent moments in Indian history, from the partition in 1947 to the demolition of the mosque of Babur in Ayodhya in 1992. The foreign minister of this same government was Atal Bihari Vajpayee, another BJS member and a future prime minister from 1998 to 2004.

The Janata coalition's stay in government lasted only two years, precisely because of a new wave of anti-Muslim violence that Advani and Vajpayee refused to condemn. Nevertheless, this stay in power was long enough to give their grouping the visibility it needed to seize the leadership of political Hinduism, and to create, in 1980, the Bharatiya Janata Party, which would control the Indian government from 1998 to 2004, and which won a majority government in the national election of 2014 under the leadership of Narendra Modi.

THE ISLAMIZATION OF THE ISLAMIC STATE OF PAKISTAN

In northwestern India, the Punjab—whose Persian-language name means the "land of the five rivers"—contained a large part of the religious and cultural variety of the subcontinent. Despite its Muslim majority—47.6 percent in 1881—it was also the homeland of Sikhism and Ahmadiyya and was, of course, home to millions of Hindus. After the British defeat of the Sikh Empire—which existed between 1799 and 1849—the Punjabis lived in relative harmony for the next century despite their religious differences. Until 1947 this province of British India was even governed by a coalition among the Congress Party, the Sikh party Shiromani Akali Dal, and the Unionist Muslim League. Then, in August 1947, it was split in two and became the epicenter of the violence of partition: by some estimates, of the 7.23 million Muslims who were forced to leave India, 5.3 million were Punjabis, and of the 7.25 million Hindus and Sikhs forced to leave Pakistan, 3.4 million were also Punjabis.[36] The victims numbered in the hundreds of thousands, and the number of women raped or mutilated was in the tens of thousands.

On a smaller scale, the same fate was reserved for the Bengalis, who were also divided by a religion-based border. But in this case, a first partition had been carried out in 1905 by Lord Curzon, the viceroy of India, separating the majority-Muslim eastern zones from the majority-Hindu western zones. With this classic tactic to *divide et impera* (divide and rule), the British authorities contributed, as Olivier Roy writes, to the creation of the "neo-ethnic category 'Muslims,'" which contained within it "subgroups with complex identities." This move forced them to adapt to an "ideal" form of Islam that was not, however, part of their culture. In Roy's view, the creation of separate religion-based electorates in 1919 and 1935 "helped to enshrine the religious marker as the determining one, which inevitably led to the partition of 1947."[37]

The Pakistan that was born in such pain in August 1947 was an imperfect creature. The idea of uniting all the Muslims of the subcontinent was quickly shown to lack validity; simply, a great number of them had elected not to leave India. Even from an ethnic viewpoint, this new political creature was unsound. When the Muslim nationalist Choudhary Rahmat Ali wrote, in 1933, a pamphlet that was considered a manifesto of the partition, he claimed to speak "on behalf of our *thirty million Muslim* brethren who live in *PAKSTAN*—by which we mean the five Northern units of India: Punjab, North-West Frontier Province (Afghan Province), Kashmir, Sind, and Baluchistan."[38] And yet in 1947 the Punjabis, Sindhi, and Kashmiris were separated by the border—some of the latter were even left in China. Also, the Afghans remained independent—except during the 1996–2001 period, when the so-called Islamic Emirate of Afghanistan was de facto a Pakistani province—and the Baluchis found themselves in three different countries—Pakistan, Afghanistan, and Iran. The Bengalis, themselves separated between two nations, are not even mentioned in Ali's text, though in 1947 they represented more than half the population of Pakistan.

In short, Pakistan was a disappointment—both for the Muslims newly arrived from India, who struggled to find a place in a country where ethnicity evidently counted for more than a common faith, and for Pakistani nationalists like Ali, whose discouragement was summed up in the title of his brochure *The Greatest Betrayal* (1947), and who lived out his days in Cambridge. It was also a disappointment for the country's powerful *ulemas*, who above all feared the secularism of Muhammad Ali Jinnah and who established two political parties—a rarity at that time in the Muslim world—to better defend their interests.[39]

The Islamists, for their part, were opposed to the birth of Pakistan for reasons not unlike those of the ultra-Orthodox Jews as regards Israel. Indeed, as the Indian philosopher Muhammad Iqbal—knighted by King George V in 1922—wrote, "Islam is non-territorial in character."[40] For the founder of the Jamaat-i-Islami (Party of Islam), Abul Ala Maududi, the association of the words *nationalism* and *Islamic* was "as contradictory a term as 'chaste prostitute.'"[41] Once Pakistan had been created, however, most of the Islamists mobilized to transform it from a "country of Muslims," which was Jinnah's vision, into a "Muslim country." But this first attempt at Islamization did not last long. The Islamists, after having purged Pakistani territory of Hindus and Sikhs, turned on the Ahmadiyya minority, the followers of Mirza Ghulam Ahmad, who, in 1889, had proclaimed himself the Mahdi (Messiah) and a new prophet of Allah. The pogroms against the Ahmadis in 1953 were halted by the state of emergency declaration, the arrest of Islamist leaders, and the sentencing of Maududi himself to death—a verdict later commuted to a few years in prison. For the country to be officially declared the world's first "Islamic state" would take a further nine years, coming only after the *ulemas*, fearful of losing their privileges, managed to impose their will on a country seized by an identity crisis and the first Constitution of Islamic Republic of Pakistan was finally approved.

Beyond the principles formally recognized in the constitution, the real Islamization of Pakistan took place in the 1970s. Two factors were decisive: the industrialization of the country, which led to intense social struggles in the late 1960s, and the secession of Pakistan's eastern province, which proclaimed its independence in 1971 under the name of People's Republic of Bangladesh.

These two factors were skillfully exploited by the scion of a family of landed aristocracy in Sind Province closely linked to the British crown, who became a minister in the governments of the military dictatorship that took power in 1958: Zulfikar Ali Bhutto. Bhutto discovered his "socialist" identity when Pakistan decided to establish privileged relations with China in 1963, in what was seen as an anti-Russian and anti-Indian move, the Sino-Indian War having just been fought in 1962. When the social crisis of the late 1960s led to the fall of the military regime, Bhutto strongly embraced anticapitalist phraseology and managed to become the most popular politician of the moment. Discreetly but decisively, he supported the military action against eastern Pakistan and, after the defeat, presented himself as the only person capable of saving the nation. He went on to become president in 1971, and then prime minister in 1973 when a new constitution was adopted.

The independence of Bangladesh, the prevalence of corruption, and the failure of the reforms advocated by Bhutto created a favorable environment for the emergence of a grand Islamist coalition uniting the parties of the *ulemas* and that of Maududi against the president. This new Islamic front, in agreement that all evil stems from the abandonment of the Prophet's path, launched a campaign for the adoption of sharia law. Bhutto responded by swapping his brand of socialism for *Musawat-i Mohammadi* (the equality of Muhammad, or Muhammad's social justice). In 1973 he called a vote on a new constitution providing guarantees for the privileges and properties of the *ulemas*, as well as the creation of an Islamic Council charged with ensuring the conformity of civil and religious laws; and he promoted a law excluding the Ahmadis from the Muslim community. Additionally, he proposed a series of laws banning gambling, horse racing, and the consumption of alcohol. Finally, four days before the military coup against him in 1977, he made Friday a legal holiday instead of Sunday.

In most discussions of the Islamization of Pakistan in the 1970s, the designated villain is General Zia ul-Haq, Bhutto's chief of staff, who overthrew him and then had him executed. Zia, it is true, based his legitimacy on Islam; but in reality, some of his decisions simply represented the implementation of "secular" Bhutto's *Musawat-i Mohammadi*. The war in Afghanistan would contribute to the Islamization of the military, but the Islamization of the rest of society rested heavily on the military regime's decision to entrust the direction of certain social services that the government was ill-equipped to manage—above all, education—to religious networks richly financed by Saudi Arabia. According to Dilip Hiro, in 1947 the number of madrasas in western Pakistan totaled only 181, rising to 893 by the start of the Bhutto era, and 2,801 by the end of the Zia era, in 1988.[42]

Hiro writes that some of their students—a word that translates as *taliban* in Pashto—having received free educations in the madrasas, were sent to save Kabul from any Iranian or Indian influence in 1995 by the government headed by Benazir Bhutto. She was the daughter of the man who, in 1973, had ordered the "mobilization of a covert Afghan anti-government guerrilla force, drawn largely from Afghanistan's growing Islamic fundamentalist movement."[43]

FROM MYTHOLOGY TO REALITY: SRI LANKA, MYANMAR, AND THE UNITED STATES

The panorama of the former British Indian Empire would be incomplete if I failed to mention two other nations in which religion has always played a leading political role: Sri Lanka and Myanmar.

It was on Salike Island—to use the name Ptolemy gave it—or what became Ceilão to the Portuguese, Ceylon to the English, and, finally, Sri Lanka ("resplendent island" in Sanskrit) that Buddhism perfected certain of its institutional tools. In 2002 Tessa Bartholomeusz wrote that, "for the defense of Buddhism—that is, of the Dharma—violence and war are permissible, even necessary, under certain conditions."[44] The text most often cited in this regard is the *Mahāvamsa*, written in the sixth century by a monk, who recounts among other tales the torment of the second-century Buddhist King Dutugamunu, who was deeply concerned for his karma after having killed thousands of Tamils in combat; the monks he summoned to discuss his plight sought to comfort him, explaining that in fact he had killed no one, for the Tamils "were heretical and evil and died as though they were animals."[45] This mythology was widely used by certain Buddhist parties involved in the 1983–2009 ethnoreligious war against Sri Lanka's Tamil separatists.

As the *Mahāvamsa* testifies, hostilities between the majority Sinhalese and the minority Tamils have been a constant in the island's history. The last phase of English domination exacerbated these hostilities through a mix of contradictory decisions: The forced importation of workers under near-slavelike conditions from Tamil areas of southern India under the Madras presidency; a sort of affirmative action—or positive discrimination—in favor of this same Tamil minority; and, finally, attempts to apply democratic principles, which led inevitably to Sinhalese political hegemony. In 1972, at the moment the republic was proclaimed, article 6 of the new constitution read as follows: "The Republic of Sri Lanka shall give to Buddhism the foremost place and accordingly it shall be the duty of the State to protect and foster the Buddha Sasana [teachings of Buddha]." This article has to count as one of the causes of the civil war, which claimed, according to the United Nations, between 80,000 and 100,000 victims over a period of twenty-five years from a population of around fifteen million in the early 1980s.

In Myanmar, as in other Buddhist countries, religion played a salient political role. One of the most prominent nationalist groupings, early in the twentieth century, was the Young Men's Buddhist Association. In the 1950s Prime Minister U Nu tried to use Buddhism as an arm of foreign policy: in 1954 he convened and presided over the Sixth Buddhist Synod and founded the World Buddhist University. The military, which had taken power in a coup d'état in 1962, overthrew U Nu and proclaimed a turn to socialism, but at the same time the military leadership was careful not to alienate the monks. According to a joke circulating in the country during the dictatorship, "Burmese TV has only two colors, green and yellow," the khaki green of military uniforms and the saffron yellow of the monks' robes. One opposition leader, U Htun Aung, said that the military "made religious discrimination official policy";[46] this was particularly true of the Rohingya, a Muslim people of Bengali origin who had been pushed into British Burma in the nineteenth century—like the Tamils in Sri Lanka. A vast military operation targeting them in 1978 sparked an exodus of 250,000 people toward the newly formed—and terribly poor—country of Bangladesh and led to a series of anti-Muslim riots that regularly struck at this population, of which the most massive occurred in 1991–92. The riots began again in June 2012, in what appears to have been a veritable campaign of ethnic cleansing led by various groups of Buddhist monks, under the eye—indulgent, to say the least—of the military and of the so-called democratic opposition.

The examples cited in this chapter do not come close to exhausting the panorama of the reemergence of religions, and religious organizations, as political actors in the 1970s. I could also mention the cases of Guatemala and Nicaragua, where, respectively, Efraín Ríos Montt and Daniel Ortega used evangelicalism and Catholic tradition to accede to power. Furthermore, some analysts even assert that the Khmer Rouge, who controlled Cambodia from 1975 to 1979, "emerged in a Buddhist milieu."[47] But these are not the only examples: beyond the three major events in the closing years of the decade—concerning Iran, Afghanistan, and the Catholic Church—which will be addressed later in greater detail, it was in the United States that the religious comeback resounded most loudly.

Today, the religiosity of Americans has become almost a stereotype, so much so that it now seems almost normal that a political competition at any level in the United States will involve the "God factor" in a crucial way. However, this too is a relatively recent phenomenon: in the decades following World War II, religion in the United States was considered more and more marginal; as Patrick Reardon put it, presidents "didn't trumpet their faith."[48] And yet in 1976 Jimmy Carter, the Democratic candidate for president, employed the religious argument, making his status as a "born-again Christian" a regular motif of his ultimately victorious campaign. Presenting himself as "the believing-president," Carter helped blaze a path that has been widely exploited since, to the point that Americans today—uniquely among developed countries—impose "informal religious tests on candidates, especially candidates for the White House."[49]

In the 1970s no one appears to have pulled together all these examples to argue the existence of a new and deeper investment in politics by religions. Thus, when the ayatollahs led the insurrection against the shah of Iran in 1978, the reaction was a mixture of stupor, incredulity, and sarcasm. This was true not only in the developed countries—where sociologists had decreed the death of God—but also in Iran, where the liberals, the pro-Russian party, and even the leftists began attending the big prayer rallies, persuaded that, once things became really serious, these holdovers of the medieval past would return to their mosques and leave politics to the politicians. They had failed to take into account that the real politicians, in Iran, were precisely the ayatollahs.

Yet some, especially in the United States, dared dream of an Islamic revolution in Afghanistan to topple its Soviet-supported government—and even in the Soviet Union's own Muslim-majority republics in Central Asia and the Caucasus. Their underlying conviction was always the same: to the extent that it still exists, religion can and must be an *instrumentum regni* (instrument of power). More rare, but no less determined, were those who believed, to the contrary, that politics can and must be an *instrumentum religionis*. This latter group could be found on the left bank of the Tiber in Rome, in the governmental palaces of Tehran, but also in the Afghan mountains, the mosques on the outskirts of Cairo, Sri Lanka's monasteries, certain ultra-Orthodox synagogues, and some Indian ashrams. They were all preparing to open a new, twenty-first-century-style "Investiture Controversy."[50]

5

THE ISLAMIZATION OF THE IRANIAN REVOLUTION

THE "LONGUE DURÉE" OF PERSIAN SHIISM

Until 1979 American Middle East policy rested on three legs: Saudi Arabia, Israel, and Iran. The latter was the most indispensable, for it offered three key advantages: it was on the front line of the strategy for containing the Soviet Union; it served as a sentinel along the Persian Gulf oil routes (and a major producer in its own right); and it provided a double counterweight in the region, as a Shiite country among Sunni neighbors and an Indo-European country among Arab neighbors.

The American schools of foreign policy were divided on the best way to ensure that Iran remained in this crucial role. Indeed, through its recent history, Tehran had shown itself to be as fickle an ally as it was a prized one: swayed by German influence in 1941; by Soviet influence in 1946, at least in the North; by the nationalist influence of Prime Minister Moham-mad Mossadegh between 1951 and 1953, who undertook to nationalize the petroleum industry; by Non-Aligned Movement influences with the Band-ung Conference in 1955 and the creation of Organization of the Petroleum Exporting Countries in 1960.

While the American foreign policy schools were united in their desire to preserve Iran's strategic role, they also shared something else in the late 1970s, as Robert Dreyfuss observed: "Each, in its own way, didn't see Kho-meini's victory coming."[1]

The realist school, represented most prominently by Henry Kissinger, advocated total and unconditional support for the shah, who was seen as the only man able to guarantee Iran's role as the "gendarme of the Gulf." But the realists were not to have their way for, as Dreyfuss points out, to them "Khomeini was nearly invisible."[2] This should not be surprising because, for many of them, religion was too insignificant to be considered one of the preponderant influences in international policy.[3] In his book *Diplomacy* (1994)—which summarizes international policy from Richelieu to Gorbachev—Kissinger keeps religion largely at arm's length, never, for example, mentioning Islam or, in a book spanning 912 pages, Ayatollah Ruhollah Khomeini.

Another foreign policy school, liberal internationalism, came to power with the Jimmy Carter administration in 1976. Wanting to revoke the blank check that had been granted to the shah and to his authoritarian policies by previous administrations, the liberals established contacts with the moderate Iranian opposition, but also with certain members of the Shi-ite clergy, though they were seen as representing "a vague force in the background."[4] The administration sent mixed signals to Iran, for it was profoundly divided between the impulses toward the liberalization of the regime, as embodied by Secretary of State Cyrus Vance, and the conviction that the shah's interests and those of the United States coincided, a view espoused by National Security Advisor Zbigniew Brzezinski.

The Carter administration's underestimation of the religious factor in Iran made things worse. According to a State Department analysis from 1972, "the Iranian clergy no longer have major political influence." For Stansfield Turner, CIA director from 1977 to 1981, "in 1977, Islam as a polit-ical force was not on our radar."[5] Here we see two complementary factors: the minimization of the political role of religious leaders and, more gener-ally, indifference toward the role of religion in Iranian society. Put them together and it is not hard to understand why Americans—along with most of the world—were caught completely off guard by the Islamic Revolution.

According to Dreyfuss, of the thousands of Americans based in Iran, including hundreds of CIA officials and specialists, "few, if any, had any familiarity with Iran's subculture, religious underground, and opposition forces."[6] And yet the unique nature of Twelver Shiism is so glaring that it is not plausible that it was completely unknown.[7] This unique nature lay not in the theological differences with Sunnism—which exist, to be sure, but which are no more important than the many theological differences between the countless tendencies, schools, movements, and sensibilities within Sunnism itself. We are talking about a historic singularity.

Indeed, the Shiism of the Safavid dynasty that ruled in Iran since the beginning of the sixteenth century has to be considered "not as a corpus but as a history," as Olivier Roy says.[8] To be more precise, as a double history: On the one hand, there was the long history of persecutions of Shiites following their definitive break with Sunnism in 680, which led them to view political power as always being "illegitimate" or at best "temporary," while awaiting the return of the Mahdi. On the other hand, there was the history dating from the Safavid period when, as Roy affirms, Shiism was transformed and took on a hierarchical structure under the influence of Persian bureaucratic and military tradition.

It is worth recalling that once before, contact with Persian culture had had a decisive effect in transforming Islam: at the birth of the Abbasid Empire in 750. Michael Axworthy defines this historic turning point as "a cultural reconquest of the Arab conquerors by the Persians."[9] In this period, Islam inherited Persian ideas, mores, traditions, and political structures; it ceased to be an Arab religion and became a universal religion, a proselytic religion—previously, conversions had been discouraged, even banned—and it ceased to be a conquering, military religion and became a sedentary religion instead.[10] According to Peter Brown, it was not Charles Martel who managed to stop the Arab war machine at the Battle of Tours in 732, "it was the foundation of Baghdad"; indeed, "the slow-moving ideals of an organized and expensive imperial administration that replaced the fearful mobility of the Bedouin armies."[11]

Thus, starting with the Safavid period in 1501, Twelver Shiism embodied continuity with the Persia of antiquity. Indeed, this version of Shiism, introduced in 1501 by Ismail I within the borders of what is modern-day Iran, falls with amazing precision into Fernand Braudel's notion of the "longue durée," a historical approach emphasizing long-term structures over discrete events. Braudel offered the example of the Reformation, the borders of which followed "rather exactly, on either side of the Rhine and the Danube, the double frontiers of the Roman Empire."[12] Yet the regions of the Middle East that are now populated by Shiites, outside of the Persian cultural zone, track closely to the areas that saw the spread of Nestorian Christianity, a political ally of the Persian Sassanid Empire—which reigned between 224 and 651—against the Orthodox Christianity of the rival Roman-Byzantine Empire and their Christian Monophysite allies. The geopolitical continuity here consists in the fact that the regions that today are on the front lines of Iranian foreign policy were on the front lines of Sassanid foreign policy fifteen centuries prior.

This longue durée view gives Shiite religious leaders a sense of historic depth which, as a general rule, their Sunni colleagues lack: the ayatollahs, according to Robert Kaplan, "in the vein of Hegel and Marx, base their moral superiority on an understanding of the purpose of history."[13]

But there is another major difference with Sunni religious leaders: like them, Iranian religious leaders have always controlled assets under mortmain, and, like them, they became substantial property owners; but, unlike them, the Iranian religious leaders directly collected and administered the zakat, the obligatory alms given by the faithful. They were thus far more powerful not only economically but politically, because those poor countrymen to whom the zakat was redistributed depended on them.

The crucial difference, however, resides in their organized clerical structure, which made it possible to give continuity to the social bonds created around the mosques and to transform them, when needed, into a political force. It was, to be sure, a potential force, for the Shiite religious leaders were mostly quietists, which is to say they were more concerned with their relationship with God than with the political authorities. However, they became a very real force when the process of secularization began to affect their interests and their properties. In those moments, the Iranian clergy displayed a capacity for resistance that was far superior to that of the comparatively weakly organized Sunni clergy.

In the mid-nineteenth century, Amir Kabir, the prime minister of Persia, attempted to begin the modernization of the country by following the model of the Turkish Tanzimat, the first great modern reform program in a Muslim state, which culminated with the promulgation of the Ottoman Constitution in 1876. In 1849 Kabir confided to the British consul in Tabriz that "the Ottoman government was able to begin reviving its power only after breaking the power of the mullas."[14] More than one hundred years later, in 1963, during an official ceremony in Qom in support of his "White Revolution," the shah delivered an angry, improvised speech in which he stigmatized "a stupid and reactionary bunch whose brains have not moved for a thousand years . . . black reaction who formed a small and ludicrous gathering from a handful of bearded, stupid bazaaris to make noises."[15]

Between these two dates, there were many attempts at reforming and modernizing the country: that of Amir Kabir, who was assassinated in 1852; that launched in 1871 by Prime Minister Mirza Hosein Khan before he was sacked in 1873; the "constitutional revolution" of 1906, crushed by the Russian military interventions of 1908 and 1910; that of General Reza Khan, in 1921, who had to scale his Kemalist ambitions downward, to the point of proclaiming himself shah in 1925; that of Prime Minister Mossadegh, who was elected prime minister in 1951 and then overthrown in an American- and British-backed coup d'état in 1953; and, finally, that of Reza Pahlavi, the White Revolution launched in 1962, against which the Ayatollah Ruhollah Khomeini distinguished himself for the first time as a political leader.

I should note that the reasons for the total or partial failure of all these reform attempts did not lie exclusively in the power of the clergy: several social factors also contributed. What is certain, however, is that all the interest groups that risked being damaged or weakened found, in the property-owning clergy, not only an attentive ear but above all a unifying political force. All these interests also met, on the other side of the barricades, a state with weak legitimacy, largely because of the ongoing history of foreign interference, whether British, American, German, or Russian. But this permanent imbalance in the history of contemporary Iran would be suddenly and violently righted in 1979 by the intervention of religion.

A NOT PARTICULARLY ISLAMIC CAST

As Vali Nasr writes, "During the whirlwind years of 1978 and 1979, the revolution did not take on a particularly Islamic cast."[16] Those who first demonstrated against the shah in 1977 were intellectuals, students, the urban middle class, the petite bourgeoisie of the bazaar, workers, and, finally, the lumpenproletariat—plus, to be sure, some members of the clergy.

These first rallies took place after the economic crisis of the mid-1970s, which had broken the momentum of a phase of extraordinarily rapid industrialization. The industrialization process had been set off by the White Revolution and then fueled by the petroleum revenues that began gushing in after the shock of 1973, when the price of crude oil had soared by 400 percent—Iran was then the world's second leading oil exporter. Economic activity had exploded in every direction, reaching into new industrial sectors: heavy industry, petrochemical, construction, but also the nuclear energy sector, with plans to build twenty-three nuclear power plants by the year 2000.[17] The massive rural flight sparked by the agrarian reforms and industrialization of the 1960s had given rise to an abundant workforce to fill these new jobs, but it had also brought the usual challenges: the growth of enormous urban slums lacking in any infrastructure; the sudden dire shortage of social services; the creation of an underclass not involved in any permanent way in productive activities and thus available for irregular work—legal and otherwise. Added atop all those elements was the suffocating presence of the state with its bureaucracy, corruption, and privileged clients who restricted and distorted competition but also its endless bans and prohibitions, enforced by a political police that was as punctilious as it was brutal. All social, labor, and even cultural activities not controlled by the state were forbidden.

Only one entity was authorized to carry on its activities, albeit under strict surveillance: the clergy. While it did represent a potential source of opposition, the government hoped to neutralize it by feeding the divisions at its core. The memory of the secularization measures of the 1960s—the nationalization of certain religious properties, the closing of madrasas, and even the threat of a state takeover of the theological training of mullahs—persuaded the majority of clerics not to meddle in politics and to limit their activities to the spiritual and charitable domains. The regime managed to lull the quietists so as to avoid pushing them into the arms of the politically active clergy. Moreover, in the face of the turbulence caused by industrialization, the network of mosques, religious associations, and sanctuaries contributed powerfully to helping maintain social peace. Iran's religious institutions kept the urbanized peasants away from politics, provided comfort to the disadvantaged through the redistribution of the zakat, and provided basic social services in areas where the state was unable to do so, or where the state chose not to—its priorities being elsewhere. Between 1974 and 1978, as the gendarme of the Persian Gulf, Iran devoted about 31 percent of its public spending to defense—in nominal terms, from $844 million in 1970 to $9.4 billion in 1977—or 9 percent of GDP.[18]

The situation in Iran bore many similarities to conditions in the other "antipopular-bureaucratic-authoritarian regimes" of the time. Its military budget was a bit higher than in other countries but not enormously so: Egypt, for example, devoted an average of 23 percent of its public spending to defense between 1966 and 1994—excluding the peak in 1973–74, when it exceeded 80 percent.[19] Inflation was also fairly average, around 10 percent between 1970 and 1978 in Iran; in Egypt during the same period, it was around 7 percent; and in Turkey, it was close to 20 percent—though it did hit 30 percent in 1977.[20] Additionally, as elsewhere in the world, the beginning of mass school attendance led to a breakup of the old structures and the birth of student protest movements that were dominated by leftists.

The repressive measures taken against the opposition were brutal in all these countries: in Iran, the authorities imprisoned, tortured, or executed political opponents in somewhat greater volumes, perhaps owing to the country's geopolitical realities. Beyond the traditionally circumspect attitude of the clergy, the country's recent past had left a heritage of strong conservative and nationalist opposition inspired by the Mossadegh experiment, and a strong pro-Russian party—the Tudeh—which of course was a favorite target for repression.

Given all these similarities to other developing countries in the Muslim world, what are the specific factors that opened the way for the success of the Islamic Revolution in Iran? I can point to at least three: a long history of foreign interventions; the political skill of certain members of the Shiite clergy; and a much more advanced stage of industrial development. But it was the interrelationship of these factors that proved decisive: namely, the political capacity of part of the Shiite clergy to channel nationalist resentment against the numerous foreign interventions at a moment of rapid economic development.

INTERFERENCE, THE CLERGY, AND DEVELOPMENT

Let us examine these three factors, one at a time.

Foreign interference. This has been, one might say, part and parcel of the history of modern Iran, which can be traced to the ascent of the Qajar tribe to power in 1794. Early in the following century, the country found itself caught in a vise between the Russian advances toward the Indian Ocean via the Caucasus and Britain's determination to protect India—a geopolitical configuration that would be repeated later in Afghanistan. The Russians and the British fought a proxy war, with the Persians suffering military defeats on both fronts; defeats that led not only to the surrendering of territory—among other things, part of Azerbaijan, the original homeland of the Safavids—but also and more important, the effective loss of political and economic independence.

From that point forward, the history of the Iranian monarchy was one of successive displays of weakness and accommodation alternating with outbursts of patriotism against a backdrop of popular revolts. The British obtained numerous concessions, regarding roads, mills, factories, mines, and public tobacco—the latter provoking a first revolt in 1892. In 1901 all the country's petroleum reserves were ceded to the Anglo-Persian Oil Company, the ancestor of BP, a decision that was behind the "Constitutional Revolution" of 1906. In 1907 Russia and Great Britain agreed to divide the country into zones of influence; subsequently, the Russians intervened militarily to restore the absolute power of the shah. The coup d'état of 1921 led by Reza Khan, an officer in the Persian Cossack brigade, was supported by the British as a way to eliminate any risk of a Bolshevik contagion in Persia. Once in power, however, Reza Khan ended up relying again on the Russians, and later on the Germans, to counterbalance the British influence. In 1935 he restored the country's historic name of Iran (land of the Aryans). Hostile to the Allies at the start of World War II, Reza Khan was ousted in a joint Russo-British intervention in 1941 and replaced by his son, Mohammed Reza Pahlavi. In 1953, after Mossadegh's brief term as prime minister, Pahlavi's authority was reestablished following the American- and British-backed coup. At that point, the Americans alone were able to obtain all the concessions that the Russians and British had enjoyed in the past, as well as judicial immunity for their military personnel.

The clergy. In the face of political authorities who were inclined both to bow to the demands of foreign Christian powers and to eat away at the prerogatives of religious leaders, the mullahs felt doubly threatened. They thus played sometimes decisive roles in the revolts provoked by the arrogance of foreigners and the servility of the Persian authorities.

The "tobacco revolt" of 1892 was launched by Ayatollah Mirza Hasan Shirazi, who called on his countrymen to save the nation from "this criminal who has offered the provinces of the land of Iran to auction amongst the Great Powers."[21] The clergy, and particularly Ayatollah Fazlollah Nuri, also played a role in the "Constitutional Revolution" of 1906: initially favorable to the movement's nationalist objectives, the ayatollah later condemned as "apostasy" its plans for the modernization and secularization of the country; he even went so far as to cooperate with the Russians in reestablishing the dictatorship of the shah. The revolutionaries hanged Nuri in 1909, apparently the only case of execution of an ayatollah in modern Iranian history.

While the clergy did not collaborate with the invaders in 1941, it was certainly relieved by the ouster of Reza Khan. And yet when he came to power he had established an extremely close relationship with religious leaders, guaranteeing their prerogatives, allowing them to complete their institutional structure, and exempting theology students from military service. Later, however, motivated as much by a desire to consolidate his authority as to modernize the country, Reza Khan took "Kemalist" measures: from the nationalization of certain clerical assets and of the religious tribunals to the banishing of self-flagellation during the Day of Ashura and forbidding women to cover their heads in public. Some of these measures were immediately revoked by his son the moment he acceded to the throne.[22]

Under the Mossadegh government, the clergy in some ways mirrored its attitude from the 1906–1909 period: it initially supported the decision to nationalize the country's petroleum resources but then progressively distanced itself from the government and, in the end, supported the CIA-orchestrated coup. According to several sources, Ayatollah Abol-Ghasem Kashani—depicted today in the schoolbooks of the Islamic Republic as the true inspiration for nationalization—was "reoriented" against Mossadegh by the intelligence services of the United States and Britain, which saw in him, as a CIA report from October 1952 makes clear, a possible alternative to the nationalist government. Shortly before the coup, Kashani reportedly even declared that "Mossadegh deserved to be executed because he had committed the ultimate offense: Rebelling against the shah, 'betraying' the country, and repeatedly violating the sacred law."[23]

Finally, there was Khomeini's stance in 1963 against the White Revolution. As we have seen, the demonstrations organized in Qom angered the shah. However, Khomeini incurred the full wrath of the regime only when he assailed the judicial immunity accorded to American military personnel and accused the shah of being a pawn of the United States and Israel.

The intervention of the Grand Ayatollah Kazem Shariatmadari, who had the shah's ear, saved Khomeini from arrest and from a probable death sentence. Instead, he was exiled, which boosted his prestige enormously, making him the leader *in pectore* of all those who seethed under the country's subordination to the geopolitical and economic interests of the United States.

If the clergy had always shown itself to be united and resolute in its defense of its assets and prerogatives, different positions toward the governing authorities began to emerge in the 1960s. Most religious leaders followed the traditional Shiite doctrine of maintaining a prudent distance from power; this majority was largely composed, in Gilles Kepel's words, of "socially conservative clerics who saw themselves as voices of conscience and reproof with respect to a government they never dreamed of overthrowing or supplanting."[24] Their most important representative was Ayatollah Shariatmadari, who was finally arrested in 1982 by the Khomeini government and held until his death. On the other side were the *politicals*, doctrinally heterodox and calling for the conquest of power. Within this latter group there were two chief factions: The first subscribed to the theories of the Third Worldist sociologist Ali Shariati, who held that the Shia should lead the "disadvantaged" to free themselves through the conquest of power. It was a sort of "Muslim liberation theology," but it explicitly rejected Marxism—which Shariati considered a "Western fallacy." The second faction embraced Ayatollah Khomeini's theory of *velayat-e faqih* (supervision of the legal expert), which advocated a takeover of power by religious leaders themselves, under the guidance of the *faqih*—that is, the most competent of the theologians, meaning the one best equipped to achieve policies closely conforming to divine law. The political groups, in particular Shariati's, remained very much the minority within the Shiite clergy until the moment when the rallies that began in 1977 changed into an insurrectional movement. When Khomeini, from his exile—first in Iraq and then in France—managed to unite the near totality of the movement under his leadership, the majority of the overall clergy rallied to his side.

Economic dynamism. In the first half of the 1970s, Iran was the most dynamic emerging power in the world. According to the World Bank, Iran's nominal GDP shot up from $10.6 billion in 1970 to $74.8 billion in 1977, and the size of its economy rose from twenty-seventh largest in the world to seventeenth. Its GDP per capita, compared to that of France, for example, was 1:3 in 1950, 1:2.8 in 1970, and 1:2 in 1976—this would later fall back to 1:4 in 1981, 1:5 in 1990, and 1:5.7 in 2012.[25] This extraordinarily rapid economic ascendance would deeply affect every social structure and class in the country. In addition to the millions of uprooted peasants, the urban middle classes were also profoundly affected. To be sure, they were growing richer; but with money came recriminations. The gap between the country's growing wealth and the manifest inadequacy of its social structures—starting with education—was, to these social classes, tangible proof that the services for which they were paying more and more taxes were not up to the level of their heightened expectations. This mechanism of social psychology is one that we would see again in China in 1989 and in India, Turkey, and Brazil in 2013: the feeling that the profits of growth are flowing mainly to speculators, politicians, a corrupt elite, and foreigners. As a general rule, when greater *taxation* is not accompanied by better *representation*, the resulting public anger can be particularly seditious.

Another phenomenon typical of rapid economic growth is a crisis of the petite bourgeoisie: by taking in enormous profits, the strongest economic groups are able to make investments that led to the ruination of their smaller competitors. In the Iran of the 1970s, it was the bazaar merchants who experienced one of capitalism's best-known paradoxes: poverty provoked by an excess of wealth.

The crisis among the industrialized countries in 1974–75 inevitably affected demand for crude oil, leading to a recession in those economies that depended on petroleum export revenues. In Iran, the spark from this imported crisis inflamed the masses, and, subsequently, the regime's brutal repression, the vacillations in American strategy, and Khomeini political intelligence transformed a revolt into a revolution.

FROM A PETIT BOURGEOIS REVOLT TO AN ISLAMIC REVOLUTION

It was the children of the middle classes who launched a movement from their university campuses in October 1977 to protest a government campaign that blamed inflation on small merchants. In Iran, the government could not use specially trained Islamist "students" to rough up the leftists on college campuses, as the Egyptian, Moroccan, Algerian, and Pakistani authorities had done. For in Iran, the Islamists were aligned with the students in opposition to the government.

The alliance that emerged was thus of a decidedly mixed complexion: there were intellectuals of Third Worldism, devout Muslims, secularists and nonbelievers, bazaar merchants, and leftist students. The clergy and the two traditional parties—the nationalist conservatives and the pro-Russian Tudeh—maintained a watchful but benevolent attitude. It is true that the political climate had become relatively less tense after the election of Jimmy Carter; still, so much political vitality and variety were particularly noteworthy in a country where, for so many years, leaders and militants hostile to the regime had been imprisoned or tortured by the thousands and executed by the hundreds.

What cemented the tactical unity of these groups was their opposition to corruption, the shameless enrichment of the elites, and the policy of submission to American interests. In short, the three targets that represented the "hijacking" of the wealth accumulated during the years of intense development.

The situation grew more ominous when, in January 1978, the police fired on a crowd in the holy city of Qom, killing dozens of people. It was at that moment that Khomeini—whose popularity up to then was greater among the political opposition than among the clergy—issued his first call for the overthrow of the shah. The network of religious structures was mobilized, and the first workers' strikes began.

The growing involvement of workers became a crucial element in the movement, even if their demands were essentially economic and would only become political later, following the government's ruthless response. Lacking any independent trade-union organization, they turned for support, guidance, and coordination to the only structures they trusted, the ones that had helped them from the moment they arrived in industrial cities: the mosques and religious associations. A very similar dynamic would be witnessed only two years later in Poland. There, too, workers would trust their faith to the parish networks; there, too, secular intellectuals would take part in grand collective masses, believing that they could use the Catholic Church as a stepping stone to gain credibility in the eyes of the working class.

Once the underemployed residents of Iran's slums joined the movement, the near-totality of mobilized social forces were under the clergy's political control; even secular politicians, certain intellectuals, and many students who still considered themselves independent were in fact following the clergy's agenda. Khomeini would quickly manage to seduce them ideologically with his anti-American harangues, his borrowings of Shariati's Third Worldist phraseology, and his calls for a redistribution of oil revenues among the disadvantaged—and, crucially, by toning down his theocratic program. On September 8, 1978, the last day of Ramadan, as Vali Nasr reminds us, a mass prayer session was improvised in the streets of one of Tehran's more elegant neighborhoods; among the faithful, Nasr saw "writers, poets and painters who I knew were not pious, or even particularly versed in Islam, lining the prayer rows and bending awkwardly in the direction of Mecca."[26] In October the leaders of the conservative party traveled to Paris, where Khomeini was living in exile, to formally pledge their allegiance; the Tudeh did the same from Tehran—the Kremlin had deluded itself into believing that an Iran without the shah could end up in its geopolitical orbit.

The Soviet leaders were not alone in their misreading of the situation. In December 1978, on the day commemorating the death of the Imam Hussein, in the middle of a general strike that would last four months, Khomeini organized a spectacular demonstration in defiance of the state of siege.[27] As Gilles Kepel recounts, at the moment when the curfew began, hundreds of thousands of Tehran inhabitants climbed up on the roofs of their buildings to raise a cry of *Allahu akbar* that resounded throughout the city.[28] It was at that moment of collective enthusiasm that everyone understood that the shah was finished and that the revolution had won. Why did the secular, Stalinist, and conservative militants join this chorus glorifying Allah? According to Tariq Ali's explanation: "It was impossible for the Iranian left to imagine that the people . . . could be serious when they chanted *Allahu akbar*. . . . All this religion was empty froth; it would be blown away by newer and stronger breezes."[29] It was not just the left, described by Ali, that disastrously underestimated the power of the clerics; as Nasr writes, "Among the secular agitators, clerics and their followers were widely regarded as harmless hangers-on to the great bandwagon of revolution."[30]

Imbued with their dogmas about the irremediable obsolescence of religion, neither the conservatives nor the Stalinists and leftists had understood that in the whole history of the revolt against the shah, it was only the mullahs that were the real political operators. The wind had changed, to be sure, but not in the direction desired by the leftists. It was a violent breeze but not at all new; to the contrary, it was extremely ancient. And it would blow for decades.[31]

6

THE GEOPOLITICAL REINVENTION OF THE HOLY WAR

A BRIEF GEOPOLITICAL OVERVIEW OF AFGHANISTAN

One of the great paradoxes of recent history is that the most successful jihad of the twentieth century was proclaimed by a Catholic American of Polish origin. Zbigniew Brzezinski, national security adviser to Jimmy Carter, speaking to a small group of mujahidin in January 1980 at the Khyber Pass between Afghanistan and Pakistan, acknowledged the sacred character of the war against the Soviet invaders: "Your cause is right," he said, "God is on your side."[1]

The success of this jihad reached far beyond its initial objective. Just as Brzezinski had promised, the mujahidin who came from all parts of the world to fight in Afghanistan credited their victory over the Red Army to God; the weapons and money given by the Americans, Saudis, Chinese, and Egyptians and distributed by the Pakistanis were merely the brute form through which God's will had been carried out. This conviction gave them the intoxicating sensation of being able to destroy any and every enemy of Islam, in any part of the world: that included the tafkir (anathematized) governments of their home countries; the Israelis; the infidels occupying former Muslim lands from Andalusia to the Crimea and current Muslim lands such as Bosnia, Kosovo, Chechnya, Kashmir, and Xinjiang; and, "Enemy No. 1," "The Great Satan," the United States, against which the infernal machine of the "holy war," touched off with help from the Americans themselves, finally turned.

Afghanistan is a geopolitical puzzle possessing several salient characteristics: a strategically crucial position both on the east–west axis between Iran and India as well as on the north-south axis between landlocked Central Asia and the Indian Ocean; an ethnic makeup that leads the Iranians to view it as one of their eastern provinces and a religious composition that encourages the Pakistanis to consider it as one of their western provinces; and, perhaps most crucially, a topographical configuration that renders it nearly inaccessible.

Since breaking away from a declining Persia in 1747, Afghanistan has been dominated—politically, historically, and culturally—by the Pashtuns, an ethnic group with a warrior mythos to which the founder of the modern state, Ahmad Shah Durrani, belonged. At the time, the country stretched from Khorasan—now part of Iran—in the West, to the Punjab and Sindh—as now part of Pakistan and India—in the East, to Tajikistan and part of Turkic-speaking Uzbekistan in the North, and as far as the Indian Ocean in the South. At the dawn of the nineteenth century, after suffering successive attacks from the Persians, Sikhs, Russians, and British, Afghanistan lost a large part of the territory that had been conquered by Ahmad Shah. Throughout the century, the country was at the center of the "Great Game"—the rivalry between the Russian and British Empires that was mentioned in our discussion of Persia. After attempts at invasion by both empires, as well as the First and Second Anglo-Afghan Wars in 1839–1842 and 1878–1880, respectively, the two great powers managed to reach agreement in 1893 on the borders of the country in such a way as to create a neutral buffer state.

Afghanistan's border with British India—the so-called Durand Line, named after the British foreign secretary of India, Mortimer Durand, who negotiated it with the Afghan emir—was designed to divide in half the territory inhabited by the Pashtuns, making most of them subjects of Her Majesty. One result of this demarcation was to produce a fourth geopolitical characteristic in Afghanistan that surfaces regularly: the Afghan Pashtuns' oscillation between collaborating with the British Raj—and, after 1947, with Pakistan—and the opposite faction, embracing the goal of reunifying the region occupied by the Pashtun. Tribal divisions within the Pashtuns merely added fuel to the fire of this already heated question—all the more so because the Russians, Indians, and Iranians were happy to fan the flames. For them, the notion of a Pashtun state represented a Sword of Damocles suspended over the head of their common rival, Pakistan.

A fifth overarching characteristic is certainly the most widely known: the profound religiosity of the Afghan population. However, the image we have of Afghanistan today—that of the Taliban, of stonings, and of the burqa—is an extremely recent form, unknown before the late 1970s. In a memoir describing his posting in Kabul between 1936 and 1944, Pietro Quaroni, the Italian ambassador, noted: "Of all the Muslim countries where I have lived, Afghanistan is certainly the most religious, but without a shadow of fanaticism."[2]

Some historians attribute this peaceful disposition to the Sufi spiritual tradition of intimate religiosity; others see it as a legacy of Mughal culture, whose religious tolerance was celebrated. In 1504, Babur, the founder of the Mughal Empire, had chosen Kabul as the capital because of the city's deeply cosmopolitan character: "In Kabul, people speak 11 or 12 languages," he wrote, "including Arabic, Persian, Turkish, Mughali, Hindi, Afghan, Pashayi, Paraji, Gibri, Birki and Laghmani . . . one can find goods there from Khorassan, from Roum [Europe], from Iraq and from China."[3] Four centuries later, Quaroni was still able to write: "In Kabul, I did more than just learn: I touched the unity of the history of the world."[4]

After 1945, Afghanistan remained officially neutral, though it was tacitly considered to fall within the Soviet sphere of influence. However, the absence of any formal agreements allowed its governments to pursue the traditional political strategy of playing on the rivalry between the two superpowers in order to obtain loans and investments from both sides. In fact, according to Husain Haqqani, between 1956 and 1969, Afghanistan received $250 million in assistance from the United States and $550 million from the Soviet Union.[5]

In 1960 the historian Arnold Toynbee described Helmand Valley—located at the center of a great irrigation and industrialization project—as "a piece of America inserted into the Afghan landscape."[6] The city of Kabul was known as the "Paris of Central Asia," and according to Thomas E. Gouttierre, director of the Center for Afghanistan Studies at the University of Nebraska, who lived there for a decade beginning in 1964, it was "one of the most beautiful places in the world."[7] To be sure, Kabul at the time was a small city of about 300,000 inhabitants, but by 1979 its population had grown to over 913,000.

Urbanization brought a typical array of problems: the University of Kabul itself was transformed into a battlefield pitting leftists against Islamists, with the latter growing steadily in power. But much of the country's life took place outside of Kabul. The urbanization process had barely begun, and the quantitative and qualitative gaps between the city and countryside were larger than they were in other countries. In the early 1970s roughly 88 percent of Afghans lived in the countryside; fifteen years later that proportion had only dropped to about 86 percent.[8] The peasants' living and working conditions, their patriarchal values, and their religious piety were essentially the same as they had been two centuries earlier. Thus the mullahs' power over people's consciences remained uncontested.

The Afghan mullahs had very little in common with their Iranian colleagues, putting aside the obvious differences in religious observance—majority Sunni instead of Shiite. In the first place, they did not constitute a truly structured clergy: in the village, they led prayers, taught, resolved family disputes, and often served as judges, but outside the village, they were connected by no institutional bonds. They also lacked the general culture of their Shiite colleagues; they had no historical depth, since their tasks had not changed in centuries. Finally, they rarely owned property and lived essentially from the donations of the faithful, except in certain cities where they received stipends from the state. To be sure, as was the case elsewhere, the poorest among the faithful were ready to deprive themselves of the most basic needs, if necessary, to be able to pay the *zakat* and provide for the mullahs' requirements; the wealthy landowners, on the other hand, had the ability to shower the mullahs with rich donations, which made the latter quite sensitive to the importance of preserving the interests of their benefactors.

The ulemas occupied a different space. Traditionally, people used to turn to these wise men to rule on the conformity of laws and decisions, public or private, with sharia—their opinions are called *fatwas*. The movement toward secularization had diminished their social prestige. When the Islamist militants began to hammer together their own fatwas and found willing audiences for their opinions, it was a blow to the most important of the ulemas' prerogatives.

Even if they did not make up an institutionally unified body, Afghan religious leaders mobilized against any assault on the traditional order. In the 1920s they led a tribal rebellion against the national constitution, a document that created the civil registry, guaranteed women's right to education, and prohibited the marriage of children. When the king imposed "Kemalist" measures on the dress of men and women, he was overthrown, and his successor hastened to return to the status quo ante.

The battle over the modernization of the country started anew in the 1950s. A key measure taken by Mohammed Daoud Khan, the prime minister of the king, who was also the king's cousin and brother-in-law, was to create a new national army capable of resisting tribal and religious pressures. As part of this initiative, officers were sent to the Soviet Union for training; while there they would observe firsthand the superior living standards of the Muslim peoples of Soviet Central Asia. Upon their return, the soldiers became committed supporters of modernization.

In July 1973 Daoud used "his" army to overthrow the king. The coup d'état also gave a timely boost to the opposing interests of Iran and Pakistan: these two countries fanned religious passions in Afghanistan and ultimately dragged it back into the whirlwind of confrontation between the superpowers, and they did so just as this confrontation was entering a new phase.

AFGHANISTAN ON THE EVE OF HOLY WAR

Iran has never really gotten over the loss of its eastern provinces in 1747. This separation came at a time of steadily waning influence; therefore, whenever minds in Tehran wistfully entertain thoughts of regaining lost grandeur, eyes inevitably turn toward Afghanistan.

In 1971 the shah of Iran organized in Persepolis a sumptuous celebration of the 2,500 years of the Persian Empire, thus offering himself to the world as the heir of Cyrus the Great and of his country's long and glorious history. In a departure from history, the $300 million spent for silken tents equipped with marble toilets, for the bottles of Dom Perignon rosé 1959, Château Lafite Rothschild 1945, and Moët et Chandon 1911 served to his 25,000 guests, came not from glorious military conquests but from oil revenues. The shah nonetheless felt that he had embarked on a historic mission: while he was transforming Iran into an industrial and military power, he began to take an interest in the "lost province" of Afghanistan. In 1974 the shah "launched a determined effort to draw Kabul into a

Western-tilted, Tehran-centered regional economic and security sphere embracing India, Pakistan, and the Persian Gulf states."[9] Washington supported this initiative. At that time, the United States had three major sources of concern in the Middle East: the recent disengagement of the United Kingdom from the region in 1971; the signing of a cooperation agreement between Iraq and the Soviet Union in 1972; and the use of the "oil weapon" by producer countries in 1973. Therefore Washington was all the more favorable to any attempt to reinforce its gendarme in the Persian Gulf, particularly if it involved an incursion into the Soviet Union's ambiguous sphere of influence in Afghanistan and India.

From Islamabad's perspective, the need to intervene in Afghanistan was felt even more pressingly. There, too, the pretext was of a historic nature, although the history was much more recent: it had to do with the Durand Line. Accepted grudgingly by Kabul, it was crossed in 1919 by the Afghan Army, leading to the Third Anglo-Afghan War. The birth of Pakistan revived the dispute and sparked an immediate crisis between the two countries, a crisis that quickly drew in the superpowers, with the United States rushing to Pakistan's assistance and the Soviet Union hurrying to Afghanistan's side. When Daoud Khan took power in 1973, he gambled on the irredentism of the Pashtuns to reinforce his prestige within the military and to subdue the Islamist rebellion that had recently arisen on political grounds. In Islamabad, Ali Bhutto was delighted at this turn of events. The nationalist card that Daoud had so maladroitly played offered Bhutto an unexpected opportunity to redeem himself from the recent humiliation of losing Bangladesh, and a chance to turn toward a country that, in the eyes of many of his compatriots, should always have been part of Pakistan all along—at least its Pashtun region. Starting in 1973, Islamabad began to arm and train on its territory three groups of Islamist Afghans with an objective of launching an attack on the government in Kabul as soon as possible.[10]

The attempted insurrection was launched in July 1975. Daoud managed to thwart it fairly easily, but his grip on power began to grow shaky. His soft-pedaling of the demands for a Pashtunistan aroused the suspicion of the army, which began aligning itself with the open opposition of the ulemas and the clandestine action of the Islamist movements financed and equipped by Tehran and Islamabad. Daoud revived the old policy of playing at several tables at once. Without breaking relations with Moscow, he engineered a rapprochement with the West and its regional allies in

Iran and Pakistan, fully aware that the objectives of his two neighbors were opposed. To establish his credibility in the eyes of the latter two—and the Americans—he excluded pro-Soviet figures from the government and began persecuting them. In April 1978, the assassination of a highly respected trade-union leader finally caused the military to turn against him, despite, according to Dilip Hiro, the Kremlin's efforts to restrain it.[11] Still, Nur Muhammad Taraki, leader of the radical wing of the pro-Soviet People's Democratic Party of Afghanistan, was soon named president of the new Democratic Republic of Afghanistan.

First-person accounts of life in Afghanistan prior to the outbreak of war always seem to give the impression of a sort of Golden Age. And yet the country was then, as it remains today, one of the poorest in the world: the rate of illiteracy hovered around 90 percent; the infant mortality rate, among the world's highest, at 25 percent; and life expectancy stuck at forty years, among the world's shortest. Nonetheless, one can readily understand that, when compared to the material and moral devastation brought on by war, the impression looking back can only be of a happy and blessed land. The retrospective accounts do differ on one point: for some, this "Golden Age" ended with the coup d'état of April 1978; for others, it ended with the Soviet invasion in December 1979. The difference in time is minimal, but it says much about the quantity and quality of the events that filled the eighteen months between those two events.

Despite the cautions of Soviet advisers, the regime born in April 1978 proceeded to institute some drastic measures: it erased peasants' debts; abolished usury; distributed land to some 200,000 rural families; excluded the mullahs from the education system; abolished forced marriages, marriages involving children, and the sale of young brides; opened new schools; and made primary education compulsory for all children. Things went relatively well in the cities, but in the countryside these measures encountered fierce opposition. Rural dwellers, while tempted by the possibility of receiving a parcel of land, were shocked by the notion of making education compulsory for women, all the more so because most of their classes would be taught by men. When the Committees for Agrarian Reform arrived in the villages, not only did the big landowners resist the changes, but they could count on the support of the mullahs and the peasants. The landowners were largely successful in persuading the mullahs and peasants that the redistribution of land and the erasing of debt amounted to pillaging and were thus condemned by the Koran. As Sahar Gul, the mullah of Laghman Province, later explained to CNN, "the Communists . . . wanted to destroy Islamic traditions: to rid Afghanistan of poverty and make everyone equal. This is against the law of Islam: God has decided who is rich and who is poor. It can't be changed by Communists. It's beyond imagination."[12] Meanwhile, the large landowners made it known that whatever decisions the reform committees might impose, they would take back their lands the moment the government delegations headed back to Kabul.

With its voluntarist policies, the government provoked a social and political divide that it dealt with through repression. Persecuted Islamists and mullahs went underground and made contact with Pakistan and Iran. In those two countries, in the meantime, things had changed. In Islamabad, the putschist General Muhammad Zia ul-Haq, the self-appointed "chief martial law administrator," had accelerated his program of Islamizing Pakistan, making religious training obligatory for the military and placing sharia tribunals on the same level as the civil courts. He had another reason for intensifying aid to the Afghan Islamists: his determination to pursue the nuclear program launched by Ali Bhutto, which the United States resolutely opposed to the point of suspending all economic and military assistance in April 1979.

In Iran, by February 1979, the ayatollahs had become the masters of the country. In Tehran, which had long feared the activism of Islamabad, a new worry emerged: that the influence of a re-Islamized Sunni Pakistan in Afghanistan might lead to a "final solution" of the Hazara problem—the Shiite minority group that accounts for roughly 15 percent of the population and is regularly persecuted by other Afghan ethnic groups. To counterbalance the influence of Islamabad and its Saudi ally, Khomeini's Iran founded its own mujahidin. The capture of the Afghan city of Herat, the former capital of Persian Khorasan, on March 16, 1979, was the spectacular operation that accelerated Soviet involvement: with the assistance of a group of Islamists in the Afghan army, the mujahidin who had come from Iran turned the local peasants against the educators sent from Kabul by Taraki's government and the Soviet military advisers. All were massacred, including the families of the latter group. The insurrection—subdued only after the arrival of three hundred Soviet tanks and airborne troops—lasted five days and left between 5,000 and 25,000 dead.[13]

THE GEOPOLITICAL ROOTS OF HOLY WAR
IN AFGHANISTAN

Soviet leaders would have gladly avoided intervening in Afghanistan. According to Dilip Hiro, before the events in Herat they had rejected twenty requests for military assistance from the Taraki government.[14] For Moscow, a direct intervention seemed sure to irreparably damage the relationship with Afghanistan.

The good rapport between the two countries was for Moscow a precious legacy of czarism, for it had the potential, at least, to assist in addressing Russia's foremost geopolitical dilemma: the lack of access to warm-water ports navigable throughout the entire year. A landlocked power—even if only *virtually* landlocked—has no hope of becoming a dominant world power. In 1905, during the war against Japan, the Russian fleet had taken seven months to sail from Saint Petersburg to the Sea of Japan, where numerous Russian warships were immediately sent to the bottom at the Battle of Tsushima Strait.

Russia's entire foreign policy from the sixteenth century to 1945 can be succinctly summed up as an effort to expand toward the "warm seas": the Mediterranean Sea—directly, via the Balkans, or indirectly, via the Black Sea—and the Pacific and Indian Oceans. Needless to say, British policy, and later, American policy, toward Russia consisted essentially of trying to prevent it from reaching these same warm seas, in particular the Indian Ocean. The late-nineteenth-century compromise on Afghanistan was an acceptable outcome for the Russians, given the conditions: it allowed them, in a manner of speaking, to get a foot in the door. Leaders in Moscow were quite aware that as long as relations among the powers remained unchanged, the possibility of opening this door wide and resuming their southward march would be impossible; but, as we know, relations between powers rarely stay static for long.

Between 1978 and 1979 they had changed a great deal. We are not talking of an upheaval but certainly a sufficiently dramatic change to concern the Kremlin. China and Japan had signed a peace treaty, which, among other things, reduced Moscow's room for maneuver in the East. On the Western front, the European Monetary System was created and a Polish pope was elected. On the Middle Eastern front, the Americans had retaken the initiative by fostering peace between Israel and Egypt, and there was a revolution unfolding in Iran. Soviet leaders hoped that the Iran of the aya-tollahs would enter their orbit after having left that of the United States; but little by little they were forced to reconsider. Taken together, these conditions enormously increased the specific weight of Afghanistan, and the Soviet leaders tried everything in their power to keep it in their sphere of influence. Their first option was to consolidate the friendly relation-ship, while limiting as much as possible the direct interference that would have produced the opposite effect.

The day after the Herat insurrection ended, Taraki traveled to the Krem-lin to ask for "practical and technical assistance, with men and arms"; in other words, the sending of Soviet troops. In Moscow, Taraki was lectured by Alexei Kosygin, the Soviet prime minister: "The entry of our troops into Afghanistan would outrage the international community. . . . Our common enemies are just waiting for the moment when Soviet troops appear in Afghanistan. This will give them the excuse they need to send armed bands into the country." Kosygin added, prophetically, "Our troops would have to struggle not only with an external aggressor, but with a significant part of your own people. And the people would never forgive such things."[15]

If the Soviets were in fact reluctant to engage in Afghanistan directly, the Americans may have forced the issue. On July 3, 1979, President Carter authorized clandestine aid—via Pakistan—to the mujahidin. Zbig-niew Brzezinski later explained the reason: "This aid was going to induce a Soviet military intervention . . . drawing the Russians into the Afghan trap."[16] The question thus arises: why was the United States so determined to draw the Russians into war, to invest \$3.2 billion in this effort—counting only the 1981–1988 period—to support an army of Islamist guerrillas whom the Americans themselves considered "scary, vicious, and fascist"[17] while closing their eyes to the Pakistani nuclear program? There were at least three reasons for this: geostrategy, containment policy, and the "loss of Iran."

Geostrategy. When the United States took over the role of "leading the world" from the United Kingdom, American strategists learned from the geopolitical doctrine formulated by the British geographer Halford Mackinder in the early twentieth century. His contention was that to pre-serve the British Empire, it was necessary at all costs to prevent the Rus-sian Empire from establishing privileged relations with what we can call a "bordering" great power—that is, Germany, Japan, or even a reunified

China—that could upset the global balance of power. Neither Mackinder nor the Americans—contrary to conventional Cold War wisdom—ever considered Russia as a significant threat in and of itself: its geopolitical and economic handicaps relegated it to a subordinate position in this potential "privileged relationship" with a neighboring littoral power; unless, that is, it was able to surmount these handicaps.

Balanced containment. This continuous geostrategic objective of the Cold War consisted in striving for a difficult balance: to weaken the Soviet Union sufficiently that it not be tempted to cross the lines established at the end of World War II, especially in Asia, but not so much as to risk losing its essential partnership against Europe.

Loss of Iran. After the revolution, Iran no longer served a role as the American gendarme of the Persian Gulf. For the United States, the control of the Gulf energy artery is doubly strategic, vital not only to ensure its own petroleum provisions but to influence the supplies reaching others. Simplistic ideologies regarding the "war for oil" masked the fact that the second objective is far more important than the first. For example, in 1981 about 22 percent of U.S. net petroleum imports came from Persian Gulf producers, the same figure as in 2011. In 2015 the United States imported much more oil from Canada than from all the Persian Gulf producers combined; at the same time, petroleum from the Middle East constitutes more than 50 percent of Chinese imports, about 60 percent of India's, more than 80 percent of South Korea's, and nearly 90 percent of Japan's.[18] The global flow of oil is fundamentally a *political tool* for the United States; it is above all for that reason—starting in 1943 with President Franklin D. Roosevelt's declaration that "the defense of Saudi Arabia is vital to the defense of the United States"—that American foreign policy doctrines treated the Persian Gulf as a zone of paramount interest, to be dominated and defended by any means necessary.

If only for simple geography, Afghanistan could not replace Iran as the gendarme of the Gulf. The Americans' goal was not to take the Soviets' place in Kabul but to prevent them from profiting from the new situation in Iran to advance their pawns in the Middle East and toward the Indian Ocean. It was necessary to get out ahead of the game. Along with countless drawbacks, the success of the ayatollahs in Iran presented an opportunity for the Americans: to play Islam against Moscow, thus making this one of the stakes of the new confrontation.

Relations between Russia and Islam reach far back into history; the relationship has generally been one of collaboration and good-neighborliness. After the mass conversions that came immediately after the Russian conquest of Kazan, the Tatar capital, in 1552, the czars opposed the Orthodox Church's desire to pursue the conversions of new Muslim subjects. Catherine II went so far as to include the latter in a plan to "transform religious authority in each community into an instrument of imperial rule," and it was then that she created the political figure of the "grand mufti."[19] To better facilitate its expansion in Asia and the Balkans, Catherine II and her successors believed that Russia had to simultaneously be both a Christian power *and* a Muslim power.

With the exception of the Stalinist period—during which the Muslim population was hardly alone in suffering the rigors of the regime—successive Soviet governments pursued the czarist policy of good relations with the Islamic world, in particular when the anticolonial struggles opened new doors for them. The competitive advantage that Moscow enjoyed was the relatively privileged condition of the inhabitants of the Soviet Union's Muslim-majority republics of Central Asia and the Caucasus when compared to most Muslims elsewhere in the world.

All the great powers attempted, at one point or another, to conquer the hearts and minds of the Muslim world and use them against their rivals: the Austrians tried this in the Balkans; the Germans in Turkey before World War I; the British in the Arab world during the same war; the French in Algeria; the Italians in Tunisia and Libya; again, the Germans in the Arab world, Iran, and India on the eve of World War II; and so on. However, the Russians, who were first to do so, benefited from their much more extensive experiences in this domain. The Americans, on the other hand, were the last to do so, and their interventions have often been clumsy and self-defeating.

For a long time—at least until the Iranian Revolution—the United States managed to compensate for its inexperience by applying its vast political, economic, and military strengths. With the coup d'état in Indonesia in 1965, the chain of countries involved in the containment of the Soviet Union in Asia was composed mainly of large Muslim countries, and it extended from the Pacific to the Mediterranean: Indonesia, Malaysia, Pakistan, Iran, Saudi Arabia, Jordan, Turkey, and, after 1972, Egypt.

The first link in this chain was put in place by President Roosevelt's declaration in February 1943 concerning the defense of Saudi Arabia. At that time, the heart of the Middle East problem was certainly not the Soviet Union, with which Roosevelt shared similar "anti-imperialist"—that is, anticolonial—aims; rather, it was the United Kingdom. Since the end of World War I, the British had been leading a desperate fight to maintain their colonial positions around the globe even as the United States was steadily nibbling away at them. The declaration of February 1943 was but one step in this process; the Casablanca Conference, Bretton Woods, the creation of Israel, and, finally, the Suez Crisis were the others. On each of these occasions, Washington and Moscow found themselves on the same side of the barricade.[20] Islam was "discovered" only later, in connection with the Korean War, when it seemed possible to use it for the containment of the Soviet Union in Asia, if not solely for that purpose.

"AMERICAN" ISLAM AGAINST SOVIET RUSSIA (AND BEYOND)

The beginnings were more than modest. "Very few people in the government even thought very much about Islam," recalled Hermann Eilts, a two-time ambassador to Riyadh, starting in 1947. Moreover, according to Eilts, "The general view in the U.S. government and in the academic world was that Islam was becoming a shrinking political factor." David Long, one of Eilts's colleagues, confirmed: "We didn't know anything . . . we wanted oil and we wanted to fight communism. We weren't really all that interested in all that crap about Islam."[21]

A first attempt involved a rather primitive campaign using comic books in Iraq in 1951; their central character had the not very subtle name of "Greedy Red Pig." In 1953 Bernard Lewis was probably the first to suggest the use of certain Sufi societies in the Caucasus "as a fifth column inside the Soviet empire."[22] Similar recommendations were later made by Donald Wilber, the CIA's Islam specialist who had helped organize the overthrow of Mossadegh.[23] But others in Washington were reluctant to exploit Islam politically, for they believed that the traditional concept of sharia as an antidote to oppression and injustice made it more of an "objective ally" of communism.

The die was cast with the coup d'état in Iran in 1953 and with the actions taken against the pan-Arab nationalism of Gamal Abdel Nasser starting in 1954. It should be noted that the United States hesitated considerably in both cases: beyond the reason mentioned above, there was a risk of strengthening the British positions in both countries—then both were seen as traditionally in London's sphere of influence.

The Americans decided to act only when they saw that there was also a possibility of striking at British interests: thus, after the coup in Iran, American petroleum companies largely replaced the British companies; and the Suez Crisis of 1956 provided the occasion to definitively oust the British from Egypt—and, in fact, from the Mediterranean Basin. American interventionism in the region, and the use of Islam to facilitate it, had three objectives: the weakening of British positions; the opposition to any attempt at unifying the Arab world; and the containment of the Soviet Union.

In 1968, however, when the British decided to withdraw their forces from "east of the Suez" by 1971 at the latest, they faced the wrath and threats of President Lyndon Johnson.[24] The American attitude appears paradoxical: after having done everything in its power to weaken the British in the region, the United States felt "betrayed" when London declared itself defeated. The fact was that American priorities had recently changed: London, by this time, no longer represented a source of concern, while Moscow had gained a solid footing in the Middle East.

The Soviet Union wanted to use its presence in the region to compensate for its loss of influence in Indonesia and for its increasingly tense confrontation with China; thus it became the leading provider of aid and arms to the Middle East, requiring the Americans to increase their military assistance by a factor of ten in the years leading up to the Six-Day War—from $44 million to $495 million, only part of which went to Israel. By way of comparison, in 1966 alone, the Soviet Union had directed $428 million to Syria.[25] Bogged down in Vietnam, the Americans counted on the British; but the British, even if they had wanted to oblige, no longer had the resources to do so.

A long period of strategic blur ensued. The Israeli-Arab wars of 1967 and 1973 and the growing importance of the oil-producing countries placed Washington on the defensive. During this period the United States faced other tests, and they were hardly negligible: it had to abandon the gold standard in 1971; sign a peace agreement with North Vietnam in 1973; and face, along with the other great industrial powers, the most serious economic crisis since World War II in 1973–1975. Furthermore, in 1974 President Richard Nixon was forced to resign following the Watergate scandal and the United States was governed for two years by a president, Gerald Ford, who had not been elected on the presidential ballot, since the vice president elected in 1972, Spiro Agnew, had resigned in 1973 over tax evasion allegations. Henry Kissinger, then serving as secretary of state, was effectively the regent during this period, and he was the principal supporter of Iran as the only trustworthy ally in the Persian Gulf. Zbigniew Brzezinski shared Kissinger's focus on a renewed American initiative in the Middle East, with the peace between Egypt and Israel representing an important step. But in the wake of the Iranian Revolution, American activism in the region led almost automatically to increased interest in Afghanistan. This was the occasion, as Brzezinski put it, to give the Soviets "their Vietnam."

Islam was the cornerstone of this Afghan involvement. President Carter wrote a letter directly to Khomeini to ask him to release the American hostages in the name of common religious values.[26] Brzezinski was more concrete: the ayatollahs' victory had advanced the cause of political Islam on the ground, making it attractive to Muslims all over the world and significantly, as concerned the United States, to those in Afghanistan and the Soviet Union. Among Brzezinski's colleagues was Richard Pipes—who was to be promoted by Ronald Reagan—who, as early as 1955, supported the notion of separating Soviet Central Asia from the rest of the Soviet Union to give birth to "a new Turkic, Muslim state oriented toward the Middle East."[27]

The use of the "Islamic weapon" also provided powerful motivation for the Saudis. They had established close relations with Pakistan starting in the early 1960s; the ayatollahs' revolution had strengthened those bonds by inaugurating a new phase of hostile competition with Iran. Indeed, Riyadh—directly or by way of the Organization of the Islamic Conference, created in Jeddah in March 1972—had made "Muslim internationalism" its preferred foreign policy tool, made all the more potent since petroleum revenues had quadrupled in this period. Suddenly, Tehran had stolen the spotlight: Islam had triumphed in Iran because it had been militant, modern, and popular. Meanwhile, the success of state-controlled Islam in

Saudi Arabia—bureaucratic, sclerotic, and elitist—was due only to oil wealth and inspired no enthusiasm. Even the fact that Iran was Shia did not seem to pose any obstacle to its newfound popularity. In November 1979 hundreds of fundamentalist Sunnis seized the Grand Mosque in Mecca, hurling the same accusations used by Khomeini against the Saudi leaders: that they were corrupt and subjugated to the United States.

Thus a heterogeneous front was created in support of the Islamist revolt and against the Taraki government in Kabul, comprising Pakistan, which already controlled an experienced network, and Saudi Arabia but also Iran, the United States, and, soon to follow, China. Their argument could not have been simpler: a people of faith linked to their most sacred traditions were being subjected to a communist dictatorship whose objective was to destroy the very foundations of their society, starting with its religion. Several Anglo-Saxon observers noted incoherencies in this premise. A year after the Taraki coup, the Irish political scientist Fred Halliday wrote in the *New York Times* that in Afghanistan "probably more has changed in the countryside over the last year than in the two centuries since the state was established."[28] His vision may have been overly optimistic, conditioned by his political convictions, but on the religious question, other observers not known for their progressive sympathies added their voices. Even the typically conservative *Economist*, on September 11, 1979, recognized that "no restrictions had been imposed on religious practice." The religious question, as reported in the *New York Times* on April 13, 1979, "is being used by some Afghans who actually object more to President Taraki's plans for land reforms and other changes in this feudal society." Even after the Soviet invasion, a BBC reporter who had spent four months alongside the rebels affirmed that they were "fighting to retain their feudal system and stop the Kabul government's left-wing reforms which [are] considered anti-Islamic."[29]

Throughout 1979 Taraki and the Soviet advisers in Afghanistan had begun to lose control of the situation, as well as of large swaths of territory. That further exacerbated divisions within the pro-Soviet party that already tended to follow old tribal fault lines. On the one side was the Khalq (People) faction led by Taraki and Hafizullah Amin, which was loyal to the Ghilzai clan; on the other was the Parcham (Flag) faction headed by Babrak Karmal, whose allegiance was to the Durrani clan.[30] The differences between Taraki and Amin led to another palace conspiracy, which climaxed in September in the murder of Taraki and a split within the miltary. Amin, who took power, attempted to soften the measures adopted by Taraki by announcing a plan for the refurbishment of mosques, distributing free copies of the Koran, and invoking Allah in his speeches. According to the Soviet services, Amin also made contact with Pakistan and the insurgents. For Moscow, this last decision seemed to indicate that, however things turned out, Afghanistan was lost.

The Politburo then decided to go all out, and on the night of December 25, 1979, some 50,000 Red Army soldiers crossed the border into Afghanistan, a number that would more than double within five years. On December 27 Amin was executed by Soviet special forces and replaced by his rival Babrak Karmal. A decade of horrific massacres was to ensue, followed by a further twenty-five years of material and moral devastation. As Kosygin had predicted when he rejected Taraki's request for ground troops, "the people would never forgive such things."

7

THE CATHOLICIZATION OF MODERNITY

E ven as the world was beginning to learn the name of Ruhollah
Khomeini, another exotic name grabbed the attention of the
global public: that of the archbishop of Krakow, Karol Wojtyła,
who was elected the 264th pope of the Catholic Church on October 16,
1978, under the name John Paul II.

At the time, few people drew any connection between Khomeini's
arrival in power and the election of the Polish pope. The first to do so, a
year later, was probably Geoffrey Godsell, an editorial writer for the *Christian Science Monitor*. Having declared Wojtyła and Khomeini to be "the two
most charismatic figures on earth," Godsell came to the point: "The Pope
and the Ayatollah are symbols within two of the world's great monotheistic religions of the deep-rooted certainties of the past which in earlier centuries gave men strength, hope, and security." He drew a conclusion that
went strongly against the prevailing wisdom, saying: "This may well be a
portent that religion rather than politics will more obviously influence the
course of human events in the coming decade."[1]

In fact, their ability to give men a feeling of "strength, hope and security" would influence the policy not just of the ensuing decade but of all
the decades to follow. And despite appearances, Wojtyła's influence is
quite likely going to prove more enduring than that of Khomeini. Indeed,
the election of the Polish pope is very probably the most significant of the

events that contributed, during the 1970s, to bringing religion back into political life—but not for the reasons most often mentioned.

John Paul II is, of course, widely seen as having played a decisive role in the fall of communism. Less well-known is the fact that Wojtyła himself dismissed that notion as "ridiculous," adding that the Eastern Bloc regimes "fell in the end because of the system's socio-economic weakness."[2] To be sure, he did not hesitate to drive a wedge between the Soviet Union, then in crisis, and its vassal regimes, helping to worsen the crisis. But for his intervention to have an effect, two preliminary conditions were required: that there was indeed a crisis under way, and that the populations of these countries were willing to follow the promptings of a religious leader. That had not been the case in 1970, for example, when the Catholic Church in Poland had played an entirely marginal role in the crisis that led to the removal of Władysław Gomułka from power.

In reality, the pontificate of John Paul II had a much more lasting impact on international relations than even his hagiographers credited him with. However, before we can consider the reasons that provoked the Catholic Church to change gears that fateful month of October 1978—when it turned to a leader who was capable of overseeing the rebuilding of the institution after a crisis of at least two centuries—we must take a look backward.

In one century—from *The Syllabus of Errors* to the Second Vatican Council—the church had moved from an attitude of intransigent hostility toward modern civilization to the recognition that the latter is *not* a "system designed expressly to weaken and perhaps destroy the Church of Christ," as Pope Pius IX declared in 1861, but rather an unavoidable step in the economic and social development of humanity.[3] A century of constant hemorrhaging of clergy and the faithful had largely proved that development could no longer be fought through nostalgia and anathema alone. To have any chance of success, the struggle against secularization had to shift gears: modernity could no longer simply be rejected; it had to be recognized, indeed celebrated, for those aspects universally considered positive, and even "Christianized" where appropriate.[4]

Yet it would not be accurate to suggest that with the Second Vatican Council, the church passed in only a matter of a few years—from October 1962 to December 1965—from the Middle Ages to modernity. The church was not situated in the Middle Ages in 1962, and it did not unconditionally accept modernity after 1965.

The transition from nostalgia for a supposed "Golden Age of Christianity"—essentially, feudal and peasant-oriented, and structured around this social order—to an opening to the changes of an industrial and urban society took much longer. It began when church leaders transformed their last feudal properties into capital, which was principally invested in the financial system and real estate; this phase corresponded to the first formulation of Catholic social doctrine, with the encyclical *Rerum Novarum* (1891) of Pope Leon XIII. The Second Vatican Council undeniably represented the major step in this transition, but its doctrinal culmination was represented by the encyclical *Centesimus Annus* (1991) of John Paul II, who recognized the "legitimacy" of profit.

Traces of this transition can be found where they might least be expected—for example, in the writings of Giuseppe Melchiorre Sarto, better known as Pope Pius X, who was famed for his condemnation of modernism and who later provided inspiration for Monsignor Marcel Lefebvre when he named his traditionalist group the Priestly Fraternity of Saint Pius X. In his encyclical *Il Fermo Proposito* (1905), Pius X in fact affirmed that the church could not live with its gaze turned continually toward the past: "It is impossible today to reestablish under the same form all the institutions which have been useful and even the only effective ones in past centuries," he wrote. He added that "the Church in its long history and on every occasion has wisely shown that she possesses the marvelous power of adapting herself to the changing conditions of civil society."

This "marvelous power of adapting," however, was never meant to imply an uncritical acceptance of modernity. To the contrary, those aspects of modernity that do not conform to doctrine, morality, or the "sacred rights" of the church have always been vigorously resisted. The strategic horizon has remained the same, reflected in the motto Pius X selected for his pontificate—*Instaurare omnia in Christo* (to restore all things in Christ)—and in the aforementioned Monsignor Marty's exhortation, in 1976, that society be adapted to the Gospel, and not the Gospel to society.

The risk that it be the Gospel that adapts itself to society—that the church submits itself to the "world" and thus loses its autonomy—was an unintended result of Vatican II. It was a serious misunderstanding, one might say, that provoked an extremely grave crisis, a crisis in which plummeting recruitment numbers and an explosion in the number of unfrocked priests were only the best-known consequences—and, for Catholic leaders, the most immediately alarming. The other aspect, much more grave when placed in context, was "the extremely confused situation, the doctrinal position of the Church [which was] not always clear," as Pope Benedict XVI articulated in an interview in 2007.[5] Let us quickly review the reasons for this "misunderstanding."

When it was convened in 1961, Vatican II was both ahead of *and* behind the times: behind, because the changes it was supposed to be taking into account had been evolving over decades, if not centuries; ahead, because the church personnel who should have been implementing its conclusions were manifestly not ready to do so. In their attempt to reconcile this contradiction, the organizers took two decisions that might have been expected to offset each other. On the one hand, they compiled the final resolutions with the intention of having them voted unchanged; on the other hand, they summoned 2,450 delegates to Rome, five-sixths of the global episcopate. The reason for the mass summoning, quite probably, was to spread as widely as possible the responsibility for carrying out difficult choices, while ensuring that the church's center kept a firm hand on the reins, and carrying this all out within a few weeks—inaugurated on October 11, 1962, the council was intended to finish its business in December 1962. In fact, it did not end until December 1965. The documents prepared by the Roman Curia were immediately pushed aside, and a relatively open discussion was imposed regarding every question on the table.

According to one anonymous cardinal interviewed in 2005 by Olivier Le Gendre, this was "a sort of putsch led by certain bishops against the Curia."[6] That thesis is plausible, for episcopal opposition to the center has always been very strong at the heart of the church, and it had grown stronger over the preceding century, at least, after Pope Pius IX had reacted to the rise of nation-states by moving toward greater centralization, aiming to curtail any temptation within the episcopates of different countries to establish themselves as national Catholic Churches. Thus many bishops interpreted the council as an occasion to exact revenge, with the result that centrifugal tendencies in the church seemed to gain an advantage over the unifying forces. Not knowing how to react, the Vatican lost control over large sectors of the Catholic world, particularly in developed countries, which were more exposed to the intellectual fashions of the moment; a new phase opened, characterized by the proliferation of unorthodox ways of living the faith, ranging along the entire spectrum not just of political options but also sociological, anthropological, philosophical, and thus, fatally, religious ones as well.

When Pope Paul VI died in the summer of 1978, the disarray was at its peak. The church had no choice but to pull itself back together, and the conclave offered the best occasion to elect a pope capable of righting the ship. No one can say what Albino Luciani—who, as Pope John Paul I, was the sovereign pontiff for just thirty-three days beginning on August 26, 1978—might have been able to do. Conversely, everyone knows what his successor, Karol Wojtyła, accomplished.

John Paul II flattered and exalted Catholics' pride in their identity, unhesitatingly resumed the path toward centralization, calmed nervous spirits, and sidelined the more undisciplined. He embodied the true spirit of the council by being both modern and antimodern at the same time. He became famous for his anticonformist gestures—which at the time were much stronger than those of Pope Francis thirty-five years later. He used every technical means offered by modernity to reach the most remote corners of the world, preferably by traveling there in person. He was the pope of stunning gestures, as when he asked for forgiveness for all the sins committed by "the men of the Church," or in his opening to the Jewish world. He cast aside the cautious and threadbare rules of traditional Vatican diplomacy to launch himself into forceful confrontation with the leaders of the superpowers: with Leonid Brezhnev in 1980; George H. W. Bush in 1991; and George W. Bush in 2003.

Then again, he was also the pope of the new Christianity, the pope who compared abortion to the Holocaust; made a ban on contraceptives an article of faith; traced the origins of the Holocaust and Joseph Stalin's massacres to Descartes and the Enlightenment; advocated for the beatification of Pius IX; sidelined, exiled, or silenced dissidents; and created 482 saints and saw the beatification of 1,340 others.[7] He was also, above all, the pope who marginalized those in the heart of the church who dreamed of modernizing Catholicism, in order to resolutely follow the path of Catholicizing modernity.

There is not the shadow of a contradiction in the pontificate of Karol Wojtyła. Rather, what we saw was the firm and resolute application of the big strategic decisions of the council: making peace with modernity even while denouncing its departures from divine law; and creating the conditions for the future reunification of the Christian world and the establishment of stable, peaceful, and fruitful relations with the world's other great religions, starting with Judaism and Islam.

Clearly John Paul II, a natural leader of the masses, was helped in his task by his pugnacious, determined, and charismatic personality; but let us not forget the audacity of the grand electors at the conclave of October 1978, who needed a man of precisely his stature to make the Catholic Church a protagonist—indeed, in retrospect, *the* protagonist—of the desecularization of the world.

PART III

THE HOLY WAR

If people worship gods and fight wars, they expect the former to take an interest in the latter.

—Peter Partner

The religious wars, almost always, were fought by princes and their armies for some tangible benefit, such as territory or trade routes. Religion was often a convenient excuse, but it was rarely the underlying purpose.

—Stephen L. Carter

8
THE CLASH OF CIVILIZATIONS

In one sense, there is no "Islam," and there is no "West."
—Graham Fuller

AN ATLANTICIST THESIS FOR THE "NEW WORLD ORDER"

The thesis of the "clash of civilizations," as we now know it in its current form, began circulating in the early 1990s, as the international order that had emerged from World War II was coming to an end. The phrase had first appeared in an article by Bernard Lewis on "The Roots of Muslim Rage," published in September 1990,[1] but he had already evoked the concept decades earlier, in the spring of 1956. Lewis spoke then of the "revolt of the world of Islam against the shattering impact of Western civilization which, since the 18th century, has dislocated and disrupted the old order."[2] The chief antagonists of the thesis, made newly fashionable in the final decade of the twentieth century, were the already so-called Islamic and Western civilizations.

The "clash of civilizations" thesis emerged from the narrow domain of geopolitical specialists in response to three major events that began in early 1990s: the Gulf War, which President George H. W. Bush insisted would help establish a "new world order"; the dissolution of the Soviet

Union; and the Yugoslav Wars. It was Samuel Huntington who brought this concept to the attention of the public, first through a *Foreign Affairs* essay in the summer of 1993, and then through his book *The Clash of Civilizations and the Remaking of World Order* (1996), an immediate best seller and one of the most discussed and controversial books of its time. After September 11, 2001, Huntington's thesis seemed almost prophetic.

Huntington's book contributed to a great debate on the future of international relations that was then already under way in the United States. Despite the 1990–91 war against Iraq, no "new order" had yet emerged; to the contrary, the breakup of the Soviet Union seemed to have produced a new phase of particularly acute international *dis*order. It was a critical moment because, since 1941, the Soviet Union had been a fundamental pillar of American global supremacy, having helped first to subdue the most formidable European competitor—Germany—and then to keep the Old Continent divided and under control. But the Soviet Union was itself a dangerous potential competitor in Asia; potential because to become an actual competitor it would have needed a far more robust economy and, as we have seen, would have required a strategic alliance with a neighboring great power that had access to open ocean warm water ports. Thus the Cold War was essentially ideological in Europe but real in Asia, to the point of transforming itself at least three times into a "hot war"— in Korea, Vietnam, and Afghanistan—as well as the proxy conflicts on the Indian subcontinent.

During the 1980s, however, the situation in Asia underwent a reversal: The Soviet Union had grown progressively weaker, losing its capacity for initiative. Japan, on the other hand, had become the most serious threat to American hegemony,[3] and China was experiencing the first of three decades of double-digit growth that would make it the "strategic competitor" of the United States in the twenty-first century. In short, the Soviet Union was fading precisely at the moment when, in addition to its traditional role as an unofficial American pillar of support in Europe, it could have served the same purpose in Asia, providing a counterweight to a threatening Japan and an emerging China.

Despite this critical situation, the fall of the Berlin Wall was widely celebrated as the definitive victory of the United States, a triumph of its system and its values. In reality, the evaporation of the Soviet Union posed more problems for Washington than it solved; all the more so on the

Old Continent. The dismantling of the Iron Curtain and, above all, German reunification had opened new possibilities for a comeback by the European powers—the agreement on the Maastricht Treaty, in December 1991, came just as the Soviet Union was falling apart. However, beside those declaring victory and touting the notion of a "unipolar world"—President Bill Clinton was prompted to cut military spending—were others urging the United States to exploit its temporary advantage. They argued that the United States must prevent the "re-emergence of a new rival"—the title of a document by Paul Wolfowitz, deputy secretary of defense under Dick Cheney, in February 1992.[4] This latter group included Richard Haass, who would oversee policy planning during the first term of President George W. Bush. Haass contended that the transformation of the world order meant that the United States must work "to see that any new 'balance' is in fact 'balanced' from our perspective," by going so far as launching "preventive attacks" if need be.[5]

If one introduces Huntington's book into this crucial debate—the second half of its title, after all, was *The Remaking of World Order*—a new dimension appears: that of Atlanticism, the current in American foreign policy that advocates a privileged relationship with Europe. In fact, a map of NATO's member countries and that of the "West"—which Huntington also refers to as "Western Christianity"—can be almost perfectly superimposed, with a few exceptions, the most noteworthy of which is Turkey, which Huntington considers a "torn country," that is, one that has betrayed its civilizational vocation.

Huntington offered the American ruling class a complete set of tools for dealing with the changes under way: he laid out a general theory, identified two major problems, formulated a hypothesis for the future of international relations, and proposed a solution. The theoretical framework: the relative strengths of the great powers change continually, and so there is never a definitive victor. The practical problems: the emergence of new rivals of the United States—notably China—and the decline of the West. The hypothesis on the future of international relations: "Islamic and Sinic [i.e., Chinese] societies . . . have reasons to cooperate with each other against the West." The solution: the common interest of the United States and Europe in fighting against their own "moral decline, cultural suicide, and political disunity" and in confronting, on an equal footing, the Muslim and Asian countries and their "assertions of moral superiority."[6]

Huntington's thesis achieved great popularity, which only grew with the new century, and not only because of the September 11 attacks. The final decade of the twentieth century had brought a new sense of optimism occasioned by the fall of the Soviet empire, as well as particularly vigorous economic growth in the United States, the beginning of an economic crisis in Japan, and the creation of the single currency in Europe. Conversely, the new century was one of disillusion and anxiety. It began with the bursting of the dot-com bubble, which led to a loss of the accumulated gains of the preceding five years.[7] That trend continued after the September 11 attacks and the unexpected difficulties encountered in Iraq and Afghanistan, and it was prolonged by the subprime crisis that began in 2007 and the ensuing explosion of unemployment. Europe, which shared in many of these problems, including major terrorist attacks on its own soil, also witnessed a crisis in its integration process after French voters rejected the European Constitution in 2005. All this took place against the backdrop of the extremely rapid rise of China, the recovery of Russia, and the emergence of new competitors.

In the space of a decade, the widespread sense in the United States and Europe had thus passed from exaltation over the triumph of the West to concern over its inexorable decline. This increasingly apparent incapacity to "govern" the world, to finally create a "new world order," led to ideological disorder and moral uncertainty, economic and social crises, and wars: in short, to the loss of clear landmarks and to a profound disquiet concerning the future. Peter Berger, let us recall, affirmed that anyone able to "provide or to renew certainty has a ready market."[8] Huntington's depiction of the world responded exactly to this demand: it was clear, it offered simple and clean demarcations between civilizations, and it helped in understanding who was inside of borders and who was beyond them. But while this representation was neat and clean and easily understandable, it had one major flaw: it simply did not exist.

THE INVENTION OF THE WEST

Among those who explain international relations in terms of civilizational blocs, many have felt the need to pay tribute to Fernand Braudel and his encyclopedic—and essential—*Grammaire des civilisations.*[9] This linkage, however, is doubtful for at least two reasons. The first, as Niall Ferguson explains in his book *Civilization: The West and the Rest*, is that the international political situation first requires one to analyze the processes of transformation, whereas Braudel "was better at delineating structures than explaining change."[10] The second, as Braudel himself explains it in the opening sentence of his book: "It would be pleasant to be able to define the word 'civilization' simply and precisely, as one defines a straight line, a triangle or a chemical element . . . [however,] the vocabulary of the social sciences, unfortunately, scarcely permits decisive definitions."[11]

One "decisive definition" that Braudel does use, if cautiously, is that of "Western civilization," or simply the "West." Braudel prefers to speak of *cultural zones*, or "areas which in turn can be subdivided into a series of districts." The civilization referred to as Western, he continues, is at the same time "American civilization" (including both North and South America), Russia, Australia–New Zealand, and Europe. Furthermore, Europe itself is the sum of a series of national civilizations—Polish, German, Italian British, French, and so on—which are in turn composed of a plethora of ever smaller subgroups—Scottish, Irish, Catalonian, Sicilian, Basque—whose mores, habits, clothing, food, languages, history, national mythologies, and other elements distinguish them from the larger whole.[12]

The invention of a "Western identity" was based on the same ideological mechanisms as in the invention of national identities. Anne-Marie Thiesse—who devoted considerable study to this subject in her book *La création des identités nationales: Europe, XVIIIe-XXe siècle*—asserts that the starting point of this invention was the search for a hypothetical common ancestry for the entire population of a single state aspiring to a *national* character. Ever since Western civilization evolved from being a matter of purely cultural interest to having a stake in international politics, it has been subjected to the same ideological vetting, starting with the establishment of its family tree. Today the most widely accepted genealogical hypothesis places its source at the confluence of Greek and Jewish culture. There was, to use the words of Joseph Ratzinger, "a theological interpretation of history," tracing the lineage of Europe—the matrix of Western civilization—from the Old Testament to medieval Christianity, by way of Greek cultural contamination.[13] The first version of this "interpretation" was seen in the works of numerous intellectuals of the late eighteenth and early nineteenth centuries, for whom medieval Europe—homogenous and pacified by the Catholic Church—had been torn apart first by the Protestant Reformation and then by the philosophy of the Enlightenment, before encountering the fire and blood of the French Revolution.[14]

The contemporary version—that of the Greek-Jewish roots of the West—includes two aspects that are often underestimated, if not altogether overlooked. The first: it simply "forgets" that Greek cultural contamination reached western Europe by way of the Arab-Muslim world—which also brought Chinese and Indian contamination with, among other things, the decimal system. The second: a common accusation lodged against Islam—that it never experienced the Reformation or Enlightenment—comes in the name of a conception of the West born from an *irreconcilable opposition* to the Reformation and Enlightenment.

The addition of Greek-Jewish roots to the romantic thesis on the Christian foundation of the West is very recent, and it could not be otherwise, for one of the least debatable currents running throughout European history is *anti-Judaism*.

But first let us consider the question of Greek heritage. In his *lectio magistralis* on Europe from 2004, Joseph Ratzinger quotes from the celebrated thesis of Henri Pirenne—published in 1937 in his book *Mahomet et Charlemagne*—on the rupture between the West and the East that occurred when, in the words of the Belgian historian, "for the first time in history the axis of Occidental civilization was displaced toward the North" by the Arab conquests.[15] Despite "this process of displacing boundaries," the future German pope wrote, "the conceptual continuity with the preceding Mediterranean continent . . . was assured by a theological interpretation of history," embodied by "the permanent *Sacrum Imperium Romanum* (Holy Roman Empire)."[16]

Several historians—among them Jacques Le Goff and Braudel himself—contested this thesis of "conceptual continuity" even before it became the founding principle of a supposed Western civilizational unity. These historians emphasize that the basis for the split between East and West can be traced to the moment when the Roman Empire divided, in 285, and particularly upon the death of Theodosius the Great in 395. By that date, the rupture was already effectively consummated, not only because of the numerous political and military vicissitudes that had gradually Germanized the western part of the empire but also because of the linguistic and cultural fractures between the Greek and Latin worlds. We know, for example, that the bishops of Rome were not present at the two councils that "settled" Christian doctrine—that of Nicaea in 325 and Constantinople in 381—not only because Rome was by then a city on the edge of the empire but because the bishops did not understand the official language of the church, which was Greek.

But the problem was not exclusively linguistic—far from it. According to Charles Freeman, it was specifically the affirmation of Christianity in the fourth and fifth centuries that led to the *destruction* of the Greek intellectual tradition, which was empirical, logical, and deductive. We must certainly recognize the contributions of the monks and Byzantine bureaucrats who helped preserve certain ancient texts, Freeman writes, while adding that transmitting them is one thing but "maintaining a tradition of rational thought" is quite another. In the Arab-Muslim world this tradition was perpetuated, nourished, and enriched, he continues, "but not in the Byzantine Empire or in the Christian West."[17] The last known astronomical observation from the ancient Greek world dates back to the Athenian philosopher Proclus, in 475. After that, we must wait until Nicolaus Copernicus, in the sixteenth century, before scientific thinking regains currency in Europe. For Freeman, far from representing the generative continuity of the West, the affirmation of Christianity had purely and simply led to "the closing of the Western mind."

The supposed Jewish heritage of Western civilization raises even greater perplexities. If an identity exists between Western civilization and Christianity, then there is also an identity between Western civilization and hostility toward Jews. This hostility has continued throughout the entire history of Christian influence on what eventually would become Europe. Many of the newer religion's early theologians expressed themselves in treatises and homilies entitled *Against the Jews*. They included Tertullian, Hippolytus of Rome, Cyprian of Carthage, Augustine, and John Chrysostom, with the latter going so far as to write: "Although such beasts are unfit for work, they are fit for killing. And this is what happened to the Jews: while they were making themselves unfit for work, they grew fit for slaughter."[18] When Christianity imposed itself as the official religion, the prior protections accorded to Jewish assets and their persons were relaxed. The turning point was the destruction of the synagogue of Callinicum—today, Raqqa, Syria—by a Christian mob in 388. Ambrose, the bishop of Milan, used this episode as pretext to touch off a power struggle with Emperor Theodosius, who had demanded that the assailants be punished and the Jews compensated for their losses: "It is lawful to set fire to the synagogues . . . if the laws forbid it, then they are bad laws."[19]

In the sixteenth century, in extremely Catholic Spain, hostility toward Jews, which up to then had been essentially religious, took on a racial element with the statutes on the *limpieza de sangre* (purity of blood). The weakening of the social weight of religion led to the birth of anti-Semitism, the modern form of this ancient hatred. Anti-Semitism is, as Bernard Lewis explains it, an attempt to find a rational justification for anti-Jewish aggressiveness, "the response of the secularized Christian, no longer able to use theological arguments, against the emancipated Jew."[20] In Europe, from that time on, there was a Christian branch and a "scientific" branch of anti-Semitism; the latter was capable of being both anti-Jewish and anti-Christian; thus Friedrich Nietzsche was one of the first to use the word *judenchristlich* (Judeo-Christian), but in a pejorative sense, to connote "chance robbed of its innocence; happiness polluted by the concept of 'sin'; well-being as danger, as 'temptation'; physiological ailments poisoned with the worm of conscience."[21]

In short, anti-Judaism seems to be a constituent element of the broader character of the West. Elsewhere in the world throughout much history, Jews have been persecuted because they are foreigners but very rarely because they are Jews. In Muslim countries, they were generally protected by the political authorities: Sultan Bayezid II welcomed to the Ottoman Empire some 200,000 Jews who had been evicted from Spain in 1492. Additionally, in 1555, when Pope Paul IV inaugurated a systematic campaign of persecution—with the papal bull *Cum Nimis Absurdum*—Suleiman the Magnificent, Bayezid's grandson, lodged an official protest and offered Ottoman protection to Italian Jews. The rare exceptions, as Bernard Lewis writes in another text, tended to be "contemptuous and dismissive rather than suspicious and obsessive." In the Middle East, it was among the Christian minorities that one would find anti-Jewish sentiment, which could "usually be traced back to European originals." At the time of the Dreyfus affair in the late nineteenth century, Lewis recalls, "Muslim comments usually favored the persecuted Jew against his Christian persecutors."[22]

The positive connotation of "Judeo-Christianity" made its appearance only after World War II. As Mahmood Mamdani writes, "The notion of a Judeo-Christian civilization crystallized as a post-Holocaust antidote to anti-Semitism."[23] Judaism was thus "rehabilitated" to the point of being made an integral part of European history. Yet another paradox rests in this ideological operation, and it is hardly a minor one: Jews were essentially a European people for nearly two millennia, but it was only after they had been nearly entirely annihilated from the Old Continent that their role was, in a way, "revalued."[24] This posthumous "revaluation" came, furthermore, through association with the same Christianity that had persecuted the Jews for some sixteen centuries. As Richard Bulliet put it, if one could ask the Jews and Christians of past centuries their reaction to the phrase "Judeo-Christian civilization," there would most likely be "majorities in both camps expressing repugnance for the term."[25]

So the idea that the West has Judeo-Christian roots is based on "weak historical depth," as Mamdani put it.[26] A more detailed study of these same roots can lead to far different, and sometimes unexpected, results. Bulliet, for example, along with many others, affirms that "the past and the future of the West cannot be fully comprehended without appreciation of the twinned relationship it has had with Islam over some fourteen centuries"; for that reason he believes that one should speak rather of "Islamo-Christian civilization."[27] The West, he adds, has many roots: not only in "Byzantine-Muslim civilization" but—and especially—in "Judeo-Muslim civilization."

THE BORDERS OF THE WEST

Adding to the difficulty in defining a civilization are the differences that emerge when one seeks to identify its members. Samuel Huntington, unlike Braudel, believes that Latin America represents a civilization of its own, distinct from the rest of the West, and that Russia is the "core state of Orthodox civilization"—also referred to as *Eastern Christianity*—and in the event of a clash, it is more likely to lean toward the Sino-Islamic alliance than toward Western Christianity.

Since the concept of Western civilization is used for political ends, its membership becomes a crucial question: the stronger the sense of common identity, the greater the cohesion when a clash occurs. Braudel, who viewed civilizations through a cultural lens, was able to include Russia among the "European civilizations bound to the West"—and this *in 1963*—at a time when almost no one would dare question the unalterable opposition between the West, or "free world," led by Washington and the Eastern Bloc, or the "Communist world," headed by Moscow.

The political notion of the West is now definitively detached from its geographic origin. While the poles made it possible for geographers to settle on the conventional positions of *north* and *south*, the Greenwich meridian has never had the same effect on our understanding of *west* and *east*—had it done so, Oxford would be in the West and Cambridge in the East. From a geographical standpoint, this means that these two cardinal points are still being used subjectively: for an inhabitant of Vancouver, San Francisco, or Santiago, what we would normally describe as the Far East lies to the west; for the Japanese, China is a western country, while for the Indians, it is a country to the east.

Geographical subjectivism has become political subjectivism.[28] As early as 1905, President Theodore Roosevelt classified Japan as a Western country based not on geographic considerations, obviously, but on political ones: "Japan is the only nation in Asia that understands the principles and methods of Western civilization." Of course, the United States withdrew this qualification in 1941, only to restore it soon after the Japanese capitulated in 1945. By this same political logic, Israel, Australia, and New Zealand are often considered Western countries. Since the Ottoman conquest of the Balkans, the Turks have considered themselves Westerners—and Europeans—a sense that grew stronger with the Kemalist revolution and the entry into NATO. And yet the vast majority of Europeans consider the Turks to be Easterners or even, through a certain stereotyped exoticism, as the very embodiment of the East.

Samuel Huntington excludes Japan, Israel, and, naturally, Turkey from the Western civilizational bloc countries but includes Australia and New Zealand. The latter two countries fit the terms of his definition, which makes "Western Christianity . . . the single most important characteristic of Western civilization."[29] And that brings us back to the "theological interpretation of history," with Christianity as the "heart" of Western civilization. One should perhaps add that this is a post–Great Schism Christianity, whose cultural and ideological unity is assured precisely by its separation from Eastern Byzantine Christianity. Huntington specifies that "Western civilization is usually dated emerging about 700 or 800 CE," the same time frame as that cited by Ratzinger.[30]

The Christian Europe invented by the counterrevolutionary intellectuals of the late eighteenth and early nineteenth centuries was also post-schismatic, but it was pre-Protestant as well: for them, Europe was united *because* it was Catholic—some romantic Protestants, including Friedrich Schlegel, Adam Müller, Friedrich Stolberg, Johann Friedrich Overbeck, and Friedrich Wilhelm Schadow, went so far as to convert to Catholicism. For Huntington, however, Western Christianity can exist as a civilizational bloc only to the extent that its indispensable Roman Catholic foundation is consolidated by the contributions of the Reformation. He leaves Latin America outside of this bloc—although he sees it as "culturally close"—precisely because it is a land where Christianity remains exclusively Catholic, indolent because of its privileged relationship with the political power, "although this may be changing," he says.[31] The contributions of the Reformation, Huntington asserts, are decisive because they reacted "to the stagnation and corruption of existing institutions . . . [they] preach work, order and discipline; and appeal to emerging, dynamic middle-class people."[32]

This vision of Protestantism as a decisive factor in Western modernity is certainly not a novelty, at least since Max Weber. However, Huntington's originality lies in his rejection of all opposition between Catholicism and Protestantism, which he sees instead—even if he would have rejected this formulation—as the two contradictory poles of the dialectical unity that forms Western civilization.

THE BLOODY BORDERS OF WESTERN CIVILIZATION

Anyone seeking to build a political identity must first grasp, or else invent, the elements shared by a certain community, nation, or civilization: that is, those aspects that, in theory, all the group's members identify themselves with. In addition to the genetic aspect—the classical heritage of "Greek philosophy and rationalism, Roman law and Latin" and, of course, Christianity itself—Huntington adds other characteristics as distinctive to the Western community: "European languages; separation of spiritual and temporal authority; rule of law; representative bodies; and, individualism."[33]

Each of the characteristics suggested by Huntington allows for some confusion. For instance, from a linguistic viewpoint, the Hungarians,

Finns, Estonians, and Basques would be excluded from the West, while the Iranians and Afghans might be included. As well, there are some objections regarding the separation between spiritual and temporal authorities, for example, more about which later. But the problem resides not so much in the choice of characteristics themselves as in the need to identify the common elements that can justify, a posteriori, a postulated unity. The circular logic in this process not only risks leading to confusion that is more divisive than unifying—as with the European languages—it also produces another source of confusion. As summed up by the *Economist*, Huntington "often distorted reality rather than imposed order on it. He skated over the fact that many of the nastiest clashes take place within civilizations rather than between them."[34]

The thesis of Western unity has always rested on fragile foundations. According to the Catholic historian René Rémond, the romantic idea of a Christian Europe "arises in considerable part from nostalgia for a past that has been largely mythologized." Indeed, Rémond goes on to add: "It would be a great illusion to represent medieval Europe as a homogenous and unified world."[35] Another Catholic historian, Paul Kennedy, adds that, unlike in the cases of the Ottoman, Chinese, or Mughal Empires, "there never was a united Europe in which all parts acknowledged one secular or religious leader."[36] To the contrary, through nearly all its history, Europe was the scene of particularly devastating internecine wars. And when this theoretical West is split in two—Europe and the United States—it happened only after a bloody and traumatic break.

In the twentieth century Western and Christian powers engaged in horrific mutual slaughter, most notably the two world wars. In addition, as we have seen, once the "tyranny of values" had replaced the principle of legal and moral equality between sovereign states, both sides justified these massacres, in part, in the name of civilization's fight against barbarism. Thus, the "civilizational principle," like the humanitarian principle before it, entered into the panoply of political tools; as such, it was used in times of war just as it was in times of peace.

In 1933, for example, the Berlin publishing house Buchdruckwerkstätte released a pamphlet entitled *Germany's Fight for Western Civilization*. The fact that the title was in English, together with its content, suggested that the purpose was to mobilize a sort of "coalition of the willing" to defend Western civilization against a supposed threat from Slavic communism and its Jewish agents, a coalition that Hitler's Germany, of course, intended to lead. During the 1905 Russo-Japanese War, it was the Russians, in the figure of Prince Sergei Petrović Trubetskoy, who had claimed to be leading the defense of Western civilization against "the yellow danger, the new hordes of Mongols armed with modern technology."[37]

Walter Russell Mead offered his own civilizational reading of the international relations of the past four centuries, but in his reading, the clash runs through and divides the Huntington West: "The clash of civilization that dominates the history of the modern world," he wrote, is "the clash between the English-speaking powers of the United Kingdom and the United States and the various enemy nations since the 17th century who have fought against them to shape the world."[38] The former powers were convinced that their confrontations with, successively, France, Germany, Italy, Japan, and Russia were fights to the death between freedom and tyranny; their adversaries, on the other hand, were persuaded that they were leading a battle of civilization against the "cold, cruel, greedy, and hypocritical" Anglo-Saxons.

Mead's thesis is seductive, and, the civilizational rhetoric aside, it evokes a fault line that is real and constant. That fault line, however, has closed and then reopened over the centuries under variable geometries: to consider only the powers that he mentions, and in the twentieth century alone, the "Anglo-Saxons" have in turn been the allies of France, Russia, and Japan against Germany in World War I; France against Russia and Germany at the start of World War II; Russia against Germany, Vichy France, and Japan starting in 1940–41; West Germany and Japan—if reluctantly—against Russia and France during the Vietnam War; and, finally, Japan and several minor Western powers against Russia, France, and Germany during the Iraq War of 2003. But above all—and Mead's thesis naturally tends to underestimate this—the two Anglophone powers have been divided on virtually every vital geopolitical question in their bilateral relationship, even if those divisions have never led, since 1812, to open conflict.

The relationship between the United States and the United Kingdom developed into the modern *special relationship* only after Britain's humiliation over Suez in 1956—and after a pointed internal strategic dust-up between Anthony Eden and Harold Macmillan that could, at least theoretically, have led to an anti-American strategic choice, such as France made on the same occasion. Ever since the American colonies declared independence from Britain in 1776, the relationship between the Anglo-Saxon powers has been characterized by latent hostility, which led to open warfare only once but which has often been seriously strained. This confrontation culminated when the United States replaced Britain as the world's leading power in nearly every dimension: economic, financial, military, political, scientific, and cultural.

Many of the crucial developments in the nineteenth century saw the two countries on opposite sides. Tensions over the U.S.–Canada border flared up repeatedly—1837, 1839, 1844, 1867, and 1898—and the British attitude during the American Civil War was far from favorable to the Union, with open war only narrowly avoided in 1861. In 1898 it was evident that the American military initiative against Spain struck more directly at British geostrategic interests than at those of Spain itself, assuring American dominance in the Atlantic and Pacific Oceans "with mathematical certainty," as the American admiral Alfred Mahan wrote in 1890.[39] The new century opened when the shift of power between Britain and the United States was already relatively imbalanced in favor of the latter. This shift culminated with the two world wars, from which Britain emerged formally victorious but only after having lost its role as the world's financial hub—as well as its colonial empire.[40] As we have seen, the United States missed no opportunity after World War II to strike at British interests.

In his book *Civilization: The West and the Rest* (2011), Niall Ferguson contends that the chief flaw in Huntington's thesis—that the post–Cold War world would be characterized by clashes between civilizations—lies in the fact that, "so far," his predictions have not come to pass: "There has been no increase in inter-civilizational war since the end of the Cold War."[41] In reality, from the end of the Middle Ages to the threatened intervention in Syria in 2013, all major conflicts between powers now considered as Western have been *intracivilizational*. Put another way, in the rhyming terms made fashionable by Huntington himself and often repeated by others—including Ferguson—there has *never* been real unity within the "West" against the "Rest." To the contrary, and as we shall see in the following pages, Westerners have continually involved Islam in their mutual divisions and hostilities.

THE PEDAGOGY OF HATE

Why do they hate us? This question gnawed at Americans after the attacks of September 11, 2001, and especially following the eruptions of joy over these attacks in several Muslim countries that were widely shown on American television. The initial shock and horror turned quickly to consternation, followed by a lasting sense of incomprehension.

Many answers were put forth, and of these, the simplest is not necessarily the least reasonable: they hate us because we have succeeded where they have failed. As Bernard Lewis wrote at the time, this feeling has nothing to do with religion but rather with something much more ordinary: envy. On this subject Lewis wrote that "it is difficult if not impossible to be strong and successful and to be loved by those who are neither the one nor the other." He added that "the same kind of envious rancor [toward the United States] can sometimes be seen in Europe," and for the same reasons.[42]

Envy is a feeling that can be exploited to political ends with a relatively minor investment and an almost certain payoff; indeed, as Thomas Sowell put it, "when people are presented with the alternatives of hating themselves for their failure or hating others for their success, they seldom choose to hate themselves."[43] Another factor, along with envy, may be the recrimination felt by a people who have a glorious history and dazzling civilization behind them: such people can easily be persuaded that they have somehow been fraudulently dispossessed of what was rightfully theirs—and often of having been the victims of those they considered their inferiors. Among such peoples there are the Arabs, to be sure; but also the Iranians, Turks, Indians, Chinese, Germans, and, of course, now the British and French. Soon enough, the Americans will be added to this list, and international relations will enter into a zone of grave turbulence. The history of the Third Reich shows us clearly enough just how far the political mobilization of "envious rancor" can go when accompanied by powerful economic and military means.

Another response has been given to the question: why do they hate us? They hate us because *we* have taught them to hate us. We taught them quite literally: the Muslims—the "they" in the question—have been drawn into disputes between Europeans since the latter began expanding across the Mediterranean Sea. Further, up until the second half of the twentieth century—and, in some cases, beyond—they thus internalized the diatribes, grudges, grievances, and hatred that the Westerners have long directed at one another.

This education has come in stages, but it has come inexorably, and it began very early. According to one hypothesis, the arrival of Muslims in Spain, in 711, was the result of an agreement between the Muslim governor of Ifriqiya—now North Africa—Musa ibn Nusair and a Christian lord, Julian (or Ollian), who was locked in conflict with Roderic, the Visigoth king of Hispania, also a Christian, who had just overthrown Achila II, a Christian, the legitimate king. In another example: it was the admiral of the Byzantine fleet in Sicily, Euphemius, a Christian, having turned against Michael II, the Christian emperor, who summoned Ziadet-Allah I, the emir of Ifriqiya, to come to his aid in 826. In the same fashion, the Ottomans were invited to the Balkans in the mid-fourteenth century by John Cantacuzene, the Byzantine emperor, who was at war with his rival John V Palaeologus. Thus the beginning of the Islamization of Europe was the collateral result of wars and rivalries among Christians.

The first episode of a formal and strategic alliance between a Christian and Muslim power dates to the sixteenth century, when Francis I, the king of France, joined his forces to those of Suleiman the Magnificent to set the Germanic Empire on its heels; which responded by forging an informal alliance with the Persian Safavid Empire to push the Ottomans back. The agreement between Paris and Istanbul—which lasted until Napoleon Bonaparte's invasion of Ottoman-controlled Egypt—is considered the longest-lasting international alliance in French history. This alliance also explains why France, the second-largest Catholic power in the world at that time, was not present at the Battle of Lepanto in 1571. In fact, France's absence greatly diminished the symbolic value of this rare, even unique, example of Christian (Catholic) unity against a Muslim power. Additionally, in the short term, the Battle of Lepanto would weaken the Portuguese, Spanish, and Venetians more than the Turks; in the longer-term, the mutual exhaustion of the Catholics and the Muslims would open the way in the Mediterranean Basin for the Protestant powers—Holland and England.

In the sixteenth century, and again in the seventeenth—when, for example, in 1622 the British helped the Persian Shah Abbas I seize control of Hormuz Island from the Portuguese—the alliances, or collusions, involved

powers of approximately equal strength. However, starting in the eighteenth century, and certainly in the nineteenth, the growing disproportion
of military and economic power made the declining Muslim empires the
pawns—and the victims—of wars being waged by the Christian powers for
control of the world. That was particularly true of the Ottoman Empire.
In 1821–1829 the Russians and British, irreconcilable rivals, supported the
Greek insurrection against Istanbul. In 1840 Great Britain, Prussia, Russia,
and Austria backed the Ottomans against the anti-Turkish ambitions of
Egypt's Muhammad Ali Pasha, who was supported by the French. In 1853
Great Britain and France supported the Ottomans against the Russians in
the Crimean War. Moreover, from the moment that Germany entered into
the great power arena, it did the same: first by organizing the Berlin Congress of 1878, which would deprive the Russians of much of the land they
had conquered in the previous year's war against the Ottomans; then, in
1881, in "orienting" France toward Tunisia to find compensation for its
loss of Alsace and Lorraine—and so that it would become a sworn enemy
of Italy, in the very year that Berlin, Vienna, and Rome had signed the
Triple Alliance.

Near the end of the nineteenth century, the Germans did not yet have
the strength to take part militarily in dividing up the Ottoman Empire;
instead they intervened with capital, piling up not just economic benefits but also psychological and political gains. The Ottomans, in fact,
saw them not as pillagers eager to impose their political control—as the
British, French, and Russians had done with their colonies—but rather as
investors assisting them in building infrastructure. One might say that the
Germans were welcomed by the Ottomans in a way that is similar to the
Chinese experience in several African countries during the first decade of
the twenty-first century. Perhaps the most important result of the German
investment in infrastructure was the construction of the Berlin-Baghdad
Railway in 1899, which would later be extended to Basra when important
petroleum deposits were discovered in the south of Mesopotamia.

In that same year, the omnipresent Lord Curzon established a British protectorate in Kuwait, about 50 kilometers south of Basra. Three years later,
it was precisely from Kuwait that the al-Saud family, political sponsors of
Wahhabism, launched its campaign to reconquer the Najd—the geographic
center of modern-day Saudi Arabia—as well as the entire eastern portion of
the Arabian Peninsula, a campaign that would continue until 1912.

During World War I, the British used every tool or weapon at their disposal to keep the Germans away from the Middle East: through outright military conquest, by November 22, 1914, they had already occupied Basra; by exploiting tribal divisions in the Arabian Peninsula; in fanning the traditional anti-Turkish feelings of the Near East; but, also making use of Zionism, by promising in 1917 to create a "national Jewish home" in Palestine as a counterweight to the Turks but also the Arabs.[44] The British naturally played the religious card as well, explicitly aiming for the rupture of Islam, even going so far as to entertain the hypothesis of creating an alternative caliphate to Istanbul in Mecca.

The caliph—that is, the vicar of the Prophet—who since 1517 had simultaneously been the Ottoman sultan, ordered the highest religious authority in the country to proclaim holy war: on November 14, 1914, the Turkish Sheikh-ul-Islam called on the faithful of the entire world to take up arms against Great Britain, Russia, France, Serbia, and Montenegro—that is, the enemies of the Ottoman Empire, allied with Germany and Austria-Hungary. It was the opportunity London had dreamed of: the call to jihad—theoretically compulsory—was rejected by the Hussein ibn Ali, the emir of Mecca, who cited doctrinal reasons—the jihad of the sword being permitted only for defensive purposes. Islam thus found itself divided into two mortally hostile camps, one aligned with the Central Powers and the other with the Triple Entente.

The legendary Colonel Thomas Edward Lawrence, better known as Lawrence of Arabia, organized and helped lead the Arab revolt against the Ottoman Turks by promising the creation of an independent Arab state. Yet in January 1916, in a memorandum to London, he had laid out his true objectives: to divide the Muslim world in the near term and the Arab world in the future. Lawrence wrote: "The Arabs are even less stable than the Turks. If properly handled they would remain in a state of political mosaic, a tissue of small jealous principalities incapable of cohesion."[45] It was an idea that the secret Sykes-Picot Agreement of 1916 between Britain and France would very soon ratify. The Russian-American duo would perpetuate this approach after World War II, and even to the present day.

In the latter half of the 1930s, a new competition arose among the Western powers, and, as Lewis put it, there again they "conducted an immense propaganda effort, in the Islamic world and elsewhere, to discredit and undermine each other." Lewis wrote, "The message they brought found many listeners, who were all the more ready to respond in that their own experience of Western ways was not happy."[46] The Arabs had been deceived by the straight-faced, but false, promises of the British and of the French. Subsequently, the revisionist powers—those interested in challenging the results of World War I—did their best to exploit their anger and frustration.

In 1937, when Benito Mussolini was handed the solid gold "sword of Islam" in Tripoli, he perhaps dreamed of becoming a new "commander of the faithful." During this period, profascist movements were forming across the parts of the Middle East ruled by the United Kingdom and France, namely, in Egypt, Lebanon, Syria, and Iraq. In 1936 nationalist and Islamist delegates from Egypt, including the young Gamal Abdel Nasser, were welcomed fraternally to the Nazi Party's Eighth Congress in Nuremberg. Later, Anwar Sadat, who collaborated actively with the Germans during the war, was arrested by the British and remained in prison until 1948.

One of the most emblematic examples of the anti-Western pedagogy taught by the Westerners to the Muslims was that of Amin al-Husseini, who had been grand mufti of Jerusalem since 1921. Al-Husseini was the very incarnation of this particular dovetailing of factors—subservience to foreign powers, nationalism, religious extremism, and racism—that has characterized the political struggle in Palestine throughout the twentieth century and up to the present day. Al-Husseini served the British against the French in Syria and the Jews in Palestine; the Germans and Italians against the British and French in the Middle East; the French against the Syrian and Algerian nationalists; the British, once again, against the Soviets and Americans in Palestine; and, finally, all those who had an interest in using the weapon of Third-Worldism to fight their battles—the Russians, Chinese, French, the Catholic Church, and, naturally, all the countries of the Third World.

Al-Husseini was named grand mufti of Jerusalem by the British, and later head of the Muslim High Council, despite his condemnation, in 1920, for having led the first pogrom against the Jews in Palestine, and despite the fact that the faithful had voted not for him but for three candidates from the Nashashibi clan who favored peaceful cohabitation with the Jews. In the eyes of the British, he personified the principle of *balance of power*, as a counterweight to the French in Syria, the Jews in Palestine, and the Nashashibi in Jerusalem—where Ragheb al-Nashashibi was mayor. The British authorities tolerated his pogroms so long as they served to restrain the ambitions of the Jewish community, but they expelled him from Palestine in 1937, when riots took an anti-British turn. At that point, al-Husseini placed himself full-time at the service of the Third Reich, first by promoting an alliance between Iraq and Germany—which led, in 1941, to a British coup d'état in Baghdad—then by issuing calls from Berlin for holy war and the extermination of the Jews, and finally by organizing the Arabische Freiheitkorps and a Muslim Schutzstaffel (SS) unit in Bosnia.

After World War II, the French, who had arrested him, released him in exchange for his support for their interests in North Africa and Syria; and the British again welcomed him to Palestine—where he proclaimed himself "president"—to help them to "cool off the Zionists."[47] Removed from office in 1948 by King Abdullah I of Jordan, al-Husseini would reappear in 1955 at the Bandung Conference as the representative of Yemen—in which he had never set foot—where he managed to make hostility toward Israel the only point of common agreement among the "nonaligned."[48] That hostility would go on to become a leitmotif of all Third World campaigns.

Al-Husseini—Muslim religious leader, agent of the British, Italians, and Germans, Nazi enthusiast and partisan of the Final Solution, collaborator of the Free French, Arab nationalist, and pioneer of Third Worldism—was hardly the archetype of an Islamism committed to wage battle to the death against the West, as is often suggested. Rather, he represented a versatile and mutable nationalism, which uses religion as a mobilizing force but remains fundamentally a pawn in the conflicts between the powers. The roots of its multiple holy wars, proclaimed in turn against the enemies of his instigator of the moment, are to be found not in the deserts of the seventh century but rather in the great capitals of the industrialized world of the twentieth century.

PLURAL ISLAM

It would be absurd to suggest that there is no specific characteristic that we can use to identify a Western civilization. There is such an element: capitalism.

In 1952, when Lucien Febvre asked Fernand Braudel to write a history of the West, the result was his celebrated essay, *Civilisation matérielle, économie et capitalisme*. In 1961, when Columbia University Press published the third edition of his *Chapters in Western Civilization*, "as a basic text in European history and Western civilization courses," Braudel included an essay on "European Expansion and Capitalism." In his *Grammaire des civilisations*, Braudel speaks of Western civilization almost as a synonym for "industrial civilization." As for the West, Braudel deserves credit for laying out a chronological, logical, and causal order; in contrast, most of those who hold up the West as an argument in political struggle are describing a mythical community that has never existed. The confusion between the notion of the West and capitalist development explains the misunderstanding, often voluntary, regarding "Westernization," which is nothing more than the global diffusion of industrial capitalism and its social consequences, an expansion that has now reached the most remote corners of the world.

It is inexact to suggest that the West and capitalism are entirely coterminous, inasmuch as this equation concerns only the next-to-last stage of a journey that can be traced on a geographic map, a journey reaching from the Red Sea to the North Sea by way of the Mediterranean Sea. We have seen that Braudel identifies its first budding in the Arabian Peninsula of the seventh century; its blossoming in Italy after the "second rupture of the Mediterranean"—that is, after the end of the Muslims' exclusive control of this sea—provoked by the Crusades; its spread to Northern Europe with the Reformation; and its triumph with the Industrial Revolution in England.[49]

So the supposed spread of a "spirit of capitalism" cannot easily be identified with a single region or religion, as has often been done, since at least the celebrated essay by Max Weber.[50] In 2012 the Spanish diplomat Luis Francisco Martínez Montes gently mocked those "economists-turned-theologians . . . [who] suggest that capitalism and globalization are essentially Protestant inventions." When Luther, Calvin, and Zwingli were at work organizing their communities and saw nothing beyond "their provincial Central European confines," he continues, the Catholics were actively working "to devote plenty of material and intellectual resources to create the first networks for the mobilization of capital, ideas and souls on a global scale."[51] In short, without Catholicism there would have been no globalization.

Martínez Montes's remarks, of course, are a rhetorical exaggeration that can be classed as doubly *pro domo sua*—since he is both Catholic and

Spanish. In fact, capitalism began its "missionary" work to conquer the world from a base in England where, through a series of favorable historical coincidences, the conditions for launching the Industrial Revolution were concentrated. England is in the West, and since capitalist development first affected a small group of Western countries, the "industrial civilization" that spread through the entire world can rightly be referred to as Western civilization. Westernization is nothing but the diffusion of capitalism around the world caused by its productivity levels being incomparably superior to those of every other economic system. Indeed, the West's six *killer apps*—competition, science, property rights, medicine, the consumer society, and work ethic—as outlined by Niall Ferguson, are among the causes, means, and effects of the spread of capitalism.[52]

It is thus possible to identify, if most cautiously, a common denominator giving historic meaning to the phrase "Western civilization." For other civilizations, however, no such defining commonality can be found, other than, naturally enough, the historic stratifications that have accumulated in the form of habits in foodstuffs, clothing, traditions, institutions, languages, and dialects, themselves often a mingling of different cultural contributions that have been "individualized" a posteriori—for example, the exact same coffee is "Turkish" for the Turks and "Greek" for the Greeks. In other words, in its unrelenting expansion, capitalism gradually destroys all the specific and individual characteristics in its path as it imposes, in the words of Jacques Berque, "the adoption of universal fashion in technology and behavior."[53]

Each of the civilizations identified by Huntington deserves to be reexamined in light of the political considerations accorded here to Western civilization; but that would draw us too far from our subject. A few pages, nonetheless, should be devoted to the supposed unity of Islamic civilization.

The idea that we can speak of Islam in the singular, and that it represents a unique and homogenous bloc—hostile to the West—has advanced quite independently of Huntington's classification and has today become widely accepted, and with serious political implications. In reality, as Graham Fuller puts it, "there is no Muslim world at all, but rather many Muslim worlds, or many Muslim countries and different kind of Muslims. . . . Islam is what Muslims think Islam is, as well as what they want it to be."[54]

Fuller's statement is based on the simple observation of the existence of Muslim communities spread across an extremely vast territorial space, from Senegal to Indonesia, and separated by differences in ethnicity, language, tradition, history, political institutions, and *religion*. It is indisputable that the Islam practiced by some adherents has very little in common with that practiced by others. This variety stems essentially from two original characteristics of Islam: its capacity for borrowing from the cultures and religions encountered along its path—a capacity that does much to explain its success and longevity—and its absence of hierarchical structures.

In its expansion, Islam has adapted, morphed, and modified itself, producing extremely different forms: ranging from certain Sufi tendencies that worship the saints, to the quietists, to the esoteric versions including those who call for a return to the purity of Islam in Muhammad's time, such as Salafism, and to the Wahhabi partisans of an absolute monotheism, which go so far as to advocate the destruction of tombs when they seem likely to be transformed into sites for cult worship. Naturally, it is possible to find combinations of these different forms: there are purely contemplative Sufis and others ready to take up arms to defend their faith; there are quietist Salafists, whose goal is simply to preach; and there are militant Salafists, who want to install their version of an authentically Islamic polity.

The absence of a central religious authority able to rule decisively on theological and juridical questions means that even the simplest definitions can become complicated. Tariq Ali describes how, during the trial of the instigators of the anti-Ahmadi pogroms in Pakistan in April 1954, the judges demanded a precise definition of what it is to be Muslim, in order to be able to rule on whether the Ahmadis were part of the family of Islam. To do so, they questioned "most of the leading ulama," but, as they wrote in their decision, "the result of this part of the inquiry has been anything but satisfactory . . . [as] no two learned divines are agreed on this fundamental." As Ali goes on to chronicle, at a time when Pakistan was not yet an "Islamic state," the judges reached a political conclusion, one that remains pertinent for those who believe that Islam constitutes a single bloc worldwide: "If considerable confusion exists in the minds of our ulama on such a simple matter, one can easily imagine what the differences on more complicated matters will be."[55]

Islam's principal sacred text is the same for all the faithful, but, in the absence of a religious authority viewed as a reference by all, its interpretations vary considerably according to different juridical schools, institutions, tendencies, sects, sensibilities, political opinions, countries of origin—or ethnicities, or clans—and even according to different ulama and muftis, indeed each individual. What's more, in the Sunnah—the law of God—besides the Koran itself there are also the hadiths—accounts of the deeds and sayings of the Prophet. And yet, in the Muslim world, there is not even agreement on the exact number of hadiths. This doctrinal confusion demonstrates the degree to which theological questions and political questions, often involving the governments of different religious communities, are closely intertwined.

In the history of Islam there has not been the succession of councils and synods that allowed the Orthodox Church to reject the Apocrypha and to isolate the four canonical Gospels.[56] Although a single version of the Koran was established in the mid-seventh century, Muslim scholars were confronted in the following century with a profusion of hadiths. According to Sadakat Kadri, one of the ulemas complained that his colleagues were "never so ready to lie as in matters of the hadith"; and another later confessed to having invented some 4,000 of them.[57] In the eighth century the traditionalist jurist Ahmad ibn Hanbal counted 30,000 hadiths, while Ibn Kathir, a fourteenth-century traditionalist jurist, in an effort to weed out heresies, limited the number of reliable *witnesses*—but not of their testimonies—to around 50,000. Needless to say, despite the authority of Ibn Kathir, the proliferation of hadiths did not stop with him; indeed, by some estimates as many as 700,000 have been tallied. This circumstance gives each group, tendency, sect, and so forth a chance to choose those that best suit its needs.

The differences between the various branches of Islam can thus be traced to a profusion of doctrinal divergences, each resting solidly on the Sunnah. But the real reasons for these differences are historic, geographic, and cultural. I shall limit the discussion here to historic reasons.

Rivalries within the *umma*—the community of faithful—existed even in the time of the Prophet: between the Quraychites, a Meccan tribe loyal to Muhammad, and the tribe of the Banu Khazraj in Medina; between the latter and their rivals in Medina, the Banu Aws; but also within the very family of the Prophet, specifically between his father-in-law, Abu Bakr, and Ali, his cousin and son-in-law. When Muhammad died, the battle to succeed him as head of the community raged, and Ali's clan—or so it appears—went so far as to hastily bury the Prophet's body in the very house where he had died, to avoid having any official funeral reinforce the authority of Abu Bakr, who had been named caliph despite Ali's opposition.

As is known, this hostility between Abu Bakr and Ali continued, eventually leading to the most dramatic break within the Muslim world, between those who later would be called Sunni—followers of Abu Bakr—and Shia— Ali's followers. A third group formed following this dispute: the Kharijites (literally, "dissidents"), against whom Ali, who had in turn become caliph, led the second internecine war in 657, a year after the first armed intra-community conflict, against Abu Bakr's clan. The Battle of Karbala in 680, where Muhammad's grandson, Hussein, was killed by the successors of Abu Bakr—the Umayyads—marked the definitive break between the Sunnis and the Shiites.[58]

Starting in the mid-seventh century, Kadri writes, the struggles and dissension within the heart of the community were so severe that "the majority of Muslims were already recalling the pre-Umayyad era as a time of almost impeccable harmony," even referring to Muhammad's four first successors as al-Khulafa'u r-Rashidun (the rightly guided caliphs).[59] This, of course, ignored the fact that three of the four had been assassinated—the third and fourth by the hand of other Muslims.

In 750, after the victory of the Abbasids over the Umayyads, an independent Umayyad caliphate arose in Spain: for the first time, there were two vicars of the Prophet. After this first great political break, the Shiite Idrisids established domination over Morocco between 789 and 985, and the Sunni Aghlabids from 800 to 909, over a territory that includes modern-day Tunisia and Algeria. In 909, another of the great dynasties of Muslim history, the Shiite Fatimids, established its authority in North Africa and in the Hejaz—a western region of what now is Saudi Arabia—which lasted until 1171. When the Crusades were first launched in the late tenth century, the divisions in the Muslim world were so numerous and so profound and the mutual hatreds so deeply rooted that, at times, certain Muslim factions allied themselves with the Christians to fight other Muslims, despite the religious obligation to defend the entire community against aggressions by infidels coming from the outside.

Basically, the only period in history during which the community of faithful was united, or at least the only period its divisions were kept in check, was during the time of the Prophet—even if the unity of the Bedouin tribes had its highs and lows. When Muhammad died, Muslim unity ended, never to be reestablished. In the modern era, more rivalries can be enumerated within the Muslim world than between Muslims and non-Muslims. If one were to draw up a far from exhaustive list of the conflicts presently under way, or of recent duration, few regions are spared. These rivalries include Berbers and Arabs; the conflict between Morocco and the Sahrawis; long-standing tensions between Morocco and Algeria; between Tripolitania and Cyrenaica; between all the countries of the Middle East—in particular, between Saudi Arabia, Turkey, Egypt, and Iran—for supremacy in the region; divisions among Palestinians; the "Black September"; Arabs, Turks, and Iranians against the Kurds; the Iran-Iraq War; the Iraqi invasion of Kuwait; the war of western Pakistan against the "bad Muslims" of eastern Pakistan; and the war by separatist guerrillas in Indonesia's Aceh Province, to mention only the most important.[60] If we added to this the incessant rivalries between Sunnis and Shiites, the civil wars, the coups d'état, the revolutions, and terrorist organizations, one would have to conclude that, at least since 1965, it is Muslims above all who have killed other Muslims, Arabs who have killed other Arabs, and even Palestinians who have killed other Palestinians.

Samuel Huntington was certainly right about one thing: "In the modern world, religion is a central, perhaps *the* central, force that motivates and mobilizes people."[61] The depiction of Islam as a bloc moved by a common will and capable of establishing global alliances is so tenacious and widespread because it constitutes an argument for political mobilization to which none of the international actors—including, and above all, the Muslim powers themselves—has any intention of dismissing, especially given the battles being fought amid the great global disorder of the twenty-first century.

9
THE CLASH OF IGNORANCE

Christian fights Christian, so why should not Mohammedans
do the same?

—Thomas E. Lawrence

RELIGION AND VIOLENCE

When it comes to political involvement, the scriptural and theological
foundations of religions play only the role of instrument.

The sacred texts, and their subsequent theological interpretations,
are used selectively and arbitrarily to support one option or another,
some of them contradictory. The use of sacred texts to justify a resort to
violence or, to the contrary, a total rejection of violence is not the exclusive
prerogative of Islam, Christianity, or Judaism; it also belongs to the other
great religions, including Hinduism and Buddhism, which are commonly
perceived as "religions of peace."

Those who attempt to restrain the propensity to violence of certain religious groups merely by offering scriptural or theological arguments are
bound to fail, since one can always find scriptural and theological grounds
to refute these same arguments—and vice versa. The only way a religion

can escape from this vicious circle is if it has a sole central authority, recognized and respected, which establishes which kind of beliefs can be seen as theologically true by the majority of the faithful at any given moment. Today—with the exception of a few close-knit but smaller communities—only the Catholic Church enjoys such authority. That does not suggest that all Catholics are ready to accept every decision emanating from Rome, either on questions of violence or on other issues; but it does suggest that there is one, and only one, official and authorized Catholic position, and those who think and act differently are in no way considered as representing the church or Catholicism.

The implications of this point are too often underestimated. Let us compare two examples of fanatics who were self-proclaimed avengers in the name of their own credos: Anders Breivik, the Norwegian responsible for the massacre of seventy-seven people, including sixty-nine young people at a Social Democrat-run summer camp on the island of Utøya in July 2011, and Nidal Hasan, the American soldier who, in November 2009, fired on his colleagues at the military base at Fort Hood, Texas, killing thirteen. While the religious motivations of Hasan, who is a Muslim, were immediately viewed as the motive for his act, the religious connection to Breivik, a self-proclaimed Catholic, was almost completely ignored. The difference between the two lay not in their motivations nor, to be sure, in the acts themselves: it lay in the fact that since Islam lacks any central authority, absolutely any Muslim can claim to be acting in its name, while that is impossible for a Catholic credibly to do. Openly dissident Catholics, like those from the Society of St. Pius X or supporters of liberation theology, are known to speak in the name of their beliefs, but no one confuses their positions with those of the church or Catholicism.

Thus the question often posed—does religion tend to worsen political tensions or to calm them?—is almost pointless: religion can be used, and is used, as a means for fomenting tensions and violence as well as, if more rarely, to support conciliation and promote peaceful relations. Those who address this question from within religious communities will often contradict one another; they are, necessarily, lined up on one side of the argument or the other—for example, within Catholicism, the group Pax Christi versus the Italian Cultural Center "Lepanto"—or are aligned with one of the countless intermediary shadings of belief. Those who attempt to respond from the outside often finish at square one. Carlo Jean, an

Italian army general and prolific geopolitical writer, for example, observes that "religions play a role of both conciliation and competition, of opposition and, at the extreme, of inflaming tensions and conflicts."[1] Russell Shorto uses another argument: religion carries within itself an element of violence, but only to the degree that it provides "an avenue of human expression"; to the thesis that "religion leads to violence" he would reply, adapting a slogan from the National Rifle Association: "Religion doesn't kill, people do."[2]

In a way, Russell Shorto is right: every religious mythology has its stories of gods inciting their followers to battle and then guiding their armies, while history testifies only to the fact of men killing other men. However, not every argument used to persuade men to fight one another has the same force or ability to mobilize; so to persuade men to fight other men requires finding the most effective means of motivation, and religion remains among the most effective. As Bernard Lewis puts it in his essay on hatred as a tool of political struggle, "religion may or may not be a source of hatred, but it certainly provides an emotionally satisfying expression of hatred."[3] Lewis goes on to add: "In fighting an enemy, it is not absolutely necessary to hate him, but it is better for morale, and therefore for military effectiveness, if one does."[4]

It cannot always be easy for the faithful, as Charles Selengut writes, to accept the fact that "at the center of the most sublime religious scriptures known to humankind is the obligation to wage war, to kill, and to maim others in the name of God. . . . The scriptures and sacred traditions of the world's religions prescribe violence."[5] Researchers have even attempted to tally the exact number of these prescriptions. Steve Wells, for example, chronicles 1,214 violent passages in the Bible, constituting some 4 percent of the text, and 527 in the Koran, or 8.5 percent of the text.[6] These figures can be considered to have only a vaguely indicative value. For one thing, they depend on the criteria and the purpose of the researcher—most modern critiques of religions seek to contest or limit their influence by resorting to coldly rationalist arguments. Additionally, this sort of counting exercise overlooks the importance of religious borrowings. For example, the Koran includes no instruction that apostates should be put to death; only a century after the death of the Prophet did the first schools of law take a stand on the question. But since Muslims consider the Pentateuch—the first five books of the Bible, which Jews call the Torah—a sacred text, it was easy for them to adopt the divine order to stone "your brother, your mother's son, or your son or daughter, or the wife you cherish, or your friend who is as your own soul," if those people attempt to "turn away from the Eternal, your God"—an order found in Deuteronomy 13:6–11.

Peter Partner writes that the "unhesitating" massacre of apostates, of which the first book of the Maccabees is an example, "was one of the most frequent characteristics of holy wars of the weak against the strong, and has remained so down to the present day." According to Partner, a specialist in holy wars, the incitement to violence, or the "propaganda," as he puts it, represented by the sanctification of combat, becomes entirely credible—indeed, desirable—in a situation where "ordinary judgment is suspended, as dust, cloud, and confusion cover men's eyes, and unfamiliar and terrible noises assault their ears." This is a moment when the natural elements can prove decisive in determining the outcome of a conflict, and "to peoples who in any case worshipped the gods of nature, battle was a time when the god who gave rain for the crops could also bring thunder, hail or storm for the benefit of one side or the other."[7] One might almost call it war as the simple continuation of nature by other means. Michel Dousse observes that, in a context where the gods govern both nature and war, people tend to embrace the god "who shows himself most vitally as the strongest and most reliable." At a time when "each nation, indeed each important city, had its own god or gods," wars represented a moment of truth. Indeed, as Dousse goes on, "it was particularly in extreme situations of violence or risk that the divinity was on notice to prove his reality and his effectiveness."[8]

In what Carl von Clausewitz was to call "the fog of war," the support of "the strongest and most reliable god" was thus the condition for victory; but in the periods between war, it was also the condition for a good harvest, the curing of the sick, and, more generally, the condition for survival at a time when surviving was a day-to-day struggle. To contextualize— that is, to view the sacred texts in relation to the historic, social, cultural, and other circumstances in which they were produced—thus becomes an obligatory exercise if one wants to discern the true political and concrete character of the use of religions in a political or military struggle. This exercise of contextualization is unknown both to the fundamentalists, for whom the sacred texts belong not to history but to eternity, and to certain of their mirror-image enemies, who also purport to cast value judgments on religions based on these same sacred texts. It took several centuries to compile the Old Testament, and throughout this long period, war was a very real part of the natural cycle, just as planting and harvesting were. Several passages in the text bear witness to this fact: in the second book of Samuel (11:1), for example, there is a reference to "the turn of the year, the time when kings go to war." Even more explicit is Ecclesiastes 3:1–11: "to everything there is a season . . . a time to plant, and a time to pluck up that which is planted; a time to kill, and a time to heal."

This is not something specific to the Middle East: Aristotle, who lived in the fourth century BCE, when Ecclesiastes was likely written, lists in his *Politics* the normal methods for securing the means of subsistence, including hunting, fishing, agriculture and pillage (ληστείας).

At the time of Muhammad, nine centuries later, raiding was considered an entirely honorable activity in Arabia, and war was part of the cycle of normal human activities: indeed, the calendar provided for "sacred months" in which fighting was to be suspended to allow commercial activities. The revelations of Muhammad were in no way considered as instigating violence but, to the contrary, as the principles of order and moderation. The Koran, Dousse asserts, "came to bring moderation and standards to the people of the desert, who were inclined to excess."[9] It established rules in places where there were none—for example, by banning personal vengeance and replacing it with the beginnings of an objective legal system, or by dictating some rather strict rules of morality—regulated the sense of honor to military ends, and, finally, imposed a level of political organization on a fundamentally anarchic society. In a society where no central power was able to impose its will, as Maxime Rodinson says, "it was not easy for any alliance of individuals or clans to endure for very long."[10] And without alliances, of course, it would have been impossible for a single tribe from Mecca to unify the entire Arabian Peninsula, let alone to vanquish two great empires and conquer the Near East, North Africa, and Persia.

The Muslims' exceptionally rapid expansion in the seventh century cannot be explained by a simple balance-of-forces calculation. To the contrary, it is among those rare cases in history in which the morale factor—so long as it is disciplined and organized—can produce effects that belie and refute the physical determinism of material considerations. Thus it was that, several centuries later, the legendary historian and philosopher Ibn

Khaldun remarked, "vast and powerful empires are founded on a religion." Khaldun went on to observe that "dominion can only be secured by victory, and victory goes to the side which shows most solidarity and unity of purpose." And it is religious fervor, Khaldun concludes, that erases "the competitiveness and envy felt by members of the group towards each other [and ensures that] the object they desire is common to all."[11]

Modern states have attempted to forge a national spirit in which all citizens recognize one another, putting aside their reciprocal rivalries and jealousies. It is no accident if people have spoken of "civil religions," for the principle is the same, and the objectives are the same as those of traditional religions. However, for reasons we have already analyzed, civil religions have proved incapable, over the long term, of competing victoriously against traditional religions; at a time when the former are in decline, the latter reemerge inevitably as the most important factors in "solidarity and unity of purpose."

THE CLASH OF IGNORANCE

One piece of evidence showing that Samuel Huntington's thesis has been successful lies in the fact that the phrases "the clash of civilizations" and "holy war" have by now become almost interchangeable. For many—particularly in Europe and the United States, but also for certain radical Islamists—a "holy war" is already under way between the Western and Islamic civilizations.

Poring through the results of six years of opinion surveys conducted by Gallup in 130 countries and regions, John L. Esposito and Dalia Mogahed reached the conclusion that the less well Muslims and Westerners know each other, the more convinced they are of the irreconcilable hostility between the two sides, and vice versa. They report: "The more Americans report knowing about Muslim countries, the more likely they are to hold positive views of those countries."[12] These results, Esposito and Mogahed conclude, thus reveal "a clash of ignorance rather than a clash of civilizations."

As is often the case, ignorance is not harmless. Indeed, the more those on one side believe that the other side is hostile to them, the more they react with hostility, thus fueling a chain of actions and of potentially infinite reactions that could, in the long term, give rise to the birth of defensive identities on both sides. Graham Fuller believes that that is exactly what happened in the early years of the twenty-first century: the foreign policy of the United States, he says, has "probably done more to forge a common-minded umma than any other factor since the time of the Prophet Muhammad." Fuller further suggests that Muslim minorities in non-Muslim countries, greatly divided until present, could discover a common identity in reaction to "serious pressure or heavy discrimination precisely *because* they are Muslims."[13] As Jean-Paul Sartre wrote, "The anti-Semite creates the Jew."[14] Or, in other words, anti-Muslim measures, wherever they take place—from Gujarat to the Central African Republic, by way of France—and in whatever form, rather than eliminating the risk of a "communitarization" could have precisely the opposite effect.

The creation of an identity is both the recognition of an existing conflict and the condition for its resurgence. It is, as Regina Schwartz explains, "the most frequent and fundamental act of violence we commit" for it is "an act of distinguishing and separating from others, of boundary marking and line drawing . . . violence is the very construction of the Other."[15] In 1997 the Italian journalist Barbara Spinelli—the daughter of one of the European Union's founders, Altiero Spinelli—provided a practical example in connection with demands that the birth of the euro be accompanied by a common European identity. Such an identity, she wrote, could not arise merely "from common designs of harmony" but rather from the identification of "the enemies we want to fight in the name of an idea of the West shared with the Americans."[16] It was thus necessary, she continued, to *invent* an enemy. As it turns out, the mechanisms for inventing an identity and for inventing an ideal enemy are, in the end, the same: again, the less well one knows those whom one has decided to transform into enemies, the easier the transformation.

But the invention of an enemy and the clash of ignorance are possible only when conditions allow; a simple pedagogical operation will not suffice. A political identity—that is, the "solidarity and unity of purpose" of the members of a community for whom "the object they desire is common to all"—is possible only if the members of this community share a common interest, whether to conquer something that they could not conquer individually or to defend something that would be impossible to defend individually. To put this more schematically: identity does not create a common interest; common interest creates an identity.

When Barbara Spinelli published her article, the possibility of building an identity around the fear of a common adversary "to fight in the name of an idea of the West shared with the Americans" was simply an intellectual aspiration, inspired by the theories of Samuel Huntington, whose book had come out the year before; but outside a narrow circle of specialists—many of whom rejected the clash of civilizations—these theses were not widely known, and Islamic extremism was not perceived as a source of major concern in the most economically advanced countries.

Other than the early experience in France, where the debate on wearing the veil began in the late 1980s, it was not until after the attacks of September 11, 2001, that such a unifying enemy finally materialized. From that date forward, anti-Muslim feelings suddenly became popular, and an ignorance of Islam is a condition for them to remain so.

We can identify a series of widely accepted beliefs that fuel this ignorance: they deal with the relationship between religion and politics, and thus with questions of democracy, sharia law, fundamentalism, violence, and jihad; with the presumed lagging development in Muslim societies; and, finally, with the roles and status of women in Muslim societies and communities. The relationship between Islam and politics and the role of women in Islam are probably the two subjects on which there is the greatest misunderstanding, so they merit a more extended discussion. Let us start with the question of the supposedly lagging development of Muslim societies.

The argument that Muslims hate the West because it has succeeded while they have failed must be relativized in three regards: from an empirical viewpoint, from a historic viewpoint, and from a geographic viewpoint.

The empirical viewpoint. Muslims do not hate the West, and polling by Gallup confirms as much. As a general rule, opinion surveys lack scientific value, but they can help to highlight trends and to establish comparisons when the sources are consistent. In this case, Gallup's findings merely confirm what is simply common sense, and they add some interesting details. For example, the percentage of those who say that they "admire nothing about the West" is extremely small: 10 percent in Saudi Arabia, 6.3 percent in Jordan, and 1 percent in Egypt; at the same time, 32 percent of Americans say they find nothing to admire in Islam. Less surprising is the fact that those Muslims surveyed do not consider the West as a single bloc: indeed, while 75 percent of those interviewed associated the adjective "ruthless" with the United States, only 13 percent associated it with France and Germany—keeping in mind that the survey was carried out shortly after the 2003 Iraq War.[17]

The historic viewpoint. It is inarguable that through much of the Middle Ages, "compared with Islam, Christendom was indeed poor, small, backward and monochromatic," as Bernard Lewis writes. Central and Western Europe were "on a significantly lower level of civilization, both moral and material, than the heartlands of Islam."[18] The decline of this onetime medieval superpower had begun, many specialists agree, in the twelfth century, and an often-cited reason is the loss of control of the seas, even if this was not the sole reason. Fernand Braudel believes that one key to Islam's success during the time of its expansion was the control of three geographic poles: the cities, the deserts, and the sea—or, more precisely, the *seas*: the Mediterranean Sea, Red Sea, Black Sea, Caspian Sea, Persian Gulf, and Indian Ocean. The loss of this maritime hegemony—starting with the Mediterranean Sea during the time of the Crusades and ending with the Indian Ocean in the sixteenth and seventeenth centuries—is also a key to explaining the gradual decline of the Muslim powers.

And as Muslim civilization retreated, European civilization moved forward. This singular succession has been explained in different ways: in one view, it was a veritable shift of power, and of the rules for applying it, as Europe seized from Islam the control of a part of the Mediterranean Basin and, at the same time, benefited from its superior scientific and philosophical culture. Halford Mackinder believes that the reason Europe was able to progress at a relatively rapid pace lay essentially in its geographic configuration: a complex network of mountains, rivers, valleys, peninsulas, and forests, which gave rise to numerous particularities extending to the vast Russian steppes. This network constituted a natural rampart behind which Europe was able to avoid the levels of destruction suffered by the Russians, Chinese, Indians, Iranians, and Turks from invading nomads.[19] Similarly, as Robert Kaplan observed, "The United States would know a similar fate, as World War II left it virtually unscathed, even as the infrastructures of Europe, the Soviet Union, China, and Japan were laid waste, granting America decades of economic and political preeminence."[20]

The geographic viewpoint. In an article published in *Le Monde* in December 2001, Daniel Cohen suggests that the perception of an "Islamic economic curse" stems from the practice of comparing the economic success, or lack thereof, of Muslim countries to that of more advanced countries; indeed, the evidence for this supposed characteristic seems to disappear when one compares these same countries to their neighbors.[21] Table 9.1 shows the result if we repeat Cohen's experiment using updated data.

Moreover, with the passage of time, even a direct comparison with the oldest industrial powers has begun to cast the latter in a less favorable light. Between 2002 and 2012, under the Islamist government of Recep Tayyip Erdoğan, for example, the economy of Muslim Turkey witnessed the most dynamic growth of any country in the entire region comprising Europe, the Mediterranean Basin, and the Middle East. Turkey's economy grew four times faster than the average rate of the European Union—in which its economy would be the sixth-largest out of twenty-nine if it were a member—and it would achieve the rare distinction of meeting the Maastricht criteria, with a public debt as a ratio of GDP less than half that of Germany in 2012, roughly one-third that of France, and just over one-fourth that of Italy.

The same criteria can be used to compare another standard frequently cited in depicting the social structure of Muslim countries as archaic, and which is one of their supposed secret weapons for "conquering" the world: the assertion that Muslim demographic growth rates are incomparably

TABLE 9.1 GDPs of Selected Muslim Countries and Their Non-Muslim Neighbors, 2012 (in Millions of U.S. Dollars)

Muslim-majority country	GDP	Non-Muslim country	GDP
Indonesia	$878.2	Philippines	$250.4
Bangladesh	$122.7	Myanmar	$53.1
Albania	$12.6	Macedonia	$9.7
Malaysia	$303.5	Thailand	$365.6
Niger	$6.6	Central African Republic	$2.2
Turkey	$794.5	Greece	$249.2

Source: International Monetary Fund, World Economic Outlook Database, April 2013.

higher than those of non-Muslim countries. Again, a comparison with neighboring countries (table 9.2) demonstrates the error in this view.

The idea of an overly prolific Muslim population feeds into existing concerns about the dwindling population of Europeans, whose demographic growth rates are among the lowest in the world. In 2012 the European fertility rate—the average number of children per woman—was around 1.6, while the global average was 2.5.[22] This concern also gave rise to the thesis of the conquest of Europe from within by Muslim immigrants with their higher average reproduction rates—a thesis that, however, is contradicted by empirical data.

As early as October 26, 1985, *Le Figaro* magazine had sounded the alarm, with a headline reading, "Will we still be French in 30 years?" and, to ensure that the reader immediately understood what was at stake, on its cover a likeness of Marianne, an iconic French national symbol, wearing a chador. But with the thirty-year anniversary of the article's publication, it is clear that the prophecy implied by the question has not come to pass. The magazine based its calculations on the hypothesis that immigrants in France would maintain the same fertility rates as in their home countries; in reality, the demographer Jean-Claude Chesnais explains, "experience demonstrates that immigrants tend rather rapidly to adopt the demographic behavior of the indigenous population."[23] Moreover, since

TABLE 9.2 Birth Rates in Selected Muslim Countries and Their Non-Muslim Neighbors (per 1,000 Inhabitants)

Muslim-majority country	%	Non-Muslim country	%
Indonesia	18.7	Philippines	25.9
Nigeria	39.9	Democratic Republic of the Congo	49.6
Bangladesh	24.8	India	24
Malaysia	20.6	Cambodia	26.5
Bosnia and Herzegovina	8.8	Croatia	9

Source: United Nations, 2005–2010.

the laws of demographic transition apply universally, fertility rates in the countries of origin have noticeably declined over time—while in France, an exception in Europe, they have risen. Thus in 2015 the fertility rate in France was 2.08, while in Tunisia and Morocco it was 1.99 and 2.13, respectively.[24]

There is thus no more a "Muslim demography" than there is a Catholic demography or an atheist demography. All those who have attempted to link the demographic question to religious inclinations are on the wrong track. In Europe, the highest fertility rates, as we have seen, are in France, a country that has become a symbol of secularization, and which has surpassed one of the most Catholic of countries, Ireland—1.99 in 2015—where fertility rates are continuing to drop. In Sweden, where only 23 percent of the people profess to believe in God, the rate is 1.88, while in Poland, where 80 percent are believers, the rate is 1.33. The least religious country in Europe, Estonia, has a birth rate of 1.59; greater than the most religious country, Romania at 1.33. The only case of a "militant demography" of a religious character is that of Israel's ultra-Orthodox Jews; but there, too, the trend is downward, and rather rapidly so, as the fertility rate has declined from 7.5 in 2005 to 6.5 in 2010—while that of Israeli Muslims has fallen over the same period from 4.6 to 3.5.[25] The politicization of the cradle is simply a road to nowhere.

ISLAM, WOMEN, AND THE WEST

Let us turn back to Islam, and to one of the most hotly debated questions of recent years: the role of the Muslim woman. Certainly, anyone who claims to have a clear and unequivocal idea about this question is destined to collide either with others whose similarly clear ideas point in other directions or else with reality.

In fact, the question is far from clear and unequivocal, because it has been contaminated by several factors: the status of women in pre-Islamic Arabic society; the role of women in the first Muslim communities and in the Koran; the superimposing of several traditional pre-Muslim elements from other populations that have become Muslim; the role of the woman in a patriarchal society of whatever religion; the extremely recent evolution of the feminine condition in industrial societies and the even more recent birth of a feminist conscience; the question of the veil; and the use of women's status in certain countries and under certain conditions—for example, in the Afghanistan of the Taliban—to mobilize popular support for war.

According to a thesis that is fairly widely accepted among specialists, Islam actually improved conditions for women in the Arab society of the seventh century, guaranteeing them the right to own property and ensuring the rights of succession, to education, and to divorce. Several hadiths testify to the respect due women, and their role in the community of the faithful and in Muslim armies would tend to confirm this change in status. Still, we must consider the particular context of the period: urbanization, which was at the origin of the Muhammadan revolution, could plausibly also be at the origin of this increased involvement of women in social life, which the Koran later confirmed—Khadija, Muhammad's first wife, was a wealthy merchant, who had hired the future prophet and later asked him to marry her, in 595. Nonetheless, the more general context remains that of a rigidly patriarchal society, where the woman's role, with only rare exceptions, was strictly subordinated to that of the man. This appears clearly in Surah 4:34, which enjoins a husband "fearing" the disobedience of his wife to first admonish her, then to no longer share a bed with her, and finally to strike her.[26]

In its later development, the religious law clearly was subjected to several influences from outside cultures. According to Hatoon al-Fassi, for example, it was the incorporation of much more restrictive rules derived from Greco-Roman legislation that made the conditions imposed on Muslim women harsher over the centuries to follow. In some cases, the influences of tradition or custom were gradually transformed into supposed religious injunctions; this was the case, for example, with female genital mutilation, whose origins reach back to ancient Egypt, and which was formally condemned by a fatwa from Al-Azhar University in Cairo only in November 2006 as a "crime against humanity." The operation is practiced today almost exclusively in Africa, including in several non-Muslim countries—South Sudan, Ethiopia, Guinea-Bissau, and among some Egyptian Copts. Another famous case is that of the Pashtunwali, part of the tradition of Pashtun tribes, a very strict honor code reminiscent, in part, of that of pre-Islamic Arabia, and which constituted the actual "juridical" foundation of Taliban rule in Afghanistan between 1996 and 2001.

Patriarchal peasant societies everywhere have always had rigorous rules and customs subordinating women. As Stephanie Coontz explains in her book on the history of marriage, "intensive agriculture or herding made a sexual division of labor within the household necessary for survival." In an agrarian economy, a married couple becomes the central unit of production, and the "desertion" of the woman can lead to the destruction of the economic system.[27] This total subordination persisted almost everywhere until the twentieth century, even if it began to be contested, particularly as a result of women's gradually increasing economic independence in industrial societies.

It was precisely the feminization of labor in industrial societies that led to the breakdown of traditional families, that is, families built on the subordination of the woman. For newly urbanized peasants, a simple glance at the lifestyle of the city revealed a threat that was seen as fatal to their economic existence, for which the patriarchal honor codes provided a social shield and a moral justification. The resultant panic explains the desperate attempt to slow the process of disintegration of families through moral imperatives, and these are all the more credible when accompanied by a religious commandment prescribing, as Pope Pius XI's encyclical *Casti Connubii* (1930) did, "the faithful and honest subordination of the woman to her husband." This terror also explains the insistence on modest clothing standards, the existence of laws forbidding adultery and excusing crimes of honor, and the instructions from religious authorities discouraging, or even forbidding, women to work.[28]

The urbanized peasants bring to the city their rural mores, which, in the case of the family, have existed for several millennia. Among these social conventions, the submission of the woman was long a general and universal rule but one that was not uniformly applied everywhere: in the past, for instance, it was more rigidly enforced in Christian countries than in Muslim countries. As Bernard Lewis writes, "The Muslim woman had property rights unparalleled in the modern West until comparatively recent times."[29] And as Noah Feldman notes, "The common law long denied married women any property rights or indeed legal personality apart from their husbands." Thus when the British replaced sharia with their own legislation in certain Muslim colonies, the paradoxical result was "to strip married women of the property that Islamic law had always granted them."[30]

In the nineteenth century, when the struggle of the Western powers to divide up a declining Ottoman Empire already carried ideological overtones, the status of women was not an issue. The Europeans, as Lewis notes, mounted campaigns against the inferior legal status reserved for Christians—and, incidentally, also for Jews—while only the British expressed concern for the fate reserved for African slaves.[31] Indeed, he concludes, "There is no evidence that any of the powers showed any great interest in improving the status of Muslim women."[32]

Possibly the first text in favor of the rights of women in a Muslim country was published in 1867, in the Istanbul-based journal *Tasvir-i Efkâr*, by the writer Namık Kemal; his article dealt in particular with the rights of women in the workplace. We do not know how his essay was greeted by the general public, but the climate was certainly propitious, for these were the years of the Tanzimat—the great reforms—between the imperial ruling of 1856, guaranteeing the equality before the law of all citizens without distinction by religion, and the Constitution of 1876. In Great Britain, the most advanced Western country of the time, the philosopher and economist John Stuart Mill had to wait until 1869 for the publication of his book *The Subjection of Women*, written in 1861; according to his biographer, Alan Ryan, this was the only book on which his publisher lost money. When it came out, Ryan adds, many of Mill's readers viewed it as the final proof of his eccentricity.[33]

The history of the women's suffrage movement shows that the British responded to demands for legal equality between men and women with amused skepticism, reflecting firmly rooted convictions. In the Britain, full equality of political rights, including the right to vote, were granted to women only in 1928, while in Azerbaijan, a Muslim country, it was in force by 1918, two years before American women won the same right. In Turkey, the right to vote was extended to women in 1930, fourteen years before France and sixteen years before Italy. Other Muslim countries—with a few exceptions, most notably Saudi Arabia, where women still do not have the vote—followed gradually as they gained independence. In Switzerland, political equality between men and women did not arrive until 1971.

Now, clothing choices should be included among the elementary rights of both men and women—that, at least, is the view of the U.S. Commission on International Religious Freedom. In its 2013 annual report, it castigated France and Belgium for restrictions, "creating a growing atmosphere of intimidation against certain forms of religious activity," notably against Muslim women who wear headscarves.

The question is a rather curious one: the clothing restrictions and outright bans imposed in France and in a few other Francophone countries or regions—including Quebec—are considered as entirely fair and normal by a large majority of the local populations, even while they are met with astonishment and incomprehension elsewhere. The story began in the France of the 1980s, at a time when a new wave of immigrants was arriving, characterized by stronger links to tradition than the preceding generations of immigrants, who by then had become largely integrated. This was one effect of the massive rural flight of the two preceding decades in certain countries of North Africa and sub-Saharan Africa, as discussed earlier in connection to the major cities of the Muslim world: a problem of quantity transformed into one of quality.

It is possible to compare the clothing norms of recent immigrants from developing countries to the linguistic behavior of immigrants moving from southern to northern Italy. So long as the number of immigrants from the South remained limited, the relatively few living in the North, who were often separated from families and their communities of origin, tended to rather quickly adopt the dialect of their new region, mastering it incomparably better than they did Italian—which at the time was little spoken in the destination regions. Yet when these migratory flows became massive in the 1960s, the new immigrants both conserved their native dialects within their communities and adopted a simplified, demotic Italian to communicate with the locals and with immigrants from other regions. Perhaps not surprisingly, the immigrants who adapted best to local dialects were more docile, even resigned, in social terms, than their comrades of the succeeding generation: the former constantly attempted to blend in with their surroundings, while the latter often proudly proclaimed their origins, particularly if they felt rejected or discriminated against by the locals. Clothing, along with other signs or objects that could be exhibited as symbols of a particular identity, ultimately played the same role; today, as Olivier Roy points out, "educated and voluntarily scarfed women . . . chose to wear [the veil] as an expression of their faith and self."[34]

Originally, the veil, headscarf, or any other clothing element designed to cover any part of a woman's body was intended simply to reduce the risk of adultery, and not only in Islamic lands. In certain places and among certain people it retains this primary function, but in other places—especially in those where Muslims are a minority—it has been transformed by some into a symbol of the moral superiority of Islam over the West, and, conversely, by others into a symbol of a conservative, fundamentally misogynistic mentality. Esposito and Mogahed noted that "in both cases, the assumption is that women are either covering or uncovering to please and obey men."[35] Certain Muslim feminists contend, even while supporting the right of women to choose not to cover their head and/or face, that a woman's dignity is in any case better preserved when she covers herself than when she does not, an opinion frequently shared by their non-Muslim colleagues.

The question of the exact amount of fabric that should cover women contains a further paradox, which has much more to do with the evolution—or, involution, depending on the point of view—of morality in industrialized countries than with Islam itself. It has been pointed out that one of the first actions undertaken by European colonizers in Africa was to force naked women to cover themselves; today, it is the right to uncover one's self that is prized as a sign of women's liberation. For instance, in the Miss Earth 2003 competition, a young Afghan woman was given the Beauty for a Cause Award for "symbolizing the newfound confidence, courage and spirit of today's women."[36]

For centuries Christians accused Islam of immorality and libertinism, of showing an immoderate penchant for the pleasures of the flesh. Peter Partner cites certain medieval Christian commentators as saying that Muslims bolstered their authority over conquered territories by authorizing sexual promiscuity. At the moment of the Reconquista, Tariq Ali tells us, the Spanish Catholic religious authorities ordered the destruction of communal bathhouses "because baths were associated with Islam and regarded as breeding grounds of sensuality."[37] Nor do we have to go as far back as 1492. I recall having been unable to learn to swim until my early adolescence because, in my native city in northern Italy, governed by Christian Democrats, the local bishop opposed the construction of a communal swimming pool, which was considered a place of dangerous promiscuity between nearly nude boys and girls.

When morality, a rampart of social order, is transformed into an ideological tool, it can be used for virtually any cause.

RELIGION, POWER, AND SHARIA

As with the other questions discussed above, the relationship between religion and politics in Islam does not lend itself to absolute or definitive conclusions.

There are several reasons for this, including, of course, the great diversity of political experiences affecting Muslims. But the chief difficulty probably resides in the impossibility of distinguishing, within Islam, between the religious and political authorities. This is one of Islam's major differences with Christianity. All Christian churches of a certain importance are, in effect, structured around one or several religious authorities who, conducting their work from within the borders of a state, are necessarily in a relationship with a political authority; throughout history this relationship has given rise to a great diversity of issues, but the result has always been a dialectic between the authorities. Sunni Islam, on the contrary, in which each believer is responsible for his or her own relationship with God—with no intermediaries—provides for no religious authority, and thus no interaction with political authorities. Theoretically, the caliph—the supreme political authority of the first Muslim communities—is also the supreme religious authority, as vicar of the Prophet and the "shadow of God on Earth."

In reality, this fusion of religious and political authority existed only during the Prophet's time. From the moment he settled in Yathrib—which would later take the name of Medina ("the city")—Muhammad "found himself the leader of a party" for his role as a peacemaker in the long civil war dividing the oasis. We know that he was invited to move to Yathrib by seventy-five eminent citizens because of his reputation for holiness—and because he had become an enemy of the rival city of Mecca. We also know that the way he consolidated his power followed a very ordinary path: the formation of an independent army and its own treasury; the channeling of the city's bellicose energies toward the outside; and the elimination of "those elements [he] was unable to assimilate and silencing opposition within the fold."[38]

Following the death of the Prophet, the authority of his successor faded, largely stripped of the saintly aura Muhammad had enjoyed; and as a consequence, the means available for exercising authority became almost exclusively political. The primary objective of the caliph was to preserve the cohesion of a community, which was essentially a confederation of tribes held together by the awareness that unity conferred greater benefits than would internecine warfare. The death of the binding element—Muhammad—risked seriously jeopardizing the tribal chiefs' calculations, and the conflicts that led to the election of Abu Bakr as first caliph testify to this climate of uncertainty. Abu Bakr had to immediately go to war against the tribes in revolt, then against the Byzantines and, later, against the Persians, with two fundamental conditions ensuring the cohesion of the community and the loyalty of the different tribes: the chance to exercise their war-making talents and the opportunity to share the resulting booty.

I have already alluded to the struggles between the factions led by Abu Bakr and Ali, which continued throughout the period of the "rightly guided caliphs." In the incessant wars of the following period—the era of the Umayyad Caliphate, which lasted between 661 and 750—"religious questions were seldom if ever brought to the fore."[39] The reign of the Abbasids between 750 and 1258 constituted not only a change of dynasty but a new balance of power: the Arab tribal federation was succeeded by a centralized regime that the caliph and his personal guard headed, supported by the army and the bureaucracy of the state and surrounded by a hierarchy of courtesans, modeled on the power structure of the Sassanid Persian Empire. This arrangement implied a certain form, however primitive, of division of powers, most notably, for our purposes, in the administration of justice: the application of sharia.

It was these new demands that imposed the necessity of transforming sharia into a well-defined juridical corpus. As we know, this attempt did not succeed and the failure lasted for fourteen centuries. Indeed, even today, sharia represents more an ambition than a code, and it is far from signifying the same thing to all Muslims. Esposito and Mogahed sum up the current situation this way: "What are Muslims calling for when they say they want sharia as a source of legislation? The answer to this is as diverse as the Muslim community."[40]

At the root of this failure was certainly the fact that the Koran is not a legal text: it provides for the punishment of only four crimes—theft, adultery, defamation, and banditry—and contains, according to Sadakat Kadri, about two hundred commandments distinguishing between that which is licit (*halal*) and that which is illicit (*haram*); even so, Kadri continues, "the practical consequences of confusing the two were rarely spelled out."[41] It was the ulema ("wise men") who were charged with compiling an oral code based on these commandments; but that is where the second likely reason for failure arose: since the Muslim community is tied to a political logic, "no ruler could accept the complete autonomy of sharia."[42] Or, as Graham Fuller puts it—in regard to the establishment of state control over Christianity under Constantine I—"for the state, theology is too important to be left to the theologians."[43]

Sharia has always had great evocative power within the Muslim community, even today—perhaps today more than ever—despite the cacophony of opinions as to what it actually contains. Its idealization stems from the fact that, since the time of the Abbasids, sharia has been considered a source of justice and balance, with its principal objective, as Noah Feldman states, being for "keeping the ruler's executive authority in check."[44] Richard Bulliet goes so far as to say that in "traditional Islamic political thought . . . all that restrained rulers from acting as tyrant was Islamic law, sharia."[45] This means that "traditional Islamic political thought" is based more on desire than on actual fact. Indeed, far from preventing a sovereign from doing whatever he pleases, the principles of sharia, in order to be approved, generally had to conform to the demands of the sovereign himself.

Bulliet further recognizes that "rulers who were tempted to go beyond the law, and thereby achieve absolute power, had to devise ways of coopting, circumventing, or suppressing the ulema."[46] The historical record contains few traces of wise men who dared stand up to the authority of the caliphs. Among the most famous in this regard were the eighth-century Persian writer Ibn al-Muqaffa, who was put to death by the caliph al-Mansur, whom he had served as private tutor; and Ahmad Ibn Hanbal, the founder of the traditionalist juridical school that bears his name, who was imprisoned, tortured, whipped in public, and forced into exile in the ninth century. In short, as Kadri put it, "The Abbasids had managed to turn God's law to the service of their regime."[47] The difficulties in interpreting Koranic dispositions, and the effects of political interference, are two reasons sharia has never become an objective body of law. Also, there are at least two other reasons of equal importance: the reluctance, if not the outright opposition, of many Muslim scholars to manipulating the law of God and, again, the absence of a central religious authority in Sunni Islam.

The first point is explained by Baudouin Dupret: for the majority of thinkers of what he calls "the classical period" of the eighth to thirteenth centuries, "sharia was largely unknowable—it referred to the rule of God, divine law. Anyone who pretended to know sharia rose, for most of the classical Muslim legal advisers, to the rank of God, thereby committing the sin (and the crime) of idolatry (*shirk*)."[48] For some scholars, the idea of drawing from the Koran a system of laws was simply absurd since, as Abdullahi An-Na'im explains, "traditional formulations of sharia can only be human and secular, because they are conditioned by the concrete experience of specific societies, rather than the direct expression of the perfection of divine revelation that is immune from human desire, whims and error."[49] These two reasons explain why—as Kadri notes, citing chronicles from the time—many ulema "were not only reluctant to pronounce on a co-religionist's sinfulness, they were manifestly terrified of doing so," to the point that some of them "feigned madness to escape the burdens of service as a judge (*qadi*)." For centuries, Kadri continues, many religious scholars shared the conviction that "only God knows the secrets of the heart," and that consequently, "any assessment of a person's innocence or guilt under the sharia was best put off until the day of Resurrection."[50] When the Ottoman sultan Mehmed II—the conqueror of Constantinople in 1453—decided to make sharia into a true legal code, he provoked scandal and the opposition of religious scholars, for whom it was inconceivable to set down on paper the laws of God.

The final reason that sharia has never become a coherent legal system, valid for the entire Muslim world, lies in the fact that the ulema have never constituted a clergy. Throughout the course of history, the ulema have never been part of an organized structure, they have never been the links in a hierarchical chain, and, above all, they have only rarely been, and in quasi-fortuitous fashion, at the head of a community of believers. The absence, with only rare exception, of these three characteristics has left them extremely vulnerable to ambient pressures and influences, in particular those exercised by political power. Thus, as Bulliet notes, "the ulema never constituted an organized challenge to their [the caliphs'] rule." While some of them probably had ambitions not of defying the authorities but at least of serving as a counterweight, or a conscience, when that did happen they were purely and simply transformed into government functionaries— subsidiary elements of those in political power. According to Bulliet, "The caliphs, along with an assortment of warlords, sometimes patronized locally popular religious figures or doctrines when they thought this might work to their political advantage." Bulliet adds, "Examples are hard to find of ulema becoming the prime facilitators of royal domination."[51]

Today, the first thing we think we know about Islam is that it makes no distinction between religion and politics, while Christianity is guided by the Gospel principle that one should "render unto Caesar what is Caesar's and to God what is God's" (Matthew, 22:21). In reality, even a most superficial examination of the history of the Catholic Church—and of Islam—suffices to make clear that things have turned out very differently.

Fuller observes, "State power in Islam was virtually always distinct from the clerics. Religious officials in Islamic states never appointed leadership and controlled the state." He also notes, "No sultan or Muslim ruler in Islamic history ever kneeled to ask forgiveness before a grand mufti in the way that Henry IV was forced to do before the pope in 1077 in Canossa."[52] When the Ottoman sultans began organizing a quasi-clerical system within the territory of their empire, in order to extend the control of their subjects along religious lines as well, the model was the caesaropapism of the Byzantine church.[53] Moreover, the first real clericalization of Islam was the work, as we have seen, of Catherine II of Russia. In short, Fuller says, "The close affiliation of religion and the state over most of Western history has affected Christianity and Christian history *vastly more than it has affected Islam and the Islamic world.*"[54]

We should also make one last observation about Shiite Islam. Bernard Lewis notes that one reason Christianity established an organizational and hierarchical structure is the very long period of persecutions it suffered before its official recognition in 313. It is an interesting thesis, which, at first glance, would seem also to apply to Shiism, which was persecuted by the Sunnis during much the history of Islam, and which established its own clerical and hierarchical structure. In reality, as we have seen, the true clerical turning point came during the Safavid era, inherited from Persian administrative culture; it is thus more an attribute of a dominant Shiism than of a persecuted Shiism. Moreover, the system has developed gradually, so much so that, as Bernard Lewis notes, "the office of ayatollah is a creation of the nineteenth century."[55] If it is true that, for Shiism, it is possible to speak of a religious authority, this authority has always been much more reserved vis-à-vis the political authorities than have Sunni religious figures, for whom, traditionally, the duty to obey the authorities, even if their power is tyrannical (*dhulm*), is preferable to *fitna*, which is disorder and conflict.

The identification between religious power and political power—the *velayat-e faqih*—was an invention of Ruhollah Khomeini dating from the

1960s. As we have seen, it was viewed with skepticism by most of his fellow ayatollahs until the eve of victory in 1979. Indeed, rather than simply demanding a restoration of "the balance between the ruler and the scholars," as Noah Feldman writes, the explicit objective of this theory—for the first time in the history of Islam since the death of Muhammad—was "to merge these two separate institutions under a single supreme jurist-ruler."[56] To Lewis, the Iranian religious leaders were thus working at "Christianizing Islam in an institutional sense . . . they have already endowed Iran with the functional equivalents of a pontificate, a college of cardinals, a bench of bishops, and, especially, an inquisition, all previously alien to Islam."[57]

By dint of infusing the diverse forms of Islam with elements foreign to its history, its "Christianization" is a result no less paradoxical than the "Islamic Republic." The latter reflects an impossible ambition of joining seventh-century traditions to the political forms that have emerged from twentieth-century struggles; with political forms necessarily overwhelming traditions. Today, we see evidence of such ideological acrobatics each time religion is used—and not only by certain Muslims—as a weapon for the regulation of society, war, or organized banditry.

10
THE BLOODY BORDERS OF RELIGION

The holy wars which have been waged in every climate of the globe, from Egypt to Livonia, and from Peru to Hindostan, require the support of some more general and flexible tenet.
—Edward Gibbon

GEOPOLITICAL IMPERATIVES

In what may be the most famous chapter in his celebrated book, Samuel Huntington wrote: "The overwhelming majority of fault-line conflicts have taken place along the boundary looping across Eurasia and Africa that separates Muslims from non-Muslims."[1] This notion has been widely popularized, to the point of being interpreted purely and simply—if erroneously—as an observation that most conflicts in the world involve Muslims.

Huntington's thesis warrants at least four observations:

1. Islam's geographical expanse covers an almost uninterrupted space stretching from Senegal to Indonesia; since the conflicts of today's world are mainly concentrated in Africa and Asia, it is almost inevitable that they would, for the most part, involve Muslim countries.

2. A majority of these "fault-line conflicts" involve confrontation between Muslim countries and non-Muslim countries for the simple reason that the countries that share borders with other countries where the dominant religion differs from theirs are "overwhelmingly" Muslim countries, as seen in table 10.1.

3. As Braudel observes, Islam "made its own series of ancient geopolitical obligations." Since conflicts are concentrated in regions of high geopolitical value, Muslims continue today to pay the price for having been able, early on, to establish their first durable presence in "the world's oldest crossroads of civilized humanity."[2] Braudel is of course referring to the geographic space linking the Mediterranean Basin to the South China Sea—both the land and maritime routes—which features the Middle East at its epicenter.

4. Finally, as Graham Fuller notes, "in a world that is fairly bloody overall, it's worth remembering that it generally takes two to make a border bloody."[3] Sometimes, on their borders, Muslims are confronted by adversaries who are no less violent, and at times even more determined, such as the Christians of Bosnia, Chechnya, and the Central African Republic, the Hindus in India, the Jews in Israel, the Buddhists in Myanmar and Sri Lanka.

Let us attempt to verify in detail Fuller's observation by also including the "internal fault lines," that is, the clashes between religious communities within various countries. If we consider a list of seventeen conflicts

TABLE 10.1 Number of Borders Between Countries of Different Religions ("Fault Lines")

	Christian	Muslim	Hindu	Buddhist	Jewish	China	Total
Christian		21	0	1	0	1	24
Muslim	21		2	2	5	5	35
Hindu	0	2		2	0	2	6
Buddhist	1	2	2		0	4	9
Jewish	0	5	0	0		0	5

Note: Ivory Coast and Nigeria are counted twice, as both are Muslim and Christian countries. China is considered separately because no religion is dominant there. North Korea is not included.

still under way as of the end of 2015 involving Muslims, which is certainly not exhaustive, we note that responsibility has not always been attributable to Muslims—far from it (see table 10.2). In the cases where the two communities clashed within the same country—Egypt, Nigeria, and India—I define the principal victim as the community that has suffered the largest number of attacks.

TABLE 10.2 Conflicts Involving Different Religious Communities, 2015

Country/Region	Muslim	Non-Muslim	Both parties	Continent
Cyprus			X	Europe
Kosovo–Serbia			X	Europe
Egypt (civil conflicts)	X			Africa
Sudan–South Sudan			X	Africa
Nigeria (civil conflicts)	X			Africa
Central African Republic (civil conflicts)		X		Africa
Syria–Iraq (against Christians and Yazidis)	X			Asia
Palestine–Israel			X	Asia
Armenia–Azerbaijan			X	Asia
Kashmir			X	Asia
Pakistan (against Christians)	X			Asia
India (civil conflicts)		X		Asia
Sri Lanka (civil conflicts)		X		Asia
Xinjiang, China		X		Asia
Myanmar (against Muslims)		X		Asia
Thailand (against Muslims)		X		Asia
Philippines (civil conflicts)	X			Asia

TABLE 10.3 Conflicts in Muslim-Majority
and Non-Muslim-Majority Countries, 2011–2012

2011									
Africa		Asia		Europe		Americas		World	
Muslim	Non-Muslim	Muslim	Non-Muslim	Muslim	Non-Muslim	Muslim	Non-Muslim	Muslim	Non-Muslim
7	5	10	9	3	3	0	4	20	21

2012									
Africa		Asia		Europe		Americas		World	
Muslim	Non-Muslim	Muslim	Non-Muslim	Muslim	Non-Muslim	Muslim	Non-Muslim	Muslim	Non-Muslim
7	5	9	7	2	2	0	9	18	23

Sources: Data for 2011 from Béatrice Giblin, *Géographie des conflits* (Paris: La documentation française, 2012); data for 2012 from *Aviation Week & Space Technology*, December 31, 2012.

More generally, a review of the conflicts under way at the beginning of the second decade of the twenty-first century (table 10.3) indicates that more of them concern non-Muslim countries than Muslim countries, albeit with a slightly higher prevalence of Muslim involvement in Asia and Africa. I have chosen two different sources, which use different criteria for their evaluations, and which examined conflicts of differing intensity, for the years 2011 and 2012.

Naturally, in considering the role religions play in these conflicts—when they do play a notable role, which is not always the case—one must keep in mind what Fuller writes in the final pages of his book: "Religion will always be invoked wherever it can to galvanize the public and to justify major campaigns, battle and wars." But, he adds, "The causes, campaigns, battle and wars are not about religions."[4] Fuller makes two good points that require, however, a bit of perspective: the adverb he uses ("always") implies that religions have always had—and in the future, always will have—this capacity "to galvanize the public and to justify major campaigns." The thesis presented in these pages, to the contrary, is that they have *only recently reacquired this capacity*, and that it promises to become more and more important in the future.

Those who have studied the role of religion in political violence and wars have generally focused on Islam, leaving aside two very important points: that all religions can be used "to galvanize the public and to justify major campaigns," and that violence is merely one form of politics, and certainly not the most important—even if, for obvious reasons, it is quicker to seize public attention. I will deal with this second point in the next chapter; for now let us concentrate on the first point: the role played by other religions in political violence.

RELIGION AND VIOLENCE IN INDIA: POLITICS

For centuries, Islam and Hinduism, but also Sikhism, Jainism, Buddhism, Christianity, and Judaism, have coexisted more or less peacefully in India; at least, as peacefully as any neighbors can coexist in a rural environment dominated by shortages and poverty. Moreover, through their mutual contacts, the two principal religions not only fought with each other but also influenced each other: Hinduism was slightly "Islamized," stressing the superiority of certain gods over others, while Islam, as Fareed Zakaria puts it, became "less Abrahamic and more spiritual."[5] Many Hindus converted to Islam, but at the same time, many Muslims converted to Hinduism and Sikhism.

Inevitably, these close encounters and intermixing had an impact on identities within the two most important religious communities on the Indian subcontinent; the coexistence of the most open and the most rigidly closed versions of Islam and of Hinduism was a constant. As a rule, the wealth, prestige, and spirit of tolerance of the Mughal Empire favored a mostly peaceful cohabitation for several centuries. The most extreme and violent forms of Islam and of Hinduism—today we would call them "fundamentalists"—gained ascendance during moments of crisis, and also when the subcontinent was drawn into the global capitalist market. The birth of nationalism, along with the political choices of the British after the Great Rebellion in 1857, ultimately separated the destinies of the Hindus and Muslims and, intentionally or not, stirred their rivalries to the point of violent confrontation.

As I have noted, the Hindus, too, found justification for violence in their sacred texts. The entire epic of the Mahabharata, which is approximately ten times the length of the *Iliad* and *Odyssey* combined, is a history of the *kshatriya*, the professional warriors whose principal occupation was to kill one another with style, with method, and according to the rules of the art. The Bhagavad Gita, the central part of the Mahabharata, which Ananda Coomaraswamy has described as a "compendium of the whole Vedic doctrine," is a history of massacres that were as horrific as they were interminable.[6] According to Graham M. Schweig, the lessons contained in the Gita are "unique even among 'holy wars.'" Indeed, he explains, "One of the important messages of the Gita is that there will always be irresolvable ethical conflicts in this world." Thus, a capacity for "returning to the struggles of this world" requires "a more elevated state of consciousness" and engages "the highest spiritual values."[7]

Several specialists have seen in the Mahabharata, in general, and in the Gita, in particular, the foundations for a Hindu theory of "just war." According to Steven J. Rosen, war, or punishment (*danda*), becomes "just" when one has exhausted three means of avoiding it: *sama*, an attempt at persuasion; *dana*, an attempt to buy peace with a gift; and *bheda*, the issuance of threats. Francis X. Clooney emphasizes that, according to the Mahabharata, for war to be "just" it must meet certain precise criteria, such as the proportionality of means, the use of "fair" weaponry—not poisoned, for example— a just cause, and clemency toward prisoners and the wounded.[8] Rosen states that, in Vedic literature, the "just war" is repeatedly recognized as an act of purification and as a social obligation: "The painter should paint. The musician should make music. And the warrior should fight. The Gita is about doing what you do with a spiritual end in mind—but do it, you must."[9]

As for the modern political struggles on the subcontinent, it was Mohandas Gandhi's victory over his successive rivals within the Congress Party that ultimately attenuated the Vedic doctrine of "necessary" violence. As is the case with Islam, Hinduism has no central religious authority capable of "guiding" the interpretation of the sacred texts, as, for example, the Catholic Church does with the Bible. As in Islam, indeed more so than in Islam, each brahmin and each individual reads in the texts of the Vedic tradition what he or she wants to read. Unlike Islam, Hinduism has not only a plurality of doctrines but also a plurality of gods, which complicates matters further.

Moreover, the perfect geographic overlap between the Hindu religion and the Indian state means that the contents of the religion are the direct result of political struggles. I alluded earlier to the conflicts within the Indian independence movement, and to the use of the Hindu tradition by Vishnushastri Chiplunkar and Aurobindo Ghose against Gandhi—and then by the latter against all others—as well as the ruling of the Indian Supreme Court setting the principles of the "eternal law" in 1966.

As for Gandhi himself, we should perhaps recall certain aspects of his biography that his subsequent beatification caused to be forgotten, but which add important context for our understanding of the political struggles of the subcontinent. When the Boer War broke out in South Africa in 1899, Gandhi—who was then living in the country—organized a recruitment campaign for the British military, creating a volunteer corps of 1,100 Indians to serve as ambulance personnel, for which he later received the War Medal. This was not long before he took a position on the racial question, writing on September 24, 1903, that "the white race of South Africa should be the predominating race."[10] He again recruited personnel for His Majesty's Army on the occasions of the war against the Zulu Kingdom of the Natal, in 1906, and yet again in 1915, in India, when he gave up ambulance service to seek actual combat: "If we want to learn the use of arms with the greatest possible dispatch, it is our duty to enlist ourselves in the army," he wrote in 1918.[11]

His position was very different at the outset of World War II. Shortly before the bombardment of London began on July 6, 1940, he wrote a famous letter in which he suggested that the British too adopt the methods of nonviolence: "You will invite Herr Hitler and Signor Mussolini to . . . take possession of your beautiful island, with your many beautiful buildings. . . . If they do not give you free passage out, you will allow yourself, man, woman and child, to be slaughtered, but you will refuse to owe allegiance to them."[12]

Gandhi's conversion to "nonviolence" was inspired not by Vedic principles but, rather, by the new geopolitical context. The United Kingdom had grown increasingly dependent on the United States, and Japan had included India as part of its Greater East Asia Co-Prosperity Sphere. Subhas Chandra Bose, the former head of the Congress Party, had taken refuge in Tokyo in 1941 to lead a notional provisional government of Free India (Azad Hind), and in March 1942 Gandhi had rejected the offer of independence from London—as, too, did the Muslim League headed by Muhammad Ali Jinnah, though for opposite reasons.[13] According to Michel Danino, it was Gandhi's refusal—which Danino explains as his "dogmatic stand on the evil nature of war, a dogma Sri Krishna rebuffs in the Gita"—that made "India's bloody vivisection unavoidable."[14]

One can view this refusal as a terrible error; but the political history of Gandhi and the military situation of the time lead to the conclusion that, at its origin, more than a "dogmatic stand on the evil nature of war" lay behind the conviction that Japan was truly poised to achieve its "co-prosperity sphere" and that Tokyo would have conceded more to the Indian nationalists than London was prepared to offer.

This quick digression reminds us that Gandhi was no stranger to this mix of religion, politics, and violence that played, in the history of modern India, a role incomparably more important than nonviolence. Moreover, the breakup of the British Raj in August 1947 brought the most horrific interreligious bloodbath of the twentieth century. The wounds inflicted by these massacres have never healed, as witness the three "official" wars between India and Pakistan; the endless war in Kashmir— with tens of thousands, and very probably hundreds of thousands, of victims; the internal conflicts in Pakistan; the violent secession of Bangladesh; the internal conflicts in India against the princely state of Hyderabad in 1948, then against the independence-minded Sikhs and against the seven states east of Bangladesh; but also the war in Sri Lanka, with the intervention of the Indian Army from 1987 to 1990; the instability of the Maldives—and a further intervention of the Indian Army in 1988; and, naturally, the permanent conflicts among Hindus, Muslims, and Sikhs within India.

An investigation by *Time* magazine in 2003 revealed that, according to official police figures, three-quarters of the victims of clashes between religious communities in India have been Muslims.[15] However, the official data are far from reliable, for it is not uncommon that the authorities responsible for preventing violence stand by without intervening or, at times, even intervene on the side of the attackers. Most of these cases can be described not as riots but as veritable pogroms, with the attackers invading predominantly Muslim neighborhoods, torching homes, and massacring the inhabitants: the number of people killed usually varies from a few dozens to several thousands, as was the case with the massacres in 2002 in Gujarat—governed at the time by the current prime minister, Narendra Modi—which claimed the lives of more than two thousand Muslims, compared to an estimated two hundred Hindus. The same techniques were used against Sikhs in 1984 during the pogroms that followed the assassination of Indira Gandhi; according to various sources, the number of victims ranged somewhere between 2,700 and 17,000. And again, the same techniques were used against Christians during the attacks in Odisha in 2008 and in the Punjab in 2010, though in these cases the numbers of victims were limited to a few dozen. The "restraint" of the assailants and the greater solicitude of the authorities regarding Christians are probably explained by the superior organization of the latter and, above all, the international attention they enjoyed, which is far from the case when dealing with Muslims or, even less so, Sikhs.

RELIGION AND VIOLENCE IN INDIA: SOCIETY

Any serious student of religious violence in India will discover that the main victims of Hindu attacks are not Muslims, nor Sikhs, nor Christians, but the Hindus themselves; indeed, it is the *dalits* ("untouchables" or the "casteless") who suffer incomparably more from violence. According to a document from the World Council of Churches in 2010, using data from 2006, each week thirteen *dalits* are killed simply because of their caste, five of their homes are torched, six *dalits* are kidnapped, twenty-one *dalit* women are raped; indeed, the report finds, a crime is committed against the untouchables every eighteen minutes. Yet those responsible are punished only 5.3 percent of the time.[16]

Religious Indian nationalists view the caste system—and thus the question of *dalits*—as a pillar of tradition, vital to maintaining social cohesion and equilibrium. One reason for the hatred of other religions is precisely that those religions make particular efforts to recruit among the *dalits*, who would like to withdraw from the caste system. Hinduism, linked as it is to the territory, is not a proselytizing religion—even if, in its "globalized" form, it could become so. Lacking any tradition of converting others, Hindus view conversions from among their midst as underhanded, which explains both the violence and the growing number of anticonversion laws. In 1978 Arunachal Pradesh became the first state to pass such laws, followed by Gujarat in 2003, Madhya Pradesh and Chhattisgarh in 2006, Himachal Pradesh in 2007, and Orissa and Rajasthan in 2008. The Parliament of Maharashtra, the state in which Mumbai is located, discussed in the fall session of 2013 its fourth proposal for an anticonversion law—all previous attempts failed due to pressure from the Catholic community.

And yet the caste question reveals the imperfect connection between tradition and religion. The caste system has belonged to Hindu tradition since the Vedic period between 1500 and 500 BCE. During this period the religion commonly known as "Brahmanism" used the Vedas to organize a system of rites, cults, and social norms, including castes. Nonetheless, as the following centuries saw the successive influences of Buddhism, Islam, and Christianity, and especially the affirmation of capitalism, the caste system lost its original social relevance and was transformed into a sort of principle of social order—sometimes all the more rigid as it moved farther from social realities—and became independent of religions.[17] While Islam, Sikhism, and Christianity theoretically reject it, several Indian emigrant communities have tended to perpetuate the system *regardless of their religion*. This is the case particularly among first-generation immigrants, in yet another example of the vital importance of the preservation of tradition among the newly urbanized or uprooted.

This, incidentally, tells us something about the question of identity, which is never fixed and immutable, and which is far less "chosen" than shaped by ambient circumstances. In other words, a Sikh who leaves the Punjab to move to New Delhi is essentially a Sikh; a Sikh who moves to London is essentially an Indian.

But let us return to the subcontinent. Violence and religion are political tools there because they are part of the social landscape, and not the opposite. In other words, it is not the Indian nationalist organizations—Viśva Hindu Parishad, Bajrang Dal, Rashtriya Swayamsevak Sangh, Shiv Sena, the Bharatiya Janata Party, and other groups and associations united under the *hindutva* federation known as Sangh Parivar—that create violence or, of course, religion.[18] Rather, they exploit, to political ends, the violence and the religion with which society is already impregnated, thereby contributing to the spread of religion and to a worsening of violence.

Within Indian society, there coexist acute forms of the most extreme sorts of unequal development: its people are still largely country-dwellers—in 2011 only 31.3 percent of Indians lived in cities, barely more than the 28.4 percent of Bangladeshis but less than the 36.2 percent of Pakistanis, 50.7 percent of Indonesians, or 52.6 percent of Chinese in 2012.[19] However, India's megalopolises are enormous—in 2011 there were 12.5 million inhabitants in Mumbai, 11 million in Delhi, 8.5 million in Bangalore, and 7.8 million in Hyderabad. India is the world's ninth-largest industrial power—its manufacturing industry accounts for 26.4 percent of GDP, a little less than Japan at 27.3 percent but much more than the United States at 19.2 percent.[20] With cutting-edge sectors in information technology, it is the second-leading Asian country in its number of billionaires and has more than Italy and France combined. Finally, at present India is the ninth-largest economic power worldwide as measured by nominal GDP, third-largest as measured by GDP purchasing power parity (PPP), but 125th overall in terms of output per inhabitant, also calculated in PPP.[21] Of all these factors, it is, above all, the coexistence of an enormous peasant mass with large urban and industrial concentrations that intensifies the urgency of preserving tradition, indeed, of sometimes reinventing tradition.

Nearly everywhere, the tradition that newcomers struggle to preserve revolves first around the patriarchal family. It should therefore be no surprise if many of the questions that seem linked to tradition, in India as well, revolve around women's role in society. India is near the top of any list of the worst places in the world for a woman to be born and is even *the* worst among the twenty largest economies.[22] As the Indian activist Shemeer Padinzjharedil has noted: "It's a miracle a woman survives in India. Even before she is born, she is at risk of being aborted due to our obsession for sons." In this regard, the situation is growing worse: the ratio in the cohort of children aged zero to six has gone from 104 boys per 100 girls in 1981 to 109.4 boys per 100 girls in 2011. Padinzjharedil adds: "As a child, she faces abuse, rape and early marriage and even when she marries, she is killed for dowry. . . . if she survives all of this, as a widow she is discriminated against and given no rights over inheritance or property."[23] According to UNICEF, 47 percent of Indian women marry before the age of eighteen, and 18 percent before they turn fifteen. A survey published in 2000 found that more than 90 percent of marriages are arranged.[24] In this regard, too, the data confirm that modernity, at least for a time, appears to worsen matters rather than improving them. As the author of the study notes, "It was widely expected that the custom of 'arranged marriage' would decline as

India modernized," adding that the persistence of the practice is "surprisingly robust."[25]

Arranged marriages have not put a brake on domestic violence—quite the contrary. According to data reported by Minister of State for Women and Child Development Renuka Chowdhury in 2006, some 70 percent of women suffer from such violence: a crime takes place every three minutes, a rape every twenty-nine minutes and a so-called dowry death every seventy-seven minutes.[26] In the latter case, the killers are for the most part unsatisfied husbands who, rather than allowing their wives to return to their parents' homes, kill them to keep the rich dowry they had brought. This crime, too, has been made worse by modernity, and rapidly so: in 2012 there was one murder every sixty-four minutes, and 90 percent of the women are educated.[27] The roots of this epidemic lie in Hindu tradition, under which the woman enjoys absolutely no rights within the family. The same tradition is found on the Indonesian island of Bali, where Hindu customary law is still applied. It should be noted that the British colonial authorities in India and their Dutch counterparts in Indonesia confirmed Hindu usage and abrogated the rights that sharia law had recognized for women.

Marriages between people of different castes or religions are subject to so-called honor crimes. Overseeing this practice, particularly in some northern Indian states, are the *khap panchayat* (councils of elders), which mete out justice in the villages in the name of traditional ways. In the cities, where the elders lack authority, it is either the laws or brigades for the promotion of virtue and prevention of vice that handle such work; in Mumbai and Delhi, young people who hold hands or kiss in public are subject to fines or can even be arrested; and in places with little police presence one finds the militias of the Shiv Sena or other, similar organizations.

In 2009, in Mangalore, the main port city in Karnataka state, a group called Sri Ram Sena ("Rama's Army") hunted for women caught drinking in bars or, worse, dancing with men, accusing them of anti-Indian behavior.

However, right-wing groups have not been alone in "religiously" exploiting social violence. The painter Maqbool Fida Husain, described by *Forbes* as the Indian Picasso, had, in the 1970s, painted pictures that some twenty years later became the target of Hindu nationalists' wrath, who viewed them as disrespectful of the Hindu gods; he was forced to flee India after his home was stormed by mobs of young Hindus. One leader of the Bharatiya Janata Party offered a kilogram of gold to anyone who would rip out Husain's eyes. The Hindu Personal Law Board went even further in 2006, promising 510 million rupees (about $7.6 million) for his head, while Akhtar Baig, a Congress Party minister, suggested a bounty of 110,000 rupees for anyone who would cut off Husain's hand.[28]

Today one hears little about these matters. Indeed, little is said about the condition of women in India, and even less about the condition of Muslim women in Indian Kashmir. The reason is that everyone these days is busy paying court to the giant of the subcontinent; even its strategic competitors—the United States and China—have established deep relationships with India. Still, if a day comes when one or more foreign powers decide to confront, or attack, India drawing on its human rights record as a pretext or justification, they will find no shortage of material in the episodes of social violence—with their numerous political patrons—and will be able to attribute them to the deeply entrenched attachment of the Indian people to their national religion.

THE BLOODY BORDERS OF BUDDHISM

No religion is foreign to violence, whether social or political, organized or spontaneous. Even Buddhism, which is often associated with its made-for-export version geared to disconcerted Westerners—featuring practices like transcendental meditation, yoga, and alternative medicines—has a long history of violence, theoretical and actual, reaching up to the present moment.

In 1891, Dutch Sinologist Jan Jakob Maria de Groot wrote that "Chinese books contain various passages relating to Buddhist monks who freely indulged in carnage and butchery . . . thus leaving no room for doubt that warfare was an integrate part of their religious profession for centuries."[29] In large measure, this exercise of violence, notably aimed at military ends or public order, can be explained through Buddhism's traditionally promiscuous relationship with political power.

Some specialists consider Buddhism—and, at times, Jainism as well—as the spiritual component of the great political upheaval that swept northern India around the sixth century BCE with the birth of the

Mahajanapadas (great kingdoms). According to this hypothesis, the religion of Siddharta Gautama—later to be known commonly as Buddha (The Enlightened One)—was born in reaction to Brahmanism; it was a sort of revenge by the *kshatriya* (warriors) who had been subordinated to the Brahmin caste. Siddharta himself was born into a clan of warrior-kings and "as a prince growing up, was inculcated in an environment imbued of practices of diplomacy and warfare."[30] Some of the Mahajanapadas—notably in the states of Kosala and Magadha, where the Gautama clan was active—quickly adopted Buddhism as a state religion, with monks supposedly filling roughly the same function as the ulema in Islam: providing both spiritual and moral guidance to the king, and serving as a counterweight to his authority.

As a general rule, the monks were influenced more by political power than political power was influenced by the monks. It was a situation not unlike that of the ulema, except for the crucial difference that the Buddhist monks immediately organized themselves on a monastic basis, with a structure inspired by the administration of the state, which often positioned them to directly assume temporal power. Testifying to this are the numerous theocratic states of Southeast Asia—the Pagan, Sukhothai, and Polonnaruwa kingdoms, among others—and, more recently, the Mongolia of Bogd Khan (1911–1919), along with the two best-known cases, those of Sri Lanka and Tibet. Even today, of the nine countries with Buddhist majorities, five make it their state religion, adding up to a density of state religions greater than anywhere else in the world except among the Muslim countries. Taken together, these traditions explain the inability of Buddhist monks "to conceive of a state without Buddhism"[31]

This close relationship with power reinforced the Indian tradition under which "*dharma* is the fact that there are rules that must be obeyed; it is the principle of order, regardless of what that order actually is."[32] This familiarity also contributed to the emergence of theories justifying power and its use of violence, whether the doctrines of "just war," expressed differently in Sri Lanka and Tibet, or the corporal punishments and torture in Mongolia. Even eschatological violence—buttressed by traditional Buddhist contempt for the body—was found in the revolts in Siam, as well as in conflicts among different schools of Buddhism, notably in Tibet.[33] Naturally, too, were the wars for the propagation and affirmation of the faith as related, for example, by the tantra of Kalachakra, one of the doctrinal supports of Tibetan Buddhism, which describes the war between the mythical kings of Shambhala and the real Muslims of the ninth century.

The theories and mythologies of the past could easily be consigned to literary anthologies—as has been the case with the Greek and Latin gods—if their evocative and mobilizing power had not reached down to modern days, transported by the conflicts of modernity.

In 1868, following the Meiji Restoration in Japan, Zen Buddhism invented a "traditional" connection to the samurai caste—the latter having been linked, since the Middle Ages, to another school of Buddhism—in order to affirm itself as the official religion of the new regime. William Johnston has emphasized the role played by the monks in the Russo-Japanese War; Brian Daizen Victoria, himself a Zen monk, has described the profound involvement of his colleagues in Japanese militarism during World War II. Among others, Victoria quotes one of the most important Zen masters of modern Japan, Daiun Sogaku Harada (1871–1961), for whom the war was "the manifestation of the highest Wisdom . . . the unity of Zen and war extends to the farthest reaches of the holy war."[34]

A few years later, and across the sea, some Buddhist monks and nuns placed themselves at the service of Maoist China's military effort in the Korean War with the same energy as their Japanese colleagues—and with the same enemy: the Americans. One eminent figure of Chinese Buddhism, the monk Juzan, wrote in 1951: "Due to our compassion, we may kill them [American imperialists]. By doing so, not only would we not violate Buddhist principles but also generate more merit. This is the necessary path to releasing suffering for happiness, and Buddhists should take it up seriously."[35]

Similar arguments were invoked in Cambodia during the same years, but this time against the French. Monks supporting the nationalist leader Son Ngoc Thanh threatened the colonial power with a holy war for the independence of the country; the monk Son Ngoc Minh, a member of the Indochinese Communist Party, insisted that the war of liberation was in keeping with the "aspirations of the Buddhist religion."[36] Later, in Thailand during the political crisis of the mid-1970s, the monk Kitthiwuttho Bhikku called again for holy war, but this time against the Communists. He declared in a speech titled "Killing the Communists Is Not Without Merit," that since they threatened both Buddhism and the nation, "their death would not produce negative karma."[37] Also in the 1970s, a similar concept was invoked by the Cambodian dictator Marshal Lon Nol when he launched a "holy war" against the Vietnamese of Cambodia. As Mahayana Buddhists, the Vietnamese were supposed to be considered "infidels" by Cambodia's Theravada Buddhists.

In recent years Thailand and Cambodia have repeatedly clashed along their border over the Preah Vihear Temple, with each country insisting that the nine-century-old edifice had played an essential role in its national and Buddhist identity. Thai monks were also behind the creation of armed anti-Muslim militias in three southern provinces—Patani, Yala, and Narathiwat—largely inhabited by Malays. As we have seen, Muslims have also been targeted by the Buddhists of Myanmar. Additionally, in Sri Lanka, since the bloody civil war against the Hindu Tamils ended, it has been the Muslims who have suffered most at the hands of Sinhalese Buddhist supremacists; the latter movement is represented, among others, by the Bodu Bala Sena religious party, organized by some of the forty thousand monks who indirectly control the country's political life.

I will conclude this expedited overview by considering the case of the tiny kingdom of Bhutan, perched high in the eastern Himalayas between India and Tibet, with a total population approximating that of Charlotte, North Carolina. Bhutan is a Buddhist country where, in contrast to Sri Lanka or Myanmar, the monks do not lead pogroms against rival religious communities but nonetheless display certain characteristics that would surely be described as fundamentalist, and which would provoke international indignation if, instead of Buddhism, the official religion of the country were Islam.

Bhutan is also known for having dropped, in 1972, the traditional accounting standard of the gross national product in favor of its own gross national happiness index, the objective of which, according to the official government site, was to "make it possible to evaluate an economy based on the spiritual values of Buddhism." It is also the first country to completely ban smoking on its soil, essentially "on religious grounds, as Buddhists here consider smoking to be a sin."[38] A less well-known distinction is that the country has taken discriminatory measures against the Hindu and Christian minorities, and even toward Buddhist minorities, as the Kadampa and Bön schools of Buddhism have been forced to merge into the Mahayana school of Drukpa Kagyu, the only version recognized by the state.

Bhutan's Hindu community is primarily formed by the Lhotshampa, who are of Nepalese origin. In 1988, according to the national census, this ethnic group constituted 45 percent of the population, but today it represents only 15–20 percent. After being subjected to a 1989 law known as the *driglam namzha* (the basic rules for disciplined behavior)—essentially, the national dress code of the majority Buddhists—between 1991 and 1992, some 100,000 Lhotshampa were expelled to Nepal, many of their places of worship were destroyed, and the faithful dispersed.

The level of harassment of the Bhutanese Hindus—little evidence of which can be found in the international news media—can be better understood when one considers the treatment of the country's Christians, who account for 12,000–15,000 of a population of some 750,000. Restrictions on proselytizing mainly target this community; among these measures is an anticonversion law, in effect since July 2011. Another example here is the obstacles to, or even outright bans on, the Christians' "Sunday meetings," which at times have been the object of violent attacks by young Buddhist militants. Nevertheless, it appears that many people have chosen to convert to Christianity because, as the author of a study published in 2011 concluded, "the rights of Christians are better looked after at the international level."[39]

It is true that in Bhutan with the Nepalese, as in Sri Lanka with the Tamils, or Myanmar with the Rohingyas, the reasons for persecution are essentially ethnic and, in the latter instance, political, and that religion is merely a pretext. This is a theme heard frequently in this book, as in every book dealing with the political role of religions; the same is true of all the complementary factors, notably the multiplying effect that religions can have on crises or conflicts of whatever sort. If the acts of violence committed in the name of Buddhism have been fewer and less well publicized than those committed in the name of other religions, they are nonetheless qualitatively comparable. And that is true, as well, of the particular form of political violence we know as terrorism.

11

TERRORISM

Anyone who would not joyously sacrifice his life for the satisfaction of exterminating a million barbarians is not a true republican.

—Karl Heinzen

POLITICAL DESPERATION BY OTHER MEANS

Terrorism is the poor cousin of political struggle. By giving a slight twist to Carl von Clausewitz's famous formulation, we could even say that terrorism is the continuation of political desperation by other means.

It is also true that terrorism, of all forms of political struggle, is that which arouses the greatest fear and anxiety. In fact, this is what explains its effectiveness: it instills in potential victims—or those who consider themselves as such—a sense of an obscure, indefinable, but permanent threat, all the more sinister when those potential victims had considered themselves sheltered from such violence. The principal reason that the media and public focused so much more—incomparably more—on the three people killed in the Boston Marathon bombing of April 15, 2013, than on the seventy-five people killed that same day in car bomb attacks across

Iraq—part of a series of attacks that claimed 1,082 lives in the first three and a half months of 2013—is that the Iraqis live in a war zone, while the athletes and spectators in Boston were considered incongruous victims, undeserving of their fate.

The differing levels of attention paid to the shootings at two American military bases—Fort Hood, Texas, in 2009 and the Washington Navy Yard in 2013, each claiming thirteen lives—stem from the fact that the man behind the first attack was Muslim and the man behind the second was Buddhist. It is true that in the first case, the culprit declared his religious motivation, while in the second, the assailant, killed during a brief gun battle, did not explain his act. Yet what interests us here is that public opinion is ready to believe the religious motivations of a Muslim killer, while it denies a priori any religious motivation when the killer is Buddhist—as if "Muslim terrorist" were a meaningful phrase while "Buddhist terrorist" made no sense at all.

In reality, it is the very notion of "religious" terrorism—of any stripe—that should be surprising; not because religions, and the religious, are not violent, but because modern terrorism is intrinsically secular. The "rise of terrorism" has followed the same path as the nation-state: it was born as a weapon—sometimes the only one—of nationalism, and it remained almost exclusively nationalist in expression until the 1980s.[1] It began evolving as the preferred instrument of certain religiously motivated groups only at the point when religion returned to the sphere of political action and the nationalist perspective began to lose its focus, the two phenomena being closely linked.

According to many historians, modern terrorism was born in the nineteenth century with movements such as Narodnaïa Volia in Russia, the Irish Republican Brotherhood, the Fenian Brotherhood, the Armenian Revolutionary Federation, and certain anti-Ottoman Balkan movements, such as the Internal Macedonian Revolutionary Organization. Nor should we forget other nationalist movements such as the Italian and Hungarian democrats, particularly active after the failure of the Revolutions of 1848; the German democrats, including Karl Heinzen, the theoretician of suicide attacks; or the Black Hand and Young Bosnia in the Balkans, both of which helped organize the assassination of Archduke Franz Ferdinand in June 1914. By this period, terrorism had also become the weapon of choice for other political tendencies: the Russian populists, as already mentioned; various nihilist and anarchist groups—Russian, Italian, French, Spanish, etc.—advocating "propaganda by the deed"; as well as the Ku Klux Klan in the United States, born in the wake of the Confederates' defeat in the Civil War.

This list of militant groups, organizations, and movements has two elements in common: all came into being in Christian countries, and all were politically weak, desperate, and/or defeated. The fact that they emerged in Christian countries does not, of course, signify that, with the exception of the Ku Klux Klan, these were Christian movements or were responding to any religious motivation; even the Irish Republican Brotherhood was strongly disavowed by the Catholic authorities. The only significance of their births in Christian countries is that modernity—the context within which terrorism emerged in the nineteenth century—was generally confined to certain Christian countries. In this period, modernity had only begun to reach into Muslim, Hindu, and Buddhist lands. Consequently, we witness no significant episodes of Muslim, Hindu, or Buddhist terrorism in this period.

The other characteristic leading to terrorism's rise in many nineteenth-century Christian countries was desperation. In politics, desperation takes hold when a determined group begins to disregard the actual relative weight of different forces. The nineteenth-century nationalists who ultimately began to theorize and practice the "propaganda of the deed" were the defeated democrats of the Revolutions of 1848 who had continued to invent their private little revolutions, heedless of the true relative weight of different forces: not only did they suffer one defeat after another, but most often they actually played into their adversary's game—as was the case with the Italian "moderates" during that country's unification, or with the "scoundrel" laws in France in the early 1890s. Subsequent politically radical groups that lacked social bases and/or were completely divorced from reality—from the Russian nihilists to the Red Brigades—followed the same path as the post-1848 democrats.

In considering terrorism from a political viewpoint, the relative-weight-of-forces question is much more crucial than the methods used. Indeed, during the twentieth century, some movements made ample use of terrorist methods, individual killings, bombings, attacks on civilians, and yet still attained their objectives. Among these were the Irish Republican Army, the Gruppi di Azione Patriotica in Italy during the Resistance, the Zionist Irgun in Palestine during the 1930s and 1940s, and the Front de Libération Nationale in Algeria. In each case, terrorism was but one means used in a more generalized political action whose chances of success depended precisely on a favorable relative-weight-of-forces, either because the movement in question was deeply rooted and its actions popular—for example, the IRA and the FLN—or because of favorable international power balances—the GAP and Irgun, or both. One might even suggest that these movements achieved their objectives in spite of, rather than because of, their terrorist methods.

"RELIGIOUS" TERRORISM

"Religious" terrorism first appears when religion becomes confused with, or simply takes the place of, politics. Some specialists go so far as to suggest that the phrase "religious terrorism" is meaningless. The justification for this position is usually summarized by explanations such as that religious motivation "is often a transparent tactic designed to conceal political goals, generate popular support, and silence opposition."[2] Another common position dismissing religious terrorism as a stand-alone phenomenon is the observation that virtually all practitioners of terrorist tactics make moral declarations, and therefore this "does not in fact distinguish religious from nonreligious terrorists, for the latter also rely upon such arguments to justify their acts."[3]

One of the first manifestations of so-called religious terrorism to emerge was Buddhist, which should not be a huge surprise, considering the traditionally close relationship of Buddhism and politics. In the 1930s the nationalist terrorist group Ketsumeidan (League of Blood) struck in Japan—which also should not be surprising, Japan being the most industrialized Buddhist country. Founded by the Buddhist preacher Nissho Inoue, the group was behind several attacks on politicians and businessmen.

It is true, chronologically, that the Ketsumeidan was preceded by the "Christian terrorism" of the Ku Klux Klan, whose avowed objective was to "re-establish Protestant Christian values in America by any means possible";[4] however, it is only partially accurate to classify the Klan as a terrorist group. The Klan's targets belonged to a well-identified group—African Americans, of course—and its main method of persecution was, primarily, the pogrom, which implies the direct or indirect participation of a significant portion of the general population. Thus a pogrom—while certainly terrifying for the targeted population—implies a separate set of circumstances from terrorism. Authentic "Christian terrorism" began to appear at the same time as most other forms of religiously motivated terrorism, that is, in the late 1970s. This occurred essentially in the form of fringe American groups of the Evangelical right, whose principal activity was an armed struggle against abortion but also, in some cases, for the affirmation of the "white race" or even for the Judaization of Israel and the Palestinian territories, which would supposedly accelerate the second coming of Christ.[5] These groups included the Army of God; the Lamb of Christ; the Christian Patriot, and the Concerned Christians. In addition, there were the individual acts of persons not directly linked to specific organizations, such as Eric Robert Rudolph, who described himself as a Roman Catholic, the man behind the bombing attack at the 1996 Olympic Games in Atlanta. As John Esposito and Dalia Mogahed wrote in 2007, "The vast majority of terrorist attacks on U.S. soil have been perpetrated by Christian terrorist groups in the past 15 years."[6]

Outside of the United States, Christian terrorist groups generally have emerged from minorities who were threatened or perceived themselves to be. This was the case with the Warriors of the Boer Nation in South Africa and, in India, of the National Liberation Front of Tripura, the National Council of Nagaland, as well as certain Christian groups linked to the Maoist rebels in Odisha.

Christian terrorism is thus primarily Protestant. This fact is not unconnected to the "freedom of conscience" that Protestantism leaves to its faithful. To the contrary, in Orthodox Christian communities, the believers are constantly guided and accompanied by their church, limiting the risks of a drift to terrorism. In the Yugoslav Wars, Serbian fighters and the Greek volunteers were certainly encouraged by their religious authorities, but their actions, as bloody as they were, cannot be described as terrorism.[7] And yet today the conditions are present in certain Orthodox countries— Russia, Serbia, Bulgaria, Romania, and, above all, Greece—for a possible "Christianization" of extremist, xenophobic, and racist groups, tempted by a sort of "Orthodox supremacist" tendency—even if, at the time of this writing, the various local churches do not appear close to encouraging this sort of development.

With regard to Catholicism, we have seen why the Catholic Church is in a position to ensure that no one can evoke the existence of such a thing as "Catholic terrorism." That applies in particular to the lone wolves describing themselves as Catholic, such as Rudolph or Andres Breivik in Norway, as well as those baptized Catholic but whose motivations were not religious—notably Timothy McVeigh, who carried out the Oklahoma City bombing in 1995, and Adam Lanza, the shooter in the Sandy Hook Elementary School massacre in Newtown, Connecticut, in December 2012.

The guerrilla priests active in Latin America in the 1960s and 1970s created a much thornier problem for the Catholic Church. Convinced that, in these countries, armed struggle was the necessary path for any good Christian to take—"Si Jesús viviera, sería guerrillero" (If Jesus were alive today, he would be a guerrilla), said Father Camilo Torres, the most famous among them—these priests were disavowed, suspended *a divinis*, or expelled. A notable case in this regard was that of Ernesto Cardenal, a Sandinist militant and later a Nicaraguan minister of culture, who was publicly reprimanded by Pope John Paul II during his visit to the Central American country in 1983.[8]

As far as we know, the church has been implicated in affairs linked to terrorism only twice: in the cases of Croatian and Palestinian terrorism. Considerable doubts surround the Irish case, even if the church has yet to express itself openly on the years of the Troubles. Martin Dillon, author of a richly reported study of the subject, writes that "the Churches in Northern Ireland have found it difficult to step out of their tribal roots." If the Catholic hierarchy has always attempted to keep its distance vis-à-vis the IRA, which was viewed as secular or, worse, socialist, "many priests subscribed to the thesis that the IRA was fighting a just war." In 1969, Dillon writes, the church favorably greeted the creation of self-defense groups that would later become the Provisional IRA (also known as Provos) as they were untainted by socialist ideals. One Republican terrorist, since retired, recalls that "the Church gave the Provos benediction, sprinkled them with holy water the way they did those who were going to fight for Franco in Spain."[9] In 1972, according to both Dillon and the Northern Ireland police, Cardinal William Conway persuaded the British authorities not to prosecute James Chesney, a Catholic priest suspected of being behind an attack in July 1972 that left nine people dead, including an eight-year-old child.[10]

Relations between the church and the Palestinians, on the other hand, have always been quite intense, at least since the Balfour Declaration of 1917 that called for the "establishment in Palestine of a national home for the Jewish people." When Catholic Palestinians published the first translation into Arabic of the *Protocols of the Elders of Zion* in their journal *Raqib Sahyun* on January 15, 1926, they should have known that it would not help relations between Arabs and Jews.[11] In less than a year, between 1948 and 1949, Pope Pius XII published three encyclicals on the 1947 partition of Palestine: the *Auspicia Quædam* in May 1948; the *In Multiplicibus Curis* in October 1948; and the *Redemptoris Nostri* in April 1949. In the latter, Pius XII, who had never publicly expressed any opinion on German policy toward the Jews during the war, declared himself to be saddened by the "concentration camps" in the Middle East, where "many, many refugees . . . [were] exposed to hunger, epidemics and dangers of all kind."

Henri Laurens, a leading French specialist on the subject of Middle East affairs, asserts that the Vatican, even while expressing ritual condemnations of terrorism, "seems ready to find reasons for these acts when the Palestinians are involved."[12] In 1974 Monsignor Hilarion Capucci, the archbishop of Caesarea for the Melkite Greek Catholic Church and auxiliary bishop of Jerusalem, was arrested while transporting guns, explosives, grenades, and munitions in his car that were intended for armed Palestinian groups. Sentenced to twelve years in prison by the Israeli authorities, Capucci was set free in 1978 after years of intense pressure from the Vatican. It is noteworthy that Capucci took refuge in Iran in 1979, where he publicly praised Ruhollah Khomeini; in 2013, at age ninety-one, he was among the most fervent supporters of President Bashar al-Assad in the Syrian Civil War.

The church's support for the "Croatian cause" in Yugoslavia was no less firm. In his autobiography, the Vatican's former minister of foreign affairs, Monsignor Agostino Casaroli, employs oblique language when referring to the Ustashi, the Catholic Croatian terrorists in exile. In the 1960s, Casaroli writes, the Croatian episcopacy avoided taking a position against Ustashi terrorism, as the government in Belgrade was demanding, because everyone was aware of the church's opposition to terrorism, "even when it is in the service of causes deemed just, and possibly not without reason." It is also quite possible, Casaroli adds, that Croatian priests in other countries "have not always exerted their influence to temper, guide, and eventually dissuade the most impetuous of their compatriots"; but the possibility that priests took part directly in terrorist actions was "easier to assert than to prove." And yet Casaroli goes on to evoke the case of a Croatian priest, a certain Father Medic, who was arrested and sentenced to prison by the German justice system as the presumed organizer of the assassination of the Yugoslav consul in Bonn. The Yugoslav episcopacy did not disavow Medic either because, as Casaroli argues, "the bishops did not have the ability to follow as closely as might be desirable the activities of their priests who have taken refuge abroad, nor to evaluate the real responsibility for acts attributed to them"; and in any case, he concludes, given the gravity of the accusation, the complaint should have been addressed directly to Rome, not to Zagreb.[13]

While terrorism is not the favored method of political violence for religious Indian extremists—who prefer pogroms—several recent episodes have led to the coining of the phrase "Saffron Terrorism." The examples of this brand of terrorism are numerous and include the bomb attack on a Muslim cemetery in Malegaon on September 8, 2006, with thirty-seven dead, attributed to the Bajrang Dal, a *hindutva* organization; the attack of February 18, 2007, on a train linking Delhi and Lahore, with sixty-eight fatalities, attributed to another *hindutva* organization, the Abhinav Bharat; the bombing of the Mecca Masjid mosque in Hyderabad on May 18, 2007, with fourteen dead, attributed to the Rashtriya Swayamsevak Sangh; the bombing of the Sufi temple in Ajmer, with three dead, attributed to the Abhinav Bharat; and the three nearly simultaneous explosions in Maharastra and Gujarat on September 29, 2008, with eight dead, attributed to the Abhinav Bharat. Furthermore, in December 2011 the Indian Intelligence Bureau declared that *hindutva* activists were being investigated in sixteen other bombing attacks across the country.

The leaders of the Bharatiya Janata Party, the main Hindu nationalist political party, insist that these accusations have been fabricated by their Congress Party rivals for political-electoral reasons. This assertion cannot be ruled out a priori. Nonetheless, it remains the case that terrorism is a rather widespread practice in India. To give a sense of the scale, the relevant *Wikipedia* page lists sixty-four major terror attacks between 1984 and 2015—bombing attacks, train derailments, assassinations, etc.—as accounting for a total of 1,934 fatalities.[14] This list does not include the full extent of the guerrilla struggles in Kashmir and Assam, nor the assassination in 1991 of Rajiv Gandhi—who was killed by a Tamil terrorist, while his mother, Indira, was killed by a Sikh bodyguard—nor the previously noted pogroms. It thus appears highly unlikely that the Hindu fundamentalists, fueled by religious hatred and having committed many other violent acts, including some of extreme cruelty—like setting people on fire, which has been fairly common during the pogroms—should have remained completely above the temptation to resort to terrorism.

And I have not even mentioned the terrorist actions of the Tamil Tigers during the twenty-five-year-long Sri Lankan Civil War. This pro-independence group was the first to create a section—the Black Tigers—devoted exclusively to suicide attacks. Specialists concur that the Tigers alone were behind more than half of such attacks throughout the world at least until the Iraq War of 2003, with 378 of them between 1987 and 2008, according to the Sri Lankan Defense Ministry. Among the victims, in addition to 106 politicians—including Rajiv Gandhi, Sri Lankan president Ranasinghe Premadasa in 1993, 7 government ministers, and 37 members of Parliament—were several thousand civilians, including some 2,150 in the 21 largest such attacks.[15]

We can draw two essential political lessons from the disastrous saga of the Tamil Tigers. The first is that a terrorist group—even when it has a clear political objective and enjoys a certain level of popular support—can continue launching attacks for twenty years without ever getting any closer to victory, inasmuch as violence is *never* the exclusive condition for political victory. The second is that it is not the hope of some eternal reward that pushes terrorists to suicide, and when that does occur, it is more the exception than the rule. The Tamil Tigers, although they are Hindu, have always been a group with a completely secular inspiration and purpose, following in the footsteps of the desperate nationalist movements of the nineteenth century. The same can be said of most other terrorist organizations, at least until 2003[16]—for example, the Kurdish groups waging a struggle for independence against Turkey, some of whom have only very recently "rediscovered" religion; and all the nationalist Palestinian groups, at least until the beginning of the First Intifada in 1987. The same also applies to Jewish terrorism.

In any discussion of Jewish terrorism, the question arises whether one is referring to the "Jewish people" or the "Jewish religious community." The question is both simple and complex, and I will not explore it deeply here. Still, it is important to note that Jewish terrorism in Palestine in the period preceding the establishment of Israel was exclusively of a political, nationalist/Zionist, and secular nature. All the armed groups—primarily Irgun, Lehi, Betar, and Haganah—made reference, in some manner and at some point or another, to the biblical borders of Israel. Also, as we have seen, David Ben-Gurion himself, though an atheist, felt a need for "traditional religious symbols in [his] self-definition."[17] On several occasions Ben-Gurion went so far as to affirm that "the creation of the new State by no means derogates from the scope of historical Eretz Israel."[18] His objective at the time was to give the political struggle a religious veneer by transforming the biblical myth into a civil religion, not to revive metaphysical beliefs that *nearly everyone* considered outmoded.

Following the birth of the new state, at least two religiously inspired terrorist groups emerged in Israel: the Brit HaKanaim, a small group active in the 1950s that favored the creation of a Halachic state—based on *Halakha*, Jewish religious law—and attacked those who did not respect the *shabbat*, the structures of public education, and the Knesset; and, Malchut Yisrael, composed of Orthodox Jews, which essentially targeted those who persecuted Jews around the world—including representatives of the Eastern Bloc but also German chancellor Konrad Adenauer. According to the historians Ami Pedahzur and Arie Perliger, the motivations of Malchut Yisrael did "not seem very different from European Muslims who identify with the suffering of Muslims in places such as Palestine, Iraq and Afghanistan and are willing under some conditions to resort to violent and radical actions."[19]

These two groups, formed by only a few dozen members at the most, were easily infiltrated and destroyed by Shin Bet, Israel's internal security service. The rebirth of Jewish terrorism in Israel mostly begins in the 1970s. Among its protagonists were Terror Neged Terror (Terror Against Terror), founded by Rabbi Meir Kahane, which carried out numerous attacks against Arabs; the Gush Emunim Underground, responsible for car bomb attacks against Arabs, as well as a plan to destroy the Dome of the Rock in Jerusalem, Islam's third most important holy site; Egrof Magen (Defensive Shield), a militia mainly active in the occupied territories, much like the Bat Ayin Underground, which was formed later; the Kach and the Kahane Chai, both of them successors to the organization founded by Kahane in the 1970s and accused of terrorist activities by the U.S. State Department; and, the ultra-Orthodox anti-Zionist group Kvutza Shelo Titpasher—commonly known as Keshet (Without Compromise). In addition to these groups, one should mention a certain number of "lone wolves," including Baruch Goldstein, who in 1994 mounted an attack on

Muslims at prayer in the Cave of the Patriarchs in Hebron that left twenty-nine dead, and Yigal Amir, Yitzhak Rabin's assassin, who announced that he had carried out a religious duty imposed by Halakha.[20]

It is nonetheless rare that the most extremist and violent Jewish religious groups are exclusively motivated by their faith: the context of the Israeli-Arab conflict makes it extremely difficult to separate religious motives from territorial and ethnic motives. Still, unlike other movements using the same arms, public opinion has a tendency to reject the religious motive, often considered as a lie, or as "cynical exploitation of Jewish law for goals that are alien to Judaism," as the judges in Tel Aviv weighing the fate of Yigal Amir wrote in sentencing him to life in prison.

And this brings us back to "Muslim terrorism," the only form whose religious motivations are never rejected.

THE GEOPOLITICS OF TERROR'S METASTASIS

As Tzvetan Todorov wrote, "All other human beings act for a variety of reasons: political, social, economic, psychological, even physiological; only Muslims, it is alleged, are always and only impelled by their religious affiliation."[21] In general, this observation is true, but it is even apparent as it applies to questions of violence and terrorism. Why do Muslims deserve this particular treatment? There are two possible answers: the first, banal in its empiricism, is that the great majority of terrorist actions since at least 2003 have been carried out in the name of Islam; the second, having to do with the absence of a central religious authority in Islam, is that Muslims, as such, are in an impossible position to reject this allegation, because for every Muslim who offers a religious basis for rejecting violence, there is another Muslim who cites a religious foundation for the justification of violence.

As we have seen, nothing in the sacred texts of Islam permits us to characterize them as "more violent" than the sacred texts of any other religion. We have also seen that it makes no sense to look at texts written centuries ago, in long-since-expired contexts very much part of ancient history, to find the causes for the recent behavior of those claiming to draw inspiration from those pages. We have seen, too, that a large number of fundamentalist Muslims would like to bring back an Islam that has never actually existed: an Islam that is anti-Jewish and anti-Christian, built on a "sharia" whose principles they alone claim to know, in the model of a theocratic regime invented in the 1960s, based on political ideas born in the nineteenth and twentieth centuries in the reviled West—nationalism, Third Worldism, and anti-imperialism—and structured around political forms also born in the nineteenth century in the West—the nation-state, parliamentarism, political parties, terrorism, and so forth.

To understand "Muslim terrorism," we must thus detach it from the metaphysical hermeneutics of the "pure Muslim," or of the "Muslim per se"—two concepts that evidently do not exist—and bring it back to its historical reality, to the conditions in which it was born in the 1980s, and in which it has since developed.

To begin with, we must point out that there was no conception of "Islamic terrorism" before the Iranian Revolution of 1979. Among all the so-called forms of religious terrorism, the form that claims its inspiration from Muhammad is thus the last, chronologically, to emerge on the scene. Its appearance dates to November 1979, with the assault on the Grand Mosque of Mecca during the hajj, the annual Muslim pilgrimage. As we have seen, this extremely bloody action can be viewed as the indirect consequence of a new climate created by the ayatollahs' seizure of power in Tehran. Although the assailants in Mecca were Sunni, their watchwords echoed those of the Shiite revolution in Iran: a return to the "original purity" of Islam, an end to corruption, and an end to the submission to American interests and Western mores. The second resounding act that drew indirect inspiration from the Iranian upheaval was the assassination of Egyptian president Anwar Sadat, and eleven other people along with him, during a military parade in October 1981. Those behind this attack, who accused Sadat of being a *kafir* (unbeliever), or even a *murtad* (apostate), said they felt a duty to rise up in anger for the sake of God: such language would have been almost unheard of before the Islamic Revolution. Also, it is noteworthy that Tehran saluted Sadat's killers as heroes.

The first widely recognized suicide attack took place a year and a half later, in April 1983, at the American Embassy in Beirut, which was organized by Shiites linked to Iran's Revolutionary Guard Corps. In fact, the first such attack of this type may have been carried out a bit sooner, in November 1982, against the headquarters of the Israeli occupying forces in Tyre, southern Lebanon, but the official version has always been that this was an accidental explosion. Regardless, the Islamic Jihad Organization and its allied group, Lebanese Hezbollah, were certainly behind the suicide attacks against the American Embassy and the American and French contingents of the multinational security force in Beirut, on October 23, 1983, which claimed 360 lives. The threshold had been crossed.

The attack in Mecca, the assassination of Sadat, and the suicide attacks in Lebanon had three elements in common: they took place after the revolution in Iran; they used methods already amply tested by nationalist terrorist groups; and, all of them, ultimately, had nationalist motivations. Indeed, those behind the assault on the Grand Mosque demanded an end to Saudi submission to the Americans and a return to national cultural roots, real or presumptive—a demand heard in any national independence struggle. Likewise, Sadat's assassins considered him a traitor for having signed the peace agreement with Israel. Equally strong in their nationalist sentiment, the Lebanese Shiites had been confronted since June 1982 with the Israeli occupation of the South of their country, their traditional bastion.

Some specialists in the field of Islam and terrorism readily assert that supposed Islamic terrorism has never been more than one of the many forms of nationalist terrorism. Robert Pape, for example, notes that "from Lebanon to Sri Lanka to Chechnya to Kashmir to West Bank, every major suicide-terrorist campaign—more than 95 percent of all the incidents—has had as its central objective to compel a democratic state to withdraw."[22] Esposito and Mogahed remind us that Osama bin Laden's first demand was that American troops withdraw from Saudi Arabia, where they had been stationed on military bases since the lead-up to Operation Desert Storm.[23] Olivier Roy points out that the difference between Hamas and the Palestinian Liberation Organization deals not with religion but with their attitudes toward Israel.[24] Before the American occupation of Iraq in 2003, Pape also notes, "Iraq never had a suicide-terrorist attack in its history."[25] As for the Soviet intervention in Afghanistan, Michael Reisman noted in 1987 that "the resistance in Afghanistan is engaged in a war of national liberation."[26] For Liah Greenfeld, even the September 11, 2001, attacks "are increasingly seen—as they should be—as one among numerous other nationalist milestones."[27]

We have seen that the "classic" Islamist movements—that is, those born in Egypt in the late 1920s, in British India in the 1930s, and in Iran in the 1960s—were originally "internationalist" and became nationalist only later. Wahhabism, the instrument used by the tribes of the Najd to conquer the Asir and the Hejaz, became the key vector for achieving Saudi ambitions, playing a role comparable to the so-called proletarian internationalism supported by the Soviet Union.[28] Olivier Roy observes that most Islamist movements display a tendency to nationalism, virtually always combined with "a search for political opening, for electoral alliances and for integration into the national political game."[29] This is hardly surprising: every movement, group, or party only *truly* participates in the political game to the extent that it represents interest groups actually existing in the society, whether they are bazaar merchants, farmers, civil servants, financiers, or industrialists. All these groups have interests that, even if they take on religious forms, are absolutely concrete; even "Islamic finance"—which some insist is a noncapitalist institution—can only function to the extent that it *assures* the remuneration of capital.

However, politics does not always respond to rational criteria. There are political movements that, for the most diverse reasons, represent no social reality or rely on weak, evanescent, or transitory social bases—for example, the lumpenproletariat, unemployed intellectuals, peasants in transition between the countryside and the city, or fly-by-night street vendors. In this case, either they cease to exist, which is what happens most frequently; or they cease to exist politically, thereby transforming themselves into cultural associations, sects, animal protection societies, and so on; or they become the passive and unconscious instruments of others (like the Italian democrats during the Risorgimento); or they turn to terrorism; or, finally, they end up in some combination of two or more of the aforementioned possibilities. This is also what happened to those Islamist movements that, though lacking a social base in their country, were convinced that it was possible to "do like in Iran."

Like the supporters of the nationalist Giuseppe Mazzini in Milan in 1853 or their epigones in the Red Brigades in 1978, those who attacked the Grand Mosque in Mecca and who assassinated Sadat were convinced that their actions would spark a popular uprising. The Soviet-Afghan War had a multiplying effect on these beliefs because the defeat and withdrawal of the legendary Red Army persuaded the mujahidin that it was Allah who had led them to victory, as he had done with Daoud (David) when facing Jalout (Goliath). Given such convictions, the relative-weight-of-forces can be seen as a mountain—one that faith can displace.

The mujahidin who had poured into Afghanistan from all corners of the Muslim world for the war against the Soviets returned home with the firm resolve to repeat what they had succeeded in doing in Afghanistan. They returned to Egypt, Saudi Arabia, Sudan, Algeria, Syria, Morocco, and other countries, persuaded that the creation of new Islamic states was both certain and imminent. Veterans of Afghanistan later became involved in four specific situations that can be said to have been at the root of the terrorist metastasis: the struggles in Bosnia, Algeria, Kashmir, and Afghanistan, again.

Some four thousand veterans of the Soviet-Afghan War flocked to Bosnia in the early 1990s to support the new majority-Muslim country—independent since April 1992, following the dissolution of Yugoslavia—in its war against the Orthodox Serbs and Catholic Croatians. Bosnian president Alija Izetbegovic, besieged in his capital of Sarajevo, warmly welcomed the arrival of the Arab Legion of Afghanistan, as well as hundreds of Iranian advisers and military instructors, Hezbollah fighters, and an estimated $150 million in Saudi assistance. However, in the end, the attempt to transform Bosnia into an Islamic republic failed because of the incompatibility between the jihadists and the local population: the city-dwellers were unsympathetic, if not downright hostile, to the call for Afghan-style sharia, and the country-dwellers were deeply rooted in a Sufi tradition that found the internationalist Salafists abhorrent. Despite this rejection, for more than three years, Bosnia was a rallying point and a sanctuary for these veterans of the Afghan jihad who, for one reason or another, had not gone back to their home countries to wage holy war.

It was in Algeria in the early 1990s, amid the economic and social stagnation caused by falling energy prices, that conditions seemed ripest for an Islamic takeover. But, in sharp contrast to Iran and other countries where Islamists had played the card of insurrection, the attempt in Algeria came through the electoral process. Having won an absolute majority in the municipal elections of June 1990, the Front Islamique de Salut (Islamic Salvation Front) carried the first round of legislative elections, in December 1991, with 47.54 percent of the vote. At that point, Algeria's military leaders intervened. Notably, they forced the head of state, Chadli Bendjedid, to step down, dissolved the FIS, and arrested the political party's leaders. This dramatic action shifted the balance of power within the wider Islamic political movement in favor of the jihadists, including a large number of veterans of Afghan fighting, who proceeded to do the one thing they had learned to do: make war. For the following decade, Algeria was racked by a horrific, atrocity-filled war, which claimed some 100,000 lives.

Following the Soviet defeat in Afghanistan, the supposedly secular Pakistani government of Benazir Bhutto and her secret services moved a number of the mujahidin toward Indian Kashmir with the explicit objective of fueling civil war there. Since the end of the 1980s, the actions of these veterans of the Afghan jihad, and the heightened response of the Indian military, have led to the deaths of tens of thousands of people. On the Afghan front, since the Soviets withdrawal in 1988–89, Islamabad has done everything in its power to impose the creation of a puppet government in Kabul; the equally unshakable will of the Iranians and the Indians—and later, again, the Russians—to avoid at all costs allowing Afghanistan to fall under Pakistan's sway explains the long and horrific war between the various factions of mujahidin. In 1996, finally, the Taliban—a group "invented," formed, trained, and equipped by Islamabad—took power in Kabul, with the discreet support of the United States.

These four episodes have one overarching feature in common: the geopolitical factor. Behind the war in Bosnia lay the determination of the German government—energetically supported by the Vatican—to impose on the international community the recognition of Croatia and Slovenia, which had declared their independence from Yugoslavia in June 1991. In Algeria, a part of the old ruling military class that had emerged following the FLN's electoral success decided to follow the path of coup d'état and bloody repression rather than see its privileges endangered, knowing that it could count on the benign neglect of the country's major economic partners—the United States, France, and Italy—which were deeply alarmed by the specter of an Islamist government in Algiers.

In Pakistan, much of the ruling class had tried, since the time of Ali Bhutto, to play the "Islamist card" in an attempt to raise the country's international prestige after the humiliating defeat in Bangladesh in 1971. Despite the support of friends as powerful as China—which helped Pakistan develop its nuclear weapons program—the United States, and Saudi Arabia, Pakistan managed only to play the role of sorcerer's apprentice, creating monsters that it has been less and less able to control: "We are fighting Pakistan's war in Kashmir," said Sayeed Salahudeen, the head of the Hizbul Mujahidin, in May 2012, "and if it withdraws its support, the war would be fought inside Pakistan."[30]

That has already been taking place with the Taliban, driven out of Kabul in 2001. According to the *South Asia Terrorism Portal*, between 2003 and 2015 acts of terrorism in Pakistan claimed a total of 59,694 lives, including 20,877 civilians, 6,370 members of the security forces, and 32,447 terrorists/insurgents (see table 11.1).

In those situations where favorable geopolitical circumstances have failed to converge, the holy warriors have sunken into a "suicidal millennarianism," as Olivier Roy describes it. Lacking any strategic perspective, these "visionaries" can transform their holy armies into Mafia-like groups, for example, exploiting the zeal of an often sincerely devoted "workforce."

TABLE 11.1 Civilian Victims of Terrorist Attacks in Pakistan, 2003–2015

Year	Total attacks	Civilian victims
2003	189	140
2004	863	435
2005	648	430
2006	1,471	608
2007	3,598	1,522
2008	6,715	2,155
2009	11,704	2,324
2010	7,435	1,796
2011	6,303	2,768
2012	6,211	3,007
2013	5,379	3,001
2014	5,496	1,781
2015	3,682	940

Source: South Asia Terrorism Portal

Alternatively, they can become the instrument of governments in order to strike internally—as in Tunisia, Libya, and Syria—or to shift the battle lines outside the country—as Pakistan has attempted to do in Afghanistan and Indian Kashmir, and, by some reports, Algeria has purportedly done in Mali. Alternatively, these groups can launch "gratuitous" acts of destruction that find justification only in the acts themselves, such as the sarin gas attack in the Tokyo subway by the Buddhist group Aum Shinrikyo in March 1995, or the massacre in Norway by Anders Breivik in July 2012, or, of course, the September 11 attacks. The capacity of these acts to inflict real harm is elevated by the very fact of their gratuitousness and thus, in large part, their unpredictability. Political analysts must give way, in these cases, to the criminal investigator and the psychiatrist.

From a political point of view, the notion of an "Islamic revolution" accomplished by a violent grab for power died in the mid-1990s. At that time, every attempt to "do like in Iran" or to "do like in Afghanistan" had failed or was failing. Recent attempts to resuscitate a jihadist state in parts of Somalia, Mali, and Syria have been largely blocked by the revolts of the affected populations, horrified by the brutal violence carried out in the venerated name of sharia.

It is true that the conditions that made possible the ayatollahs' victory in Iran were unique, beginning with the presence of a clergy capable of taking the leadership of broad-based insurrectional movement. Yet it is equally true that economic and social crises in certain rapidly developing economies have created among the "urbanized peasants" of the Muslim world a demand for "sharia"—that is, for social justice—that was as urgent as it was incoherent. The ten years of blind and senseless terrorism that culminated in the massacre of September 11 can be seen as the "lost decade" of political Islam.

PART IV

THE HOLY ALLIANCE

Whenever the Church of England dealt with a human problem she was very likely to call in the Church of Rome.

—Rudyard Kipling, *Kim*

The Christian religion and other religions can offer their contribution to development *only if God has a place in the public realm*, specifically in regard to its cultural, social, economic, and particularly its political dimensions.

—Pope Benedict XVI

12
DIALOGUE AMONG CIVILIZATIONS

THE ROOTS OF WESTERN RAGE

The current transitional phase of international relations is often described as being a historic turning point comparable to the sixteenth century: a substantial reorientation of the world's geopolitical axes, characterized by the "return of Asia" after centuries of decline and of parallel affirmation of the West.

If this description corresponds to reality, it means that the very foundations of the legal and ideological structures built on this phase of Western hegemony would be under threat. Entities to which we have grown so accustomed over the centuries that they seem almost part of nature—the principle of sovereignty, the nation-state, liberalism with all its manifestations—would be subjected to a global challenge.

If that challenge played out exclusively on legal or ideological terrain, the problem would be relatively minor: during the past century, Westerners, and Europeans in particular, showed themselves capable of considerable flexibility, able to adapt to the different ideological and institutional vicissitudes of their continent. What makes the challenge more likely to yield major geopolitical complications is the fact that it has manifested itself concretely, for the most part, through a generalized deterioration in living conditions for the populations of countries that were among the first to industrialize. Countries that previously had occupied the highest positions in the hierarchy of industrialized nations now run the risk of grave social disruption—and thus political and, finally, geopolitical disruption.

This risk is even greater in the United States. Its short history has been almost entirely marked by "sustained and perpetual growth," justifying "an expected and continuous improvement," as described by Ernest Gellner[1]—the exception being the Great Depression, though Americans emerged from it headed toward the most prosperous period in their history. This led them to falsely conclude that any crisis, even the most profound, can only be temporary and lead to an even more favorable situation. Robert J. Samuelson has calculated that "since 1950, the U.S. economy has grown slightly more than 3% annually. But projections for the future are just above 2%."[2] For Samuelson, this slowdown represents not a passing circumstance but rather a "new economic norm." He goes on to conclude that such "prolonged slow growth threatens to upend our political and social order."

A growing number of observers have been studying the possibly traumatic psychological consequences of economic decline in the United States. Along with Samuelson, they include Stephen S. Cohen and J. Bradford DeLong, who have observed that "when the money drains out," a great power can count "for a considerable time" on maintaining an elevated living standard for its citizens, thanks to the international placement of its debt; still, "the end is inevitable: you must become, recognize that you have become, and act like, a normal country. For America, this will be a shock."[3]

In his celebrated 1990 essay on the roots of Muslim rage, Bernard Lewis explained the hostility and rejection of some in the Muslim world toward Western societies in these terms: "In part this mood is surely due to a feeling of humiliation—as a growing awareness, among the heirs of an old, proud, and long dominant civilization, of having been overtaken, overborne, and overwhelmed by those whom they regarded as their inferiors."[4] The same words could be used to describe the nascent roots of Western rage in general, and American in particular, today and in the years to come.

In a small group of countries that perceive themselves as the incarnation "of an old, proud, and long dominant civilization"—notably Britain, France, and the United States—these feelings of frustration and rage sometimes manifest themselves with greater virulence. It was the crushing victory of the United States in World War II that transformed the non-Soviet

Allied front into the "West," or at least the Huntingtonian version of the West. So the ideology of Western unity is a way of representing what seems to be an undeniable fact: if the United States should fall, all of its "Western" allies would fall with it. That is what happened to the Eastern Bloc with the fall of the Soviet Union, providing a spectacular proof of such common destinies—and risks.

It is thus understandable that the relative decline of certain old industrial powers inserted into the Western alliance with the United States after World War II—including Japan—is represented as the "decline of the West." The emergence of new powers among those that the British, French, and Americans regarded as their inferiors—not necessarily for racial reasons but simply because they had brought them to submission—is thus seen as a sort of break with the natural order of things, an act of insubordination, an aggression against "our" way of life, and finally an attack on the West. The attempt to safeguard the privileges accumulated by the old powers thanks to their dominant position in the international division of labor thus takes on the ideological form of the "defense of Western values."

This ideological campaign succeeds despite the fact that these supposed values—at least those invoked in denouncing "others" for their "obscurantism"—are too recent to allow any claim of being rooted in civilizations past. The "liberty, equality, fraternity" triad dates to the eighteenth century, but it was not until the twentieth century that it became part of the structure of the democratic rule of law. As for "individual rights," whose absence in the "obscurantist" countries is deplored by the West, their origins are much more recent. As late as 1975 adultery was still a criminal offense in France, and as of 2013 it remained a crime in twenty-two American states, including Michigan, where a penalty of life in prison remains technically on the books.[5] Also in this recent past, several Western countries, including France and Italy, still envisaged so-called honor crimes; abortion, divorce (in Italy), and the sale of contraceptive products were still illegal; most women did not work.[6] As late as the 1970s, in the Italian countryside, typically women wore traditional veils; and everywhere, homosexuals were mocked, discriminated against, and sometimes legally persecuted. In Germany, the crime of sodomy was abolished in 1969; in the United States, the Supreme Court held, in 1986—in ruling on Bowers v. Hardwick—that to suggest that "a right to engage in such conduct is deeply rooted in this Nation's history and tradition" was "facetious." It was not until 2003 that the Supreme Court reversed itself and eliminated homosexuality from the penal code. In Italy, it was eliminated in 1927, with the justification that "this shameful vice is not sufficiently widespread to demand the intervention of penal law."[7]

The "values" being defended against the "obscurantists" can thus hardly be said to be part of some long-standing "Western tradition." Nevertheless, this ideological fiction makes sense to us at a visceral level, "without having to be explained rationally, without our having to give it much thought," as Raphaël Liogier observed.[8] The reason is that it offers an easy explanation for the relative deterioration of the living conditions of part of the population of the formerly advanced countries: we have fewer social benefits, nonexecutive salaries are lower, retirements start later, and so on, *because* we are suffering through the invasion of an army of "new barbarians" who pillage and destroy our social model with the goal, implicit or explicit, of replacing our "values" with theirs.

This "defense of values" takes the most varied forms, ranging from a true call to arms to a more benign and ecologically correct call to "defend the planet" against the new polluters—based, of course, on the presumption that "our" ecological values and the well-being of the entire planet coincide. Naturally, the call to arms does not yet target the true strategic competitors of the United States or Europe. Rather than pointing a finger directly at China, India, or Russia, the sense of encirclement is blamed on "intermediary enemies"—such as George W. Bush's "axis of evil"—or else "subsidiary enemies"—such as Muslims of every possible gradation, from al-Qaeda to the believer prostrated in prayer.

James Woolsey, director of the CIA from 1993 to 1995; Alexandre de Marenches, head of French counterespionage from 1970 to 1981; Eliot A. Cohen, a former top adviser to Condoleezza Rice while she served as secretary of state; and, above all, Norman Podhoretz, one of the best-known neoconservative intellectuals, are among those who have helped popularize the phrase "World War IV" to describe an obviously asymmetric and unconventional war in which the West is purportedly engaged against Islamic terrorist groups. According to Marenches, this war began in the early 1990s, well before the "global war on terror" became a mantra of international politics.

In another work, Raphaël Liogier studied the psychological motivations behind the legal measures and anti-Muslim sentiments in Europe, and in

France, in particular. Liogier, too, established a relationship between the European identity crisis and what he calls the "anti-Muslim paranoia" based on psychological distress. Europe, which had "commandeered the world," and which had shaped it, has been destined, "since the mid-twentieth century," to be but "a simple part" of a universe that once "was its own"; it is condemned to "again become a mere fraction of humanity, its erstwhile project." The French suffer more than others from this downgrading, Liogier continues, because they have always imagined themselves as being the originators of "European universalism."[9]

This distress drapes itself in motivations that, once again, have little basis in reality, in particular the notion that France is the favored victim of an invasion of clandestine Muslim immigrants who live "at the crown's expense," that is, on the shoulders of the honest taxpayer. In reality, "France is among the countries that welcomes the fewest foreigners"; clandestine immigrants constitute only a minuscule share of the total, the majority of which are *not* Muslim; immigrants are exactly as likely to be in the workforce as the "native" French; and finally, immigrants produce more wealth than they cost in benefits.[10] According to a study in 2010 on the financial contributions of immigrants in France, the state received €60.3 billion from this segment of the population in 2005, while outlaying €47.9 billion.[11]

Perhaps the most eloquent demonstration of the divide between fear and reality comes from the fact that the distrust of Muslims is felt with the same virulence in the United States as in Europe, although the population of Muslim origin in the United States is incomparably smaller, between 0.5 and 1 percent of the population, one-tenth the level of France. To be sure, the United States was traumatized by the September 11 attacks; but that carnage seems to have had only a relatively small influence on the unfavorable opinion that roughly one-half of Americans feel toward Muslims. John Esposito and Dalia Mogahed point out that a survey in 2006 found a 7-point increase in negative opinions when compared to another survey conducted a few months after the 2001 attacks.[12]

Some observers have yielded to the temptation of explaining this paranoia through another paranoia: they attribute the irrational fear of immigrants, and of Muslim immigrants in particular, to a conscious and deliberate plan. Unquestionably, certain groups will not hesitate cynically to incite or encourage these concerns in order to gain political advantage

TABLE 12.1 Net Migration of France and of the Twenty-Five-Nation
European Union, 1991–2002

Year	France	EU-25
1991	0.6	2.5
1992	0.6	2.9
1993	0.3	2.2
1994	−0.1	1.7
1995	−0.3	1.8
1996	−0.3	1.7
1997	−0.2	1.2
1998	−0.1	1.5
1999	0.8	2.1
2000	0.8	2.6
2001	1	3
2002	1.1	3.7

Note: Net migration equals immigration minus emigration as a percentage of a population.

Source: Eurostat, *Le guide statistique de l'Europe* (Luxembourg: Office of the Official Publications of the European Community, 2004).

or to compel immigrants to accept worse-than-average working conditions. However, there is no "architect" lurking conspiratorially in the wings—whether it be Big Government, Big Capital, the Trilateral Commission, the Elders of Zion, or any other occult force—to conjure up this obsession with immigrants or Muslims. Any society passing through a crisis will rather spontaneously find its scapegoats: the fate reserved by the Hutus for the Tutsis in 1994 in Rwanda—some 800,000 massacred with machetes and nailed clubs in 100 days—or the massacre of Srebrenica—forty years after the last Nazi concentration camp was closed—demonstrate clearly that the lessons of history are completely lost on us.

TABLE 12.2 Immigrants in France by Year, 1994–2008 (in Thousands)

Year	Non-Muslim immigrants	Muslim immigrants	Total number of immigrants	Ratio
1994	83	31	119.5	2.68
1995	75	25	106.2	3.00
1996	75	25	105.9	3.00
1997	80	37	127.4	2.15
1998	92	52	155.9	1.77
1999	90.5	46	145.1	1.97
2000	95.5	55	160.4	1.74
2001	104	67	182.7	1.55
2002	111.5	81.5	205.7	1.37
2003	114.5	86.5	215.4	1.32
2004	112.5	84.5	211.9	1.33
2005	123	79.5	217.3	1.55
2006	120.5	77.5	212.7	1.55
2007	116	70	199.7	1.66
2008	120.5	76.5	211.1	1.58

Source: Institut national d'études démographiques, 2008. The calculation of the number of Muslims and non-Muslims is an estimate by the author based on the countries of origin.

In reality, if some greater force were able to act with deliberate intention in this situation, chances are that it would act in the opposite direction: it would work to overcome these irrational prejudices. The motivation would come not from any fuzzy civic-mindedness but for practical reasons. The reasons were clearly illustrated by the European Commissioner for Home Affairs, Cecilia Malmstrom: "When I meet ministers responsible for labor policies," she said in 2011, "they almost all speak of the need for immigrant workers—and it's true, we need hundreds of thousands, millions in the long-term." Yet, she continued, "When the ministers go and speak in front of their national publics, this message is not to be heard at all." The reason for this, as Malmstrom noted, is that "the need for immigrants is hard to explain in a climate of high unemployment, riots in the streets, financial crisis and people in extreme difficulties."[13] In short, these ministers are not in a position to openly enact policies that they fully realize are indispensable for the medium- and long-term health of their own country; they are, in some ways, "prisoners" of the ideologies of their voters.

Still, the need for immigrant labor is only one of the reasons that certain leading politicians and religious organizations have attempted to reverse the rising curve of the "clash of civilizations" by offsetting it with projects for an "alliance among civilizations."

THE DIALOGUES OF THE EUROPE SUPERPOWER

In May 1997 Ayatollah Mohammad Khatami was elected as the fifth president of the Islamic Republic of Iran. His election, according to one Iranian opposition web site, was programmed in an effort to revive good relations with the Europeans at the moment of their historic transition to the euro.

The matter was given urgency since the Court of Justice in Berlin had recently recognized the involvement of the Iranian Supreme Leader, Ali Khamenei, and President Akbar Hashemi Rafsanjani in a murderous attack in Berlin in 1992.

Khatami is a pure product of the Khomeini-ist inner circle: married to Khomeini's granddaughter, he became minister of culture and Islamic orientation in 1982, during the great purges in Iran's universities.[14] Nonetheless, his electoral victory in 1997 over the conservative Ali Akbar Nateq-Nouri elevated him, in European eyes, to the rank of "reformer," giving the Europeans indispensable political cover not only to renew relations but to "lead to a global dialogue in 1998," as Nicolas Dufays writes. From that point, Dufays continues, a series of initiatives was launched aimed at reaching an agreement on trade and cooperation, accompanied by a political dialogue between Europe and Iran. As Dufays concludes, "In short, this multiplication of dialogues attests to the European desire to seize the opportunity represented by the Khatami presidency to encourage internal reforms."[15]

One of Khatami's first major initiatives on the international stage aimed to establish a dialogue. The Iranian president proposed a grand "dialogue among civilizations," with the announced intention of countering the theory of clashing civilizations made famous a year earlier by Huntington's book. The proposal was received favorably at the United Nations. On November 16, 1998, the General Assembly approved Resolution 53/22, proclaiming 2001 the "United Nations Year of Dialogue Among Civilizations," with the stated objective of nurturing "a dialogue which is both preventive of conflicts—when possible—and inclusive in nature."

Through no fault of either the UN or Iran, 2001 will certainly not be remembered as a year of dialogue among civilizations and of prevention of conflicts. Iran did, however, bear responsibility for two other events, incomparably less important than the September 11 attacks but still significant. In July 2001 thirteen Jews were found guilty of spying on Iran and were sentenced to lengthy prison terms; and in December of that year Rafsanjani raised the possibility of a nuclear bombardment of Israel, adding that "Jews shall expect to be once again scattered and wandering around the globe the day when this appendix is extracted from the region and the Muslim world." President Khatami's silence in both matters seemed not to have damaged his self-made image as a "man of dialogue," an image that both the UN and the Europeans had decided to recognize.

The "dialogue among civilizations" initiative should be interpreted less as an ideological response to the thesis of a clash of civilizations than as a geopolitical one. Huntington's thesis, as we have seen, bolstered the Atlanticist panoply of tools, offering theoretical support for consolidating a Western alliance against the emerging competitors in Eurasia. Khatami's thesis, in contrast, aimed to detach Europe from the United States by sending signals from the region where U.S.-European frictions have always been most intense—the Middle East. In the 1990s, Germany, Italy, and France had been among the top five most important economic partners of Iran. Khatami's extended hand offered them a means of contesting the Iran Foreign Oil Sanctions Act, the American law passed in September 1995 to sanction foreign companies that exported petroleum technology to Iran.

For the Europeans, the economic interests involved were reason enough to believe in the "dialogue among civilizations" despite the arrests of the

Jews and the threats of a nuclear annihilation aimed at Israel. However, in 1997, an even more important dimension entered the picture: the strategic dimension. With the adoption of the euro, Europe intended explicitly to assume the role of a superpower offering a strategic alternative to the United States. Among other things, this involved defining a sphere of influence, based both on the primary zones of economic interest and on the regions with which Europe had long maintained relations—in some cases "millennial relations," as Nicolas Dufays has described the relationship with, in particular, Iran.

Beyond the pacifist rhetoric, it was doubtless that this potentially anti-American strategic dimension appealed to the bulk of the UN General Assembly. Among the backers of the initiative that led to the passage of Resolution 53/22 were all the European countries, including the United Kingdom; the traditional "anti-American front," headed by Russia, China, and India; as well as a large number of African and Asian countries. Conversely, among those abstaining, along with the United States and Israel, were nearly every Latin American country, including Cuba. The list of those favoring a "dialogue among civilizations" was read in alphabetical order so it was impossible to miss the fact that it was led by Afghanistan, which, in 1998, had been under Taliban control for two years; it was from there that, in August 1998, the order went out for the bombing attacks on the American embassies in Nairobi and Dar es Salaam.

The UN committee charged with organizing the official events of the Year of Dialogue Among Civilizations was composed of twenty individuals of international prestige, including Jacques Delors, the former president of the European Commission; Richard von Weizsäcker, the former German president; Amartya Sen, the Nobel-winning economist; Hans Küng, the renowned theologian; and Nadine Gordimer, the South African Nobel literature laureate. The characteristic shared by most committee members was a clearly drawn religious identity; apart from the overrepresentation of Catholics—hardly an irrelevant detail—nearly every major religion was represented. There were seven Catholics in all, but also two non-Catholic Christians, three Muslims—two Sunnis and a Shiite—two Jews, a Confucian, a Buddhist, and four others of no obvious religious affiliation. An Italian Catholic, Giandomenico Picco, was named coordinator for the group and served as the personal representative of the UN secretary-general.

The UN initiative—or more accurately, the UN-endorsed Iranian initiative—effectively accepted two key elements of the thesis that it was meant to combat: the division of the world based on civilizational blocs, and the identification of civilizations with religions. An official summary of the committee's work states that "since harmony among religions is essential for cultivating a culture of hope for the human family, interreligious dialogues are an integral part of the Dialogue among Civilizations."[16] The initiative became more concrete with the creation of a permanent institution, the Foundation for Dialogue Among Civilizations, based in Geneva and presided over by Ayatollah Khatami himself; as well as of a World Public Forum, equally described as fostering a "dialogue of civilizations." The latter organization's mission statement explains that the "implementation of the 'Dialogue of Civilizations' program is closely connected with interconfessional dialogue that brings together representatives of world religions to face the global challenges of extremism and terrorism."[17]

These permanent entities constitute a sort of inertial prolongation of the Khatami initiative endorsed by the UN, though without the initial geopolitical impetus. In fact, on June 16, 2003, the authorities in Tehran had rejected a report from the International Atomic Energy Agency on the evolving Iranian nuclear situation, marking the beginning of a crisis that the Europeans could no longer ignore. Iran repositioned itself on the international scene following the American invasion of Iraq, which in a single stroke had seriously weakened the European position in the region, while strengthening that of Iran. Despite the efforts of the European Union's high representative for foreign policy, and the creation of the E-3—France, Germany, and Britain—charged with negotiating with the Iranian authorities, the latter refused to accede to European requests. From that point on, the nuclear file became the principal subject of Euro-Iranian relations, pushing aside the ambitious but ephemeral "dialogue among civilizations."

A FAILED "ALLIANCE"

It was in this context that in 2004 Prime Minister José Zapatero of Spain, speaking from the podium of the UN General Assembly, relaunched the initiative while promoting the "dialogue" to the rank of an "Alliance of Civilizations." This proposal, advanced in cooperation with Prime Minister

Recep Tayyip Erdoğan of Turkey, had the explicit objective of presenting an alternative to the "global war on terror," which was launched by the George W. Bush administration, in part, to justify the occupation of Iraq. Once again, the General Assembly immediately appropriated the idea as its own, making it an organ of the UN: the Organization of the Alliance of Civilizations, headed by High Representative Jorge Sampaio, a former president of Portugal.

The Zapatero-Erdoğan initiative was clearly meant to be both the continuation of and an enlargement of the "dialogue among civilizations" proposed by the former Iranian president in 1998. Its goals were clearly more ambitious, an "alliance" having a much broader political meaning than a simple "dialogue." Yet the principal reason for this deepening lay surely in the fact that the "Iranian card" had been undercut by the war in Iraq and the eruption of the nuclear crisis. The election of Mahmoud Ahmadinejad to the Iranian presidency in 2005 put an end to it for good.

Zapatero and Erdoğan had the ideal profile to embody this new phase: Zapatero had been elected prime minister in 2004—a few days after the Madrid terror attacks of March 11—on a platform in which a central plank was the withdrawal of troops from Iraq; while Erdoğan, the leader of Turkey's main Islamist democratic political party, had won election the previous year and had then distinguished himself by taking the surprising position—given his country's long and close friendship with the United States—of refusing to allow American warplanes to use the Incirlik air base in southeastern Turkey as a launching point for operations in Iraq.

The run-up to the war had been a period of fierce confrontation between, on the one side, the European Union duo—Germany and France—plus a few other European nations and Russia and, on the other side, the United States, allied with other European countries, notably the United Kingdom, Italy, Spain, and the entire former Eastern Bloc. France, in particular, cast this confrontation as *the* founding moment of a *Europe-puissance* (European power) finally capable of standing up to the American *hyperpuissance*, a termed popularized in Europe by Hubert Vedrine, the French foreign minister from 1997 to 2002. In this context, the Alliance of Civilizations represented a new opportunity to establish the specific personality of a "benign" European power, as opposed to the warmongering image of America.[18] It also represented an opportunity to establish a sphere of influence in the Mediterranean Basin among the countries—nearly all of them—that were also opposed to the invasion of Iraq. It was certainly not by accident that Vedrine was named as the official representative of France to the "alliance."

The Alliance of Civilizations appeared much more solid than the "Dialogue" that had preceded it, notably because the Muslim partner in this case—Turkey—lent itself better to the cause than did Iran. There were at least three reasons for this: Turkey's secular institutions; its democratic system, which made it more reliable; and its historic alliance with the United States, an alliance that it "betrayed" at the decisive moment of the confrontation in 2003 in order to align itself with the "benign" alternative to the Americans. A fourth reason, but a more hypothetical one, is that Turkey is considered by many as a potential "core state" of the Muslim world, to use Huntington's terminology: "Turkey has the history, population, middle level of economic development, national coherence and military tradition and competence to be the core state of Islam."[19] Even if the unification of Islam—behind a core state, a caliph, or anything else—appears to be extremely unlikely, the possibility that Turkey could take the lead of even a part of the Muslim world certainly justified serious attention.

Despite what had seemed like a propitious beginning, in the eyes of the French-German leadership of Europe, this initiative, too, failed to achieve its geopolitical objective. The Organization for the Alliance of Civilizations still exists as such: it continues to organize colloquia, meetings, seminars, forums, and conferences; and, since March 1, 2013, it has had a new high representative—Nassir Abdulaziz Al-Nasser, Qatar's former ambassador to the United Nations. Nonetheless, it has lost its early shine precisely because it lost the geopolitical purpose that had guided it from birth.

France, one of its most enthusiastic sponsors, was also indirectly behind the decline in its political importance. The defeat of the European Constitution in France's 2005 referendum had an abrupt braking effect on the process of continental integration, particularly its political aspect. As a result, EU foreign policy initiatives lost some of their potency, including, of course, the alliance launched the preceding year by Zapatero and Erdoğan. Moreover, in the campaign leading up to the referendum in France, Turkey had become a key issue, even if it had no direct relationship to the question before voters. When forces opposed to the EU constitution began to argue that it would serve as a Trojan horse for Turkish entry into the EU, the backers of the constitution, trailing badly in the polls, joined in with the anti-Turkish declarations in an effort to neutralize this argument. The result was that the referendum of 2005 not only undercut the European process, it also left the French as among the European peoples most hostile to Turkey's eventual accession to the European Union.[20] This was no small problem for an alliance in which Ankara was supposed to be a pillar. Added to that was the American decision, announced in February 2006 by Condoleezza Rice, to also join the organization, helping further undercut, from within, its anti-American objectives.

In the end, the Alliance of Civilizations was little more than an empty shell. Yet it had contributed, however briefly, to spreading the belief that the world is divided along civilizational fault lines and that these correspond, for the most part, to religious fault lines.

THE DIALOGUE AMONG RELIGIONS

Despite Zapatero's rigorously secular background and his partnership with the leader of the most secular of the Muslim countries, the Alliance of Civilizations initiative fell squarely in the ideological zone defined by the relationship between "Western civilization," which is regarded as mainly Christian, and "Muslim civilization." Moreover, the histories of Spain and Turkey situated them particularly well to serve as "bridges" between the two civilizational blocs. Based on their own backgrounds, the two copresidents, Federico Mayor Zaragoza, a Spaniard, and Mehmet Aydın, a Turk, personified this religious dimension: the former was a Catholic scientist and one-time Christian-Democrat deputy, the latter a Sunni theologian. The document approved at the United Nations during the 2005 World Summit made explicit what had been implicit, as member countries committed themselves to support different initiatives on dialogue among cultures and civilizations, including the dialogue on interfaith cooperation. The conviction on which the Organization of the Alliance of Civilizations was based was the same as had characterized the initiative of 1998: the divisions between the world's civilizations can be healed through dialogue between religions.

This same conviction led to the birth of several organizations in the first decade of this century. They include the Tony Blair Faith Foundation, created in 2008; the Centre for Dialogue at La Trobe University in Victoria, Australia, in 2006; the Berkley Center for Religion, Peace and World Affairs at Georgetown University, in 2006; the International Center for Religion & Diplomacy in Washington, D.C., in 1999; and the Doha International Center for Interfaith Dialogue, in 2008. Although they explicitly make dialogue between religions the key to cooperation among civilizations, these organizations were not the creation of religious institutions. Amartya Sen— who was, however, a member of the committee that promoted the Year of Dialogue Among Civilizations (or perhaps precisely because of that)— notes that since "unique categorization along so-called civilizational lines . . . closely follows religious divisions [an inevitable consequence] is generally magnifying the voice of religious authority."[21]

Thus it should come as no surprise that certain religious groups and movements have created their own organizations dedicated to encouraging "dialogue among civilizations." These include the Interfaith Encounter Association, the Elijah Interfaith Institute, and the Jordanian Interfaith Coexistence Research Center, all initiatives—two Jewish and the other Muslim—that sprang up in the Middle East. As did the Interfaith Center of New York and the United Religions Initiative of San Francisco, with ties to the Episcopalian Church, America's Anglicans; the transnational movement inspired by the Turkish-American theologian Fethullah Gülen; a Saudi organization, the International Islamic Forum for Dialogue; an older entity, the World Conference of Religions for Peace, founded in 1970 and present in more than seventy countries; and, finally, the historic Parliament for the World's Religions, founded in Chicago in 1893 by Presbyterians, and relaunched one hundred years later in the same city based on a policy document—*Towards a Global Ethic*—written by the Catholic theologian Hans Küng, himself a member of the UN committee of 1998.

These organizations are the fruit of initiatives by groups or movements linked to one faith or another, but they are not religious institutions as such. There are specific reasons explaining the absence of institutional initiative. In general terms, one can say that Sunni Islam and Hinduism are intrinsically unable to take initiatives involving the totality of their faithful, because they lack single central authorities or structures able to disseminate a directive to all followers. To be sure, a large number of Muslim and Hindu associations have taken part in dialogue initiatives with other religions and, in particular, with the followers of other religions, but there is nothing institutional about these initiatives, as they have no authority to represent all Muslims or Hindus.

The various Protestant denominations, and in particular the tens of thousands of evangelical groups and churches, suffer from the opposite problem: there are too many decision-making centers to allow one to speak of a *single* position or a *single* Protestant initiative.[22] The various Protestant positions, attitudes, and doctrines are as numerous as they are contradictory. The so-called Historic Adventist Church—one of about twenty Adventist churches in America, which broke from the rest of the movement in the late 1950s—in opposition to dialogue with certain evangelical groups, purchased advertising space along American highways for a ten-year period beginning in 1993 to inform motorists that the pope is the Antichrist. At the other extreme, Nancy Wilson, the moderator (world leader) of the ultraliberal Metropolitan Community Churches, with 222 congregations in thirty-seven countries, accused Pope Benedict XVI of having been an "un-Catholic pope" because of his opposition to same-sex marriage; after his resignation, she urged people to pray for the election of a "truly Catholic pope."[23]

Anglicanism and the Orthodox Churches have hierarchical structures similar to that of the Catholic Church; still, their polycentrism—a problem also affecting the Buddhist galaxy, if in other forms—prevents them, too, from taking positions that commit their entire following.

Almost all the Orthodox countries have a national church and sometimes more than one, as is the case of Ukraine, Estonia, Macedonia, and Greece—with each of them de facto independent from all the others. Thus decisions taken by the patriarchal authorities in Moscow or Sofia, for example, are viewed as binding on, respectively, all followers of the Russian Orthodox Church or of the Bulgarian Orthodox Church, but not on the faithful of other Orthodox communities.[24] As a general rule, and outside institutional contacts with Catholics, Orthodox leaders are skeptical, to say the least, when it comes to interreligious dialogue. Vsevolod Chaplin, secretary of the department for relations between the church and the society of the patriarchate of Moscow (2009–2015), is convinced that Orthodoxy can represent the future of Europe and "of the whole world" if—and only if—it is able to preserve its identity and not give in to the temptation of a "dialogue of civilizations."[25] On the other hand, one of Chaplin's colleague, Bishop Hilarion, who heads the external relations department of the same patriarchate, defended such a dialogue.[26]

As for the Anglican community, it is divided into thirty-eight "provinces," which, while declaring themselves to be in full doctrinal communion with one another, are under no obligation to obey the community's center—Canterbury—the primacy of which is purely formal. The decisions taken during the synodal Lambeth Conferences, which bring together all Anglican bishops every ten years, are "recommendations." For that reason, the Network for Inter Faith Concerns, created in 1988 by the 12th Lambeth Conference, cannot be considered as a true structure of the Anglican Church.

Among the great religions of the world, only the Catholic Church is institutionally involved in ecumenical and interreligious dialogue. The Second Vatican Council created official bodies to fulfill this task; they, therefore, embody a strategic will to make a "holy alliance" among the world's great religions the key to a long-term geopolitical strategy.

13
THE CATHOLIC ALLIANCE

History teaches us that Providence uses great social upheavals
for the good of His Church.
                    —Cardinal Vincenzo Vannutelli

THE POWER OF STATELESSNESS

The road that led the Catholic Church from holy war to holy alliance was
long and tortuous. The three crucial steps came rather recently, at least in
terms of the long history of the church: the Italian occupation of Rome—then
under direct rule of the papacy—in 1870, World War I, and the decolonization
period following the conclusion of World War II. The end of the church's temporal power forced it to recognize the advantages of the "power of statelessness." During World War I the glacial wind of the "suicide of Europe" struck
it with full force, leading it to take the first tentative steps toward a strategy
of continental unification. Decolonization, for its part, sounded the death
knell of a time when the propagation of faith could advance in tandem with
colonial conquests: the borders of religions were set in place once and for all.

It took a century for the Catholic Church to move from heaping curses
on the "Piedmontese usurpers" of the Papal States to recognizing "the

Providence of the Lord" in Italian unity.[1] Yet the end of temporal power proved to be a double blessing: it finally allowed the church, as Cardinal Giacomo Biffi wrote in 1999, although only "after differences and sometimes violent opposition," to affirm the "near-consubstantiality between the Catholic faith and the national [Italian] identity."[2] At the same time, the loss of temporal power allowed the church to discover the virtues of what Jakub Grygiel calls the "power of statelessness": the advantage of being relieved of the obligation to govern.[3]

During the struggle over Italian unification, the power of statelessness was something a pope could not possibly have imagined. More than one thousand years in the exercise of temporal power had persuaded Catholic leaders that its loss would inevitably lead to the loss of the church, particularly since Italy's annexation of the Papal States' last remaining territorial possessions had left the Vatican "completely bereft in the face of dramatic new budget problems."[4] The fiasco of the first attempt to resort to *soft power*, as it would be called today, contributed to the growing disarray surrounding Pope Pius IX and his entourage: on September 30, 1870, ten days after the Italian *bersaglieri* had entered Rome, Pius IX, in the encyclical letter entitled *Respicientes ea*, excommunicated all those who had "perpetrated the invasion, the usurpation and the occupation of the provinces of our domain," including their "commanders, instigators, assistants, advisers, affiliates and anyone else." However, not only did the Italians continue to attend mass and receive communion, but also King Victor Emmanuel II, the man responsible for the invasion, was able to continue enjoying the comforts of religion, both during the remainder of his life and at the moment of his death.

For several years, the church devoted a considerable share of its energies to attempts to restore the papacy's temporal power and to recover the territories "stolen" from it. Already in 1865, four years after the proclamation of Italian unity but five years before the Italian conquest of Rome, Pius IX wanted "a European war to set matters right again in the Holy See," as the British envoy informed his superiors in London.[5] In the months following the capture of Rome, pontifical diplomacy was mobilized with the goal of obtaining a military intervention by any power willing to help return the pope to the throne. In addition to a campaign that involved virtually every bishop in the world, the Vatican addressed explicit requests for military intervention against Italy to Spain, Belgium, Austria, and also

Protestant Prussia. Even the French capital, under Prussian siege at the time, was approached for help. In the end, the only country to send a note of protest to the Italian government was Ecuador.

In the years that followed, the Holy See's international prestige entered a period of steady decline. The disappearance of the state and of its territory was not, however, the principal cause for this; in fact, the church had retained a number of its former prerogatives even without a state: a sovereign, a prime minister, a government, and above all, an international network made up of papal nuncios, primates, cardinals, and simple bishops. The loss of influence had much more to do with the decline in its moral prestige, due certainly to the spread of secularization but also to the decision to wage a veritable war against modernity and, after 1870, to tirelessly press its heavy-handed demands for the restoration of the Papal States.

From a diplomatic viewpoint, the crisis with Italy had produced catastrophic results: relations with Austria-Hungary had cooled, and the United States had withdrawn its diplomatic representative in 1867, followed by Switzerland in 1873, Britain in 1874, and France in 1905.[6] In 1914, the Holy See exchanged ambassadors with a very small group of countries, nearly all of them in Latin America, with a single European power, Austria-Hungary, as well as with the kingdoms of Prussia and Bavaria, by this point part of the German Empire. As Stewart Stehlin writes, "By the first decades of the 20th century, it appeared as if the Vatican might become a *quantité négligeable* in world affairs . . . and it appeared to many observers as if the Papacy for the Christian world, like the Caliphate for the Moslem world, was on the way out."[7]

And yet World War I, one of the greatest challenges ever confronted by the church, turned this prediction on its head. During the war the church found itself facing "moral, legal and diplomatic problems immeasurably greater than those posed during earlier conflicts."[8] However, despite the objective challenges, the church survived surprisingly well. Indeed, "Catholics' enthusiastic rallying to the war" produced a happy consequence: "reintegrating them into the nation, where, on the eve of 1914, and especially in France and Italy, they had been seen almost as immigrants from within."[9]

A crucial factor favoring this reversal of fortunes was this: while the church was facing a political crisis externally following Italian unification, it was also undergoing a formidable internal consolidation as it moved to centralize and strengthen papal power. For Pius IX, the memory of his first eviction in 1849, and then the progressive weakening of his sovereign prerogatives, as well as the loss of a first portion of the papal territories in 1860, had led him and his advisers to move to reinforce the "immaterial" authority of the head of the church. It was to this end that Pius IX convened a so-called ecumenical council to approve the theses contained in the *Syllabus* of 1864 and, more important, to vote a new dogma: papal infallibility.[10] The respected German theologian Ignaz Dollinger, one of the most prestigious opponents of this dogma, viewed it as the final step in a long process of centralization to the detriment of the authority of the bishops.

The other factor strengthening the pope's authority and prestige among the faithful is the very same one that had weakened it on the diplomatic front: Pius IX's declaration that, amid the crisis with the Italian state and the capture of Rome, Italy was holding him "prisoner." This depiction of the pope's "martyrdom" in the very heart of the global capital of Catholicism— often embroidered with details that were as cruel-sounding as they were fabricated—gave rise to an unprecedented cult of papal personality among Catholic faithful around the world, to the point that it gave birth, according to Marcel Launay, to a veritable phenomenon of "papolatry"—or papal idolatry—particularly in France.[11] The growing popularity of photography also contributed to the birth of this new cult, as images of the vicar of Christ were widely disseminated for the first time among the faithful. It was at this point that English Catholics, and then Belgians, French, and Austrians, launched the "St. Peter's Pence" collection; in addition to helping resolve some of the church's economic problems, this effort provided a new element of cohesion for Catholics around the world, who felt engaged in a mission that concerned far more than simply raising money.[12]

Church authorities gradually realized that "temporal power had been a burden for the Holy See . . . the possibilities for working more and better for the diffusion of Catholicism in the world . . . increased rapidly with the loss of that power."[13] In short, they recognized that any political actor relieved of the obligation of raising taxes, building infrastructure, organizing production, calling citizens to arms, and coercing them to go to war enjoys two considerable advantages over those political actors who must oversee a state: it becomes more popular, and it can devote its best energies to building on this popularity and transforming it into organization. As Grygiel writes, the nonstate actors "are considerably more capable of achieving their objectives and maintaining their social cohesion without a state apparatus."[14]

This new awareness was considerably accelerated by the chief political consequence of the attitude adopted by the church during World War I: a noticeable improvement in the political status of Catholics in the world, which helped lay the foundation for the long-range Catholic strategy of the *reconquista* of public spaces.

THE *COMPLEXIO OPPOSITORUM*

In 1923 Carl Schmitt published his *Romischer Katholizismus und politische Form*, one of the first political essays about the Catholic Church. This short essay opens with a definition of the church as a *complexio oppositorum* (complex of opposites): "One might say," Schmitt writes, "that there appears to be no antithesis it does not embrace."[15]

It is not surprising that this phrase, now almost proverbial, was coined in the aftermath of World War I when the church, with its extraordinary dialectical capacity to unite within its bosom the most disparate positions, managed to win its riskiest wager. Indeed, during this conflict, it succeeded in being both the ardently patriotic and violently bellicose church of the different national clergies and, at the same time, the intransigently and universally pacifistic church of the Roman center.

In July 1914, the Vatican was caught in the middle of a confrontation that saw two-thirds of all Catholics in the world mobilized on opposing fronts: 124 million on the side of the Allies, and 64 million on the side of the Central Powers.[16] Church authorities reacted by playing an unprecedented, and risky, card—probably the only one available to them—of a fragile dialectic between the center and the periphery. On the one hand, Rome, if half-heartedly, withdrew its initial support from Vienna—which it had affirmed at the time of the ultimatum to Belgrade—and chose the path, for the first time, of observing the most scrupulous neutrality. Thus Pope Benedict XV, in a speech to cardinals entitled *Nostis Profecto*, condemned "an unprecedented carnage which, if it continues on, could be for Europe the beginning of the end of the level of civilization to which Christianity had elevated it." He later went on to implore the relevant governments in August 1, 1917, to cease this "useless slaughter," which risked leading "Europe, so glorious and flourishing . . . to its own suicide"—words judged to be so inappropriate and inopportune by the governments involved that nearly all viewed Benedict XV as an "agent of the enemy." At the same time, to strengthen his authority, the pope promulgated a new code of canon law, conceived, according to Giorgio Feliciani, as a tool of modernization, homogeneity, centralization, and discipline.[17]

Yet Benedict XV was perfectly aware that this pacifist posture could not apply to the national episcopates, for it would risk provoking a series of national schisms and the birth of different patriotic Catholic churches, the worst nightmare for the church, tantamount to its dissolution. That is why, at the very beginning of the conflict, Benedict XV wrote the encyclical *Ad Beatissimi Apostolorum Principis*, as a firm reminder that "to obstinately resist a legitimate human power is to resist God and to prepare for eternal punishment"—an imperative that implied "the obligation to obey, not only in a mundane way, but religiously, that is to say as a duty of conscience, all those who command by virtue of their authority." This declaration was received in the various countries as an implicit authorization for the enthusiastic backing by Catholics for the war.

This rallying behind the war took place at both material and ideological levels. On the one hand, the clergy provided its unconditional support to the mobilization; at the same time, social structures linked directly or indirectly to the church were committed to the cause. In the Paris region alone, sixty-one religious buildings were placed at the disposition of the Red Cross, and 12,544 nuns were mobilized.[18] In Italy, parishes oversaw 11,932 charitable organizations, 8,088 groups collecting money and clothing, 4,177 administrative or informational offices, 1,963 child-care centers, and 3,084 committees for mobilization and civilian assistance.[19] According to a calculation by John Pollard, the Vatican's international spending on charity and assistance efforts totaled 82 million lire at the time—the equivalent of nearly 100 million euros at their 2002 value.[20]

The now common notion of the church's attitude during World War I is strongly influenced by the changes that followed the Second Vatican Council: today everyone remembers Benedict XV's calls for peace and almost no one recalls the mobilization of church spiritual and social structures in support of national military efforts. Yet, at the time, affected governments clearly saw a very different view: while the calls for peace ended up having no effect, the activism of Catholics on the ideological and, more important, the material front proved useful and at times indispensable.

"Immigrants within" until 1914, Italian, French, and German Catholics were welcomed after the war into their respective political communities, either directly or indirectly. In France, the more controversial points of the law of 1905 on church and state separation were amended as the Catholic Church desired. In Italy, discussions aimed at resolving the "Roman question" began almost as soon as the war had ended. In Germany, the consequences were perhaps even happier, if one considers that Catholics had managed to go in the space of forty years from the pariah status to which they had been relegated by the *Kulturkampf*—part of Bismarck's effort to eradicate the influence of Catholicism—to the dominant role exerted by the Catholic party Zentrum on the administrative structures and successive governments of the Weimar Republic.

In the United States, the fierce prewar anti-Catholicism of many Protestants receded to the point that Governor Al Smith of New York, a Catholic, was able to take part in the Democratic Party presidential primaries in 1924 and even become the party's—ultimately unsuccessful—candidate in 1928. On the diplomatic front, in 1919 the Holy See had relations with twenty-four countries, roughly half of the global total at the time, though not with Italy, France, the United States, or Russia—all of which, however, had unofficial representatives at the Vatican. Some states had established formal relations during the war; and at its conclusion, most of the new countries born from the collapse of the European empires—including entirely Lutheran countries, like Finland and Estonia—immediately sought international legitimacy through connections to the oldest political power in the world. By 1930 the number of countries with diplomatic relations with the Holy See had reached thirty.

In light of the church's regained authority, one can understand the sense of the remarks made in March 1917 by Vincenzo Vannutelli, dean of the College of Cardinals, during an internal meeting: "History teaches us that Providence uses great social upheavals for the good of His Church."[21] Following World War I, the church's objective was no longer to restore the sovereignty of the Papal States but rather to "restore the sovereignty of Our Lord," as Pope Pius XI, successor to Benedict XV, wrote in the encyclical *Quas Primas*, which was issued on December 11, 1925. He went on to state that this sovereignty "consists, we need scarcely say, in a threefold power which is essential to lordship. . . . It would be a grave error, on the other hand, to say that Christ has no authority whatever in civil affairs."

Even if, at first glance, the reference to the church's authority in civil affairs seems to relaunch the old demand for the restoration of the Papal

States, the true goal was actually far more ambitious: to create a "totalitarian regime of the church." As Pius XI himself put it in a speech to a delegation of French Christian unionists of September 18, 1938, borrowing for rhetorical purposes Mussolini's favorite adjective, "if there is a totalitarian regime—totalitarian in both law and fact—it is the Church, because man belongs totally to the Church. . . . The Church truly has the right to exert the totality of its power over individuals."

This argument for total power over individuals does not conflict with the insistence on the principle of respect for legitimate authorities for, as Benedict XV outlined in the November 1, 1914, encyclical *Ad Beatissimi Apostolorum Principis*, there is an "obligation of obeying the commands of those in authority . . . unless their commands are against the laws of God." This is not only because "human authority fails where religion is set aside" but also, and more important, because "those who resist any legitimate authority, resist God, much more impiously do they act who refuse to obey the Bishop, whom God has consecrated with a special character by the exercise of His power."

The claim to the primacy of divine authority over public authority had been part of the history of the Catholic Church since, on Christmas Eve in the year 800, Pope Leon III placed the imperial crown on Charlemagne's head. The real novelty thus resides not in the intentions of a succession of popes, but rather in the reception with which the church's latest stance was met: World War I had made clear to the various governments that they again needed the church and that, given the violent confrontations of the era of imperialism, they would need it even more in the future. Another milestone had thus been established along the path to the *reconquista* of public spaces.

TO THE "FAR ENDS OF THE EARTH"

The loss of the church's temporal power had allowed it to discover the virtues of the *power of statelessness*, and World War I had glorified those of the *complexio oppositorum*. Decolonization was another of the traumas of history that forced the church to undertake a radical reconsideration of the conditions for its survival and growth. This reconsideration led not to the discovery of further virtues but rather to finding the key to the strategy of *reconquista* of public spaces in an era of globalization: the holy alliance.

The end of the colonial empires had three major consequences for the church: (1) it was the final and most significant act in the crisis of waning European influence in the world; (2) it closed off forever the principal avenue used through the centuries for propagating the Catholic faith, that is, by following or preceding the armies of Catholic countries; and (3) it gave greater weight and visibility, within ecclesiastical structures, to Catholic personnel from the former colonies. In 1648 the religious borders inside Europe were fixed by the Peace of Westphalia; decolonization fixed the religious borders of the entire world (see table 13.1).

In the encyclical *Quas Primas* (1925), Pius XI noted with admiration "how many countries have been won to the Catholic name through the unremitting labor and self-sacrifices of brave and invincible missionaries," while also noting "the vastness of the regions which have yet to be subjected to the sweet and saving yoke of our King." In the official English translation, the adjectives "fortissimi e invitti" (brave and invincible) have been omitted. With decolonization, this language and the activities it described were no longer possible. Until then the world had been the vast field for a competition with the "heretics" (the Protestants, in the jargon of the Catholic Church), the "infidels" or "pagans" (all non-Christian religions), and the "schismatics" (the Orthodox). As to the "deicidal people" (the Jews), the first official Christian persecutions in the fourth century "extinguished the passion for proselytizing."[22]

With decolonization, this competition was no longer possible. Since the leaders of the new countries did not, in fact, have the means to assure real sovereignty, they acted with firmness in establishing the external forms of sovereignty; thus the principle of *cuius regio eius religio* was applied literally, with the aim of making dominant religions into part of the supposed "national" character of the new states. The fact that these religions were sometimes, especially in the case of sub-Saharan Africa, the religions of the former colonial powers did not pose a major obstacle. From that time on, there were no longer any regions available to be subjected to the "sweet and saving yoke of our King." The mission of carrying the Catholic religion to the "far ends of the Earth," entrusted by Jesus to the Apostles, would now have to follow another path, unless the church was prepared to spark new conflicts not only with its former religious competitors but also, and above all, with the leaders of the new states.

TABLE 13.1 Continents of Origin for Cardinals (by Pope), 1903–2013

Pope	Europe		Americas		Africa	Asia	Oceania	Total	% Europe	% A+A+LA*
	Entire continent	Italy	United States and Canada	Latin America						
Pius X (1903–1914)	47	18	3	0	0	0	0	50	94	0
Benedict XV (1914–1922)	31	18	1	0	0	0	0	32	96.9	0
Pius XI (1922–1939)	69	44	4	2	0	1	0	76	90.8	3.95
Pius XII (1939–1958)	36	13	6	9	1	3	1	56	64.3	23.21
John XXIII (1958–1963)	37	21	5	6	1	3	0	52	71.2	19.23
Paul VI (1963–1978)	83	39	14	16	12	13	5	143	58	28.67
John Paul I (1978)	0	0	0	0	0	0	0	0	0	0
John Paul II (1978–2005)	128	48	22	36	18	23	4	231	55.4	33.33
Benedict XVI (2005–2013)	52	26	10	9	8	11	0	90	57.7	31.11

*Africa–Asia–Latin America

Source: Based on data from Salvador Miranda, The Cardinals of the Holy Roman Church (Miami: Florida International University Library, October 2007).

The church, however, has not completely abandoned the territorial principle. As Andrea Riccardi writes, "the Church is interested in all lands, to the point that it includes them all in the jurisdiction of dioceses (at least theoretically), without excluding any."[23] In other words, since all the regions of Earth belong to God, they have been divided and structured in such a way as to be able to welcome, when the time comes, the territorial organization of the only legitimate representative of God on Earth, namely, the Catholic Church.

According to certain Catholics deeply impregnated with the ideologies surrounding decolonization, this merely represents a continuation, by inertia, of the old way of conceiving the expansion of Catholicism, a legacy henceforth stripped of any practical involvement; to them, the "territorial" mission is simply no longer on the agenda. And yet Pope John Paul II asserted in the encyclical *Redemptoris Missio*, on December 7, 1990, that "the criterion of geography, although somewhat imprecise and always provisional, is still a valid indicator of the frontiers toward which missionary activity must be directed." Pope Francis, for his part, stated in a message for World Mission Day, on May 19, 2013, that this activity "is not only about geographical territories, but about peoples, cultures and individuals." The difference in nuances as to "the criterion of geography" lies in the fact that John Paul II was writing at a time of *shifting* of borders, while Francis was speaking at a time of the *weakening* of borders, a weakening caused by the fact that "peoples, cultures and individuals" cross them today more often and much more easily than was the case before.

On January 6, 2001, John Paul II also noted in the apostolic letter *Tertio Millennio Adveniente* that "in situations of hostility and of persecution," the work of missionaries can go "to the point of the supreme test of shedding their blood." Still, the activities aimed at extending the authority of the church to the "far ends of the Earth" essentially take other forms: from individual conversions—sometimes highly symbolic, like those of Tony Blair, Jeb Bush, and Newt Gingrich, or, in Italy, of the Egyptian-born journalist and politician Magdi Allam—to the competition on the "religious free market," in keeping with the American model, but also to re-evangelization, which is to say the return to the fold of lost sheep.[24] In Francis's message one detects a relative diminution of the importance of the professional missionary, to the benefit of everyday missionary activity, a sort of militant evangelization for which each believer is responsible wherever he may be, so long as he never forgets "a fundamental principle for every evangelizer: one cannot announce Christ without the Church" (message for World Mission Day).

That said, the militant church rebuilt by John Paul II, and to which Francis hopes to, according to his aforementioned speech, impart a "paridigmatic dimension that affects all aspects of Christian life," is surely the principal vector for enlarging the influence of the Catholic Church and even—as is the case in certain countries—for reversing the trend in the levels of participation in religious functions. Yet it is still not sufficient for the task of extending the church's influence to the "far ends of the Earth."

If this strategic objective cannot be attained through competition with the "heretics," "infidels," and "schismatics," then the church must try to attain it in collaboration with them. Participants in the Second Vatican Council were urged to update this language, removing in a single stroke "heretics," "infidels," and "schismatics," as well as "deicides," and to discover that all other religions also "try to counter the restlessness of the human heart" and "often reflect a ray of that Truth which enlightens all men." The church of the Second Council also exhorted "her sons, that through dialogue and collaboration with the followers of other religions, carried out with prudence and love and in witness to the Christian faith and life, they recognize, preserve and promote the good things, spiritual and moral, as well as the socio-cultural values found among these men," as proclaimed in the *Nostra Ætate* declaration of October 28, 1965.

Thus common values in the "spiritual and moral, as well as the socio-cultural" realms have become the basis for "dialogue" and "collaboration" with the faithful of other religions. The beginning of the desecularization process in the 1970s made the return of God into the public sphere the goal of a veritable "alliance." As the Catholic Church is the only religious institution with such deep roots, organization, and global prestige—as well as a wealth of accumulated experience unequaled by any other human organization or institution—it is also the only one concretely able to lead this alliance and direct its missionary agenda.

So the "dialogue" and "collaboration" proposed by the church are not, at least not exclusively, "defensive" efforts to keep religions from being used as a pretext for conflict between civilizations. The alliance proposed by the Catholic Church has an "offensive" value and ultimate objective: to promote a return of religion to the center of public life. To most of those who promote "dialogue" or "alliances" between civilizations, conflicts would best be prevented if religions were to withdraw completely from the public sphere and inhabit a solely spiritual space. For the church, religions should occupy a larger place in the public sphere, in order to help direct major political decisions and thus eliminate the causes of these conflicts at their roots. In the view of the former group, we need less God; but for the church, we need more. That is why, in the eyes of the church, the alliance among civilizations can only be a Catholic-led alliance.

14
THE HOLY ALLIANCE

Together we can build the future, and the history, of humanity
—Pope John Paul II

THE DOUBLE TESTIMONY OF THE JEWS

In the *City of God* (book 18, chapter 46), Augustine turns to Psalm 58 to affirm, about the Jews: "You shall not slay them, lest they should at last forget Your law: disperse them in Your might" so that they will be, "by their own Scriptures, a testimony to us that we have not forged the prophecies about Christ."

The linkage Augustine draws between Jews and the biblical "adversaries . . . who commit iniquities . . . wicked traitors and evildoers" and who, Psalm 59 demands, should be dispersed "all over the Earth" is of course entirely arbitrary. Nevertheless, it has served as a theological basis for the hostility and persecutions inflicted by Christians on Jews for more than fifteen centuries.

And yet since World War II the attitude of the Catholic Church toward Jews has undergone a profound transformation: they have gone from the status of black sheep, against whom one must take "energetic measures to preserve both the faith and morals of her [the church's] members and society itself against the corrupting influence of error," to quote Pius XI's encyclical entitled *Humani Generis Unitas* (On the Unity of the Human Race, 1839), to that of "older brothers," in the language of Pope John Paul II, and even of "our fathers in faith," during the reign of Pope Benedict XVI. Moreover, as Pope Francis told representatives of the Jewish community of Rome on October 11, 2013, "paradoxically, the common tragedy of war has taught us to journey together."

None of those who attended Francis's meeting rose to point out to the pope that the tragedy experienced by Jews during the World War II was not "common" at all; perhaps this discretion reflected the determination of Jews to pursue, at any cost, a rapprochement with the Catholic Church. And yet what Francis said seems to comport with an analysis by the American historian John Connelly: it was not the unique nature of the fate reserved for Jews that persuaded the church to abandon its traditional anti-Judaism but precisely "*this* sense—the sense of common suffering of Jews and Christians," the conviction that Catholics, like Jews, had suffered through "the violence of the pagan juggernaut."[1]

This explosion of the pagan juggernaut led to the opening of a dialogue on the theological and historical differences between a handful of intellectuals representing the two communities; but as soon as the Christians started to explain their viewpoint to the Jews, as Connelly notes, "they began to realize how obscene much of their own teaching sounded when spoken in the shadow of the war's crimes."[2] According to Connelly, this sudden new awareness was behind the creation of an International Council of Christians and Jews, and of the convening of the Seelisberg Conference in 1947. The conference's final document—concerning the definitive end to any and all Christian vilification of the Jewish people—was approved by the Christian religious authorities, including the Catholics. This outcome was far from certain, as William Simpson notes, since "at the time of the Conference, fifteen years before the convening of the Vatican Council, the possible reaction of the Catholic authorities to an appeal to all Churches in the name of both Catholics and Protestants was still a matter of some uncertainty."[3]

The *nihil obstat* of the ecclesiastical authorities from Rome to the final Seelisberg document demonstrates that a small group of determined Catholic theologians—nine of the seventy participants at the conference were Catholic—were able to achieve their desired goal. But other factors certainly contributed to the change in attitude by the church toward Jews, factors linked to the unique tragedy of the Holocaust. Three of these factors appear to have been particularly important.

First, the church urgently needed to relieve itself, at least a posteriori, of any possible blame for co-responsibility in the colossal slaughter. The problem, even beyond the history of hostility reaching back to the very doctrine of Christianity, had to do with the recent and deafening silence of Pope Pius XII during the war. Among the first to express his surprise at this silence was Ernst von Weizsäcker, then the German ambassador to the Holy See, writing to his superiors in Berlin regarding the roundup of Jews from the ghetto in Rome. Having written on October 17, 1943, to signal his fear that the pope would likely "take a clear position" against the roundup, Weizsäcker wired one week later that, "even though he was urged to do so by many parties, the Pope took no position against the deportation of the Roman Jews. . . . He has done everything, in this delicate situation, as not to jeopardize the relationship with the German government and German authorities in Rome."[4]

Second and third, the attitude of American Catholics and the creation of the state of Israel surely played a role in the evolution of the church's position on Jews. The entry of the United States into World War II and the weight of the American Jewish community had led the country's bishops on November 14, 1942, to express their "revulsion against the cruel indignities heaped upon the Jews in conquered countries."[5] It is thus not unlikely that, at the end of the war, the Catholic authorities in Rome adopted a less hostile posture toward the Jews in order to eliminate any possible grounds for discord with Washington, where many of the thorniest questions about the organization of the postwar world were being decided, in particular, on the future treatment of Germany and Italy.

The hostility of the Holy See toward the birth of the state of Israel is well-known: "If Palestine belonged exclusively to the Jews," Vatican secretary of state Luigi Maglione wrote to the apostolic nuncios in the spring of 1943, "the Catholics' religious feelings would be injured and they would justly fear for their rights."[6]

These "just" fears were also theological in nature: the very existence of a "Jewish homeland" undercut the traditional interpretation of Psalm 58. Indeed, Augustine wrote that God "did not content himself with saying:

'You shall not slay them, lest they should at last forget Your law,' but he added, 'Disperse them.'" Therefore, for the Jewish people, wandering in the world was the condition of their survival.

With the birth of the state of Israel, this condition had simply disappeared. Also, despite attempts to "historicize" the biblical prophecy—the Jews had been dispersed long enough to bear "testimony" to the four corners of the Earth—it was inevitable that one day a pope would assert that Augustine was purely and simply mistaken in his anti-Jewish theology. Indeed, Francis did so in his interview with *La Repubblica* of October 1, 2013: "Augustine . . . made some very harsh statements about the Jews, of which I have never approved."[7]

In short, the official attitude of the church began to change, despite numerous reservations and internal opposition. In 1955 Pius XII slightly modified the Good Friday liturgy, in which Catholics, for centuries, had prayed for the conversion of the *perfidi Iudæi* (perfidious Jews). In 1959 Pope John XXIII dropped the adjective *perfidi*, and a new version of the Roman missal was published in 1962. Finally, in 1966 Pope Paul VI promulgated a new missal, again modified in 1969, in which the prayer for the "conversion of the Jews" became a prayer "for the Jewish people, the first to hear the word of God." John XXIII's intention was that the council convened in 1959 should specifically approve ecumenism—that is, the movement for the reunification of Christians—and the rapprochement with the Jews. But the church as a whole was clearly not yet ready.

John XXIII charged the German cardinal Augustin Bea with the task of preparing a document, the *Decretum de Iudæis* (Decree About Jews), to submit to the assembly; but the document was blocked by the conservative wing of the council and, finally, by the Middle Eastern prelates. As Thomas Stransky, a close adviser to Bea, later acknowledged, "We did not grasp the fact that in the Middle East, religious politics and political religion are the norm." Diplomatic circles in Arab countries, almost all of which maintained relations with the Holy See, mobilized against a text they viewed, Stransky said, as "a positive support of their enemy." An Egyptian bishop, quoted by Stransky, went so far as to admit that "if we do not display our opposition, we would not even be able to return to our homes."[8] The Syriac patriarch, Ignace Tappouni, in the name of the four Middle Eastern patriarchs, officially demanded that the document be withdrawn.

However, as Stransky went on to observe, "most setbacks became blessings in disguise." Indeed, in an exemplary case of the heterogony of ends, it was precisely the difficulties encountered in attempting to deal with the accusations of anti-Semitism that led to a transformation of the *Decretum de Iudæis* into a more general document, broadened to deal with relationships with other religions—Islam, Hinduism, and Buddhism—the declaration known as *Nostra Ætate* (In Our Time, 1965). Thus, through this single document, the church found itself in a position to pursue two different, if convergent, objectives: to renew the status of Jews as "witnesses," but this time as witnesses to the horrors to which a society can descend if it ceases basing itself on the law of God; and, at the same time, promoting a sort of common front with the other religions of the world that "seek to counter the restlessness of the human heart," as outlined in *Nostra Ætate*.

THE POPES AND ISLAM: WAR

About the attitudes of the church toward the Muslim religion in the early 1960s, Ralph Stehly writes: "Before the opening of the council, the Catholic hierarchy as a whole . . . did not seem unduly preoccupied by questions concerning Islam."[9] According to Michel Lelong, the European bishops continued to be "inattentive to this rather serious question of Islamo-Christian relations," at least until the 1970s.[10]

The fact is that, in the eyes of the Catholic authorities, Islam had become a nonproblem: broken up and dispersed over an enormous geographical area, with a great variety of distinct characteristics; in states often hostile to one another, sometimes weakened by civil wars, and nearly all strongly secularized. Indeed, Islam ceased to possess either of the two qualities that it had always presented in the past: it was no longer an enemy nor a model.

Once the church decided to open a dialogue with Islam, it set aside fourteen centuries of sometimes extremely violent hostility. Over the past fifty years, in their efforts to veil the past, top Vatican leaders have described the relationship with Islam through a mixture of euphemism and understatement, at times even simply glossing over the reality. According to the *Nostra Ætate*, "In the course of centuries not a few quarrels and hostilities have arisen between Christians and Moslems." According to John Paul II (1985), "We have generally misunderstood each other";[11] and to Benedict

XVI (2005), "Unfortunately, relations between Christians and Muslims have not always been marked by mutual respect and understanding."[12] Finally, Cardinal Jean-Louis Tauran, president of the Pontifical Council for Interreligious Dialogue, stated via *Radio Vaticana* on November 4, 2008, that there is no need to speak of opening a new dialogue between Islam and Christianity for "in reality, we have been in dialogue for 1,400 years!"

Diplomatic language, to be sure, has its demands. So do historical and political analysis, but the latter are based on events as they actually occurred. Through most of history, the attitude of the Church of Rome toward Islam has been marked by deep-seated hostility, often involving actions of an extreme violence, even by the standards of the time. In this hostility one finds, in turn, and often in combination, misunderstanding, jealousy, fear, slander, and also opportunism.

According to Bernard Lewis, this hostility sprung from the fact that no religion can allow itself to be seen as overtaken by a new religion that questions its "veracity and finality"; inasmuch as each religion presents itself as eternal, "anything subsequent [is] therefore necessarily false and harmful and [can] not be tolerated." It is true, Lewis continues, that "medieval Islam and medieval Christendom spoke the same language"; but the fact was that "using the same methods of argument and reasoning or similar notions of what religion is about" simply meant, at the time, that "Islam and Christendom could disagree meaningfully . . . when Christians and Muslims called each other infidels, each understood what the other meant, and both meant more or less the same thing."[13]

I cited misunderstanding as one element of the hostility toward Islam: this stemmed from the fact that it was long simply unclear that Muhammad's version was a new religion; many people viewed Islam as a new Christian heresy, bearing certain affinities with Arianism; others saw in it a new form of Judaism. The majority of Christians and Jews in the territories conquered by the Arabs in the early Muslim conquests accepted the new regime fairly readily; it brought them both peace and religious tolerance. Still, a minority resisted, and certain Christian theologians produced a rich anti-Muslim literature, which included themes of divine retribution, the carrying out of apocalyptic prophecies, the approach of Judgment Day, and also denunciations of Muhammad as an impostor, a magician, a madman, an epileptic, or the Antichrist plotting with the devil—and of Islam itself as a perverse, idolatrous, and lascivious religion. This final aspect captured the imaginations of theologians and Christian preachers, who speculated excitedly over the quantity and quality of sexual relations in the Muslim paradise; for Theophanes the Confessor, a Constantinople monk of the eighth century, women and their seductions constituted the vanguard of the Muslim armies.[14]

The Christian reaction was not uniform; it evolved as and when Christians found themselves confronted with the Muslim expansion. Greek Christianity was the first to react, followed by Arian Christianity in Spain and, finally, Roman Christianity, which is to say the future Catholic Church. The Bishop of Rome, in an opportunistic move, profited indirectly from the Muslim expansion to break away from the rest of the Orthodox Christian Church. Indeed, the Arabs, with their conquests in the Middle East and North Africa, eliminated three of the five most important patriarchates— Alexandria, Jerusalem, and Antioch—that were best placed to assume the leadership of the whole Christian world. A century later, in a direct threat to the southern borders of the Byzantine Empire, these same Arabs mobilized all the military energies of Constantinople; the emperors were unable to defend their positions in Italy, in particular, the Exarchate of Ravenna, the Greek foothold on the peninsula, which were conquered in turn by the Lombards and the Franks and ceded by the latter to the bishop of Rome, who made it the heart of his future Papal States.

The conquest of the Byzantine territories in the Middle East and North Africa, the conquests of Visigoth Spain and Sicily, the sieges of Constantinople in 674–678 and again in 718, the incursion into the land of the Franks, as well as the sacking of Rome in 846 by Saracen pirates, transformed theological concerns into more practical concerns. According to Jean Flori, it was this final episode that prompted Pope Leon IV to issue the first clear statement "in the Christian West" on the divine compensation awaiting soldiers who died while fighting "the enemies of the holy faith."[15] This laid the ground for similar promises by later popes, most often, though, during conflicts with other Christians. For example, the speech of Pope Leon IX to the German soldiers fighting the Normans in 1053 preceded the call of the First Crusade by Pope Urban II at the Clermont Council in 1095.

A number of specialists have pointed out that, over the centuries, when the Christian authorities made reference to Islam they never named it directly, as if it did not deserve to be treated as a religion. In the language that the Christian clerics transmitted to the intellectuals of their period and, finally, to the broader society, the connotation has always been eth-nic: the "Moors," "Saracens," or "Turks," and never the "Muslims." Thus when King Francis I of France entered into an alliance with the Ottoman Empire, and merchants throughout the Christian world made a fortune by selling arms and all sorts of goods to the sultan, Pope Clement VII issued a papal bull in 1527 banning the sale of anything to "the Saracens, Turks and other enemies of the Christian name."

Among Latin Christians there was no significant production of anti-Muslim theology: the followers of Allah certainly did not receive the same attention—sometimes obsessive—reserved for the Jews. Other than a few rare exceptions, it was the Christians of the East or Spain who had theo-logical disputes with the Muslims, not the Christians of Rome. The key rea-son for this absence of dialogue lies quite simply in the absence of contact.

In all likelihood, this absence of contact was principally due to the Arabs' very limited interest in conquering western Europe, which they viewed as "a remote, unexplored wilderness inhabited by exotic, pictur-esque and rather primitive people from whom there was nothing to fear and less to learn."[16] At times, certain western European cities or regions were the targets of isolated, one-time raids—such as the incursion into Touraine in 732, or the sacking of Rome—but not of conquest. Along with the limited attractions of the European lands, one should add the risk of imperial overstretch, a risk with which the Arabs were rapidly confronted. It was largely the implications associated with imperial overstretch that led to the loss of Spain, which in 750 became an independent caliphate. The concept of imperial overstretch was first analyzed in its theoretical form by Arab thinker Ibn Khaldun, who lived between 1332 and 1406. In his *Muqadimmah*, Khaldun wrote that "each dynasty has a certain amount of provinces and lands, and no more . . . the greatness of a dynasty, the extent of its territory, and the length of its duration depend upon the numerical strength of its supporters."[17]

When contact was established—during the Crusades—the time was not exactly propitious for theological discussions. There is reason to believe that religious objectives of the Crusades, while indispensable to the mili-tary mobilization, were not entirely central to the motivations of the papacy. For Rome, it was important first to assume the "protection" of the Greek Christians only a few decades after the Great Schism of 1054, and just a few years after the Battle of Manzikert in 1071 between the Byzantine and Seljuk Empires, which had allowed the latter to pour into Anatolia. It was also important to guarantee a sort of "open door" *ante litteram* to the Christian powers engaged in trafficking with the Levant. Finally, it was important to enlarge the sphere of influence of the Church of Rome, and not only in the Middle East. This is demonstrated by the interdiction placed on Spanish Catholics from taking part in the Holy War to concentrate their forces against two enemies on the Iberian Peninsula—the Saracen and Arian Christians—as well as by the papal bull from Pope Eugene III in 1147, which effectively exempted the Germanic tribes from participating in the Second Crusade to direct them instead toward the Slavic lands of the East, where the looming breakup of the Kievan Rus' was opening some interesting geo-religious perspectives.

Peter Partner asserts that the Crusades, moreover, represented a crucial political moment for the Church of Rome: on the one hand, the taxes imposed by the popes to finance the Crusades represented "a development that had important results for the centralization of the Latin Catholic Church"; on the other, the Second Crusade transformed the papacy into the heart of the era's diplomatic activity and "in one way it was the first major step towards the concept of European collective security."[18]

According to Partner, the conquest of Jerusalem did little to alter the Catholic misreading of Islam; this was the case until, in the twelfth century, the abbot of Cluny, Peter the Venerable, and, a few decades later, Francis of Assisi treated Islam for the first time as a religion—even if their clear objective was to convert Muslims to the sole "true religion."

The Crusades also marked the beginning of a gradual reversal in the power balance between the Christian principalities and the Muslim caliphates, sultanates, and emirates. They were also the occasion for the formation of hybrid alliances between Muslims and Christians against other Muslims and Christians, a practice that would become common in the centuries to follow, and of which the most successful example—at least until the Crimean War, in the second half of the nineteenth century—was the alliance between Francis I of France and the Ottoman sultan Suleiman the Magnificent, as he is known in the West.

Rome did not, however, shy away from attempting to oversee an eventual system of European collective security, with the Turkish menace serving as the galvanizing impulse: the ephemeral "Holy League" of Lepanto in 1571 is probably the best-known example. Europe, nonetheless, progressively escaped from the authority of the Catholic Church, in a process of which the Reformation and the Peace of Westphalia were the first, and most decisive, steps. As this process unfolded, the adversaries of the church sometimes used Islam against Rome: this was the case with certain Protestants who, at the beginning of the Reformation, saw the Muslim religion as an objective ally against a common foe, and it was even more the case with several eighteenth-century intellectuals who used Islam "as a weapon against Christian dogma and the Catholic clergy."[19] Henri de Boulainvilliers, in 1730, and Edward Gibbon, in 1788, attributed to Islam all the qualities that the church lacked. As Boulainvilliers put it, "For them, the maceration, the fasting, the flagellation and the disciplines are unknown," and Muhammad was "an incomparable statesman and a legislator superior to all those produced by ancient Greece."[20] For Gibbon, he was "a wise and tolerant lawgiver, the founder of a rational, un-dogmatic, priest-free religion and society."[21]

If, as late as the sixteenth century, the church accused Calvin of "Islamizing tendencies," by the time of the Enlightenment the polemical force of this argument had grown drastically weaker. Islam had ceased, centuries earlier, to be seen as a threat, and when the European powers began occupying Muslim lands—the Russians in Crimea, the English in India, the Dutch in Indonesia, and the French in Algeria—it had become a "recessive" religion. Finally, the abolition of the caliphate in 1924, and the secularist path taken by the governments of most Muslim countries created by decolonization, ultimately made Muslim religious piety socially marginal, and the church gradually lost all interest in this religion—except in the Middle East, where Christians and certain Muslim authorities shared their hostility toward a Jewish national home.

At the time of the Second Vatican Council, it was of course the bishops and the patriarchs from the Middle East who demanded that the *Decretum de Iudæis* be withdrawn. When two American cardinals and a German threatened to quit the council if the peace with the Jews was not signed, the urgent need for a compromise led certain Arab prelates to propose a broader document, in which the reference to Judaism would be softened by placing it in the middle of references to the other great world religions, led by Islam. At the time, Judaism was the only "problematic" religion; Buddhism, Hinduism, and Islam had the role of "buffer religions." Things have changed considerably since then.

THE POPES AND ISLAM: COLLABORATION

The French writer Pascal Brucker coined an apt description of the current feeling of Catholic authorities toward Islam: Ramadan envy.[22] In France, according to data compiled by Brucker in 2009, seven of every ten Muslims fasted during Ramadan, representing a 60 percent increase over twenty years, and the percentage of those who describe themselves as believers is double the rate among Catholics, with peaks in the fifteen to twenty-four age cohort.

Beyond the subtle Freudian allusion, Brucker's reference to Ramadan is far from being metaphorical. It was precisely by pointing to this "arduous month of fasting" that, in 1991, John Paul II indicated to faithful Catholics "an example of obedience to divine will, a proof of the importance of prayer and discipline, and a testimony to ascetic simplicity in our use of the goods of this world." This was a potential model for Catholics whose piety had suffered amid the distractions of the "goods of this world," but it was also a plan for a unity of action with Islam. Indeed, for the pope, these values should be offered "to all humanity as a religious alternative to the attractions of power, of money, and of material pleasures."[23]

It was not until the 1970s that the church discovered the strength of Muslim religiosity, together with its possible implications. And yet some Christians had long ago called attention to the degree to which contact with Muslim religious practices could be beneficial to both evangelization and re-evangelization.

In 1856 Jean Hippolyte Michon, an eccentric and visionary priest, suggested to Pius IX that he leave behind the squabbles of Italy and relocate to Jerusalem, where he could work on reunification with the Christians of the East and also more closely observe "the men of Islam." By studying "the Arab element from the point of view of its affinity with Christianity" as had never been done before, Michon asserted that Islam could be held up as a model. He argued that "the Arab is the most religious of all people. . . . God is permanently in his thoughts. The Arab converses familiarly with God; he understands Him, he sees Him in his mathematically spiritualistic dogma; he seems to breathe Him with the air." Moreover, according to Michon, Muslims have "naturally Christian souls."[24]

Michon's books were condemned by the church and included in the *Index Librorum Prohibitorum*.[25] Early in the following century, other

Frenchmen, having come into contact with Muslim religiosity, emphasized how helpful it might be in the spiritual reconquest of secularized Europe. In 1901, for instance, Charles de Foucauld wrote: "Islam produced a profound upheaval within. . . . Seeing this faith, these souls living in the continual presence of God, gave me a glimpse of something greater and more true than our worldly pastimes."[26] Additionally, as the protagonist in the novel *Le voyage du centurion* (1916) by Ernest Psichari put it, "for many of the French who no longer have faith, but who still feel the regret, Islam exerts a profound attraction."[27]

Decolonization represented a real turning point in the Catholic perspective on Islam. Still, for much longer to come, the idea of collaborating on an equal—formal—footing with other religions remained hidden behind the principle of "Catholicization," meaning the conversion of the faithful of the entire world to the one true religion.

In 1964, at his Sunday homily during Pentecost, Pope Paul VI announced the creation of a Secretariat for Non-Christians, "an organ which will have quite different functions but a structure analogous to that for separated Christians," which was created in 1960 by John XXIII. The pope placed this new secretariat in a missionary context aimed at linking the spread of the church to "the far ends of the Earth." For Paul VI, the fact that "the world is not yet Catholic" represented a source of pain for all who have "a truly Catholic heart." The missionary, the pope concluded, "walks in paths that must make the world Catholic."

Even while stating that "the true religion is unique, and it is the Christian religion," Paul VI nevertheless announced, in his encyclical *Ecclesiam Suam* of August 1964, his intention to work with non-Christian religions with the goal of "promoting and defending common ideals in the spheres of religious liberty, human brotherhood, education, culture, social welfare and civic order." Since no rapprochement was possible on the theological level, it was proposed in practical terms, with a few clearly stated objectives. In July 1967, during the papal visit to Turkey, he was even more explicit, specifically addressing Muslims, "all those who worship the one and only God are called to establish an order of justice and peace in the world."

Since that time, meetings, conferences, and seminars have been held to encourage dialogue between Catholics and Muslims. In 1975 the Islamic-Christian Research Group was created, the first in a series of entities through which the Catholic Church maintains and encourages dialogue with Islam. Listed in 2010 by Jean-Louis Tauran, the others included the Libyan-based World Islamic Call Society, founded in 1976; the Islamic-Catholic Liaison Committee, in 1995; the joint committee with Al-Azhar University of Cairo, in 1998; the Royal Institute for Interfaith Studies of Amman, in 1994; and the Islamic Culture and Relations Organization of Tehran, in 1995. The most recent is the very official Catholic-Muslim Forum, which first met in the Vatican, in 2008.

Paul VI's successors confirmed the disposition outlined in the encyclical of 1964, emphasizing the practical objectives—in other words, the political goals—of dialogue with Muslims as well as the need to elevate this dialogue to the level of a true alliance. In November 1979, John Paul II placed what he openly described as "collaboration" into a framework that was not just *tactical*, aiming to achieve a series of specific objectives, "social justice, moral values, peace and freedom," but also *strategic*, aimed at returning religion to the center of political choices. During his visit to Ankara, John Paul II asserted: "Man has rights that cannot be violated, but at the same time he must respect the law of good and evil that is based on the order established by God." In February 2000, at Al-Azhar University, he proposed a veritable pact of joint action: "Together," he said, "we can build the future and the history of humanity."

To achieve what Benedict XVI, during his May 2009 trip to Amman, called an "alliance of civilizations between the Western world and the Muslim world," the major difficulty facing the church is to find, to use Henry Kissinger's famous quip, Islam's "telephone number"; that is, to find, in the vast Muslim galaxy, a possible interlocutor. The church avoided the temptation of conferring this distinction on any particular Muslim religious authority, for that would raise the risk, indeed the certainty, of provoking endless jealousies and recriminations. The difficulties encountered in dialogue with the Orthodox Christian world are instructive: the choice, rather logical in the end, of giving priority to contacts with the patriarch of Constantinople fanned the resentment of the Patriarchate of Moscow and ended by complicating the task rather than facilitating it. It is thus easy to imagine what could happen in the Muslim world, where any individual, or almost any, can be his own patriarch.

In simplified terms, the Catholic Church took three approaches in its search for interlocutors in the Muslim world: grassroots activities, concerning a whole series of practical and immediate questions; contacts with institutions recognized by various states; and attempts to provoke responses and position-taking by individuals available for dialogue and sufficiently prestigious within their respective communities.

As concerns grassroots activities, the church has for some years been addressing itself directly to the Muslim faithful and to their needs, both practical and even religious. In France, for example, young Muslims can attend Catholic schools, which help them sidestep the public-school ban on wearing conspicuous religious symbols; moreover, there are only some 31 Muslim schools in the country, compared to the 9,005 Catholic establishments tallied in the 2012–13 school year.[28] The result is that some 10 percent of the students in French Catholic schools now identify as Muslim. Furthermore, the higher-education training program for imams in France is conducted by the Catholic Institute of Paris, after several public universities refused to do so. Finally, the church supports the construction of places of worship for Muslims, the right to halal meals, and the extension of Muslim chaplaincy services to the army and prisons, even at the cost sometimes of conflict with the public authorities and, often, rankling a certain number of Catholic faithful. With the exception of a few particular cases, the attitude of the French Church merely mirrors locally the indications of the universal church.

It is nonetheless clear that the involvement of the church in favor of Muslim communities does not resolve the problem of who can represent them and thus does not resolve the problem of identifying institutional interlocutors with whom to establish official contact. Often, the Catholic authorities of different countries bypass this difficulty by establishing contacts with those Muslim authorities recognized by the respective states—such as the leaders of Muslim councils in France, Belgium, or Germany—particularly when it concerns questions involving national political life. However, this is hardly an ideal solution, for two key reasons: the church, by depending on a state-recognized institution, loses some of its autonomy; and authorities recognized by states are not always representative of their respective communities.

The church greatly prefers to manage its relations with other religious communities directly, and to select its own interlocutors. The Catholic-Muslim Forum—currently the most important venue for contacts between the two religions—was born in reaction to a letter from 138 prominent figures in the Muslim world criticizing the much-disparaged *lectio* of Benedict XVI in Regensburg in September 2006. Certain observers contended that the polemical assertion of Byzantine emperor Manuel II—who said that Muhammad had brought nothing but "the evil and the inhuman"—quoted by the pope in Regensburg was explicitly intended to provoke a reaction. The reaction came in the form of the 138 Muslim dignitaries. According to Lelong, the 138 are "important Muslim figures representative of their community"; but the author, a long-time advocate of closer collaboration between the Catholic Church and Islam, presents as undeniable something that can, even generously, only be described as wishful thinking: by definition, Sunni Islam has no "important Muslim figures representative of their community," at least not in an institutional sense.[29]

Viewed from this angle, the problem is irresolvable; the church can only hope that what Lelong affirms a bit too categorically comes as close as possible to reality: namely, the views of these dignitaries carry the weight of authority within the global Muslim community. They will certainly not be able to convince those who view Christians as enemies, or simply as foreigners, in their relations with Islam, but they may hope for a favorable welcome from all those Muslims who, for one reason or another, aspire to relations of peaceful coexistence or even collaboration with Christians, at the national or international level.

Whether the outcome was desired or an unintended consequence, it is clear that the lesson of Benedict XVI at Regensburg resulted in a highly significant initial consequence: for the first time, Muslim eminences from different communities and countries reached agreement on both theological and practical questions, even if their document does not rise above the lowest common denominator.

During the First Seminar of the Catholic-Muslim Forum, the Catholic demand to confront concrete and immediate problems prevailed over the theological discussion sought by the Muslim delegation. Four of the fifteen points in the final declaration insisted on the question of the "right of individuals and of communities to practice their religion in private and in public." This was not merely an assertion of principle: it went to the concrete question of reciprocity, a question on which the church is so insistent that certain commentators see it as the sole reason for its interest in dialogue with Muslims. In Catholic countries, church officials say, Muslims enjoy near-total religious freedom and are not persecuted because of their faith; so the same guarantees are sought to protect the rights of Catholics—and more generally of all Christians—in Muslim countries.

Still, the reasons for the "collaboration" between the church and Muslims are more profound and more strategic. It is by collaborating with them that the church hopes, over time, to make the growth of its own influence coincide with the "far ends of the Earth."

"EXTRA ECCLESIAM, NULLA SALUS"

"Better a turban than a tiara." Legend has it, that it was by sticking to this principle that Constantinople, the capital of Eastern Christianity, preferred to give itself over to the Turks rather than to Rome. In reality, in 1439 its political and religious authorities had given themselves over to the pope when, at the Council of Florence, they signed an unconditional capitulation in hopes of saving the city, the last intact remnant of the former Eastern Roman Empire. But once they had come back to the capital, the Byzantine ambassadors who, in Florence, had signed the "decree of union" with the Latin Church were disavowed. Anticipating a jolt of democracy, the clergy and the people prevented the emperor from invoking his imperial prerogatives to impose a union with the Catholics, and they resigned themselves instead to the arrival of the Turks.

Historians generally date the beginning of "Orthodox rage" against the Church of Rome to the Fourth Crusade. Launched in 1202 with the intention of retaking Jerusalem from the Arabs—who had reconquered it in 1187—the crusade climaxed with the capture and pillaging of Constantinople. The Kurdish historian Ibn al-Athir, who lived through this period, recounts that "all the Rums [the Greeks] were killed or robbed." According to Amin Maalouf, "the sack of Constantinople was one of the most degrading acts in history." But, he continues, it was also a twofold strategic error: the wealth of Constantinople and of the Byzantine lands turned the Catholic knights away from Jerusalem, which would never be recaptured; and from that time on, Greek Christians would never again doubt that the domination of the turban was far preferable to that of the tiara.[30]

However, the roots of Orthodox rage run deeper still, to the time when Rome profited from Byzantine difficulties amid Arab advances in Asia Minor to liberate itself from Constantinople's political and religious tutelage and found a new Roman Empire in the West. The capture of Constantinople by the crusaders in 1204 was merely the most famous, and perhaps the bloodiest, chapter in a long history lasting more than a millennium, during which the Catholic concept of the unity of Christians has always been based on their submission to the authority of the pope.[31]

With a view to absorbing other Christian communities, the church made massive use of the instrument of "union." The mechanism consisted of progressively annexing sectors of Eastern Christianity, even while conceding to them the right to retain their rituals and habits, notably the ordination of married priests. This process first drew in the Maronites, shortly after the creation of the Latin Patriarchate of Jerusalem in 1099, then the Syriacs, Melkites, Chaldeans, Armenians, and Copts. With the exception of the Maronites, the union of other churches with Rome provoked splits within the respective communities, in which "the feeling of nationality prevailed over all other considerations," as Hyppolite Desprez noted in 1853.[32] The most important union, in every respect, was that which was imposed on the Orthodox faithful in the territories conquered in 1596 by the Polish-Lithuanian Commonwealth—now in Belorussia and Ukraine—which gave birth to the Catholic Church of Kiev, the Ruthenians, known pejoratively as the Uniate Church.

The hostility between Christians of the East and of the West was thus at its zenith precisely on the eve of the Thirty Years War in Europe, which originally pitted Catholic states against Protestants. As we saw in the early pages of this book, the ravages provoked by that war helped spur the decision of the European states to progressively exclude religious pretexts from their political and military disputes, starting with the Peace of Westphalia in 1648. From that time forward, the breakups, excommunications, schisms, dialogues, and reunifications within the Christian world were gradually drawn back into a sphere affecting religious institutions almost exclusively, while only rarely involving the political or military authorities of different states.

Thus it was that the Catholic Church found itself in the nineteenth century embattled on three fronts: confronting the eastern "schismatics," the Protestant "heretics," and the advancing forces of secularization. In less than a century, the papacy lost Rome four times: in 1798–1799, after the first French conquest; in 1809–1815, with the annexation of the Papal States by the French Empire; from February to July 1849, with the ephemeral Roman Republic; and, finally, in 1870, with the Italian conquest. All these reversals, rather than disquieting Pius IX, reinforced him in his intransigence; in the restorations of the pontifical throne in 1799, 1815, and 1849, the pope saw not the hand of the great powers fighting over Europe but the hand of God or, put another way, the will of God being achieved through the secular arm of the great powers. One reason that Pius IX proclaimed himself a "prisoner" of the Italians lay in his certainty that God would again restore the power of the pope.

Faced by the common enemy of secularization, the different Christian churches began accusing one another of having sparked the "revolution" by destroying the unity of the Church of Christ; the accusation became a regular refrain in Catholic literature until the first half of the twentieth century. For Pius IX, it was, as the encyclical *Quanta Cura* in 1864 outlined, "the heresies and errors which, being adverse to our Divine Faith, to the doctrine of the Catholic Church, to purity of morals, and to the eternal salvation of men, have frequently excited violent tempests, and have miserably afflicted both Church and state." Behind the opposing barricade, an unidentified "Russian diplomat" explained in 1850 that "the origin of Protestantism is linked to the usurpations of Rome; for the usurpation . . . sparked the revolt."[33]

These mutual accusations were not unrelated to the geopolitical dynamics of the time, notably the rivalry between the extremely dynamic Russian Empire and the Ottoman Empire, which was in a state of decay. Russia was fast expanding in every direction: toward Siberia, Central Asia, the Mediterranean, and Central Europe. It was in the context of Russian advances in the direction of Central Europe that the dissolution of the Uniate Catholic Church—decreed in 1839 by Czar Nicholas I—took place, following the principle of "one land, one Church" that was typical of Orthodox tradition, a notion as dear to the emperor as to the patriarch.

The acceleration of the Ottoman crisis in the mid-nineteenth century opened a breach that all parties attempted to fill: in 1841 a joint Anglican-Lutheran bishopric was created in Jerusalem; in July 1847 the first Russian ecclesiastical mission was sent to the capital of the Holy Land; and simultaneously Rome decided to reestablish the Latin patriarchate there. At the same time, notions of a geo-religious reorganization of the region began to be sketched out.

In 1856 the Jesuit Ivan-Xavier Gagarin proposed a reconciliation of the churches of the East and the West that would leave Russian Orthodox worshipers with their rites and institutions but would free them from

"Byzantinism," that is, from their subordination to a national political power—which, however, constituted the real raison d'être of Orthodoxy. Thus, Gagarin continued, "hundreds of Russian missionaries would rush forth, crosses in hand, for the conquest of the vast Asian continent. . . . Islamism would be taken by surprise, at the same time that it is being attacked on the shores of the Mediterranean."[34] In 1862 Father Emmanuel d'Alzon, founder of the congregation of the Assumptionists, laid out an opposing theory, aiming to hinder Russian ambitions in Constantinople by creating a, "zone of Catholic populations" between Russia and Turkey, thanks to which "the Porte [the Ottoman central government] could hope for a prolonged existence."[35]

These proposals clearly reflect a fundamental misunderstanding of the geopolitical weakness of Catholicism in the second half of the nineteenth century. Nevertheless, it was precisely this weakness that fueled papal intransigence. In the encyclical *Quanto Conficiamur Moerore* (1863), Pius IX reminded those who remain "obstinately separated from the unity of the Church and also from the successor of Peter" of the evangelical principle according to which "he who is not with me is against me, and he who does not gather with me, scatters" (Luke 11:23). In the encyclical *Satis Cognitum* (1896), Pope Leon XIII also devoted considerable energy to bringing "back to the fold, placed under the guardianship of Jesus Christ, the Chief Pastor of souls, sheep that have strayed."

It was not until after World War I that were there signs of a first timid opening of the Catholic hierarchy. And yet, "beginning in 1925, Rome's attitude began to harden."[36] In the encyclical *Mortalium Animos* (1928), Pius XI issued a brusque reminder that "this Apostolic See has never allowed its subjects to take part in the assemblies of non-Catholics: for the union of Christians can only be promoted by promoting the return to the one true Church of Christ of those who are separated from it, for in the past they have unhappily left it." Roger Aubert explains this hardening by the irritation provoked by the "doctrinal liberalism" of the ecumenical conference held in Stockholm, in 1925, as well as by the necessity to "offer some reassurance to the intransigent faction in the College of Cardinals," in order to reach a compromise with the Italian government on the "Roman question." Aubert adds that "the hopes of rapprochement with Russian Orthodoxy now appeared much less certain," although he does not say why.[37]

The fact is that, as Peter Kent and John Pollard write, after 1917 "the Holy See sought to exploit the chaos in Russia by sending missionaries," and to do so it made several "attempts to seek good relations with the Bolsheviks between 1917 and 1929."[38] In 1924, David Alvarez relates, Pius IX "instructed his nuncio in Germany, Monsignor Eugenio Pacelli, to continue the secret talks with Soviet diplomatic representatives that had been going on for almost a year in Berlin."[39]

The Vatican thus again displayed its geopolitical reflex to always follow—even at the cost of sudden detours—the guiding star of Catholic interests. Concerning its relations with the Orthodox churches, there was a precedent in 1914: the ink on the concordat the Holy See signed on June 24 with Serbia had not yet dried when the Vatican threw its support behind Vienna's ultimatum to Belgrade. The interests of 40,000 Serbian Catholics suddenly vanished in the face of the strategic imperatives with Austria-Hungary.

This geopolitical reflex has not disappeared, despite the passage of time, the work of ecumenical councils, and the various openings. It revealed itself again in April 1941, at the moment the Independent State of Croatia was created, when Alojzije Stepinac, the archbishop of Zagreb, invited believers to cooperate with the new regime and to pray "that the Croatian nation become the Divine nation, loyal to Christ and his Church."[40] On May 20, 1941, Ante Pavelić, the regime's new leader—and the man who, in 1934, had ordered the assassination of King Alexander I of Yugoslavia in Marseille—was received by Pope Pius XII on a "private visit." Despite its private character, this visit was described on page 1 of the L'Osservatore Romano the following day.

This reflex appeared again in 1991–92, when the Vatican offered its firm and unconditional support for the independence of Slovenia and Croatia. If the widely reported network of arms purchases by the Institute for the Works of Religion—commonly known as the "Vatican Bank"—for the Croatian Army via Lebanon remains unproven, the engagement of the pope and of his secretary of state, Angelo Sodano, in favor of a "humanitarian intervention" in the war was clear and reiterative. On December 5, 1992, in a speech to the Food and Agriculture Organization of the United Nations, Pope John Paul II demanded that "humanitarian intervention be made obligatory in situations that gravely threaten the survival of peoples and of entire ethnic groups." From an Orthodox standpoint, the Catholic Church aligned itself with Croatia, Slovenia, and then Bosnia for the same reasons that it supported the Austrian ultimatum in 1914 and the dictatorial regime of Ante Pavelić in 1941: to make the Drina River the last rampart of Catholicism in Europe.

On Easter in 1944 Pius XII published the *Orientalis Ecclesiae* encyclical devoted to "the happy return of our separated brethren in the East to Us and to the one Church of Jesus Christ." If "the Divine Spirit enlighten[s] the minds of Eastern peoples with His heavenly light," he wrote, then "there shall be one flock in one fold, all obedient with one mind to Jesus Christ and to His Vicar on Earth." In that same month, Ante Pavelić's troops were busy massacring Orthodox believers, Jews, Roma, and partisans. At war's end, the death toll was put at 50,000 Serbians, 13,000 Jews, 12,000 Croats, and 10,000 Roma.[41] One can understand why, all other implications aside, Eastern Christians remain, even today, highly suspicious of anything that is even vaguely connected to the tiara.

UT UNUM SINT

After the election of Joseph Ratzinger to lead the Catholic Church in 2005, some analysts observed that a German pope might have a better chance of reaching agreement with the Russian Church than would a Polish pope. At the time, Russian energy giant Gazprom and German corporations E.ON and BASF were finalizing an agreement for the construction of Nord Stream, the gas pipeline linking Russia to Germany via the Baltic Sea, expressly designed to circumvent Poland and other transit states. The accord led the then Polish minister of defense Radosław Sikorski to speak of a "Ribbentrop-Molotov energy pact."[42]

Throughout history, there have always been groups in Germany and in Russia that favored a rapprochement between the two countries. We should not forget that the key to the geopolitical strategic outlook of Karl Haushofer—a man unfairly dubbed by some as "Hitler's geopolitician"—consisted precisely in a German–Russian alliance. But nor should we forget, when speaking of the Catholic Church, that Rome has its own political agenda, and that while it is affected by the entirety of relations between states, it tends to jealously protect its autonomy. Benedict XVI renewed ties with the Patriarchate of Moscow not because he was German but because the strategy of the church demanded it.

Similarly, the election of Karol Wojtyła as pope in 1978 presumably was not meant as a gesture of defiance toward Moscow. The archbishop of Krakow was selected for other qualities—the fact that he was *not* Italian, his age, his intransigence on moral questions, his good relationship with Jews, and so forth. Indeed, in 1978 the Vatican's agenda was still dominated by the opening to the regimes of Central and Eastern Europe, for which a good relationship with Moscow was necessary. Wojtyła's election was nonetheless perceived by the Soviets as interference in their sphere of influence; subsequently, the inflexibility of his character, the emergence of the Solidarity movement, and the 1983 Euro-missile Crisis seemed to confirm their suspicions. John Paul II had thus long been considered an anti-Russian pope by the time he decided to reorganize the Catholic dioceses of Russia, in 2002, a decision that provoked a return to the "religious Cold War" between the Vatican and the Patriarchate of Moscow.

In fact, the Catholic Church is not, and will never be, either pro-Russian or anti-Russian, pro-German or anti-German, or, for that matter, pro-Orthodox or anti-Orthodox; it will always be favorable to anything that advances the influence of Catholicism in the world and will always be opposed to anything that risks slowing its advance or, worse still, causing its retreat. Since the decolonization process began following World War II, it has been ecumenism and cooperation with other religions that have provided the pivot of the strategy aimed at reaching to the "far ends of the Earth." However, any time the church has an opportunity to advance its pawns and draw an immediate advantage from a particular situation, it is unlikely to decline to do so, even if it risks offending the sensitivities of its allies. All of which makes considerably more sense if one applies to the church the famous maxim of Lord Palmerston: "Nations have no permanent friends or allies, they only have permanent interests." The Yugoslav Wars and the reorganization of the Russian dioceses in 2002 are two examples of this.

The independence movements in Zagreb and Ljubljana had suddenly opened the possibility of creating two new Catholic states in the heart of Europe, one of which—Croatia—was making Catholicism its *only* truly national characteristic. The transformation of the apostolic administrations of Moscow, Saratov, Novossibirsk, and Irkutsk—created shortly after the collapse of the Soviet Union—into dioceses demonstrated the determination to reinforce the Catholic structure despite the harsh reaction of the

Orthodox hierarchy. Moreover, the existence of diocesan structures of the Patriarchate of Moscow in several Christian countries offered an opportunity to invoke the principle of reciprocity.

For many observers, the apostolic constitution *Anglicanorum cœtibus* falls into the same category. This constitution, made public in November 2009, provides for "personal ordinaries for Anglicans entering into full communion with the Catholic Church." Still, it appears to respond more to a need to offer a canonic framework for those Anglican pastors who had *already* decided to leave the Anglican community and to return to the Catholic fold, many of whom are married. One year before the promulgation of the *Anglicanorum cœtibus*, the Jesuit Keith Pecklers had suggested that "the last thing the pope would wish to do is support any kind of division [within the Anglican Communion.]"[43] Indeed, dialogue and the passage of time are likely to offer the Catholic Church much more valuable and lasting results.

Caution and dialogue thus remain the dominant postures of the church. In 2004 Igor Kowalewskj, the Catholic spokesman for the joint committee in charge of relations between the two communities in Russia, stated that "it would be absurd, and even paranoid, to think that we Catholics can convert Russia to Catholicism. There is no strategy for converting Russia."[44] The strategy is a different one, and it requires relations with the Orthodox hierarchies to be both frank and cordial; it is on this basis that it will be possible to give birth to what journalist Sandro Magister calls a "holy alliance" between Rome and Moscow.[45]

The landscape had changed considerably between the time of Pius IX's anathematizing of "heresies and errors" and Benedict XVI's "holy alliance." But Catholic intellectuals had long since begun to prepare the fields for change. In 1910 the priest and German theologian Maximilian von Sachsen, who was brother to the king of Saxony, had published an article proposing a union between the Catholic and Orthodox Churches based on a recognition of the mistakes of the Western Church and guarantees that the Eastern Church could conserve its dogmatic and ritualistic traditions.[46] The theologian-prince was immediately disavowed by the hierarchy, provoking an intervention from Pope Pius X, in the form of the *Ex quo* letter on December 26, 1910, and the inclusion of his text in the *Index Librorum Prohibitorum*; but the ice had been broken.

Outside the Catholic world, the first glimmerings of ecumenism appeared after World War I, starting with the birth of a Lutheran-inspired

movement Life and Work in 1925 and of an Anglican-inspired initiative
Faith and Order in 1927, which in 1948 came together to found the ecumenical World Council of Churches. According to Aubert, the Vatican,
even while asserting that "there was no question of its sitting equal-to-
equal with other Christian denominations," unofficially encouraged the
meetings between various Anglican and Catholic figures under the leadership of the archbishop of Brussels, Désiré-Joseph Mercier, from 1921 to
1925. In Rome, the Belgian Benedictine monk Lambert Beauduin organized
encounters in 1921 with Orthodox believers who had left Russia after the
revolution; while the church discreetly, but officially, encouraged this
in 1924, it withdrew its support from the monk in 1928 and transferred
him away from Rome in 1931.[47] A few rare strains of ecumenical thought
emerged in the Catholic world during the 1930s as well. In Germany, the
two most representative figures of this movement were the theologian
Robert Grosche, who founded the review *Catholica* in 1932, and Max Josef
Metzger, who in 1938 founded the Una Sancta Brotherhood for dialogue
with Lutherans. In 1944 Metzger was executed by order of the German
authorities. In France, such an approach was advocated by people like the
abbots Paul Couturier and Laurent Remillieux, who promoted meetings
with francophone Protestants in 1937, as well as Henri de Lubac and Yves
Congar. These initiatives resumed after World War II, objectively aided by
the Catholic Church's determined support for the unification of Europe
but always officially rejected by the hierarchy. The French "ecumenists"
were sidelined and their work censured—all the more so because they
were suspected of colluding with the worker-priest movement, which was
condemned, in 1954, by Pius XII.

If one compares the quantity and quality of grassroots Catholic initiatives in favor of ecumenism with the firm positions rejecting it issued in
Rome, one forms the impression of a particularly bitter struggle within
the Catholic world over the proper path to follow to reach the "far ends
of the Earth," after the upheavals of the two world wars, and as decolonization was beginning. However, the acceptance by the Catholic hierarchy of the final declaration of the Seelisberg Conference in 1947, which
marked the official end of Christian anti-Judaism, signaled that the possibility of taking common positions with other Christian denominations was
no longer taboo. On December 20, 1949, the instruction *Ecclesia Catholica*
issued by the Vatican's Holy Office recognized in the aspirations to unity

of "many dissidents" the inspiration of the Holy Spirit, but it also reaffirmed the principle according to which "the only true union [takes place] by the return of the dissidents to the only true Church of Christ." The pope himself, in proclaiming in 1950 the dogma of the Assumption of the Virgin Mary, dug a bit wider the theological divide separating Catholics from other Christian denominations.

In 1952, on the other hand, the Dutch priest Johannes Willebrands was authorized to establish the Catholic Conference for Ecumenical Questions, to maintain contacts with the World Council of Churches. In 1954, there was a new distancing from this movement, and the observers to the ecumenical conference were recalled. And yet, at the same time, Angelo Roncalli, a former longtime diplomat to Sofia and Istanbul—where he encountered Orthodox patriarchs—had in his library the works of Yves Congar, though these had been condemned by the Holy Office, in particular *Disunited Christians: Principles for a Catholic Ecumenism*, which was published in 1937. This demonstrates that, in spite of official positions, the debate was continuing at the highest level.

When, in 1958, Roncalli was elected pope with the name of John XXIII, this debate led to the creation of a Secretariat for Christian Unity, headed by Willebrands and Augustin Bea, and then to the convening of a council "which the pope placed expressly in the perspective of the reunion of Christians."[48] Delegations from other Christian denominations were invited, according to Aubert, following a personal decision of the pope, "against the opinion of the majority of the Curia." In all, ninety-three observers representing twenty-eight churches took part in the work of the council.[49] The decisions of the assembly resulted, among other things, in documents on ecumenism and on relations with non-Christian denominations, followed by the creation of new administrative subdivisions, which, within the official structures of the church, were given the mission of developing dialogue with the other major religions.[50]

In January 1964, it was in this climate that Paul VI met with the patriarch of Constantinople, Athenagoras I, in Jerusalem, the first meeting of the heads of the two Christian communities since 1439; one year later, the reciprocal excommunications of 1054 were revoked. In 1966, Paul VI also met with the archbishop of Canterbury, Michael Ramsey, thus opening the way for the creation of the International Anglican-Roman Catholic Commission. In 1967, a joint Lutheran-Catholic international commission was also established. All these initiatives gave rise to regular contacts, primarily centered on theological questions, even if key obstacles lay elsewhere: on the questions of married priests, the ordination of women, and, above all, the issue of papal primacy, proclaimed unilaterally by Rome.

In his encyclical *Ut Unum Sint* (Let Them Be One, May 1995), John Paul II called for the opening of a debate on the question of papal primacy, in order "that we may seek—together, of course—the forms in which this ministry may accomplish a service of love recognized by all concerned." This more open language may explain the insistence with which Jorge Mario Bergoglio, upon his election to head the church, referred to his own role as that of the bishop of Rome, rather than as pope.

The shared horizon in which a new form of papal primacy might become possible was indicated by Benedict XVI in a speech in September 2011 to the leaders of the Evangelical Church in Germany. Responding to remarks by the pastor Nikolas Schneider, for whom churches must come together to face the challenge represented by the "suppression of God" in modern society, the pope called for a "joint commitment to the Christian *ethos* in our dealings with the world."[51] The greatest risk facing ecumenism, Benedict XVI said, would be "to yield to the pressure of secularization, and become modern by watering down the faith." He held up the example of Martin Luther, for whom "the decisive hermeneutical criterion in the interpretation of the Sacred Scripture [was] 'what promotes the cause of Christ.'"

Promoting the cause of Christ: this is the action plan that the Catholic Church proposes to the rest of Christianity. So confident is it of its means, and so sure is it of its objectives, that it can look even to the father of the Protestant Reformation to offer a testimonial to this holy alliance.

15
ALL ROADS LEAD TO ROME

There is no power but from God.

—Pope Leo XIII

It is right to obey God rather than men.

— Pope John XXIII

Laws made by men . . . must not be in contradiction with natural laws, that is with the eternal law of God.

— Pope John Paul II

HOLY IGNORANCE

Some of the same factors that led to the "return of God," beginning in the 1970s, are behind what Olivier Roy calls "holy ignorance," a phenomenon he believes has helped fuel a trend toward the creation of an "interreligious front against materialism and neo-paganism."[1]

The "tectonic movements" typical of globalization that "blur territories and identities," according to the French political scientist, invalidate the thesis of a clash of civilizations—but also of an alliance, one might add—by severing "traditional links between religions and culture."[2] Roy's "holy ignorance" is, literally, the product of this separation: it results when religions are detached from their cultural roots. Some examples of this are the movements within Sunnism calling for a return to the so-called pure Islam of the seventh century throughout the world, regardless of subsequent cultural stratifications; Shiism, which is tending to reshape itself across the broader Middle East, from Lebanon to Afghanistan, on the Iranian model; and fundamentalist evangelism, which applies the same set of beliefs, behaviors, and rituals to countries as different as the United States, Brazil, and South Korea, supplanting local cultures, religions, and traditions.

The trend toward a "holy alliance," Roy continues, goes hand in hand with "a desire for greater visibility in the public sphere that no longer takes on the form of cultural visibility but becomes a display of religious 'purity,' or of reconstructed traditions." Roy reaches the same conclusion as Peter Berger regarding the spectacular success of the various religious fundamentalists, but he comes to it by a different path: "Fundamentalism is the religious form that is most suited to globalization, because it accepts its own deculturation and makes it an instrument of its claims to universality." Further, in order to adapt to the regime of the free movement of ideas, "the religious object must appear universal, disconnected from a specific culture that has to be understood in order for the message to be grasped."[3] In the standardized universe of globalization, religions standardize themselves as well; that allows them to find areas of agreement and to meet common demands.

In Roy's view, this standardization presents two complementary aspects: an internal uniformization, via a "normalizing orthodoxy [that] absorbs and marginalizes sub-groups [and] multiple identities"; and an external uniformization, via an "orthopraxy" that leads to the adoption of certain common behaviors in the defense of similar values as well as in cultural practice—with, for example, a tendency toward "clericalization" even in religions that have never known a clergy.[4] There exists, of course, a permanent tension between an orthodoxy that is ever more inward-turned and an orthopraxy that grows ever more similar to other religious groups. Thus, Roy suggests, the spread of fundamentalism provokes both a multiplication of confrontations between religious communities and, at the same time, a multiplication of "ecumenical events, inter-faith dialogues and religious coalitions against secularization."

Roy's analysis allows us to identify three crucial features: the link between globalization and the return of religions; the growing weight of fundamentalist movements; and the coexistence of trends both toward conflict between communities and of intercommunity dialogue.[5] These three aspects are linked by their objective character: globalization determines the conditions for a return of religions in their most fundamentalist form, that is, in the form that lends itself both to conflict and to alliance.

The return of religions depends on globalization, but only to the extent that that phenomenon amplifies existential uncertainties without offering a visible path to the future. Globalization, *like any other phase of capitalist development*, produces these "tectonic movements that blur territories and identities" that Roy discusses. Still, the approximately sixty million Europeans who left the Old Continent between 1870 and 1910 to resettle in the New World—a period now recognized as the "first wave of globalization"—did not give rise to a desecularizing movement. The reason is that, at the end of their travels, these migrants met situations both worryingly uncertain and reassuring: not only extremely dynamic socioeconomic development but also a solid political context. During the "economic miracle" years of the 1950s, the protagonists of the massive rural flights in France, Italy, Spain, and Japan met similar situations: in no case was urbanization accompanied by a religious resurgence.

Since the 1970s, as a general rule (China remains an exception, even among emerging powers), the uncertainties have become more worrying to the extent that the economic outlook has ceased to be reassuring: the future often seems to offer more difficult living conditions than in the past, and this in a context in which traditional political landmarks have grown indistinct or have simply disappeared. The current situation confirms the paradigm suggested by Pippa Norris and Ronald Inglehart: "All things being equal, *the experiences of growing up in less secure societies will heighten the importance of religious values*, while conversely, *experience of more secure conditions will lessen it*."[6]

The return of religions has been marked today by the affirmation of the most conservative, orthodox, and traditionalist movements, and by the failure of liberal tendencies. The reason is linked to the characteristic cited in the previous paragraph: the uncertainties as to the present and the absence of alternative possibilities for the future mean that, as Meera Nanda asserts, "religions continue to find new work to do in secular societies *without* giving up, or even diluting, the essential religious impulse which seeks help and solace from beings with extraordinary powers who are supposed to exist beyond the confines of time and space."[7] Peter Berger is even more explicit: it is the "religious movements with beliefs and practices dripping with reactionary supernaturalism" that have "widely succeeded."[8]

The phrase "reactionary supernaturalism," which Berger borrows from the Lutheran theologian Wolfhart Pannenberg, consists of two parts: first, of supernaturalism, its permanent characteristic; and, second, its contemporary feature, which is reactionary because it "arise[s] as a reaction against the problematic of the Enlightenment."[9] It is indeed this latter aspect that forms the basis for a unity of action by different religious denominations; in its political dimension, "the reaction against the problematic of the Enlightenment," is the will, common to the dominant branches of the world's major religions, to mend the fracture that took place in the eighteenth century when, in Joseph Ratzinger's words, for "the very first time in history, a purely secular state arose, which abandoned and set aside the divine guarantee and the divine ordering of the political sector."[10]

The contradiction between the identity barriers of orthodoxy and the ecumenical openings of orthopraxy is an essential point to consider. This is a searing contradiction for the naturally fundamentalist groupings, that is, those religious branches—Evangelicalism, Salafism, Wahhabism, *Hindutva*, and ultra-Orthodox Judaism—that were born as fundamentalists and which would disappear if they ceased to be fundamentalists. To cite one example: for the ultra-Orthodox Israeli Jews of the Degel HaTorah— as for all other fundamentalists—any form of reconciliation (orthopraxy) "with secularism, which moved hundreds of thousands of children from religious education through deception and corruption," is simply impossible; while at the same time (orthodoxy), "any Jew who believes in the 13 Articles of Faith can never acquire a friendship with those who deny faith in the Creator of the world."[11] The contradiction between orthopraxy and orthodoxy is insurmountable: Degel HaTorah, which represents a fraction of the Lithuanian wing of the non-Hasidic Haredim in Israel, has condemned itself to a lone struggle against secularism, its fundamentalist ways leading it into ever deeper isolation—the group's latest split took place in October 2013.

In those religious communities within which orthodoxy and ortho-praxy manage to coexist, the contradiction is much less harrowing. There is, still, a delicate balance, which can lead to the risk of a split, as with the Anglicans, or of strident cacophony, as within the Patriarchate of Moscow. The contradiction exists as well, of course, for the Catholic Church, though it suffers less from this, for it is—let us not forget—a *complexio oppositorum*, able to accommodate any contrast within itself. Thanks to its autonomy and its long experience, it has learned to deal with any contradictions and to draw every possible advantage from them. The church is orthodox—the doctrine proclaimed by the pope represents *the* truth—but not fundamentalist—other religions also "often reflect a ray of truth."[12]

After the centrifugal forces that emerged following the Second Vatican Council, the church returned to its "normalizing orthodoxy" under the pontificate of John Paul II. By fighting against both the more liberal and the more traditionalist tendencies, it has "absorbed and marginalized the sub-groups, the multiple identities,"[13] and thus facilitated both its opening and its ecumenism. Also, owing to its nature as a *complexio oppositorum*, it has been able to fully assume its "reactionary supranaturalism" and make this the pivot of its holy alliance strategy.

THE MINORITY CHURCH

In his encyclical *Redemptoris Missio* (December 1990), John Paul II wrote that "statements about the missionary responsibility of the Church are not credible unless they are backed up by a serious commitment to a new evangelization in the traditionally Christian countries." In other words, if the church fails to strengthen its authority in tradition-ally Catholic countries, its influence in other regions of the world and among followers of other religious denominations will lose a great deal of its force.

The new evangelization, the establishment and strengthening of bonds with other Christian denominations and the collaboration with certain fringes of the Muslim and Jewish worlds, are parallel and simultaneous initiatives and should reinforce each other. The re-evangelization of tradi-tionally Christian countries is, nevertheless, the priority, in terms not just of timely urgency but also of maintaining credibility.

As for its worldwide credibility, the church of "normalizing orthodoxy" imagined by Karol Wojtyła and Joseph Ratzinger has won its bet: between 1978 and 2014 the number of seminarians in the world nearly doubled from 63,882 to 116,939; between 1990 and 2014 the number of priests worldwide rose from 403,173 to 415,792; and between 1980 and 2014 the number of permanent deacons soared from 7,654 to 44,566.[14]

These numbers, of course, hide regional disparities that at times are quite profound: the recruitment of priests has been progressing steadily in Asia, Africa, and Oceania, more slowly in the Americas, but remains in decline in Europe. At the same time, the recruitment of permanent deacons is a phenomenon essentially seen in the United States, almost 40 percent of the total, and in Europe, at 33 percent. In some of the countries that the secularist vulgate considers as irreversibly secularized—like Italy, the United States, and the United Kingdom—various studies suggest a slow but perceptible increase in participation in Catholic religious functions.[15] The future will tell whether the "Latin American method" imported by Pope Francis—getting out of the parishes and going to meet people—will succeed in bearing fruit in the other countries of the old Christian tradition.

Yet Joseph Ratzinger has written that "statistic is not one of God's measurements. . . . We're not a business operation that can look at the numbers to measure whether our policy has been successful and whether we are selling more and more."[16] Naturally, numbers are important too, as is well-known in Rome, because if that were not the case, the Vatican would not go to the trouble of publishing an annual Pontifical Yearbook, providing data on the church's ecclesiastical personnel. However, the sense of Ratzinger's remark is that the successes of the church cannot be measured exclusively in quantitative terms but should be viewed foremost by its qualitative achievements.

Ratzinger is the first high-ranking church official to take note of the fact that, on the societal level, "a widespread Christian atmosphere no longer exists."[17] Yet Ratzinger also drew some practical conclusions. It is time, he said, for the church to set aside—once and for all—its dreams of recreating an "osmosis" between Christianity and society, and to concentrate instead on building a church that compensates for its quantitative weakening through qualitative reinforcement: a "minority Church [which] will live in small, vital circles of really convinced believers."[18] Ratzinger was not, of course, recommending the minority state in which his church found itself; he was merely acknowledging a typical product of secularized societies. In another text, he showed how this handicap could be turned into an advantage: "Here we must agree with Toynbee, that the fate of a society always depends on its creative minorities. Christian believers should look upon themselves as just such a creative minority."[19]

Once elected pope, Joseph Ratzinger also made clear that quality should take precedence over quantity for the church's leaders; thus the priesthood must no longer be an expedient for obtaining a social promotion—as was often the case during the era when a widespread Christian atmosphere existed—but must instead reflect a choice that, given the difficulty of taking that step, is all the more mature and considered. According to the post-synodal apostolic exhortation *Africæ Munus*, issued on November 19, 2011: "Following Christ on the path of the priesthood entails making decisions. It is not always easy to live up to these. Christ . . . demands a radical decision which we sometimes find difficult to understand and live out." Even if the church does everything in its power to overcome the marginalization of the "religious fact," it intends, nevertheless, to profit from this trend by increasing its followers' sense of belonging and training pastors who are both more aware and more combative. As Pope Francis told the editor of *La Repubblica* in October 2013, "Personally, I believe that the fact of being a minority can even constitute a strength."[20]

It is largely thanks to this choice of identity consolidation and redefinition—orthodoxy *plus* orthopraxy—that the church again became a point of reference for its faithful, first, and then for all those who "seek freedom from the anguish of our human condition," to quote the *Nostra Ætate*. However, that does not mean that every problem has been resolved; quite the contrary. Further, the most difficult problem to resolve, paradoxically, deals with its core leadership. The leadership circle is a small group that is steeped, according to Massimo Franco, in a "long chain of conflicts, maneuvers [and] betrayals in the shadow of St. Peter's Dome . . . a legacy of hostility, of personal grudges, of factional struggles [and] of economic vendettas with legal implications," which, in the end, claimed an illustrious victim: Pope Benedict XVI himself.[21]

The "singular tribal structure" that Franco denounces was not, however, born during the pontificate of Joseph Ratzinger. The latter, during the *Via Crucis* of Holy Week in 2005, had minced no words: "So many stains in the Church, and particularly among those who, in the priesthood, should belong to her totally! So much pride and self-sufficiency!" When he was elected pope one month later, Benedict XVI had invited the faithful to pray for him, "that I may not flee for fear of the wolves." Nevertheless, the evidence strongly suggests he failed in his efforts to tame the wolves.

In fact, since the beginning of the church's history, signs of "conflicts, maneuvers, [and] betrayals" have always been part of life in the shadow of St. Peter's Dome, even long before the dome itself was built. Perhaps, because of a life's journey that was more intellectual than political, Joseph Ratzinger was too naive; or perhaps, to the contrary, he was not naive at all but wanted, through the spectacular gesture of his resignation, to accelerate the attempted solution of the problem of a church leadership that was so inwardly turned and self-referential that it bordered on the autistic. This "self-referentiality" did not pose a serious problem during the time when the church had the advantage of being a state religion and when its chief concern was, as Gramsci wrote, "to defend . . . the privileges that, it proclaims, are the bequest of its own divine essence."[22] However, it did become a substantial obstacle as the church began having to struggle against a secularized ambient atmosphere and found itself confronting other cultures and other religions even on its own territory, and sought to establish fruitful alliances with these groups in order to counter secularization.

Thus Benedict XVI's successor was elected with the specific mandate of throwing his full weight into a far-reaching cleanup operation. It may seem strange that some of those who themselves are compromised by the "hostility, personal grudges, factional struggles and economic vendettas" should now throw their weight behind someone charged with eliminating these "stains," that is, with draining the water from the pool in which they swim. Yet one should never forget that, as *Limes* observed in an op-ed of 1993: "What for a state is the national interest, for the Holy See is the Catholic interest." The notion of national interest suggests that differing interests within a country agree on measures that, while requiring some parties to give something up, will lead over the long term to advantages benefiting all. Before the conclave that elected Jorge Mario Bergoglio, the cardinals reached agreement to take a step backward in order to put the entire Catholic Church in a position to take one larger step forward.

In every country, from the moment when different private interests identify a national interest, each of them begins pulling in their own direction, trying to make others pay the highest price in the sharing of responsibilities. Within the church, exactly the same dynamic prevails. Thus one should not prejudge the results of Francis's attempt—as he outlined in his speech to the 65th General Assembly of Italian bishops in May 2013—to jolt the church's pastors out of "the torpor of laziness, pettiness and defeatism . . . and to burn away [their] sadness, impatience and rigidity." What is certain is that the Argentinian pope's strongest ally in this initiative is precisely the strategic prospect of the "holy alliance."

THE "NATURAL MORAL LAW"

During his meeting with the Jewish community of Rome in October 2013, Francis said: "Among the many things that can unite us is our common witness to the truth of the 'Ten Commandments,' the Decalogue, as a solid foundation and source of life for our society, which is so disoriented by an extreme pluralism of choice and direction, and marked by a relativism which leads to no longer having sure and solid points of reference."

These words remind us of the point of convergence that the church proposes to other religions: the "natural moral law"—the Decalogue—as opposed to "relativism"—the possibility of choosing among different moral doctrines, or refusing them all. The *Catechism of the Catholic Church* recognizes that several moral doctrines exist but holds that only one of them is "natural"; it expresses the "original moral sense which enables man to discern by reason the good and the evil, the truth and the lie." The political implication of this idea is clear. As Benedict XVI proclaimed in the encyclical *Spe Salvi* (November 2007): "Power" must open itself to the "saving forces of faith, to differentiation between good and evil"; the alternative is that man "becomes a threat for him and for creation."

For this thesis to become the binding cement of collaboration with other religious denominations, three conditions must first be fulfilled: society must be truly "disoriented" and thus in search of "sure and solid points of reference"; society must accept, or at least not contest, the thesis of natural moral law; and other religions must share the same definition and contents of natural moral law, at least in its broad terms.

The first two conditions are linked: with few exceptions, the thesis of a natural moral law is not contested because it makes it possible to give meaning, direction, and theoretical order to a society that is losing its direction, meaning, and order. What is accepted, or at least not contested, is not so much any specific content of the proposition advanced by the church as the very principle of a moral law, capable of guiding society, particularly in the absence of any alternative proposition. In general, secular thought, incapable of finding meaning in the contradictions of modernity, has not limited itself to simply declining to propose an alternative moral doctrine but has sought to give this renunciation a "democratic" motivation, by entrusting each individual to choose his or her own moral code—or not to choose any at all.

It is in this state of moral entropy that the church has managed to plant its flag almost without opposition. Still, there is no shortage of reasons to feed doubts about its "natural moral law."

In its *Catechism*, the church explains that the natural moral law "is *universal* in its precepts and its authority extends to all men," and that it is "*immutable* and permanent throughout the variations of history; it subsists under the flux of ideas and customs." The coexistence between *universality* and *immutability* may seem problematic at times. For example, the *immutable* character of the "the primacy of the husband with regard to the wife and children, the ready subjection of the wife and her willing obedience," as prescribed in the name of natural law by Pius XI in his encyclical *Casti Connubii* (1930), could provide some common ground with large sectors of Islam, Hinduism, Judaism, and Orthodox Christianity, and of nearly all the Anglicans of Africa and Asia; but it is unlikely that it could be recognized as *universally* acceptable.

The fact—seemingly banal but only rarely invoked in discussions of natural moral law—is that nothing is immutable and permanent. As Roy puts it, "A religion's normativeness is always subject to revision," but also "the definition of what is anathema is fluid." Christianity, Roy explains, has known several historical incarnations: a "sect" in the Roman Empire; the official religion of that same empire; a cult adopted and adapted by Germanic, Hungarian, and Slavic tribes; organizer of the Crusades; official motivation of the *conquistadores*; and missionary vanguard of European colonization. As regards moral mutability, Roy reminds us that the condemnation of birth-control practices is very recent, "after a period of blame mixed with relative indulgence"; and that "pedophilia in the Church," though always condemned, was for a very long time "treated as a minor concern" and only now is viewed as "unacceptable."[23] The death penalty was only officially abolished in the Vatican in 1969; but the *Catechism* states that when "the guilty party's identity and responsibility have been fully determined, the traditional teaching of the Church does not exclude recourse to the death penalty."

There is no shortage of examples. Divorce has not always been vigorously rejected. The Christian emperors did not abolish it, and the Byzantine emperor Justinian—who was behind the large-scale persecutions and forced conversions of pagans—even expanded the accepted conditions. Further, Charlemagne, according to Edward Gibbon, had "nine wives or concubines, the various indulgence of meaner or more transient amours, the multitude of his bastards whom he bestowed on the church, and the long celibacy and licentious manners of his daughters, whom the father was suspected of loving with too fond a passion," without being sanctioned by the church.[24] According to James Kent, it was toward the end of the first millennium that laws on divorce became more restrictive, at a time when the stability of the nuclear family had become a condition for the economic survival of the peasants. Yet it was not until the Lateran Council of 1215 that marriage was proclaimed a sacrament; while Kent contends that this decision was taken only in 1563, at the Council of Trent.[25]

To have any credibility today, natural moral law would have to wish away many practices and divine commandments found in the Old Testament. To mention only a few of the best-known: polygamy, practiced by Abraham, Jacob, and especially Solomon, who had 700 wives, accepted and even regulated by God himself (Exodus, 21; Deuteronomy, 21; Deuteronomy, 17); the obligation to "not leave alive anything that breathes . . . in the cities of the nations the Lord your God is giving you as an inheritance" (Deuteronomy, 20); and the injunction to stone adulterers (Deuteronomy, 22), apostates (Deuteronomy, 13), those who work on the day of rest (Numbers, 15), blasphemers (Leviticus, 24), women who pass themselves off as virgins but who are not (Deuteronomy, 22), and even "stubborn and rebellious" children (Deuteronomy, 21). Such measures may have had social relevance in the eighth or seventh century BCE, but today they are considered as unacceptable.

If the thesis of natural moral law is rarely contested by secular observers, a fortiori it is not in other religious circles. In the three "religions of the Book," there are of course extreme fundamentalist minorities, sometimes quite vociferous, convinced that all the sanctions provided in the Old Testament constitute God's law and should be applied to the letter. Sometimes these minorities are quite large: according to a Gallup survey of 2011, for instance, 30 percent of Americans "interpret the Bible literally, saying it is the actual word of God."[26] As a general rule, however, believers do seek "sure and solid points of reference," rules and moral codes that may sometimes be strict—especially as regards family matters—but which are not barbaric. The Catholic Church has, in a sense, "cleaned house" for the other religions, by drawing from the Bible only those precepts that can be presented today as "naturally" moral, while forgetting those that have become unacceptable. But the church has done much more: on the basis of these principles, it has laid out some common objectives toward which the social and political actions of believers should be directed, whatever their religion—those that Joseph Ratzinger had called the "non-negotiable values."

In 2002 the Congregation for the Doctrine of the Faith, headed at the time by Ratzinger, had published a *Doctrinal Note on Some Questions Regarding the Participation of Catholics in Political Life*. In this text, Ratzinger was reaffirming that there is indeed a "moral law rooted in the nature of the human person, which must govern our understanding of man, the common good and the state." He continued: "Democracy must be based on the true and solid foundation of non-negotiable ethical principles, which are the underpinning of life in society." These principles are the rejection of abortion and euthanasia; the protection and advancement of the family and of traditional marriage; and a freedom of education—that is, the equivalence of public education and private religious education.

This was a sort of common platform, based on precise and absolute "non-negotiable" demands, toward which the followers of other religions could converge. This was seen recently in France when the various religions became near united in their opposition to state-sanctioned same-sex marriages. Yet the possibilities for this struggle over "natural morality" are more ambitious: as Alberto Melloni writes, "Catholicism's commitment is not measured in results or problems but rather in the willingness to affirm one's right/duty to express oneself against the cultures of separation and the 'religion' of secularism." Moreover, Melloni adds, "outside the Church, as well, there is nostalgia for a time when a specialized agency was charged with unknotting the tangle of values."[27] Eric Hanson describes this prospect clearly: the church, he says, aims to become a "primary ethical broker" between society and the political world.[28] In doing so, it can pull together similar forces from other religious families, among whom the law of God takes priority over the laws of man.

THE "ETHIC OF DUTY"

In *The Clash of Civilizations*, Samuel Huntington asserted that, in understanding the decline of the West, one should assign moral factors more weight than economic or demographic factors: "increases in antisocial behavior," "family decay," "general weakening of the work ethic," and the "rise of the cult of personal indulgence." These are, in Huntington's eyes, some of the trends that gave "rise to the assertions of moral superiority by Muslims and Asians."[29]

The Catholic Church shares Huntington's analysis of the relative weight of critical factors, but, as for the "clash of civilizations," it comes to quite different conclusions. The clash that most concerns it takes place in the world not *vertically*, meaning between nations and blocs of nations, but *horizontally*, which is to say between different ethical models within each nation or bloc of nations. The moral horizon that the church proposes to the world, and which it finds in other religious communities, is that of the "ethic of duty," as opposed to the "drift to individualism."

Benedict XVI devoted the most passionate lines of his social encyclical *Caritas in Veritate* (2009) to the "duty of universal solidarity. . . . Many people today would claim that they owe nothing to anyone, except to themselves. They are concerned only with their rights," he wrote, adding that "an overemphasis on rights leads to a disregard for duties." Along the same lines, Pope Francis, in the first lines of his exhortation *Evangelii Gaudium*, asserted that "whenever our interior life becomes caught up in its own interests and concerns, there is no longer room for others."

These few lines demonstrate that the church justifies its position not through traditional morality but rather through an analysis of the seemingly irresolvable internal contradictions of our society. Structurally based on individualism, capitalist society in the end separates human beings from the only true *nature* that defines them: that of social animals—that is, animals incapable of surviving in isolation from one another. As was the case with the encyclical *Humanæ Vitæ*, to the church, in the words of Joseph Ratzinger, "falls the role of prophetic contradiction." The church, he explained, "may never simply align herself with the zeitgeist. The Church must address the vices and perils of the time."[30] It is thus not a question of *opposing* modernity, but of offering a *different way*, not allowing oneself to be dragged along by modernity, but rather dominating it, and *steering* it.[31]

In 2010 the "Vaticanist" Paolo Rodari wrote: "On bioethical issues, [the Catholic Church] is more in tune with the Anglicans and the Orthodox than with the progressives."[32] For Hilarion Alfeyev, external relations director of the Moscow Patriarchate, a series of specific questions—abortion, surrogate motherhood, fetal therapy, homosexuality, and so on—can form a basis of mutual understanding in order to oppose, together, "a completely atheistic and secularized Europe, where God is excluded from society and religion is confined to the private sphere." Writing in *L'Osservatore Romano* in 2010, the Russian Patriarch Kirill I criticized "pagan anthropocentrism, [which] appeared in European culture at the time of the Renaissance," cultivated by "elements of Protestant theology and of philosophical thought of Jewish origin."[33] Kirill I goes on to say that this culminated in the philosophy of the Enlightenment and the French Revolution. Further, he concluded that this philosophy finally became institutionalized, namely, the "refusal of the normative signification of tradition." The identical conclusion had been reached by Joseph Ratzinger, who attributed to the French Revolution the end of the "divine guarantee and the divine ordering of the political sector."[34]

Since the nomination in 2004 of a homosexual bishop in New Hampshire, the Anglican Communion has been virtually divided into two camps: a considerable number of prelates from Africa, Asia, Australia, Latin America, and certain communities in the United States and the United Kingdom did not take part in the latest Lambeth Conference because, in the shorthand used by the *Economist*, "they would not share the communion cup with gay-friendly Americans."[35] Another article in the same issue explains that, in reality, "only a small minority in America's well-groomed Episcopal churches or the Church of England's underpopulated pews finds clerical homosexuality non-negotiably bad nowadays." To the contrary, "many in Africa and other parts of the 'Global South' do," and, moreover, they view "efforts to enforce liberal values as 'colonial.'"[36]

The question of homosexuality—and a fortiori of homosexuality among the clergy—is much more delicate than it may appear to observers from certain countries that have only recently become gay-friendly. If the great majority of Europeans and Americans now view homosexuality as socially acceptable, the perception in the rest of the world is very different, as one can see in table 15.1.

Any major religious organization—including especially the Catholic Church—that aspires to increase its global presence and influence must

TABLE 15.1 Level of Acceptance of Homosexuality in Selected Countries, 2007–2013

Country	2007	2013	Change
France	83%	77%	–6%
Spain	82%	88%	6%
United Kingdom	71%	76%	5%
Italy	65%	74%	9%
Mexico	60%	61%	1%
United States	49%	60%	11%
Israel	38%	40%	2%
South Korea	18%	39%	21%
Russia	18%	16%	–2%
China	17%	21%	4%
Turkey	14%	9%	–5%
Ghana	4%	3%	–1%
Nigeria	2%	1%	–1%
Egypt	1%	3%	2%

Note: Numbers are based on affirmative responses to the question, "Should homosexuality be accepted?"
Source: Pew Global Attitudes Project, Washington, D.C., March–April 2013.

take into account the social and political constraints in traditional societies. Following a joint appeal by about twenty Hindu, Muslim, and Christian religious associations, the Supreme Court of India, on December 11, 2013, reestablished article 377 of the penal code punishing "carnal intercourse against the order of nature"—a crime first introduced into Indian law by the British in 1860. Dominic Emmanuel, director and spokesman of the Catholic Archdiocese of Delhi, declared that "the verdict re-established the law of nature."[37] India, it is important to note, is the country in which the Catholic Church has enjoyed the highest rate of priest recruitment in the world.

The disproportionate importance held by the issue of homosexuality within Anglicanism can be explained more by its internal implications than by the question itself; indeed, the appointment in 2004 of the afore-mentioned New Hampshire bishop cast a sudden light on the incompat-ibility between "conservatives" and "liberals" that goes far beyond their differing views on homosexuality. According to Giulio Meotti, the former group—the "Anglo-Catholic and evangelical branch"—numbers "eleven thousand priests and 291 bishops—of a total of about 780—and represents 35 million Anglicans in the world—of a total of 80 million."[38] Its leader, Meotti writes, is the bishop of Rochester, Michael Nazir-Ali, a former stu-dent at Saint Patrick's Catholic secondary school in Karachi, who became an Anglican at the age of twenty.

In his book on the "triple jeopardy for the West"—which he identifies as aggressive secularism, radical Islamism, and multiculturalism – Nazir-Ali mentions homosexuality only once, to reaffirm his opposition to same-sex marriages.[39] Yet he is behind the concept of "founding ideals," which is very close in both form and content to that of Benedict XVI's "non-negotiable values." Interviewed by Meotti in 2008, the Anglican bishop of Rochester praised the sovereign pontiff of the time as a "clearly evangelical pope" and criticized those in the Enlightenment who "rejected Christianity, lead-ing to the excesses of the French Revolution . . . and a bloodbath in France." For Nazir-Ali, "once the Christian consensus was destroyed, nothing else replaced it, other than an infinite self-indulgence."[40]

Nazir-Ali considers multiculturalism and radical Islam as two dangers for the West, on the same level as secularism, but this does not make him hostile to Islam; quite the contrary. For him, radical Islam represents a break with Muslim tradition; and, despite this break, it "uses tradition to unleash conflict within Islam and toward the outside." Nazir-Ali considers, nonetheless, that it is possible—indeed necessary—to hold dialogue with "cultural" Muslims, Sufis, for example, "in the name of the common vision of God's love for man."

At a time when Islam has become a sort of exemplar of the return of religion to the public sphere, many of those who want religion to move in this direction end up referring, for one reason or another, to the

Muslim example. Thus within the Patriarchate of Moscow, Arch-priest Vsevolod Chaplin, while a fierce critic of the dialogue between civilizations, did not hesitate to single out Chechnya as a model of moral austerity, writing: "Numerous norms of Islamic law are in effect in Chechnya, in Ingushetia or in Dagestan, and it would be a mistake . . . to say that this is necessarily a bad thing."[41]

Along the same lines, Baruch Efrati, a rabbi in the West Bank community of Efrat, allows that while Islam is mistaken about the prophets, it is a religion that is "relatively honest: it educates a bit more for a stable life of marriage and creation, where there is certain modesty and respect for God." He believes that Europe is becoming Islamicized and that this is "a good thing," so long as it does "not harm the people of Israel."[42]

If Efrati is personally hostile to any suggestion of contacts with Christianity, which he considers idolatrous, the notion of an alliance of religions has many defenders within Judaism.

Among those is Jonathan Sacks, a former chief rabbi of the United Hebrew Congregations of the Commonwealth, who speaks a language that is very close to that of the Catholic Church: "You cannot defend a civilization on the basis of moral relativism," he said at a conference in 2009.[43] Freedom of conscience, he went on, was developed in the seventeenth century, "not on moral relativism but on moral absolutes: the non-negotiable dignity of the human person, the sanctity of human life, the imperative of conscience," that is, on what is known as the "Judeo-Christian heritage." For Sacks, "the idea that you can lose the moral foundations of freedom without eventually losing freedom itself is simply absurd."

Joseph Weiler, the former president of the European University Institute in Florence, is one of the organizers of the Cairo Meeting, which brings together Jews, Christians, and Muslims for a "dialogue among cultures." Weiler is in perfect accord with the Catholic Church and with all those who believe that conflicts in today's world are due not to an excess of religion but rather to an excess of secularism. Dialogue can only succeed, Weiler said in 2011, on the basis of "a common ground, without putting differences aside, but taking into consideration the importance of the religious factor."[44]

This common ground was clearly staked out by the protagonists of the March 2011 meeting between the Grand Rabbinate of Israel and the commission of the Catholic Church in charge of relations with Jews: in order for the gains of modern society to be "sustainable," according to their final document, they must be placed into "a higher anthropological and spiritual framework that takes into account 'the common good,' which finds its expression in the religious foundation of moral duties." In other words, what is needed is a "specialized agency charged with unknotting the tangle of values."

THE COMMON ASPIRATION TO SHARIA

In classic Islam, the function of the ulemas consisted, at least in theory, of guaranteeing—that is, both certifying and ensuring—the conformity of political power with the law of God: a caliph who did not respect the law of God was no longer worthy to govern. The proposal to make religions the "primary ethical broker" between society and politics seems to be based on the model of the classic ulemas; it should thus ring familiar in Muslim ears. Nonetheless, over the past century, many Muslims have evolved politically in a direction opposite to that taken by the Catholic Church. The more the church recognized the *power of statelessness*, the more the theories calling for the establishment of an Islamic state seemed to proliferate.

The church knows by experience that the risks of a theocracy are much greater today than are its advantages. Religious parties, even when they do not seek the establishment of a theocratic regime, are exposed to some of those same risks; in the case of the Islamist parties in countries that witnessed the "Arab Spring," they were weighed down by their inexperience, by the complexity of the problems they had to face, by the political immaturity of the emerging social sectors that they represented, and, above all, by an extremely troubled international situation. Their failure can lead to three possible outcomes: a weakening of their credibility, without necessarily harming Islam; a negative impact on the supposed moral superiority of the religion; or a revival of the most extremist, even overtly jihadist, movements. As a general rule, the more a party or a regime insists it is based on a religion, the more its failures risk negatively affecting the religion.

The risk of damaging the credibility of religion itself is certainly the risk most feared by religious leaders. That is what occurred in Iran. Religious sentiment in Iran—82.5 percent of Iranians say that religion occupies an important place in their lives—is the lowest in the entire Middle East.[45] Moreover, a similar survey found that Iran's population is less religious than a broad range of different countries, for example, Cambodia (96 percent), Philippines (95.5 percent), Romania (92 percent), Turkey (89.5 percent), Brazil (86.5 percent), and South Africa (84.5 percent), and even the state of Mississippi (85 percent).[46] Many Iranians have "turned away from Shiite convictions and embraced atheism, skepticism, Sufism, Sunni Islam, the Bahai faith, evangelical Christianity, Zoroastrianism, Buddhism, and New Age and Latin American mystical trends," according to the Shiite theologian Mehdi Khalaji. But, he adds, the loss of credibility of the theocratic regime provoked an even more unexpected—almost unbelievable—effect: "the rise of Persian Salafism," a movement that considers Shiism "superstitious," "heretical," even out-and-out "apostate."[47] Finally, its official slogans notwithstanding, Iran is also the least anti-American country in the Middle East; Robert Kaplan recalls that after the September 11 attacks, "Iranians held vigils for the victims in the streets of Tehran, even if crowds in parts of the Arab world cheered on the attacks."[48]

However, the divide that has opened between society and the official ideology of the Iranian regime is evident not only on the political level. The government of the ayatollahs has been unable to prevent a "new bourgeoisie with middle-class values" from following the universal path toward secularization.[49] This trend to secularization is visible not only in the dress and clothing expedients being adopted to get around the proscriptions of Islamic modesty, or in the numbers of plastic surgeries—the highest in the world and proportionally seven times the level of the United States; secularization is also evidenced by other more significant, and measurable, social behaviors.[50] For example, the decline in the population fertility rate from 3.9 percent in 1986 to 1.2 percent in 2012; the rise in the average age at marriage from twenty to twenty-eight for men and from twenty-four to thirty for women; and the tripling of the number of divorces, from 50,000 in 2000 to 150,000 in 2010.[51] Today one marriage in 3.76 ends in divorce, a rate "almost comparable to Britain," according to Afshin Shahi.

The aspiration of making religion into a pillar of social and political life is not unique to Muslims. According to a survey by Gallup in 2007, 46 percent of Americans would like to make the Bible a source of legislation, and for 9 percent of them it should be *the only* source of legislation.[52] In 1999, 53 percent of Poles favored giving religion greater influence over politics.[53]

In 2009 Yaacov Neeman, the Israeli minister of justice, declared that Halakha—rabbinical jurisprudence—should become part of the legal foundation of the Hebrew state because "the Torah gives the complete response to every question we face."[54] Tariq Ali has pointed out that fundamentalist religious parties receive proportionally fewer votes in Pakistan than in Israel.[55] In Sri Lanka, the *Economist* notes, former president Mahinda Rajapaksa had established Buddhist "vice-and-virtue squads" in order to achieve his plan for creating "a society with good values and ethics."[56]

It is certain that in almost every part of the world there is—more or less widespread, more or less clearly—a tendency to turn to religion to resolve, or at least alleviate, the numerous complex problems posed by contemporary society, and which traditional political parties seem incapable of dealing with. We might call this a "common aspiration to sharia," that is, to a superior form of justice able to restore balance amid our everyday injustices, whatever the faith of those who worship. As Sadakat Kadri notes, "Every faith community in the United States, from the Amish to the Zoroastrians, has equivalent ways of doing right by God. The only difference is that Muslims call their quest the sharia."[57]

The question of whether God's law precedes that of man is asked, according to Noah Feldman, in the same terms as a problem raised by the constitutions of liberal states: "Americans," he writes, "have never fully resolved the question of whether the inalienable rights of life, liberty and property pre-exist the U.S. Constitution or derive from it."[58] While leaving the sort of room for ambiguity that is useful in any negotiation, the Catholic Church has provided its own answer to the question: a response that seems capable of bringing some order to the common aspirations for sharia.

ALL ROADS LEAD TO ROME

In its aforementioned *Doctrinal Note on Some Questions Regarding the Participation of Catholics in Political Life* (2002), the Congregation for the Doctrine of the Faith asserted that secularism must be understood as the "rightful autonomy of the political or civil sphere from that of religion and the Church—*but not from that of morality*." In their *Catechism* (1992), Catholic authorities had, however, explained that "natural moral law . . . hinges upon the desire for God and submission to Him, who is the source and judge of all that is good." We can thus infer that, if the civil and political sphere must not be autonomous from the moral sphere, and if the latter is based on our submission to God, ergo the civil and political sphere must be based on submission to God, which is to say, submission to the Catholic Church, knowing that "the Church is competent in her magisterium to interpret the natural moral law," as Pope Paul VI, among others, reminded us in his encyclical *Humanæ Vitæ* (1968).

By reaffirming the need for the subordination of political authority to religious authority, the church merely confirms its raison d'être. As discussed earlier, the structural cause of the separation between the Latin and Greek Churches lay precisely in their differing relationships with political power in the two parts of the Roman Empire. In the Greek East, where power was solid, the church submitted and accepted a "subsidiary" role—Caesaropapism. In the Latin West, where political power—both central and local—was ebbing, the church progressively replaced it. In the celebrated definition of Thomas Hobbes in his classic *Leviathan*, "Papacy is no other than the ghost of the deceased Roman Empire, sitting crowned upon the grave thereof."

In fact, the real founding act of the Catholic Church goes back to the decision in 800 CE to proclaim Charlemagne the emperor of the West. The pope's gesture of placing the crown on the king's head, even if it did not reflect the true power relationship, symbolically marked the reversal of the Byzantine ritual of proskynesis, in which the spiritual leader would prostrate himself before the Basileus. All the subsequent history of the Catholic Church, from the humiliation of Holy Roman Emperor Henry IV at Canossa to the struggle with the pro-Soviet Hungarian government, and including the Gallicanism of Napoleon, is an endless "investitures controversy," that is, an unending struggle to affirm and consolidate the primacy of religious power over political power.

In the encyclical *Diuturnum* (1881), Leon XIII quoted Saint Paul as saying that "there is no power but from God," and that "the prince is the minister of God." This is why Pius IX, in 1874, according to *La Civiltà Cattolica*, had urged a group of French pilgrims visiting Rome to do away as soon as possible with a "great affliction which plagues contemporary society: this is called universal suffrage." Nor did the doubts concerning the wisdom of popular sovereignty change quickly: for John XXIII, as outlined in the encyclical *Pacem in Terris* (1963), "It is of course impossible to accept the theory which professes to find the original and single source of civic rights and duties, of the binding force of the constitution, and of a government's right to command, in the mere will of human beings, individually or collectively." He continued: "Since the right to command is required by the moral order and has its source in God, it follows that, if civil authorities pass laws or command anything opposed to the moral order and consequently contrary to the will of God, neither the laws made nor the authorizations granted can be binding on the consciences of the citizens, since God has more right to be obeyed than men." John Paul II confirmed, in turn, that "the law established by man, by parliaments and by every other human legislator must not contradict the natural law, that is to say, the eternal law of God."[59] As outlined by Benedict XVI in a speech to the International Congress on Natural Moral Law on February 12, 2007, "No law made by man can override the norm written by the Creator without society becoming dramatically wounded in what constitutes its basic foundation." The church, Pope Francis wrote in his *Evangelii Gaudium*, "proposes in a clear way the fundamental values of human life and convictions which can then find expression in political activity."

This conviction that religion is the final—and only—recourse for those who aspire to peace and justice not only applies to the internal political life of each country but holds as well, and even more surely, to the global system of international relations.

After World War I, in the encyclical *Pacem Dei Munus* (1920), Benedict XV said he was prepared to support the League of Nations, so long as its members were united "under the Christian law." Pius XI, vexed by the unfavorable response to this condition, pointed out in the encyclical *Ubi Arcano* (1922) that "no merely human institution of today can be as successful in devising a set of international laws which will be in harmony with world conditions as the Middle Ages were in the possession of that true League of Nations, Christianity."

In 1945 the church decided to move through more discreet channels. According to the Jesuit Joseph S. Rossi, it managed to place its own "consultants" into the American delegation to the United Nations in an effort to "'catholicize' the UN Charter." However, following what Rossi calls "the UNCIO's failure to mold the UN in the spirit of Pope Pius XII and his predecessor Benedict XV," the pope turned a cold shoulder to the new international body, to the point of mentioning it publicly only twice between 1948 and 1956.[60] The Holy See gained permanent-observer status at the UN only in 1964.

Pacem in Terris was the first encyclical addressed not just to Catholics but "to all men of goodwill." This is perhaps why Pope John XXIII made a point of confirming, from its very first lines, the traditional position of the church: "Peace on Earth—which man throughout the ages has so longed for and sought after—can never be established, never guaranteed, except by the diligent observance of the divinely established order."

Nearly fifty years later, in his encyclical *Caritas in Veritate* (2009), Benedict XVI aligned himself explicitly with the *Pacem in Terris*, writing: "There is urgent need of a true *World Political Authority,* as my predecessor Blessed John XXIII indicated some years ago." The adjective "true," as well as the capital letters and italics reserved for the phrase "*World Political Authority*"—which, of course, had not yet been established, since there was still "urgent need" of it—signify clearly that, in the eyes of the Catholic Church, the United Nations, or any other organization claiming to exercise supranational power, is no more than a global authority by default, incapable of making "*a commitment to securing authentic integral human development inspired by the values of charity in truth*" and "conditioned by the balance of power among the strongest nations." In effect, it lacks the essential characteristic that is "outlined" in the *Pacem in Terris*: "Representatives of the State have no power to bind men in conscience, unless their own authority is tied to God's authority, and is a participation in it." Only on this condition, Benedict XVI continued, would it be possible to realize "the construction of a social order that at last conforms to the moral order, to the interconnection between moral and social spheres, and to the link between politics and the economic and civil spheres."[61] Pope Francis evoked the same concept in *Evangelii Gaudium*, borrowing the words of Paul VI: "Peace . . . is fashioned by efforts directed day after day towards the establishment of the ordered universe willed by God."

In their letter of October 13, 2006, to Benedict XVI, thirty-eight leading Muslim personages declared that the pope "is arguably the single most influential voice" in helping advance the dialogue among religions.[62] This influence—explicitly recognized or not—is beyond question: the pope is the only religious authority who speaks to international assemblies and before whom heads of state bow, not by virtue of the importance others accord him, as is the case with the Dalai Lama and others, but because of the importance of the institution he represents. He may decide to refer to himself more modestly as the *bishop of Rome*, and he may even go so far as to accept formal equality with the heads of other Christian communities; he will remain, nonetheless, the *primus inter pares*, endowed with a greater authority that is real, not just symbolic. Going forward, he can speak in the name of all Christianity, and even of other religions, once he embodies the "common aspiration to sharia." Benedict XVI did precisely this in the *Caritas in Veritate*: "The Christian religion and other religions can offer their contribution to development *only if God has a place in the public realm*, specifically in regard to its cultural, social, economic, and particularly its political dimensions."

That is the goal of the holy alliance.

CONCLUSION

RELIGION AND INTERNATIONAL POLITICS
IN THE TWENTY-FIRST CENTURY

If a man knows not to which port he sails, no wind is favorable.

—Seneca the Younger

Over at least the past four decades, religion has regained a place in the public scene. All evidence would indicate that this trend will continue in international relations, as in other areas. In the months that this book was being written, religion was used as a pretext to explain, justify, or glorify political and military confrontations in Mali, Nigeria, the Central African Republic, Kenya, Iraq, Myanmar, Sri Lanka, India, and even Ukraine. It has been a central feature of the "Arab Spring," and it continues to play a dramatic role in those countries where revolutions have been abortive: Syria, Egypt, Yemen, and Bahrain. Libya, for its part, remains a hotbed of potential trouble for the entire region, where mujahidin—who are as zealous as they are heavily and richly armed—are ready to place their capital of "holy wars" at the service of one interest or another, either local or international.

It has taken some time for the return of religions as political actors to be considered as not just a curiosity of history but a general trend. Nonetheless, even today, in some countries where the secularization process has gone on for centuries, the dominant opinion is that the "Return of God" is of no direct concern; that it essentially affects only emerging countries lacking in solid political traditions. Some even see it as a matter of interest only for Muslim-majority countries.

The failure to understand the universal character of this desecularizing movement is particularly acute in France, where the belief prevails that the 1905 law on the separation of church and state settled the matter once and for all. The impacts of this misunderstanding—based on a quasi-Pavlovian legalistic tropism—can be almost laughable. During their respective electoral campaigns of 2007 and 2012, Nicolas Sarkozy and François Hollande both addressed the 1905 law of separation of state and church: the former, to suggest an easing of its terms, with the idea of appealing to Catholic authorities and believers; the latter, to propose that it be engraved in bronze in the constitution, with the idea of winning over the supposedly Jacobinist and anticlerical masses. It appears that neither candidate had read a document from the Conference of French Bishops of 2005, in which they expressed the wish that the 1905 law not be modified: "It would appear wise to us to not touch this equilibrium through which our country has been able to achieve a certain calming and healing." Neither Sarkozy nor Hollande carried out his plans; had they done so, they would have obtained a result precisely the opposite of what they intended.

In politics, as in many other domains, such flawed assessments often lead to misfortune, with more or less serious results. In Hollande's case, pursuing a frontal confrontation with the church over same-sex marriages produced three undesirable forms of collateral damage: it allowed the church to test its own ability to mobilize, proving again that it was among the strongest forces—if not *the* strongest—in France; it gave the church the opportunity to consolidate the Conference of Religious Leaders in France—founded on November 23, 2010, it includes Orthodox, Protestant, Muslim, Jewish, and Buddhist dignitaries—around a common objective; and, it made France—according to a Gallup survey in the spring of 2013—the only Western country where homosexual relations were considered much less acceptable in 2013 when compared to 2007. Moreover, Hollande's central objective with this operation—to burnish his image as a statesman—also failed, as his public approval ratings continued their inexorable descent until setting a negative record among all the presidents of France's Fifth Republic.

<hr />

In the United States, it is now nearly impossible to run for almost any elective office without putting one's solid religious credentials on display. John McCain, the failed Republican presidential candidate in 2008, learned this lesson the hard way: suspected of being lukewarm on the matter, he felt obliged to try to offset this major weakness by choosing as his running mate a fundamentalist evangelical heavyweight, Sarah Palin. In the same election campaign, Barack Obama broke two records that proved decisive in his ultimate victory: he spent more money than any candidate in United States history, and he mentioned God more frequently than any major party candidate before him. Indeed, it was Obama who, in reversing the principle enunciated by John F. Kennedy—"I believe in an America where the separation of church and state is absolute"—asserted in 2006 that "secularists are wrong when they ask believers to leave their religion at the door before entering into the public square."

The interest for politicians in this new religious "Great Awakening" goes beyond the possibility of exploiting it for immediate political benefits, whether electoral or military. One critical front that has opened up with the acceleration and intensification of international competition has been that of social services: with the exception of a few emerging countries, nearly every country in the world has been forced to trim its financing and administration of public services in areas ranging from health and education to disaster management, culture, or even sports. In nearly every part of the world, religious groups and institutions have been called on to fill the breach with their networks of social assistance and protection. According to research conducted at Georgetown University, in 2000, the latest figures available, the Catholic Church alone operated some 80,000 hospitals and clinics, 14,000 retirement homes, nearly 9,000 orphanages, just over 1,000 universities, and some 125,000 elementary, middle, and high schools. If one considers that even in highly secularized France the number of Catholic institutions of learning has grown from 8,847 in 2010 to 9,005 in 2012, one can easily imagine how rapidly Catholic social services are developing in other parts of the world.

The proposal for a "Big Society," the flagship policy of David Cameron's election campaign in 2010, was intended precisely to transform this weakening of the state's social competence into a motif of free-market and populist propaganda. In the slogan "take power away from politicians and give it to the people," the "people" were the local authorities and charitable organizations—often branches of religious groups or institutions—involved in administering social assistance in those areas where the British state lacked the means, or the will, to do so. It is significant that, two years after his election, Cameron advocated a "Christian fightback," asserting that "the values of the Bible, the values of Christianity, are the values that we need."

For his part, in his encyclical *Caritas in Veritate* (2009), Pope Benedict XVI stated no less than thirteen times his explicit offer to shoulder a share of the social responsibilities, calling for action aimed at "gradually *increasing openness, in a world context, to forms of economic activity marked by quotas of gratuitousness and communion*"—that is, openness to charitable and other voluntary activities within organizations administered directly or indirectly by the church. Such actions, Pope Francis later made clear in his apostolic exhortation *Evangelii Gaudium* (2013), should not be limited to "activities or programs of promotion and assistance" but should above all be characterized by "an attentiveness which considers the other 'in a certain sense as one with ourselves.'" This is a plus, when compared to almost any state social structure, which can only reinforce the sense of the historic superiority of religions and churches over public institutions.

⸺✦⸺

Another reason politicians seek to profit from the reemergence of the religious phenomenon is, finally, the international context. Religions often constitute an element of stability, providing an anchor to tradition that can be particularly useful in an era of instability and change. Clearly, the more solid and influential religion is, the more capable it is of fulfilling this auxiliary political role. Thus the governments of Muslim countries often present themselves as the heralds of the religious cause, aiming to exploit the religious faith of their subjects in the sense of justice that Islam represents to them; but the more Islam bows to private interests, the less effective it becomes.

Orthodox-majority countries claim the unconditional support of their respective churches, helping consolidate their identity and contributing to the maintenance of social and political order. This support is, however, ineffective on the international level, since the range of helpful action for these churches almost never extends beyond their national borders. Countries with Lutheran majorities, as well as Anglican Britain, are barely supported by their churches, which suffer from the same limits as their Orthodox counterparts on the international level, without, however, offering the same advantages on the national level, despite the fact of often being state religions.

The Catholic Church, on the other hand, can exert its influence equally on the national and international levels; it is thus extremely rare for any country to close its doors to the church. Since 1993 Israel has had diplomatic relations with the Holy See; and even Saudi Arabia saw fit to invite Benedict XVI for a visit, while rejecting his request to allow places of Catholic worship to open in the country. As for the relationship with China, the current impasse does not appear to depend on the will, or lack thereof, of Beijing.

The United States is among the countries that have been shaken most by the current shifting of the world's geopolitical axis; that might explain the disproportionate weight held by leaders who come from America's Catholic community—which represents between 25 and 30 percent of the general population—in key political, military, and judicial institutions. At the start of the second Obama administration, the vice president, the entire Joint Chiefs of Staff, one-third of Congress, the Speaker of the House of Representatives, as well as the House majority leader, the national security advisor, the CIA director, and the FBI director were all Catholic. Further, as of January 2015, 38 percent of American governors and six of the nine Supreme Court justices were Catholic. Never before in the short history of the United States have Catholics enjoyed such political visibility and importance.

⸺ ⣿ ⸺

As the United States tries to leverage, and gain advantage from, the position of the Catholic Church—which seems even more likely in the future—the church also reciprocates. For at least the past half century, Rome has adopted the entrepreneurial mentality of the American model: the "free market of faith," which is often considered the most important factor behind Americans' greater than average religiosity. The church also draws another advantage in principle from this model: in any system based on free competition, the best-equipped competitor nearly always prevails. Moreover, any relationship with the world's leading power will have an effect on the influence of the church—even, and perhaps above all, when the latter takes its distance from the United States. Finally, the generosity of American Catholics provides a very large part of the funding on which the global church relies.

During the last conclave, American prelates played a particularly visible role, contributing in a not insignificant way to the election of a pope whom Andrea Riccardi has described as being "quasi-pan-American." The nineteen American cardinals constitute not only the second largest national contingent in the Sacred College but also the largest contingent of cardinals from the United States in the entire history of the church—yet another sign of an ever closer relationship.

Whatever weight the American component carries, we should not forget that the church does not rely on the United States to affirm its power on the international level, any more than it does on any other political or economic power. It does not reject a priori any support—material or political— but only so long as it is able to preserve its freedom of movement in every situation.

This book has emphasized the potential role that the Catholic Church could play in national and international life of the twenty-first century. In these pages, the term "strategy" has been used to refer to the possible long-term objectives of Rome in a historical era in which the mission of carrying the word of Jesus to the "far ends of the Earth" coexists with the impossibility of doing so through the old method of conquest and conversion. However, this strategy has not been thought out, discussed, and codified by a general staff in the way that, for example, the military doctrines of great powers are—such as the Schlieffen Plan in the Second Reich—or even, *si parva licet*, the "electoral strategies" of the parliamentary parties. Rather, it is referring to the practical form that, in each historical era, the church's accumulated experience takes; experience that is unique in the world, allowing it to inscribe its action and its views into a framework of time and space that has nothing in common with those of any other human organization or institution.

The strategy of the church flows "naturally" from this accumulated experience. In fact, the church knows perfectly well where it wants to go—to the "far ends of the Earth"—and it also knows, from its very long historical and political practice, how to go about this: by thoroughly defending its autonomy and independence; remaining conscious of objective constraints; and, avoiding, as much as possible, any frontal collision with them. The church knows how to combine rigidity in strategic principles with extreme flexibility in daily practice; it is a *complexio oppositorum*. John Paul II and Benedict XVI established that certain values are "nonnegotiable," even while knowing perfectly well that in everyday life, most of their followers, and some Catholic leaders, not only negotiate those values but transgress them with ease. If the church really required of its followers a rigid respect for its moral prescriptions, it would no longer be a great global political force—perhaps the greatest and most important global political force—but merely a sect of limited standing, completely without political influence, like any other sect. The current Jesuit pope from Argentina clearly understands this difference.

—⚬⚬⚬—

Since the election of Jorge Mario Bergoglio, numerous observers claim to have detected a revolution: an end to the rigidities, Roman centralism, and the prohibitions of years long past. At the time of writing, it is still too soon to have a well-defined idea of what, plausibly, the church will be under and after the reign of Pope Francis. With the exception of Joseph Ratzinger, who, when he was elected pope, was already fairly well-known, one must always wait a few years to understand the political imprint of a new pope. This is truer still when we are dealing with a Jesuit: many people seem to forget that Bergoglio is a Jesuit, which is to say a member of the most *political* order in the history of the church.

Yet the Argentinian pope's public speeches have already allowed us to distinguish two particular traits: the frequent use of the title "bishop of Rome" rather than "pope" and the charismatic accent, the promotion of the image of a church that is both "joyous" and "outgoing," that is, in a state of permanent mission.

The first trait is generally interpreted as a subtle wink to other Christian denominations, a formal and highly symbolic step backward on the question of the primacy of Peter, historically claimed by the Church of Rome. The second trait is a product of the competition with the Pentecostalist and charismatic evangelical movements, which, especially in Latin America, have eaten away at the Catholic influence owing, exactly, to their state of permanent mission, to their close-level contacts with the populace, and to the people's aspiration to move out of poverty and accede to the relative benefits of the middle class.

And yet Francis does not turn his back on the political advantage embodied in the Ratzingerian line about an "ethic of duty." In only the second paragraph of the *Evangelii Gaudium*, he reminds readers that "the great danger in today's world . . . is the desolation and anguish born of a complacent yet covetous heart, the feverish pursuit of frivolous pleasures, and a blunted conscience." While Francis does not reject this notion, he attempts to give it, in his own words, "a fitting sense of proportion." Thus when a parish priest "speaks about temperance ten times but only mentions charity or justice two or three times, an imbalance results," and the most important of virtues can be overlooked. The priest should thus not be "obsessed with the disjointed transmission of a multitude of doctrines to be insistently imposed."

The "new proportion" of Francis's church seems to have as its pivot the charismatic concepts of "joy," "mercy," and "missionary enthusiasm." If observers often speak of his charisma, it is not by chance. Jorge Mario Bergoglio knows perfectly well that a smiling face and a modest lifestyle are important aspects of an image that can only shore up, but not replace, the political power of the church: a power made of organization, centralism, networks, and solid principles around which the "holy alliance" can be built. A Jesuit will always be the best-placed person to know this.

─── ❦ ───

In conclusion, I should again point out that in politics, as in other domains, there is no such thing as an unequivocal and absolute trend; and that one face of uneven development is uneven religious development. The trend toward desecularization provides the indispensable historical context for any possibility of creating a "holy alliance" among the great religions of the world. However, this trend to desecularization coexists with certain trends toward secularization, both in different countries and, at times, within the same country.

Many countries are in the process of modernizing, that is, of following "roughly the same fairly simple 'model,'" as Fernand Braudel has put it, of every process of industrialization. The effects of this process are also more or less uniform. So if the economic and social development of Turkey, Brazil, India, or China gives the impression of "sustained and perpetual growth" capable of supporting "the expectation of incessant improvement," as Ernest Gellner has articulated, it is highly likely that many of those who have reached the psychological status of the "middle class" are beginning to adopt more and more secularized models and styles of living. It is even possible that these trends ultimately lead to a new religious form, more individualistic and more secularized, while remaining rigorously fundamentalist. The struggle of certain ultra-Orthodox Jewish women to win the right to pray at the Wailing Wall could be a symbol of this new religious form.

The global shift of power under way today will certainly result in the populations of the developed countries living in ever more uncertain conditions; but it is also possible that the populations of the so-called emerging countries, in the future, will be able to live in conditions that seem to them to be less and less uncertain. Such an eventuality could yield a paradoxical result: a more religious Europe and United States at odds with an increasingly materialistic Asia, Latin America, and Africa.

Just the sort of thing that could feed new "clashes of *civilizations*."

NOTES

INTRODUCTION

1. Nicholas Spykman, "Geography and Foreign Policy," *American Political Science Review* 32, no. 1 (February 1938): 28.
2. Sadakat Kadri, *Heaven on Earth: A Journey Through Shari'a Law from the Deserts of Ancient Arabia to the Streets of the Modern Muslim World* (New York: Farrar, Straus and Giroux, 2012), 278.
3. Eric O. Hanson, *The Catholic Church in World Politics* (Princeton: Princeton University Press, 1987), 257–58.
4. Mirza Abu Taleb Khan, *Travels of Mirza Abu Taleb Khan in Asia, Africa, and Europe, During the Years 1799, 1800, 1801, 1802, and 1803*, trans. Charles Stewart (London: Broxbourne, Watts, Herst, 1814), 81.

1. THE DEATH OF GOD

1. Peter Berger, *The Desecularization of the World: Resurgent Religion and World Politics* (Grand Rapids, Mich.: Eerdmans, 1999), 2. Berger presented his original thesis in *The Sacred Canopy: Elements of a Sociological Theory of Religion* (Garden City, N.Y.: Doubleday, 1967).
2. Berger, *The Desecularization of the World*, 3.
3. Max Weber, "Science as a Vocation," in *From Max Weber: Essays in Sociology*, trans. and ed. Hans Heinrich Gerth and Charles Wright Mills (New York: Oxford University Press, 1946), 129–56.

4. John Elson, "Is God Dead?," *Time*, April 8, 1966. The title of the cover article was essentially symbolic. Indeed, some of the articles published in this issue answered the question in the negative. It is interesting to note that three years later (December 26, 1969), *Time* published a related cover article titled "Is God Coming Back to Life?"

5. Fernand Braudel, *A History of Civilization*, trans. and ed. Richard Mayne (New York: Penguin, 1994), 64.

6. Marshall G. S. Hodgson, *The Venture of Islam: Conscience and History in a World Civilization* (Chicago: University of Chicago Press, 1974), 132.

7. Gallicanism and Josephinism represented efforts to advocate for the national Catholic Church to take a certain distance from Rome, by submitting it to the authority of the state. The roots of Gallicanism go back to the fourteenth century, just as modern France was beginning to take shape. Josephinism is an Austrian phenomenon dating to the eighteenth century.

8. Olivier Roy reminds us that the death sentence given to the young nobleman Jean-Francois de la Barre—for refusing to remove his hat as a Catholic procession passed—was a reflection of the political will of the Parliament of Paris, which was Gallican and wanted to establish its Catholic legitimacy.

9. Joseph Ratzinger, *Europe: Today and Tomorrow* (San Francisco: Ignatius Press, 2007), 11.

10. Georg Wilhelm Friedrich Hegel, *The Philosophy of Right*, trans. S. W. Dale (Kitchener, Ont.: Batoche Books, 2001), 265.

11. Rudolf Kjellén, *Der Staat als Lebensform* (Berlin: K. Vowinckel, 1924), 45.

2. THE RETURN OF GOD

1. Fernand Braudel, *A History of Civilization*, trans. and ed. Richard Mayne (New York: Penguin, 1994), 14.

2. Paul Davidson, "Making Dollars and Sense of the U.S. Government Debt," *Journal of Post Keynesian Economics* 32, no. 4 (Summer 2010): 663–66.

3. World Bank, "Central Government Debt (% of GDP)," http://data.worldbank.org/indicator/GC.DOD.TOTL.GD.ZS, accessed September 8, 2015.

4. Stephen D. King, *When the Money Runs Out: The End of Western Affluence* (New Haven: Yale University Press, 2013), 43.

5. Sigmund Freud, *The Future of an Illusion* (New York: Norton, 1990), 40.

6. Ernest Gellner, *Nations and Nationalism* (Ithaca: Cornell University Press, 1983), 22, 23.

7. Peter Berger, *The Desecularization of the World: Resurgent Religion and World Politics* (Grand Rapids, Mich.: Eerdmans, 1999), 7.

8. King, *When the Money Runs Out*, 7.

9. Karl Marx, *Critique of Hegel's Philosophy of Right* (Cambridge: Cambridge University Press, 1970), 131.

10. *Les Trente Glorieuses* (The Glorious Thirty) is a phrase coined by the economist Jean Fourastié to describe the period of vigorous economic growth by most developed countries between 1945 and 1974.

11. Marx, *Critique of Hegel's Philosophy of Right*, 131.

12. Karl Marx, *Manifesto of the Communist Party* (Rockville, Md.: Manor Thrift, 1980), 9.

13. Benedetto Croce, *History of Europe in the Nineteenth Century*, trans. Henry Furst (New York: Harcourt, Brace & World, 1933), 24.

14. Ibid., 25.

15. Owen Chadwick, *The Secularization of the European Mind in the Nineteenth Century* (Cambridge: Cambridge University Press, 1975), 10.

16. Carl Schmitt, *The Tyranny of Values*, ed. and trans. Simona Draghici (Washington, D.C.: Plutarch Press, 1996), 25.

17. Carl Schmitt, *The Concept of the Political*, trans. George Schwab (New Brunswick, N.J.: Rutgers University Press, 1996), 54.

18. The thesis of collaboration/confrontation between the United States and the Soviet Union during the Cold War is very much a minority opinion but deserves greater attention. Rather than elaborate on this argument here, I would refer the reader to Manlio Graziano, *Essential Geopolitics: A Handbook* (amazon.com, 2011), 68–73.

19. François Lelord, *Hector and the Search for Happiness* (London: Gallic Books, 2010), 68.

3. GOD'S REVENGE

1. Bernard le Bovier de Fontenelle, *A Week's Conversation on the Plurality of the Worlds*, trans. William Gardiner (London: E. Crull in the Strand, 1728), 160.

2. José Casanova, *Public Religions in the Modern World* (Chicago: University of Chicago Press, 1994), 211.

3. René Rémond, *Religion et société en Europe: Essai sur la sécularisation des sociétés européennes aux XIXe et XXe siècles (1789-2000)* (Paris: Seuil, 1998), 46.

4. René-Georges Coquin, "Écueils 'théologiques' éventuels, dans le passage, pour les chrétiens d'Égypte, du copte à l'arabe," *École pratique des hautes études, Section des sciences religieuses Annuaire*, vol. 103, no. 99 (1990): 17.

5. Ali A. Allawi, *The Crisis of Islamic Civilization* (New Haven: Yale University Press, 2009), 9–10.

6. Tariq Ali, *The Clash of Fundamentalisms: Crusades, Jihads and Modernity* (London: Verso, 2003), 11.

7. Mohammad Qayoumi, "Once Upon a Time in Afghanistan," *Foreign Policy*, May 29, 2010.

8. Elisabeth Bumiller, "Remembering Afghanistan's Golden Age," *New York Times*, October 18, 2009.

9. Stephen Farrell, "Baghdad Jews Have Become a Fearful Few," *New York Times*, June 1, 2008.

10. Joel Beinin, *Workers and Peasants in the Modern Middle East* (Cambridge: Cambridge University Press, 2001), 139.

11. Armand Frémont, "La terre," in *Les Lieux de mémoire*, vol. 3, ed. Pierre Nora (Paris: Gallimard, 1997), 400.

12. Fareed Zakaria, "Culture Is Destiny: A Conversation with Lee Kuan Yew," *Foreign Affairs* 73, no. 2 (March–April 1994): 109–26.

13. Unless stated otherwise, all the quotations from encyclicals can be found on the official Vatican website.

14. Wu Jiao, "Religious Believers Thrice the Estimate," *China Daily*, February 7, 2007.

15. David Aikman, *Jesus in Beijing: How Christianity Is Transforming China and Changing the Global Balance of Power* (Oxford: Monarch, 2003), 303.

16. Etiane Caloy Bovkalovski de Souza and Marionilde Dias Brepohl de Magalhães, "Os pentecostais: Entre a fé e a política," *Revista Brasileira de História* 22, no. 43 (São Paulo: Associação Nacional de História, 2002): 85–103.

17. John Micklethwait and Adrian Wooldridge, *God Is Back: How the Global Revival of Faith Is Changing the World* (New York: Penguin, 2009), 3.

18. Olivier Roy, *Holy Ignorance: When Religion and Culture Part Ways* (Oxford: Oxford University Press, 2013), 197–98.

19. José Casanova, "Religion and Conflict in Latin America: Conversation with Otto Maduro," *Telos*, no. 58 (January 1983): 185–95. See chapter 6.

20. "WEC in Africa," WEC International, http://www.wecinternational.org/where-is-wec/africa.php.

21. Ali, *The Clash of Fundamentalisms*, 29.

22. Maxime Rodinson, *Muhammad* (London: I. B. Tauris, 2002), 88.

23. A *hadith* is an act or a saying attributed to Mohammad. Along with the Koran, the hadith form the *Sunnah*, which is the full panoply of rules that all the faithful are meant to follow.

24. Vali Nasr, *The Rise of Islamic Capitalism: Why the New Middle Class Is Key to Defeating Extremism* (New York: Free Press, 2009), 23.

25. Patrick Haenni, *L'islam de marché: L'autre révolution conservatrice* (Paris: Seuil, 2005), 10.

26. Djallal G. Heuzé, "Évolutions socioreligieuses en Inde," *Revue Tiers Monde*, no. 204 (2010): 155.

27. Meera Nanda, *The God Market: How Globalization Is Making India More Hindu* (New York: Random House, 2010), 91.

28. Nasr, *The Rise of Islamic Capitalism*, 255.

29. Nanda, *The God Market*, 199.

30. Ibid., 91.

31. Gilles Kepel, *The Revenge of God: The Resurgence of Islam, Christianity, and Judaism in the Modern World* (Cambridge, Mass.: Polity Press, 1994), 150.

32. The Non-Aligned Movement was founded in 1955 at the Bandung Conference in Indonesia. Organized by Indonesia, Burma (Myanmar), Ceylon (Sri Lanka), Pakistan, and India, it brought together representatives of twenty-nine Asian and African countries, including Egypt, China, and Japan. Its announced objective

was to create a bloc of countries independent of both the United States and the Soviet Union.

33. See Manlio Graziano, *The Failure of Italian Nationhood: The Geopolitics of a Troubled Identity* (New York: Palgrave Macmillan, 2010).

34. Beinin, *Workers and Peasants in the Modern Middle East*, 136.

35. Ibid., 148.

4. RELIGION AND POWER IN THE 1970S

1. Gilles Kepel, *Jihad: The Trail of Political Islam* (London: I. B. Tauris, 2006), 63.

2. The Great Awakening refers to the powerful wave of religiosity in Britain and its American colonies in the mid-eighteenth century. It was applied to the 1970s context by economist Robert Fogel in his work *The Fourth Great Awakening and the Future of Egalitarianism* (2000), although it is limited in use in this instance to the spread of "Protestantism" in the United States.

3. Robert Dreyfuss, *Devil's Game: How the United States Helped Unleash Fundamentalist Islam* (New York: Henry Holt, 2006), 149.

4. Ibid., 148.

5. Ibid.

6. John L. Esposito, *Unholy Wars: Terror in the Name of Islam* (New York: Oxford University Press, 2002), 84.

7. Historians will have to say just how much the Muslim Brothers served, once again, as a stepping stone for other political forces after the Arab Spring of 2011 and the Egyptian Armed Forces coup d'état of July 2013.

8. Olivier Carré and Gérard Michaud, *Les frères musulmans (1928-1982)* (Paris: Gallimard, 1983), 65–82.

9. Cynthia Myntti, *Paris Along the Nile: Architecture in Cairo from the Belle Époque* (Cairo: American University in Cairo Press, 1999), 6.

10. Ibid.

11. Operation Badr is a reference is to the Battle of Badr, Mohammed's first military victory, on March 17, 624.

12. Joel Beinin, *Workers and Peasants in the Modern Middle East* (Cambridge: Cambridge University Press, 2001), 158.

13. Gilles Kepel, *The Revenge of God: The Resurgence of Islam, Christianity, and Judaism in the Modern World* (Cambridge, Mass.: Polity Press, 1994), 25.

14. Gilles Kepel, *Muslim Extremism in Egypt: The Prophet and Pharaoh* (Berkeley: University of California Press, 1985), 134.

15. Kepel, *The Revenge of God*, 25.

16. Farhad Khosrokhavar, "Les paysans dépaysannés et la Révolution iranienne," *Cahiers d'Études sur la Méditerranée Orientale et le Monde Turco-Iranien*, no. 27 (1999): 159–79.

17. In 1959 the two sides had reached an agreement on Sumatra oil, and between 1959 and 1962 trade between Indonesia and Japan shot up by more than 50 percent.

At the same time, China had adopted its "united front" strategy, consisting, in part, of a rapprochement with Japan with an anti-Russian objective. The disputes between President Sukarno and London stemmed from Indonesian hostility toward the Federation of Malaysia, a British protectorate comprising Malaysia, Singapore, and the colonies of Borneo (Sabah, Sarawak, and Brunei), which were also the target of a pro-Chinese guerrilla campaign.

18. Peter G. Boyle, ed., *The Churchill-Eisenhower Correspondence, 1953–1955* (Chapel Hill: University of North Carolina Press, 1990), 136.

19. William Blum, *Killing Hope: U.S. Military and CIA Interventions Since World War II* (Montreal: Black Rose, 1998), 195.

20. Tariq Ali, *The Clash of Fundamentalisms: Crusades, Jihads and Modernity* (London: Verso, 2003), 379.

21. Robert Gellately and Ben Kiernan, eds., *The Specter of Genocide: Mass Murder in Historical Perspective* (Cambridge: Cambridge University Press, 2003), 290.

22. Tarzie Vittachi, *The Fall of Sukarno* (London: Andre Deutsch, 1967), 138.

23. Geoffrey Robinson, "The Post-Coup Massacre in Bali," in *Making Indonesia*, ed. Daniel S. Lev and Ruth McVey (Ithaca: Cornell Southeast Asia Program Publications, 1996), 141.

24. In the 2014 elections, the National Awakening Party, a moderate democratic Islamist formation, saw its share of the vote jump up by some 4 percent, while the two pro-sharia Islamist parties lost around 2 percent.

25. Norimitsu Onishi, "In Indonesia, Islamists Lost Political Ground," *New York Times*, April 24, 2009.

26. Ardavan Amir-Aslani, *La guerre des Dieux: Géopolitique de la spiritualité* (Paris: Nouveau Monde, 2011), 281.

27. Shlomo Sand, *The Invention of the Jewish People* (London: Verso, 2009), 254.

28. Yakov M. Rabkin, *Au nom de la Torah: Une histoire de l'opposition juive au sionisme* (Québec: Presses de l'Université Laval, 2004), 18.

29. Menachem Begin headed the anti-British/anti-Arab terror group Irgun from 1943 to 1948. Irgun was responsible for attacks on British targets starting in 1944, including the bombing of the King David Hotel in Jerusalem in 1946. The group's terror policy toward Palestinian Arabs reached its zenith with the massacre of the village of Deir Yassin in 1948, for which Begin took responsibility. The British authorities promised a bounty of 10,000 pounds for his capture, "dead or alive."

30. Pew Research Center, "Countries with the Largest Muslim Populations," April 2, 2015, http://www.pewforum.org/2015/04/02/muslims/pf_15–04–02_projectionstables74/.

31. The Vedas are "revelations" first transmitted orally, from brahman to brahman (Hindu priests who reside at the summit of the caste system), then written between the years 1800 and 1500 BCE.

32. Fernand Braudel, *A History of Civilization*, trans. and ed. Richard Mayne (New York: Penguin, 1994), 244.

33. Ali, *The Clash of Fundamentalisms*, 232.

34. Sumathi Ramaswamy, *The Goddess and the Nation: Mapping Mother India* (Durham: Duke University Press, 2010), 2.

35. Meera Nanda, *The God Market: How Globalization Is Making India More Hindu* (New York: Random House, 2010), 8.

36. "Refugees in India," *Wikipedia*, last modified December 30, 2016, https://en.wikipedia.org/wiki/Refugees_in_India.

37. Olivier Roy, *Holy Ignorance: When Religion and Culture Part Ways* (Oxford: Oxford University Press, 2013), 79.

38. Choudhary Rahmat Ali, *Now or Never; Are We to Live or Perish Forever?*, pamphlet published in Cambridge, U.K., January 23, 1933, http://www.columbia.edu/itc/mealac/pritchett/00islamlinks/txt_rahmatali_1933.html.

39. In Pakistan, the word *ulema* is used to describe all religious Muslims—not just Muslim theologians—whose social role (especially through the educational network of madrasas) only grew under British rule.

40. Inamullah Khan, *Islam in the Contemporary World* (Karachi: Umma, 1967), 11.

41. Sadakat Kadri, *Heaven on Earth: A Journey Through Shari'a Law from the Deserts of Ancient Arabia to the Streets of the Modern Muslim World* (New York: Farrar, Straus and Giroux, 2012), 253.

42. Dilip Hiro, *Apocalyptic Realm: Jihadists in South Asia* (New Haven: Yale University Press, 2012), 16–162.

43. Robert G. Wirsing, *Pakistan's Security Under Zia, 1977–1988: The Policy Imperatives of a Peripheral Asian State* (New York: St. Martin's Press, 1991), 30.

44. Tessa J. Bartholomeusz, *In Defense of Dharma: Just-War Ideology in Buddhist Sri Lanka* (London: Routledge, 2002), 145.

45. Thera Mahanama-sthavira, *Mahavamsa: The Great Chronicle of Sri Lanka* (Fremont, Calif.: Asian Humanities Press, 1999), 252.

46. Kyaw Zwa Moe, "A Radically Different Dhamma," *Irrawaddy*, June 22, 2013.

47. Debarshi Dasgupta and Pranay Sharma, "Buddha Mortified," *Outlook*, July 22, 2013.

48. Patrick J. Reardon, "JFK and the Cafeteria Bishops: 50 Years After Kennedy Asserted Independence from the Pope, the Tide Has Turned," *National Catholic Reporter*, August 10, 2010.

49. Corwin Smidt, Kevin den Dulk, Bryan Froehle, James Penning, Stephen Monsma, and Douglas Koopman, *The Disappearing God Gap? Religion in the 2008 Presidential Election* (New York: Oxford University Press, 2010), 18.

50. The Investiture Controversy (eleventh to twelfth centuries) was the first great conflict between the Catholic Church and the Holy Roman Empire to establish who—the pope or the emperor—had the right to name bishops. This episode was seen to symbolize the struggle for supremacy between the religious and political power centers.

5. THE ISLAMIZATION OF THE IRANIAN REVOLUTION

1. Robert Dreyfuss, *Devil's Game: How the United States Helped Unleash Fundamentalist Islam* (New York: Henry Holt, 2006), 222.

2. Ibid.

3. Daniel Philpott analyzed some 1,600 articles published between 1980 and 1999 in four specialized reviews (*International Organization, International Studies Quarterly, International Security*, and *World Politics*) and found that only six of them dealt with religion.

4. Dreyfuss, *Devil's Game*, 223.

5. Ibid., 229, 230.

6. Ibid., 230.

7. Twelver Shiism represents the majority current of Shiism (about 90 percent). Under this doctrine, Mohammed had twelve successors (hence the name), dubbed imams, of whom the last—the Mahdi—did not die but has been hidden away since the year 874, to reappear on Day of Judgment. The Twelvers constitute the majority of the population in Iran, Iraq, Azerbaijan, and Bahrain and are the largest Muslim community in Lebanon. It should be noted that, in Sunni belief, the imam is simply the person who leads prayers.

8. Olivier Roy, *The Failure of Political Islam* (London: I. B. Tauris, 1994), 168.

9. Michael Axworthy, *Iran: Empire of the Mind: A History from Zoroaster to the Present Day* (New York: Basic Books, 2008), 81.

10. Graham Fuller tells us that under the Umayyad Caliphate (661–750), only 10 percent of conquered peoples converted to Islam, whereas under the Abbasids Caliphate, the number rose to 40 percent (it was not until the end of the eleventh century that we can speak of generalized conversions). See Fuller, *A World Without Islam* (New York: Little, Brown, 2010), 90.

11. Peter Brown, *The World of Late Antiquity: AD 150–750* (London: Times & Hudson, 1971), 202.

12. Fernand Braudel, *La Méditerranée: L'espace et l'histoire* (Paris: Flammarion, 1985), 163.

13. Robert D. Kaplan, *The Revenge of Geography: What the Map Tells Us About Coming Conflicts and the Battle Against Fate* (New York: Random House, 2012), 275.

14. *Encyclopaedia Iranica*, vol. 1, no. 5 (London: Routledge & Kegan Paul, 1985), 960.

15. Baqer Moin, *Khomeini: Life of the Ayatollah* (London: I. B. Tauris, 1999), 88.

16. Vali Nasr, *The Rise of Islamic Capitalism: Why the New Middle Class Is Key to Defeating Extremism* (New York: Free Press, 2009), 117.

17. It is worth noting that in 1976, the Ford administration had authorized Tehran to acquire everything needed to master the complete nuclear fuel cycle; and yet two years earlier (August 23, 1974), a CIA report had warned that "if [the shah] is alive in the mid-1980s . . . and if other countries [i.e., India] have proceeded with weapons development we have no doubt Iran will follow suit." See "Special National Intelligence Estimate: Prospects for Further Proliferation of Nuclear Weapons" *National Security Agency*, last modified August 23, 1974, http://nsarchive.gwu.edu/NSAEBB/NSAEBB240/snie.pdf.

18. Robert E. Looney, "The Role of Military Expenditures in Pre-Revolutionary Iran's Economic Decline," *Iranian Studies* 12, no. 3–4 (1988): 54.

19. "Military Expenditure (% of GDP) in Egypt," *Trading Economics*, http://www.trading-economics.com/egypt/military-expenditure-percent-of-gdp-wb-data.html, accessed August 14, 2015.

20. "Inflation Rate," *Trading Economics*, http://www.tradingeconomics.com/country
-list/inflation-rate, accessed October 15, 2015.
21. Roy Mottahedeh, *The Mantle of the Prophet: Religion and Politics in Iran* (Boston: Oneworld, 2000), 216–17.
22. Zohreh Salehi Siavoshani, "The Role of the Clerics and the Religious Forces in the
Iranian Movement of the Nationalization of Oil Industry," *Historia Actual Online*, no.
26 (Fall 2011): 7–19.
23. Richard Yann, "Ayatollah Kashani: Precursor of the Islamic Republic?," in *Religion
and Politics in Iran: Shiism from Quietism to Revolution*, ed. Nikki R. Keddie (New Haven:
Yale University Press, 1983), 108.
24. Gilles Kepel, *Jihad: The Trail of Political Islam* (London: I. B. Tauris, 2006), 41.
25. My own elaboration from data at http://www.indexmundi.com/.
26. Nasr, *The Rise of Islamic Capitalism*, 119.
27. Al-Hussein ibn Ali (626–680) was Shiism's third imam. He died during the Battle of
Karbala, which marked the definitive victory of the Sunnis over the Shiites. The
Day of Ashura, which commemorates the event, is Shiism's most important rite.
28. Kepel, *Jihad*, 208.
29. Tariq Ali, *The Clash of Fundamentalisms: Crusades, Jihads and Modernity* (London: Verso,
2003), 131.
30. Nasr, *The Rise of Islamic Capitalism*, 134.
31. The epilogue of history is tragedy. Starting in the spring of 1979, gangs of *pasda-
ran*, young men from the Iranian lumpenproletariat, were sent to disperse those
demonstrators who were hostile to the ayatollahs and to rid the universities of
leftist elements. Conservatives were chased from power and then arrested. The
Islamist movement of the Mujahedin-e-Khalq (the people's mujahedin), which
was close to the positions of Ali Shariati, was eliminated. The Tudeh Party,
which supported Khomeini until 1982 and accused women who protested the
law on wearing the chador of "bourgeois deviationism," was outlawed, its leaders killed or forced to make televised statements on the superiority of Islam
over Marxism.

6. THE GEOPOLITICAL REINVENTION OF THE HOLY WAR

1. *Cold War*, season 1, episode 20, "Soldiers of God," produced by Jody Gottlieb, aired
1998 on CNN.
2. Pietro Quaroni, *Il mondo di un ambasciatore* (Milan: Ferro, 1965), 139.
3. Zehir-Ed-Din Muhammed Badur, *Memoirs of Zehir-Ed-Din Muhammed Badur, Emperor
of Hindustan*, trans. John Leyden and William Erskine (London: Oxford University
Press, 1921), 225.
4. Quaroni, *Il mondo di un ambasciatore*, 103.
5. Husain Haqqani, *Pakistan: Between Mosque and Military* (Washington, D.C.: Carnegie
Endowment for International Peace, 2005), 165.

6. Nick Cullather, "Damming Afghanistan: Modernization in a Buffer State," *Journal of American History* 89, no. 2 (September 2002): 512.

7. Elisabeth Bumiller, "Remembering Afghanistan's Golden Age," *New York Times*, October 18, 2009.

8. "Urban Population (% of Total)," World Bank, http://data.worldbank.org/indicator /SP.URB.TOTL.IN.ZS, accessed September 8, 2015.

9. Diego Cordovez and Selig S. Harrison, *Out of Afghanistan: The Inside Story of the Soviet Withdrawal* (New York: Oxford University Press, 1995), 15.

10. Robert G. Wirsing, *Pakistan's Security Under Zia, 1977-1988: The Policy Imperatives of a Peripheral Asian State* (New York: St. Martin's Press, 1991), 30. See chapter 4.

11. Dilip Hiro, *Apocalyptic Realm: Jihadists in South Asia* (New Haven: Yale University Press, 2012), 44.

12. *Cold War*, season 1, episode 20.

13. Olivier Roy, *Islam and Resistance in Afghanistan* (Cambridge: Cambridge University Press, 1990), 108.

14. Hiro, *Apocalyptic Realm*, 48.

15. Martin Walker, *The Cold War and the Making of the Modern World* (London: Fourth Estate, 1993), 253.

16. "Brzezinski: Oui, la CIA est entrée en Afghanistan avant les Russes," *Le Nouvel Observateur*, January 15, 1998.

17. Gabriel G. Tabarani, *Jihad's New Heartlands: Why the West Has Failed to Contain Islamic Fundamentalism* (Bloomington, Ind.: AuthorHouse, 2011), 91.

18. "International Energy Statistics," Energy Information Administration, https:// www.eia.gov/beta/international/data/browser/#?ord=CR&cy=2014&v=H&vo=0&s o=0&io=0&start=1980&end=2014, accessed October 1, 2015.

19. Robert D. Crews, *For Prophet and Tsar: Islam and Empire in Russia and Central Asia* (Cambridge, Mass.: Harvard University Press, 2006), 2.

20. The Soviet Union was represented at Bretton Woods by Andrei Gromyko, who signed the final act of the conference. But once World War II was over, the Soviet Union did not ratify the agreement because it had not obtained the loan of $10 billion that it had demanded as a precondition (to understand the enormity of this request, consider that spending for the entire Marshall Plan, from 1947 to 1951, totaled $15 billion). See John Ikenberry, "The Political Origins of Bretton Woods," in *A Retrospective on the Bretton Woods System: Lessons for International Monetary Reform*, ed. Michael D. Bordo and Barry Eichengreen, 155–97 (Chicago: University of Chicago Press, 1993).

21. Robert Dreyfuss, *Devil's Game: How the United States Helped Unleash Fundamentalist Islam* (New York: Henry Holt, 2006), 90.

22. Eric Walberg, *Postmodern Imperialism: Geopolitics and the Great Games* (Atlanta: Clarity Press, 2011), 69.

23. Dreyfuss, *Devil's Game*, 123.

24. The phrase "East of Suez," from a poem by Rudyard Kipling, reflects the extent of British interests beyond the European theater. In 1968, British possessions in the

Middle East still included Oman, the Emirates (known then as Trucial Oman), Qatar, and Bahrain.

25. Michael B. Oren, *Six Days of War: June 1967 and the Making of the Modern Middle East* (New York: Presidio Press, 2002), 28.

26. In November 1979, fifty-two employees of the American Embassy in Tehran were taken hostage; they were held for 444 days and released only when Ronald Reagan became president, in January 1981. The episode of the letter is described by Carter's chief of staff, Hamilton Jordan: "I was amused at the idea of the Southern Baptist writing to the Moslem fanatic. What will he say to the man? I thought. Maybe he'll sign the letter 'The Great Satan.'" See Hamilton Jordan, *Crisis: The Last Year of the Carter Presidency* (New York: Putnam, 1982), 35–51.

27. Richard Pipes, "Muslims of Soviet Central Asia: Trends and Prospects," *Middle East Journal* 9, nos. 2–3 (Spring–Summer 1955): 308.

28. Fred Halliday, "Tough Choices for Afghanistan's Regime and Its Opponents," *New York Times*, May 18, 1979.

29. Dave Holmes and Norm Dixon, *Behind the US War on Afghanistan* (Chippendale, New South Wales: Resistance Books, 2001), 26.

30. Another such division existed between, on the one hand, the Taliban and its onetime leader Mullah Omar (pronounced deceased in 2013), who are Ghilzai and, on the other, Hamid Karzai, the Afghani president from 2001 to 2014, who is Durrani. It is worth noting that from 2014 onward, the respective roles have switched: the new president, Ashraf Ghani Ahmadzai, is Ghilzai, and the new leader of Taliban, Mullah Akhtar Mohammad Mansoor, is Durrani.

7. THE CATHOLICIZATION OF MODERNITY

1. Geoffrey Godsell, "1980s: Ayatollah, Pope Embody Rise of Religion," *Christian Science Monitor*, January 2, 1980.

2. John Paul II, *Memory and Identity: Personal Reflections* (London: Orion, 2005), 88.

3. The *Syllabus of Errors*, "containing the most important errors of our time," was written by Pope Pius IX and published on December 8, 1864. Among the errors that Catholics were to reject were rationalism and socialism but also "progress, liberalism, and modern civilization." Pius IX's declaration of 1861 is from his address *Iamdum Cernimus* (March 18, 1861).

4. An example of this "re-Christianization" was a 2005 speech in Krakow by Monsignor Giovanni Lajolo, in which the then "minister of foreign affairs" of the Catholic Church declared: "It is from Christianity that have sprung forth . . . the great principles of equality, of liberty and of fraternity." See "Se i cristiani sono esclusi dall'Europa," *Avvenire*, September 10, 2005.

5. Johannes Nebel, "Dopo il Concilio fui troppo timoroso," *Corriere della Sera*, October 19, 2007.

6. Olivier Le Gendre, *Confession d'un cardinal* (Paris: JC Lattès, 2007), 250.

7. There was a trend during the twentieth century to canonize more and more new saints. Pius X proclaimed an average of 0.3 saints per year during his pontificate; Benedict XV, also 0.3; Pius XI, 1.8; Pius XII, 1.65; John XXIII, 1.66; Paul VI, 5.25; and John Paul II, 17.2. Under Benedict XVI, the rate fell to 5.5 per year (without counting the 813 "martyrs of Otranto," canonized on the very day he announced his resignation).

8. THE CLASH OF CIVILIZATIONS

1. Bernard Lewis, "The Roots of Muslim Rage," *Atlantic Monthly*, vol. 266, no. 3, (September 1990): 47–60.
2. Bernard Lewis, "Middle Eastern Reaction to Soviet Pressures," *Middle East Journal*, no. 10 (Spring 1956): 130.
3. America's "Yellow Scare" of the late 1980s was felt intensely. Japanese exports had left the United States with a growing trade deficit, and the Japanese had gained the advantage in certain industrial sectors that the Americans had long dominated, such as the automotive industry. Japanese firms had also made a series of highly symbolic purchases (including Columbia Pictures, CBS Records, Rockefeller Center, and Radio City Music Hall in New York, and even the famous Pebble Beach golf course in California).
4. "Excerpts from Pentagon's Plan: 'Prevent the Re-Emergence of a New Rival,'" *New York Times*, March 8, 1992.
5. Richard Haass, *The Reluctant Sheriff: The United States After the Cold War* (New York: Council on Foreign Relations, 1997), 31.
6. Samuel Huntington, *The Clash of Civilizations and the Remaking of World Order* (New York: Simon & Schuster, 1996), 169, 288.
7. See Chris Gaither and Dawn C. Chmielewski, "Fears of Dot-Com Crash," *Los Angeles Times*, July 16, 2006.
8. Peter Berger, *The Desecularization of the World: Resurgent Religion and World Politics* (Grand Rapids, Mich.: Eerdmans, 1999), 7.
9. Fernand Braudel, *Grammaire des civilisations* (Paris: Arthaud, 1987). The book was actually written in 1962–63 as the textbook for a history course, but the French Ministry of Education eventually rejected it. The English edition is *History of Civilization*, trans. and ed. Richard Mayne (New York: Penguin, 1994).
10. Niall Ferguson, *Civilization: The West and the Rest* (London: Penguin, 2011), xxvi.
11. Braudel, *A History of Civilization*, 3.
12. Ibid., 12.
13. Joseph Ratzinger, *Europe: Today and Tomorrow* (San Francisco: Ignatius Press, 2007), 13.
14. Among the most important such works one should mention those by Frenchmen Louis de Bonald (*Théorie du pouvoir politique et religieux*, 1793, and *Réflexions sur l'intérêt général de l'Europe*, 1814), Étienne Antoine Boulogne (in the review *Annales littéraires et morales*, 1804), Joseph de Maistre (*Du pape*, 1819), and Hugues-Félicité Robert de

La Mennais (*Essai sur l'indifférence en matière de religion*, 1817–1823); Germans Novalis (*Die Christenheit oder Europa*, 1799), Friedrich Schlegel (*Lessings Geist*, 1804), August Wilhelm Schlegel (*Vorlesungen über dramatische Kunst und Literatur*, 1808), and Adam Heinrich Müller (*Die Elemente der Staatskunst*, 1808–09); a former Calvinist pastor from Switzerland, Pierre de Joux (*Lettres sur l'Italie considérée sous le rapport de la religion*, 1825); and Italians Giovanni Marchetti (*Della socialità della religione cristiana, specialmente della cattolica*, 1804, and *Della Chiesa quanto allo stato civile delle città*, 1817), and Antonio Rosmini (*Il Panegirico alla santa e gloriosa memoria di Pio VII*, 1831).

15. Henri Pirenne, *Mohammed and Charlemagne* (New York: Routledge, 2008), 184.

16. Ratzinger, *Europe*, 13.

17. Charles Freeman, *The Closing of the Western Mind: The Rise of Faith and the Fall of Reason* (New York: Vintage, 2002), xix.

18. John Chrysostom, "Homilies Against the Jews [Adversus Judeaus]," Preterist Archive, http://www.preteristarchive.com/ChurchHistory/0386_chrysostom_adversus-judeaus.html, accessed October 15, 2015.

19. Marcel Simon, *Verus Israel: Les relations entre juifs et chrétiens dans l'empire romain (135–425)* (Paris: E. de Boccard, 1948), 266.

20. Bernard Lewis, *From Babel to Dragomans: Interpreting the Middle East* (Oxford: Oxford University Press, 2004), 187.

21. Friedrich Nietzsche, *The Anti-Christ, Ecce Homo, Twilight of the Idols, and Other Writings* (Cambridge: Cambridge University Press, 2005), 22.

22. Bernard Lewis, *What Went Wrong? The Clash Between Islam and Modernity in the Middle East* (New York: Oxford University Press, 2002), 154.

23. Mahmood Mamdani, *Good Muslim, Bad Muslim: America, the Cold War, and the Roots of Terror* (New York: Doubleday, 2004), 36.

24. In 1888, 88.6 percent of the world's Jews population lived in Europe; by 1948, their number had fallen to 32 percent of the total, and in 2010, to 10.8 percent. See Museum of Jewish History, "Databases," http://www.jewishgen.org/databases/; and Jewish Federation of North America, "Berman Jewish Databank," http://www.jewishdatabank.org, both accessed October 15, 2015.

25. Richard W. Bulliet, *The Case for Islamo-Christian Civilization* (New York: Columbia University Press, 2004), 6.

26. Mamdani, *Good Muslim, Bad Muslim*, 244.

27. Bulliet, *The Case for Islamo-Christian Civilization*, 45.

28. For some years political subjectivism has been contaminating the North–South divide as well, a concept often used to draw ideological more than geographical distinctions, as in the classification of Australia in the "North" and Haiti or Mongolia in the "South."

29. Huntington, *The Clash of Civilizations*, 70.

30. Ibid., 46.

31. Let us remember that Huntington was writing in the first half of the 1990s, when the growth of Evangelicalism in Latin America seemed irresistible. Since then, much has changed, in part because of a new attitude of the Catholic Church, made official at

the Fifth General Conference of the Bishops of Latin America in 2007 and spread to the rest of the world with the election of Jorge Mario Bergoglio as pope in 2013.

32. Huntington, *The Clash of Civilizations*, 111.

33. Ibid., 70–72.

34. Lexington, "Huntington's Clash," *Economist*, December 30, 2008.

35. René Rémond, *Religion et société en Europe: Essai sur la sécularisation des sociétés européennes aux XIXe et XXe siècles (1789-2000)* (Paris: Seuil, 1998), 130, 151.

36. Paul Kennedy, *The Rise and Fall of the Great Powers: Economic Change and Military Conflict from 1500 to 2000* (New York: Random House, 1987), 4.

37. Niall Ferguson, *The War of the World: History's Age of Hatred* (London: Penguin, 2006), 54.

38. Walter Russell Mead, *God and Gold: Britain, America and the Making of the Modern World* (New York: Knopf, 2007), 13.

39. Alfred Mahan, *The Influence of Sea Power Upon History* (Cambridge: Cambridge University Press, 2010), 52.

40. Nor should we forget that before the two wars broke out, numerous analysts had raised the possibility of (and even bet on) an alliance forming between Britain and Germany.

41. Ferguson, *Civilization*, 312.

42. Bernard Lewis, "Targeted by a History of Hatred," *Washington Post*, September 10, 2002.

43. Thomas Sowell, *Black Rednecks and White Liberals* (New York: Encounter Books, 2005), 77.

44. On this subject, Robert Kaplan remarked that, "just as the Arabs never succeeded in capturing the mountain fortress of Anatolia, the Seljuks, deep inside those very fortresses, never quite succeeded in maintaining stable rule over the heart of Islamdom—the Fertile Crescent and the Iranian plateaus." If one substitutes the Ottomans for the Seljuks, the relationship between the Turks and the "Fertile Crescent" remained the same. See Robert D. Kaplan, *The Revenge of Geography: What the Map Tells Us About Coming Conflicts and the Battle Against Fate* (New York: Random House, 2012), 53.

45. Mark Curtis, *Secret Affairs: Britain's Collusion with Radical Islam* (London, Serpent's Tail, 2010), 9.

46. Lewis, "The Roots of Muslim Rage," 56.

47. Richard Breitman and Norman Goda, *Hitler's Shadow: Nazi War Criminals, U.S. Intelligence and the Cold War* (Washington, D.C.: National Archives, 2011), 21.

48. *Le Monde* reported on April 20, 1955, that "the anti-Israeli resolution was the only point of agreement at the conference." See Léon Poliakov, *De Moscou à Beyrouth: Essai sur la désinformation* (Paris: Calmann-Lévy, 1983), 55.

49. Braudel, *A History of Civilization*, 87.

50. It is noteworthy that three authors with sensibilities as varied as Fernand Braudel, Samuel Huntington, and Graham Fuller all see "some resemblance" (Huntington) or even "striking echoes" (Fuller) between the Protestant and Muslim work ethics. See Graham Fuller, *A World Without Islam* (New York: Little, Brown, 2010), 120. The same thesis is supported by certain French sovereigntists in order to stigmatize a supposed convergence between "Anglo-Saxon (neo)-liberalism" and Islam against

European civilization. As Richard Millet wrote, "Islamism is but a spectacular variant of Protestant capitalism." Millet, *Fatigue du sens* (Paris: Pierre-Guillaume de Roux, 2011), 149.

51. Luis Francisco Martínez Montes, "The Catholic Origins of Globalization," *Globalist*, June 1, 2012.

52. Ferguson, *Civilization*, 12.

53. Braudel, *A History of Civilization*, 111.

54. Fuller, *A World Without Islam*, 8.

55. Tariq Ali, *The Clash of Fundamentalisms: Crusades, Jihads and Modernity* (London: Verso, 2003), 179.

56. These included the Council of Rome (382), the Synods of Hippo (393), and Councils of Carthage (397 and 419), the latter three coming after Christianity had become the state religion. Among the rejected Gospels, specialists list ten "Gnostic" Gospels (nearly all from the second century), four "Judeo-Christian" Gospels (second century), eight "infancy Gospels" (second to eighth centuries), a Gospel of Peter (second century), six fragmentary Gospels, twelve lost Gospels, and also other "false (Gnostic) Gospels," according to an account from Epiphanius, bishop of Salamis (fourth century). As for the Koran, it was the third caliph, Othman, who ordered the publication of a single text in 651 and the destruction of all other existing versions. No such fate was possible for the hadiths.

57. Sadakat Kadri, *Heaven on Earth: A Journey Through Shari'a Law from the Deserts of Ancient Arabia to the Streets of the Modern Muslim World* (New York: Farrar, Straus and Giroux, 2012), 63.

58. Shiism in turn can be divided into six main families: Twelver, Ismaelite, Zaydite, Alawite, Alevi, and Kaysanite. The latter three are not always considered as Shiite; plus some fifteen subfamilies (most famously the Druze), and other tendencies that define themselves as Muslim (Ibadism, Azraqite, etc.) as well as nonrecognized heterodox Muslims. The "official" divisions within Sunnism can be boiled down to four principal juridical schools, but today there are countless divisions and divergences concerning theology, politics, and, especially, the daily lives of the faithful.

59. Kadri, *Heaven on Earth*, 51.

60. In September 1970 Jordan (a majority-Palestinian country) unleashed military operations against the Palestine Liberation Front, leading to 20,000 deaths, most of them among Palestinian refugees. When the PLO fled to Lebanon, civil war engulfed that country.

61. Huntington, *The Clash of Civilizations*, 66.

9. THE CLASH OF IGNORANCE

1. Carlo Jean, "Ragione e oscurantismo," *Aspenia*, no. 42 (2008): 39.

2. Russell Shorto, *Saints and Madmen: Psychiatry Opens Its Doors to Religion* (New York: Henry Holt, 1999), 145–46.

3. Bernard Lewis, *From Babel to Dragomans: Interpreting the Middle East* (Oxford: Oxford University Press, 2004), 198.

4. Lewis notes that neither Christianity nor Islam requires hatred of the enemy; but, he adds, history teaches us that feelings of contempt by "those who possess the truth to those who reject it with contempt" can transform into hatred when the believer becomes jealous of the infidel and fears his power. Thus it is this dynamic that for Lewis explains Christians' hatred of Muslims and Muslims' tolerance of Christians during the Middle Ages. For the same reasons, centuries later the situation was reversed.

5. Charles Selengut, *Sacred Fury: Understanding Religious Violence* (Lanham, Md.: Rowman & Littlefield, 2008), 15.

6. Steve Wells, *Drunk with Blood: God's Killings in the Bible* (Moscow, Id.: SAB Books, 2010), 28.

7. Peter Partner, *God of the Battles: Holy Wars of Christianity and Islam* (Princeton: Princeton University Press, 1998), 19, 4.

8. Michel Dousse, *Dieu en guerre: La violence au cœur des trois monothéismes* (Paris: Albin Michel, 2002), 8.

9. Ibid., 196.

10. Maxime Rodinson, *Muhammad* (London: I. B. Tauris, 2002), 111.

11. Tariq Ali, *The Clash of Fundamentalisms: Crusades, Jihads and Modernity* (London: Verso, 2003), 13.

12. John L. Esposito and Dalia Mogahed, *Who Speaks For Islam? What a Billion Muslims Really Think* (New York: Gallup Press, 2007), 155.

13. Graham Fuller, *A World Without Islam* (New York: Little, Brown, 2010), 8, 142.

14. Jean-Paul Sartre, *Anti-Semite and Jew* (New York: Schocken, 1948), XI.

15. Regina M. Schwartz, *The Curse of Cain: The Violent Legacy of Monotheism* (Chicago: University of Chicago Press, 1997), 5.

16. Barbara Spinelli, "Le occasioni perdute dell'euro," *La Stampa*, December 15, 1997.

17. Esposito and Mogahed, *Who Speaks For Islam?*, 141.

18. Bernard Lewis, *Islam and the West* (New York: Oxford University Press, 1993), 9.

19. Halford J. Mackinder, *Democratic Ideals and Reality: A Study in the Politics of Reconstruction* (Washington, D.C.: National Defense University, 1942), 72.

20. Robert D. Kaplan, *The Revenge of Geography: What the Map Tells Us About Coming Conflicts and the Battle Against Fate* (New York: Random House, 2012), 358.

21. Daniel Cohen "Y a-t-il une malédiction économique islamique?," *Le Monde*, December 2, 2001.

22. Keep in mind that the simple replacement rate for the population is conventionally set at 2.1 children per woman, which means that, not counting immigration, Europe would lose an estimated 70 million inhabitants between 2010 and 2060.

23. Jean-Claude Chesnais, *La démographie* (Paris: Presses Universitaires de France, 2002), 119.

24. Central Intelligence Agency, *The World Factbook*, continually updated, https://www.cia.gov/library/publications/the-world-factbook/, accessed October 15, 2015.

25. Dov Friedlander, "Fertility in Israel: Is the Transition to Replacement Level in Sight?," in United Nations Secretariat, Division of Economic and Social Affairs, Population Division, *Expert Group Meeting in Completing the Fertility Transition* (New York, 2002), 443.

26. I will not delve into the discussion generated by this verse (for example, the mistranslation of the verb *DaRaBa*, which has at least ten different meanings: to hit, but also to ignore, to leave, to condemn, to travel, etc.), not only because of my ignorance of the subject but also because what matters here is the historic interpretation of the text, all the more so if there is room for linguistic ambiguity.

27. Stephanie Coontz, *Marriage, a History: From Obedience to Intimacy, or How Love Conquered Marriage* (New York: Viking Penguin, 2005), 66.

28. In Italy, the penal code provision calling for a prison sentence of up to one year for an adulterous woman was abolished only in 1969; in France, it was the reform of 1975 that eliminated both the crime of adultery and the "honor crime" provision (reducing the penalty for the murder of lovers caught in flagrante delicto); in Italy, the law on "honor crimes" was abolished only in 1981.

29. Bernard Lewis, *What Went Wrong? The Clash Between Islam and Modernity in the Middle East* (New York: Oxford University Press, 2002), 83.

30. Noah Feldman, "Does Shariah Mean the Rule of Law?," *New York Times*, March 16, 2008.

31. According to Braudel, the dimensions of the slave trade in Islamic country were still very substantial in the nineteenth century: he cites an 1877 study estimating at 500,000 the number of African slaves transported annually to Muslim countries. Trafficking to the Muslim countries, Braudel explains, exceeded European trafficking because the latter was limited by the inherent difficulties of long maritime voyages.

32. Lewis, *What Went Wrong?*, 85.

33. Alan Ryan, *John Stuart Mill* (London: Routledge and Kegan Paul, 1974), 125.

34. Olivier Roy, *Globalized Islam: The Search for a New Ummah* (New York: Columbia University Press, 2004), 192.

35. Esposito and Mogahed, *Who Speaks For Islam?*, 110.

36. Ibid., 132.

37. Ali, *The Clash of Fundamentalisms*, 37.

38. Rodinson, *Muhammad*, 215.

39. Fernand Braudel, *A History of Civilization*, trans. and ed. Richard Mayne (New York: Penguin, 1994), 70.

40. Esposito and Mogahed, *Who Speaks For Islam?*, 35.

41. Sadakat Kadri, *Heaven on Earth: A Journey Through Shari'a Law from the Deserts of Ancient Arabia to the Streets of the Modern Muslim World* (New York: Farrar, Straus and Giroux, 2012), 50.

42. Olivier Roy, *Holy Ignorance: When Religion and Culture Part Ways* (Oxford: Oxford University Press, 2013), 114.

43. Fuller, *A World Without Islam*, 48.

44. Noah Feldman, *The Fall and Rise of the Islamic State* (Princeton: Princeton University Press, 2008), 7.

45. Richard W. Bulliet, *The Case for Islamo-Christian Civilization* (New York: Columbia University Press, 2004), 62.

46. Ibid.

47. Kadri, *Heaven on Earth*, 58.

48. Alain Gresh, "Il y a charia et charia," *Le Monde diplomatique*, August 20, 2012. The sin of *shirk* (literally "to associate") is among the gravest in Islam. Generally translated as "idolatry" or "polytheism," it consists of associating someone or something to God and making that person or thing an object of adoration or worship.

49. Abdullahi Ahmed An-Na'im, "Political Islam in National Politics and International Relations," in *The Desecularization of the World*, ed. Peter Berger (Washington, D.C.: Ethics and Public Policy Center, 1999), 117.

50. Kadri, *Heaven on Earth*, 55, 50.

51. Bulliet, *The Case for Islamo-Christian Civilization*, 28, 65.

52. Fuller, *A World Without Islam*, 122.

53. Caesaropapism is the intervention of political authorities in religious affairs. The first example is that of Constantine I, who presided over the Council of Nicaea in 325, during which it was the emperor himself—at the time still a pagan—who decided on the official doctrine of Christianity (the creed), as he would do again repeatedly during his reign.

54. Fuller, *A World Without Islam*, 12.

55. Lewis, *What Went Wrong?*, 114.

56. Feldman, *The Fall and Rise of the Islamic State*, 11.

57. Lewis, *What Went Wrong?*, 109.

10. THE BLOODY BORDERS OF RELIGION

1. Samuel Huntington, *The Clash of Civilizations and the Remaking of World Order* (New York: Simon & Schuster, 1996), 239.

2. Fernand Braudel, *A History of Civilization*, trans. and ed. Richard Mayne (New York: Penguin, 1994), 41.

3. Graham Fuller, *A World Without Islam* (New York: Little, Brown, 2010), 139.

4. Ibid., 286.

5. Fareed Zakaria, *The Post-American World* (New York: Norton, 2008), 156. The Mughal conquest of the sixteenth century was in fact the third encounter between Islam and the subcontinent. The first Arab merchants to convert to the new religion settled in the Kerala region during Muhammad's lifetime, mixing with the local populations; it was these merchants who brought the decimal system developed by the Indians to the Middle East, from where it spread to Europe. In the North, the Umayyads conquered Sindh region in the eighth century, and the Abbasid caliphs promoted the translation of the sacred Indian texts from Sanskrit into

Arabic. Between the tenth and twelfth centuries, the Turko-Persian dynasty of the Ghaznavids conquered the Punjab and founded the sultanate of Delhi, which was finally absorbed into the Mughal Empire in 1526.

6. Ananda K. Coomaraswamy, *Hinduism and Buddhism* (New York: Philosophical Library, 1943), 5.

7. Graham M. Schweig, "Foreword," in *Holy War: Violence and Bhagavad Gītā*, ed. Steven J. Rosen (Hampton, Va.: A Deepak, 2004), vii.

8. Francis X. Clooney, "Pain but Not Harm: Some Classical Resources Toward a Hindu Just War Theory," in *Just War in Comparative Perspective*, ed. Paul F. Robinson (Aldershot, U.K.: Ashgate, 2003), 202.

9. Steven J. Rosen, *Holy War: Violence and Bhagavad Gītā* (Hampton, Va: A Deepak, 2004), 30.

10. Goolam Vahed, "Gandhi, Indian Opinion, and the Making of Indo–South African Identity, 1903–14," *Comparative Studies of South Asia, Africa and the Middle East* 35, no. 2 (August 2015): 354–60.

11. Mahatma Gandhi, *Complete Works*, vol. 14 (New Delhi: Publications Division, Ministry of Information and Broadcasting, 1965), 440.

12. Mahatma Gandhi, "To Every Briton," in *The Gandhi Reader: A Sourcebook of His Life and Writings*, ed. Homer A. Jack (Bloomington: Indiana University Press, 1956), 345.

13. The chief concern of Indian Muslims, of course, was that they might find themselves completely at the mercy of the Hindu majority once the British departed. That is why, unlike the Hindu nationalists, the Muslims supported the military effort of the British Empire during World War II.

14. Michel Danino, "Sri Aurobindo and the Gita: The Problem of Non-Violence vs. Dharmic Action," in *Holy War: Violence and Bhagavad Gītā*, ed. Steven J. Rosen (Hampton, Va.: A Deepak, 2004), 52.

15. Alex Perry Bombay, "India's Great Divide," *Time*, August 11, 2003.

16. "Now We Are Fearless: Facts About Dalit Women," *World Council of Churches*, http://www.overcomingviolence.org/en/resources/campaigns/women-against -violence/now-we-are-fearless/dalit-fact-sheet.html, accessed October 1, 2015.

17. One might say that the caste system represents, for traditionalist Hinduism and the nationalist right, what the system of corporatism represented for Italian Catholics and Fascists until World War II.

18. *Hindutva* is an ideology built around the idea of protecting Indian and Hindu tradition (which are considered the same thing) against elements viewed as foreign, such as Islam, Christianity, socialism, and the West.

19. United Nations Population Division, *World Urbanization Prospects*, 2011 Revision (2005–2010 est.), http://esa.un.org/unpd/wpp/publications/Files/WPP2011 _HIGHLIGHTS.pdf, accessed October 1, 2015.

20. Central Intelligence Agency, *The World Factbook* (2013–14 edition), https://www.cia .gov/library/publications/the-world-factbook/, accessed October 15, 2015.

21. International Monetary Fund, 2015.

22. See "Afghanistan Worst Place in the World for Women, but India in Top Five," *Guardian*, June 15, 2011. According to *The Global Gender Gap Report 2013*, India ranked

very high (9th) in terms of political empowerment for women but had the sec-ond-lowest position (135th) for women's health and survival. It ranked 124th in economic opportunity and 120th in educational attainment. (*The Global Gender Gap Report 2013* is published by the World Economic Forum, in collaboration with fac-ulty at Harvard University and the University of California, Berkeley.) For the worst among the twenty largest economies, see Lyric Thompson, "The Worst Place to Be a Woman in the G20," Amnesty International, June 19, 2012.

23. Nita Bhalla, "India Advances, but Many Women Still Trapped in Dark Ages," *Reuters*, June 13, 2012.

24. World Health Organization Media Center, "Child Marriages: 39,000 Every Day," March 7, 2013.

25. Patricia Uberoi, "Family, Kinship and Marriage in India," in *Students' Britannica India: Select Essays*, ed. Dale Hoiberg (New Delhi: Encyclopædia Britannica India, 2000), 156.

26. Renuka Chowdhury, "India Tackles Domestic Violence," *BBC News*, October 26, 2006.

27. "Crimes Against Women," (Indian) National Crime Records Bureau, 2013.

28. Husain, despite his Muslim origins, received no support from the Indian ulema. To the contrary, they accused him of apostasy and blasphemy.

29. Jan Jakob Maria de Groot, "Militant Spirit of the Buddhist Clergy in China," *T'oung Pao*, vol. 2, no. 2 (1891): 127–39.

30. Michael K. Jerryson and Mark Juergensmeyer, *Buddhist Warfare* (New York: Oxford University Press, 2010), 10.

31. Ibid., 13.

32. Wendy Doniger O'Flaherty, *The Origins of Evil in Hindu Mythology* (Berkeley: Univer-sity of California Press, 1976), 94.

33. The number of schools of Buddhism would suggest that such clashes have been frequent through history. Drawing on information from a variety of sources, and making no pretense of being exhaustive, we were able to count eighteen principal schools of Hinayana, including Theravada (in Thailand, Laos, Cambodia, and Sri Lanka), plus ten older branches; several schools of Mahayana, two of them Indian and ten others medieval Chinese, from which offshoots developed later in Japan, Korea, and Vietnam; some forty schools born in Japan from the Buddhism of Nichi-ren; and, finally, the newer religious movements (Soka Gakkai, Reiyukai, Rissho Ko-sei Kai). The other large branch was that of the schools of Vajrayāna, including the Sino-Japanese tantric schools, with some 20 million followers, and the four main schools of Tibetan Buddhism, with 15–20 million adherents.

34. Brian Victoria, *Zen War Stories* (Abingdon, N.Y.: Routledge Curzon, 2003), 67.

35. Jerryson and Juergensmeyer, *Buddhist Warfare*, 142.

36. Matthew O'Lemmon, "Buddhist Identity and the 1973 Cambodian Buddhist Holy War," *Asian Anthropology* 10, no. 1 (2011): 121–38.

37. Louis Gabaude, "Approche du bouddhisme thaï," in *Thaïlande contemporaine*, ed. Sté-phane Dovert (Paris: L'Harmattan, 2001), 41.

38. Simon Montlake, "Tiny Bhutan Aims to Become First Smoke-Free Nation," *Christian Science Monitor*, November 24, 2003.

39. I. P. Adhikari, "Kagyupa Only," *Himāl South Asian*, January 2011, http://old .himalmag.com/component/content/article/3551-kagyupa-only.html.

11. TERRORISM

1. The "red" terrorism of the 1970s can also be linked to nationalism via the ideology of "proletarian nations," invented by the Italian nationalists of the 1910s, taken up later by Fascism and recycled by certain pro-neutrality and anti-American groups, whether Catholic, Third Worldist, or Maoist.

2. Michael A. Sheehan, "Terrorism: The Current Threat," lecture at the Brookings Institution, Washington, D.C., February 10, 2000.

3. Terry Nardin, "Review: Terror in the Mind of God, by Mark Juergensmeyer," *Journal of Politics* 63, no. 2 (May 2001): 683–84.

4. Robert Michael, *A Concise History of American Antisemitism* (Lanham, Md.: Rowman and Littlefield, 2005), 137.

5. According to certain "literalist" Christians, the Bible (notably the books of Ezekiel and Daniel) states that the Last Judgment will take place when all Jews have returned to their biblical homeland.

6. John L. Esposito and Dalia Mogahed, *Who Speaks For Islam? What a Billion Muslims Really Think* (New York: Gallup Press, 2007), 76.

7. Takis Michas, *Unholy Alliance: Greece and Milosevic's Serbia* (College Station: Texas A&M University Press, 2002), 109–19.

8. One of these guerrilla priests, the Franciscan Silvano Girotto, having returned to Italy after the 1973 coup d'état in Chile, infiltrated the Red Brigades, contributing decisively to the arrest of its leaders.

9. Martin Dillon, *God and the Gun: The Church and Irish Terrorism* (London: Orion, 1997), 103, 129, 141.

10. "Cardinal Conway Was Wrong to Send a Terrorist Priest to Another Parish," *Catholic Herald*, August 25, 2010.

11. Esther Webman, "Adoption of the Protocols in the Arab Discourse on the Arab-Israeli Conflict, Zionism, and the Jews," in *The Global Impact of the Protocols of the Elders of Zion: A Century-Old Myth*, ed. Esther Webman (Abington, N.Y.: Routledge, 2011), 176. Unlike many other historians, Webman affirms on this same page that the very first translation from French into Arabic was made by an Egyptian priest, al-Khuri Anton Yamin, who published the book "in the mid-1920s" under the title *Mu'marat al yahudiyya 'ala al-shu'ub* (The Jewish Plot against the Nations).

12. Henri Laurens, "Le Vatican et la question de la Palestine," in *Nations et Saint-Siège au XXe siècle*, ed. Hélène Carrère d'Encausse and Philippe Levillain (Paris: Fayard, 2000), 311.

13. Agostino Casaroli, *Il martirio della pazienza: La Santa Sede e i paesi comunisti (1963-1989)* (Turin: Einaudi, 2000), 221, 222.

14. "List of Terrorist Incidents in India," *Wikipedia*, last modified September 21, 2015, https://en.wikipedia.org/wiki/List_of_terrorist_incidents_in_India.

15. Robert Pape, *Dying to Win: The Strategic Logic of Suicide Terrorism* (New York: Random House, 2005), 139–54.

16. According to Yoram Schweitzer, 68 percent of all suicide attacks between 1980 and 2000 were perpetrated by nonreligious groups, and 20.6 percent were by openly religious groups (Yoram Schweitzer, "Suicide Terrorism: Development and Characteristics," International Institute for Counter-Terrorism, April 21, 2000). Robert Pape writes that this trend continued until 2003. See Pape, *Dying to Win*, 3. The United Nations Assistance Mission in Afghanistan reported the first two suicide attacks in Afghanistan in 2003, a number that rose to 140 in 2006 and 239 in 2008 (UN Assistance Mission in Afghanistan, Suicide Attacks in Afghanistan, 2001–2007, September 9, 2007). According to other sources, between 2003 and 2010 there were 336 suicide attacks in Afghanistan, 303 in Pakistan, and 1,003 in Iraq. See Jennifer Hesterman, *Soft Target Hardening: Protecting People from Attack* (Boca Raton, Fla: CRC Press, 2015), 194.

17. Shlomo Sand, *The Invention of the Jewish People* (London: Verso, 2009), 254.

18. State of Israel, *Israel, the State and the Nation* (Government Yearbook, 5716/1955), 320.

19. Ami Pedahzur and Arie Perliger, *Jewish Terrorism in Israel* (New York: Columbia University Press, 2009), 32.

20. Ibid., 98–110.

21. Tzvetan Todorov, *The Fear of Barbarians: Beyond the Clash of Civilizations* (Chicago: University of Chicago Press, 2010), 97.

22. Robert Pape, "The Logic of Suicide Terrorism," *American Conservative*, July 18, 2005.

23. Esposito and Mogahed, *Who Speaks For Islam?*, 92.

24. Olivier Roy, *L'islam mondialisé* (Paris: Seuil, 209), 37.

25. Pape, "The Logic of Suicide Terrorism."

26. Michael W. Reisman, "The Resistance in Afghanistan Is Engaged in a War of National Liberation," *American Journal of International Law* 81, no. 4 (October 1987): 906–9.

27. Liah Greenfeld, "Nationalism and Terrorism," *Project Syndicate*, September 10, 2012.

28. Petroleum revenues have clearly played an essential role in the global expansion of Wahhabism, and thus in Saudi foreign policy. Saudi Arabia's official theologians have long insisted on the fact that the petroleum income is a gift from God to the land of Islam's birth, even if the oil wells are far from the holy sites and around 70 percent of them are in a region populated by Shiites (10–15 percent of the Saudi population), often considered by many Sunnis as "bad Muslims"—or not Muslims at all.

29. Roy, *L'islam mondialisé*, 36.

30. Zafar Mahmood Sheikh, "Normalization of Indo-Pak Ties Hurts Kashmir Cause: Salahuddin," *Arab News*, May 30, 2012.

12. DIALOGUE AMONG CIVILIZATIONS

1. Ernest Gellner, *Nations and Nationalism* (Ithaca: Cornell University Press, 1983), 22.

2. Robert J. Samuelson, "The Shutdown Heralds a New Economic Norm," *Washington Post*, October 14, 2013.

3. Stephen S. Cohen and J. Bradford DeLong, *The End of Influence: What Happens When Other Countries Have the Money* (New York: Basic Books, 2010), 2–3.

4. Bernard Lewis, "The Roots of Muslim Rage," *Atlantic Monthly*, vol. 266, no. 3, (September 1990): 47–60.

5. Brian Dickerson, "Adultery Could Mean Life, Court Finds," *Detroit Free Press*, January 15, 2007.

6. In the United States, in 1950 only 34 percent of women worked; the figure had risen to around 43 percent in the 1970s. Today some 60 percent of American women are part of the active workforce. See Howard N. Fullerton Jr., "Labor Force Participation: 75 Years of Change, 1950–98 and 1998–2025," *Monthly Labor Review* (December 1999): 3–12.

7. Emilio Dolcini, "Omosessualità, omofobia, diritto penale," *Stato, Chiese e pluralismo confessionale*, no. 16 (2012): 1–10.

8. Raphaël Liogier, *Souci de soi, conscience du monde: Vers une religion globale?* (Paris: Armand Colin, 2012), 6.

9. Raphaël Liogier, *Le mythe de l'islamisation: Essai sur une obsession collective* (Paris: Seuil, 2012), 207–9.

10. Marie Bellan "Immigration: Quel enjeu pour l'économie française?," *Les Échos*, April 26, 2011.

11. Xavier Chojnicki, Cécily Defoort, Carine Drapier, and Lionel Ragot, *Migrations et protection sociale: Étude sur les liens et les impacts de court et long terme* (Lille: Université Lille II, July 2010).

12. John L. Esposito and Dalia Mogahed, *Who Speaks For Islam? What a Billion Muslims Really Think* (New York: Gallup Press, 2007), 45.

13. Tony Barber, "Fortress Europe: Immigration," *Financial Times*, 14 June 2011.

14. Between 1980 and 1983, Iranian universities were closed to allow a "cultural revolution," which led to the exclusion of a large number of professors—somewhere between 700 and 8,000 out of a total of 12,000, according to various sources—and of 200,000 students.

15. Nicolas Dufays, "Les Relations de l'Union européenne avec la République islamique d'Iran: Une tradition de dialogue," *Émulations*, no. 7 (2010): 421–35.

16. Giandomenico Picco and Ahmed Kamal Aboulmagd, *Crossing the Divide: Dialogue Among Civilizations* (South Orange, N.J.: School of Diplomacy and International Relations, Seton Hall University, 2001), 68.

17. "About Us," *World Public Forum*, http://wpfdc.org/about-us/about, accessed October 1, 2015.

18. In 2002 Robert Cooper of Britain, the political adviser of Javier Solana, secretary general of the Council of the European Union, coined the concept "liberal

imperialism" for Europe, writing: "What is needed then is a new kind of imperialism, one acceptable to a world of human rights and cosmopolitan values . . . an imperialism which, like all imperialism, aims to bring order and organization but which rests today on the voluntary principle." See Robert Cooper, "The New Liberal Imperialism," *Guardian*, April 7, 2002.

19. Samuel Huntington, *The Clash of Civilizations and the Remaking of World Order* (New York: Simon & Schuster, 1996), 178.

20. An October 2011 opinion poll by the Institut français d'opinion publique found that 68 percent of French citizens were hostile to Turkey's entry into the European Union; a survey by the same organization in 2005 placed the level of hostility at 50 percent. In a Eurobarometer survey in July 2006, French attitudes toward Turkey were more negative than the European average on all eight questions asked.

21. Amartya Sen, *Identity and Violence: The Illusion of Destiny* (London: Penguin, 2007), 10–15.

22. According to the 2010 edition of *The Cambridge Dictionary of Christianity*, there are 20,800 Protestant denominations in the world, while the 2001 edition of the *World Christian Encyclopedia* puts the figure at 33,820, and the 2005 publication of *The Routledge Companion to the Study of Religion* cites 38,000 Christian denominations around the world, the enormous majority of them evangelical.

23. Nancy L. Wilson, "Is the Pope Catholic?," *Huffington Post*, February 2, 2013.

24. Two large communities define themselves as "Orthodox." The first—calling itself the "Church of the Three Councils" because it rejects all decisions taken starting with the fourth council, at Chalcedon, in Asia Minor, in 451—includes the Coptic Church, the Ethiopian Church, and the Armenian Church. The second, referred to as "Greek-Orthodox" or "of the Seven Councils," includes fifteen "canonical" churches, recognized by the entire community, plus seventeen "autonomous" churches, of disputed status, as well as thirty-five "independent" churches, which are not recognized by the rest of the Orthodox community.

25. Interfax, "Eastern Christian Countries Capable of Altering Humankind in 10 Years—Archpriest Chaplin," *Interfax*, May 14, 2012.

26. Interfax, "Religious Factor in International Relations," *Interfax*, October 24, 2013.

13. THE CATHOLIC ALLIANCE

1. Remarks by Pope John XXIII to Amintore Fanfani, president of the Italian Council of Ministers, April 11, 1961.

2. Giacomo Biffi, *Risorgimento, Stato laico e identità nazionale* (Casale Monferrato: Edizioni Piemme, 1999), 44.

3. Jakub Grygiel, "The Power of Statelessness," *Policy Review*, no. 154 (April/May 2009): 35–50.

4. Alberto Caracciolo, *Roma capitale: Dal Risorgimento alla crisi dello Stato liberale* (Rome: Edizioni Riuniti, 1956), 147.

5. David I. Kertzer, *Prisoner of the Vatican: The Pope's Secret Plot to Capture Rome from the New Italian State* (Boston: Houghton Mifflin, 2004), 17.

6. Pope Leon XIII attempted to slow France's loss of influence by ordering, in 1892, Catholics to rally behind republican institutions, but he managed only to confuse his flock—giving rise to the legend that the pope had been kidnapped, imprisoned in the "caves of the Vatican," and replaced by a look-alike—without managing to ease the pressure from the anticlerical forces. The Dreyfus affair, finally, sharpened the dispute between Catholics and republicans until the law on the separation of church and state was passed in 1905.

7. Stewart Stehlin, "The Emergence of a New Vatican Diplomacy During the Great War and Its Aftermath, 1914–1929," in *Papal Diplomacy in the Modern Age*, ed. Peter C. Kent and John F. Pollard (Westport, Conn.: Praeger, 1994), 75.

8. Roger Aubert, "Le demi-siècle qui a préparé Vatican II," in *Nouvelle histoire de l'Église*, vol. 5: *L'Église dans le monde moderne*, ed. Ludovicus Jacobus Rogier, Roger Aubert, and David Knowles (Paris: Seuil, 1975), 584.

9. Ibid., 588.

10. This dogma affirms that the pope is infallible when he expresses himself *ex cathedra*, that is, in the accomplishment of his pastoral function and his role as the supreme teacher of Christian doctrine in matters of faith and morality. Contrary to widespread belief, the conditions for any papal declaration being considered "infallible" are very strict, and the cases in which it has been invoked have been rather rare.

11. Kertzer, *Prisoner of the Vatican*, 107.

12. "St. Peter's Pence" has become an annual collection of funds destined for Rome. In 1870 the total French contribution amounted to 40.9 percent of the total; in 2007, when the last country-by-country breakdown was released, France's share was only 3.68 percent, with American Catholics being the most generous, 28.9 percent, followed by the Italians and the Germans. In 2011 receipts for Saint Peter's Pence totaled $69.7 million.

13. Arturo Carlo Jemolo, *Chiesa e Stato in Italia negli ultimi cento anni* (Turin: Einaudi, 1948), 42.

14. Grygiel, "The Power of Statelessness."

15. Carl Schmitt, *Roman Catholicism and Political Form* (Westport, Conn.: Greenwood Press, 1996), 7.

16. Andrea Riccardi, "In te, Domine, speravi; non confundar in æternum," *Giorni nella Chiesa e nel mondo*, no. 5 (May 2005).

17. Giorgio Feliciani, "La codificazione del diritto canonico e la riforma della curia romana," in *Elio Guerriero*, ed. Annibale Zambarbieri (Cinisello Balsamo: Edizioni Paoline, 1990), 293–315.

18. Jacques Fontana, *Les catholiques français pendant la Grande Guerre* (Paris: Les éditions du Cerf, 1990), 282, 372.

19. Giordano Bruno Guerri, *Gli italiani sotto la Chiesa: Da san Pietro a Mussolini* (Milan: Mondadori, 1995), 256.

20. John F. Pollard, *Money and the Rise of the Modern Papacy: Financing the Vatican, 1850–1950* (Cambridge: Cambridge University Press, 2005), 115.

21. Eugenio Pacelli, "Circa la situazione della Santa Sede in Italia," *Limes: Rivista italiana di geopolitica*, no. 3 (1993): 109–22.

22. Shlomo Sand, *The Invention of the Jewish People* (London: Verso, 2009), 174.

23. Andrea Riccardi, "La potenza profonda," *Limes: Rivista italiana di geopolitica*, no 1, (August 2009): 11.

24. According to a survey by the *Pew Forum on Religion & Public Life* in 2009, 44 percent of Americans say they have given up the religious community of their own families. This statistic takes on added interest when one considers that 200,000 Americans converted, or reconverted, to Catholicism from 1997 to 2009, for a growth rate of 11 percent, while the overall population grew by 8.5 percent.

14. THE HOLY ALLIANCE

1. John Connelly, *From Enemy to Brother: The Revolution in Catholic Teaching on the Jews, 1933–1965* (Cambridge, Mass.: Harvard University Press, 2012), 175.

2. Ibid., 176.

3. William Simpson, "The Ten Points of Seelisberg: A Significant Anniversary," *Revue SIDIC*, no. 1 (1977): 21–25.

4. Liliana Picciotto, "The Vatican and the Anti-Jewish Persecution," *Centro Primo Levi Online Monthly*, March 26, 2012, http://primolevicenter.org/printed-matter/the -vatican-and-the-anti-jewish-persecution/; Léon Poliakov, *Il nazismo e lo sterminio degli ebrei* (Turin: Einaudi, 1955), 397. Since a complete record of the attitude of the central authorities of the Catholic Church toward the Holocaust is not yet available, it is impossible to comment confidently on the true reasons for Pius XII's silence— but the silence is undeniable.

5. Robert Michael, *A Concise History of American Antisemitism* (Lanham, Md.: Rowman & Littlefield, 2005), 150.

6. *Miscellanea historiæ ecclesiasticæ*, vol. 9 (Louvain: Publications Universitaires de Louvain, 1984), 488.

7. Eugenio Scalfari, "Papa Francesco a Scalfari: Così cambierò la Chiesa," *La Repubblica*, October 1, 2013.

8. Thomas Stransky, "The Genesis of Nostra Aetate," *America Magazine: The National Catholic Weekly*, October 24, 2005.

9. Ralph Stehly, "Le concile de Vatican II (1962–1964) et l'islam," http://stehly.chez -alice.fr/vatican.htm, accessed October 1, 2015.

10. Michel Lelong, *Les papes et l'islam* (Monaco: Éditions Alphée, 2009), 56.

11. Speech in Casablanca, August 19, 1985.

12. Meeting with representatives of some Muslim communities, Cologne, August 20, 2005.

13. Bernard Lewis, *Islam and the West* (New York: Oxford University Press, 1993), 5–7.

14. Jean Flori, *Guerre sainte, jihad, croisade* (Paris: Seuil, 2002), 125–26.

15. Ibid., 157.

16. Lewis, *Islam and the West*, 13.

17. Abd Ar Rahman bin Muhammed ibn Khaldun, *The Muqaddimah*, trans. Franz Rosenthal (Princeton: Princeton University Press, 2015), 216–18.

18. Peter Partner, *God of Battles: Holy Wars or Christianity and Islam* (Princeton: Princeton University Press, 1998), 108.

19. Lewis, *Islam and the West*, 89.

20. Henri de Boulainvilliers, *La vie de Mahomed: Avec des réflexions sur le religion mahométane et les coutumes des Musulmans* (Amsterdam: Chez Francois Changuion, 1731), 85, 225.

21. Lewis, *Islam and the West*, 96. As a general rule, however, the Enlightenment thinkers attacked Islam as they did every other major religion. The *Encyclopédie* of d'Alembert and Diderot, for example, described the Koran as a "book brimming over with contradictions, absurdities and anachronisms," although its morality was considered as superior to that of Christianity.

22. Pascal Bruckner, "Invidia del Ramadan," *Il Sole 24 Ore*, August 29, 2009.

23. Message to Muslims for the end of Ramadan, April 3, 1991.

24. Jean Hippolyte Michon, *La Papauté à Jérusalem* (Paris: Chez E. Dentu Libraire, 1856), 49–51.

25. *Index librorum prohibitorum* is a list of works that Catholics were not authorized to read. Established in 1559, it was abolished on June 14, 1966.

26. Frédérique Neau-Dufour and Ernest Psichari, *L'ordre et l'errance* (Paris: Éditions du Cerf, 2001), 216.

27. Ernest Psichari, *Le voyage du centurion* (Paris: L'Harmattan, 1994), 119.

28. For the Muslim schools, see "L'émergence de l'enseignement musulman," *Al-Kanz*, October 11, 2014. According to an article published by *Le Monde* on June 13, 2014, entitled, "Un collège musulman «sous le choc» après le refus de l'État de le prendre sous contrat," in 2014, there were only about twenty Muslim schools in France. Concerning the number of Catholic schools, see "Les chiffres clés de l'enseignement catholique," Enseignement catholique actualités, no. 343 (February–March 2012).

29. Lelong, *Les papes et l'islam*, 167.

30. Amin Maalouf, *Les Croisades vues par les Arabes: La barbarie franque en Terre Sainte* (Paris: Editions Jean-Claude Lattès, 1983), 254.

31. Orthodox Christianity, being fundamentally territorial and national, normally does not aim at the conversion of peoples who do not live within the national territory. A notable exception was the conversion of the Muslim Tatars following the conquest of Kazan by Ivan the Terrible in 1552. The czars later banned the practice to avoid transforming the conquered peoples of Central Asia into a potential fifth column for the eternal Turkish enemy.

32. Hyppolite Desprez, "L'Église d'orient," in *Revue des Deux Mondes*, vol. 4 (Paris: Bureau de la Revue des Deux Mondes, 1853), 54.

33. Anonymous, "La Papauté et la question romaine au point de vue de Saint-Petersbourg," in *Revue des Deux Mondes*, vol. 5 (Paris: Bureau de la Revue des Deux Mondes, 1850), 124.

34. Ivan-Xavier Gagarin, *La Russie sera-t-elle catholique?* (Paris: Charles Douniol Libraire, 1856), 84–85.

35. Constantin G. Patelos, *Vatican I et les évêques uniates: Une étape éclairante de la politique romaine à l'égard des orientaux, 1867-1870* (Turnhout, Belgium: Bibliothèque de la Revue d'histoire ecclésiastique, 1981), 48.

36. Roger Aubert, "Le demi-siècle qui a préparé Vatican II," in *Nouvelle histoire de l'Église*, vol. 5: *L'Église dans le monde moderne*, ed. Ludovicus Jacobus Rogier, Roger Aubert, and David Knowles (Paris: Seuil, 1975), 652.

37. Ibid., 652–53.

38. Peter C. Kent and John F. Pollard, "A Diplomacy Unlike Any Other: Papal Diplomacy in the Nineteenth and Twentieth Centuries," in *Papal Diplomacy in the Modern Age*, ed. Peter C. Kent and John F. Pollard (Westport, Conn.: Praeger, 1994), 17.

39. David Alvarez, *Spies in the Vatican: Espionage and Intrigue from Napoleon to the Holocaust* (Lawrence: University Press of Kansas, 2002), 135. Jonathan Luxmoore and Jolanta Babiuch report that, a few months after the revolution of October 1917, "some Vatican sources" referred to a "positive evolution in Russia." The same authors note that a Catholic vicariate was created in Siberia in 1921 and was transformed in 1923 into the diocese of Vladivostok. See Jonathan Luxmoore and Jolanta Babiuch, *The Vatican and the Red Flag: The Struggle for the Soul of Eastern Europe* (London: Geoffrey Chapman, 1999), 9–10. According to Stewart Stehlin, "Moscow initially showed interest, but was not willing to negotiate on matters considered vital to the Vatican, such as the founding of religious school in Russia." See Stehlin, "The Emergence of a New Vatican Diplomacy During the Great War and Its Aftermath, 1914-1929," in *Papal Diplomacy in the Modern Age*, ed. Peter C. Kent and John F. Pollard (Westport, Conn.: Praeger, 1994), 81.

40. Michael Burleigh, *Sacred Causes: The Clash of Religion and Politics, from the Great War to the War on Terror* (New York: HarperCollins, 2006), 263.

41. These are conservative estimates from the Croatian economist Vladimir Zerjavic, though they are rejected by the Wiesenthal Center. The most pessimistic historians speak of 322,000 Serbians, 255,000 Croatians, 77,000 Muslims, 26,000 Jews, and 16,000 Roma. In 1945 Pavelić and other dignitaries were welcomed at the San Girolamo monastery in Rome, which, according to Hrvoje Matković, was later the scene of the creation of the Hrvatski državni odbor, the Ustashi terrorist network that remained active until the proclamation of Croatian independence in 1991.

42. Andrew E. Kramer, "Russia Gas Pipeline Heightens East Europe's Fears," *New York Times*, October 12, 2009.

43. "Anyone for Schadenfreude?," *Economist*, August 7, 2008.

44. "La Chiesa cattolica in Russia non segue alcuna strategia di proselitismo," *Zenit*, September 8, 2004.

45. Sandro Magister, "Tra Roma e Mosca è nata una santa alleanza," March 24, 2010, http://chiesa.espresso.repubblica.it/articolo/1343399. These lines were written long before the historical meeting between Pope Francis and the patriarch of Moscow, Kirill II, in Havana in February 2016.

46. Aubert, "Le demi-siècle qui a préparé Vatican II," 524–27.

47. Ibid., 652–53.

48. Ibid., 678.

49. Ibid., 679.

50. According to the official website of the Holy See, the Pontifical Council for Promoting Christian Unity maintains relationships with certain Orthodox Churches of the Byzantine tradition (eight patriarchates, including those of Constantinople and Moscow, and five autocephalous churches), the six Eastern Orthodox Churches, the Apostolic Assyrian Church of the East, the Anglican Communion, the World Lutheran Federation, the World Methodist Council, the World Reformed Alliance (Calvinist), the World Baptist Alliance, the Christian Church of the Disciples of Christ (American Protestant), certain "classical" Pentecostalist Churches, the World Evangelical Alliance, the international Old Catholic Church of Utrecht, and, of course, the Ecumenical Council of Churches. The Commission for Religious Relations with Judaism—as surprising as it may seem—is an organ of the Council for Christian Unity. In the Pontifical Council for Interreligious Dialogue, there is a commission for relations with Muslims; no other religion is mentioned.

51. Benedict XVI, "Pope's Speech to Lutheran Leaders," *Catholic Herald*, September 23, 2011.

15. ALL ROADS LEAD TO ROME

1. Olivier Roy, *Holy Ignorance: When Religion and Culture Part Ways* (Oxford: Oxford University Press, 2013), 134.

2. Ibid., 1.

3. Ibid., 5, 6.

4. Ibid., 208.

5. Roy prefers to speak of the "transformation" and the "reformulation" of religions rather than of their "return." It is true that religions *have always been there*, despite the progress of secularization, but have been essentially confined to the countryside, where the eye of the sociologist is rarely on them. It is in the contact with the city or, more precisely, the industrialized city—with the uprooting and separation between religion and culture that occurs there—that the "transformation" takes place.

6. Pippa Norris and Ronald Inglehart, *Sacred and Secular: Religion and Politics Worldwide* (New York: Columbia University Press, 2004), 18.

7. Meera Nanda, *The God Market: How Globalization Is Making India More Hindu* (New York: Random House, 2010), 189.

8. Peter Berger, *The Desecularization of the World: Resurgent Religion and World Politics* (Grand Rapids, Mich.: Eerdmans, 1999), 4.

9. Cornelius A. Buller, *The Unity of Nature and History in Pannenberg's Theology* (Lanham, Md.: Rowman & Littlefield, 1996), 110.

10. Joseph Ratzinger, *Europe: Today and Tomorrow* (San Francisco: Ignatius Press, 2007), 21.

11. Shahar Ilan, "Reconciling Conscription," *Haaretz*, April 21, 2008.

12. *Nostra Ætate*, Declaration on the Relation of the Church to Non-Christian Religions, October 28, 1965, § 2.

13. Roy, *Holy Ignorance*, 208.

14. "L'Annuario Pontificio 2016 e l' 'Annuarium Statisticum Ecclesiae' 2014," *Bollettino Sala Stampa della Santa Sede*, March 5, 2016.

15. According to the Center for Applied Research in the Apostolate (CARA) at Georgetown University, the percentage of American Catholics who take part in church functions at least once a week has grown from 22 percent in 2000, to 23 percent in 2005, to 24 percent in 2012. According to CARA, between 1980 and 2008 such participation also rose in Italy and Brazil (CARA, "Frequently Requested Church Statistics," October 21, 2014). The Christian Research Institute has found that, in the United Kingdom, "the Roman Catholic Church is continuing to enjoy a rise in attendance at Mass," as the *Telegraph* reported in 2010 (see Jonathan Wynne-Jones, "Churches Halt Decline, New Research Shows," December 19, 2010). A few years before the same author reported that the number of practicing Catholics in the United Kingdom had passed the number of Anglicans: 861,000 to 852,000 (see Jonathan Wynne-Jones, "Britain Has Become a Catholic Country," *Telegraph*, December 23, 2007).

16. Joseph Ratzinger, *Salt of the Earth: Christianity and the Catholic Church at the End of the Millennium: An Interview with Peter Seewald* (San Francisco: Ignatius Press, 1997), 16.

17. Joseph Ratzinger, *Il sale della terra: Cristianesimo e Chiesa cattolica nella svolta del terzo millennio. Un colloquio con Peter Seewald* (Cinisello Balsamo: Ed. S. Paolo, 1997), 222. This quote is translated here directly from the Italian version, because in the English edition the concept has been slightly but significantly changed with the sentence, "We can no longer take for granted a universal Christian atmosphere" (see *Salt of the Earth*, 265).

18. Ratzinger, *Salt of the Earth*, 222.

19. Joseph Ratzinger and Marcello Pera, *Without Roots: Europe, Relativism, Christianity, Islam* (New York: Basic Books, 2006), 80. As to this minority status, we must emphasize that the church is in less of a minority position than any of the forces with which it competes. As René Rémond has written, "Even in the most secularized societies, the religious presence, when viewed statistically . . . is by far, among social factors of voluntary nature, the most massive." See René Rémond, *Religion et société en Europe: Essai sur la sécularisation des sociétés européennes aux XIXe et XXe siècles (1789–2000)* (Paris: Seuil, 1998), 274. As an example: the demonstrations in France against the proposed retirement reforms of October 12, 2010, were, according to the labor unions, "the most massive of the past 20 years," with 3.5 million participants—1.23 million according to the police. If, as reported by *Libération* on February 13, 2013, the number of practicing Catholics in France is close to six million, that would mean that each week, the number of people participating voluntarily in Catholic functions would be twice—or even five times more, if one uses the police estimate—the

number of people the unions are able to mobilize only once every twenty years. To complete this picture we should add that, according to differing sources, the number of French Catholics who take part in a religious function at least once a week is between 4.5 and 15 percent of the population, that is, anywhere between 2.8 million and 9.5 million people.

20. Eugenio Scalfari, "Papa Francesco a Scalfari: Così cambierò la Chiesa," La Repubblica, October 1, 2013.

21. Massimo Franco, "Dietro il sacrificio estremo di un intellettuale le ombre di un 'rapporto segreto' choc," Corriere della Sera, February 12, 2013.

22. Antonio Gramsci, Prison Notebooks, vol. 2 (New York: Columbia University Press, 1996), 274.

23. Roy, Holy Ignorance, 30, 31–32.

24. Edward Gibbon, The History of the Decline and Fall of the Roman Empire, vol. 6 (Philadelphia, William Y. Birch & Abraham Small, 1805), 193.

25. James Kent, Commentaries on American Law, vol. 2, second ed. (New York: O. Halsted, 1832), 104.

26. See Jeffrey M. Jones, "In U.S., 3 in 10 Say They Take Bible Literally," Gallup Poll, July 8, 2011.

27. Alberto Melloni, Chiesa madre, chiesa matrigna: Un discorso storico sul cristianesimo che cambia (Turin: Einaudi, 2004), 100.

28. According to Hanson, a "primary ethical broker" is "an institution which is traditionally recognized by the majority of a national society to have the responsibility to articulate the primary ethical concerns of that society." By citing the examples of the Philippines and Latin America, where the church at the time had just accompanied the transition toward democracy, Hanson enlarges the role of "primary ethical broker" to the directly political domain. See Eric O. Hanson, The Catholic Church in the World Politics (Princeton: Princeton University Press, 1987), 257–58.

29. Samuel Huntington, The Clash of Civilizations and the Remaking of World Order (New York: Simon & Schuster, 1996), 304.

30. Ratzinger, Salt of the Earth, 241, 82.

31. The objective of the Humanæ Vitæ (1968) was not to oppose any given method of contraception while authorizing any other approach but rather to oppose the neo-Malthusian catastrophism of the era; fifty years later, in the face of a full-blown demographic crisis, this encyclical has often been described as "prophetic."

32. Paolo Rodari, "Alle prese con la zona grigia: Perché sui temi bioetici c'è più sintonia con anglicani e ortodossi che con i progressisti," Il Foglio, May 26, 2010.

33. Kirill I (Vladimir Michajlovič Gundjaev), "Norme di fede come norme di vita," L'Osservatore Romano, May 17, 2010.

34. Ratzinger, Europe, 21.

35. "The High Price of Togetherness," Economist, August 7, 2008.

36. "United We Fall," Economist, August 7, 2008.

37. "Is SC Verdict on Section 377 a War Between Gay Rights, Humanity?," Firstpost, December 12, 2013.

38. Giulio Meotti, "Il cantico del prof. Nazir-Ali," *Il Foglio*, September 28, 2008.
39. Michael Nazir-Ali, *Triple Jeopardy for the West: Aggressive Secularism, Radical Islamism and Multiculturalism* (London: Bloomsbury, 2012), 22. "Multiculturalism" is a term with many diverse meanings and usages, some of them quite different from one another. In addition to designating the coexistence of different cultures within a country, it can also refer to policies intended to assure equal status for different cultures or political communities, authorizing different cultural and religious communities to enjoy their specific status. Nazir-Ali uses it in this latter sense.
40. Meotti, "Il cantico del prof. Nazir-Ali."
41. Vsevolod Tchapline, "Ces dames sont priées d'aller se rhabiller," *Courrier International*, January 27, 2011.
42. Kobi Nahshoni, "Islamization of Europe a Good Thing," *Jewish World*, November 11, 2012.
43. Jonathan Sacks, "Religion in Twenty-First Century Britain," 2009 Annual Theos Lecture, November 4, 2009.
44. Mattia Ferraresi, "Prof. ebreo spiega che il nemico del dialogo in Egitto è la secolarizzazione," *Il Foglio*, January 5, 2011.
45. Gallup, "State of the States: Importance of Religion," *Gallup*, January 28, 2009.
46. Gallup, "Religion Provides Emotional Boost to World's Poor," *Gallup*, March 6, 2009.
47. Afshin Shahi, "Erotic Republic: Iran Is in the Throes of an Unprecedented Sexual Revolution. Could It Eventually Shake the Regime?," *Foreign Policy*, May 29, 2013.
48. Robert Kaplan, *The Revenge of Geography: What the Map Tells Us About the Coming Conflicts and the Battle Against Fate* (New Work: Random House, 2012), 281. We should not forget that the Iranian authorities were reportedly deeply hopeful that in the wake of the September 11 attacks, the United States would strike, in one way or another, at Iran's traditional enemies: Iraq, Saudi Arabia, Pakistan, and Pakistan's Taliban puppet government in Afghanistan.
49. Ibid., *The Revenge of Geography*, 277.
50. Tehran Bureau, "The Beauty Obsession Feeding Iran's Voracious Cosmetic Surgery Industry," *Guardian*, March 1, 2013.
51. Shahi, "Erotic Republic."
52. Magali Rheault and Dalia Mogahed, "Majorities See Religion and Democracy as Compatible," *Gallup News Service*, October 3, 2007.
53. Sciences Humaines, "Qui sont les fondamentalistes chrétiens?," *Sciences Humaines*, June 15, 2011.
54. Adrien Jaulmes, "Et si la Torah se substituait à la loi israélienne," *Le Figaro*, December 10, 2009.
55. Tariq Ali, *The Clash of Fundamentalisms: Crusades, Jihads and Modernity* (London: Verso, 2003), 195.
56. "Sri Lanka's Moral Policing: Young Lovers and Naked Women Had Better Watch Out," *Economist*, October 28, 2010
57. Sadakat Kadri, *Heaven on Earth: A Journey Through Shari'a Law from the Deserts of Ancient Arabia to the Streets of the Modern Muslim World* (New York: Farrar, Straus and Giroux, 2012), 278.

58. Noah Feldman, *The Fall and Rise of the Islamic State* (Princeton: Princeton University Press, 2008), 13.

59. John Paul II, *Memory and Identity: Personal Reflections* (London: Orion, 2005), 150–51.

60. Joseph S. Rossi, *Uncharted Territory: The American Catholic Church at the United Nations, 1946-1972* (Washington, D.C.: Catholic University of America Press, 2006), xii. The UN Conference on International Organization, better known as the San Francisco Conference, brought together fifty-one allied nations which, from April 25 to June 26, 1945, drafted the Charter of the United Nations.

61. The mission of this "true" world authority would be "to manage the global economy; to revive economies hit by the crisis; to avoid any deterioration of the present crisis and the greater imbalances that would result; to bring about integral and timely disarmament, food security and peace; to guarantee the protection of the environment; and to regulate migration." We should note that the publication of the encyclical, originally planned for 2008, was delayed to the following year in response to the global financial crisis.

62. Muslim Religious Leaders, "Open Letter to His Holiness Pope Benedict XVI," *Islamica Magazine*, October 12, 2006.

BIBLIOGRAPHY

Adhikari, I. P. "Kagyupa Only." *Himal South Asian*, January 2011. http://old.himalmag .com/component/content/article/3551-kagyupa-only.html.

Aikman, David. *Jesus in Beijing: How Christianity Is Transforming China and Changing the Global Balance of Power*. Oxford: Monarch, 2003.

Ali, Choudhary Rahmat. *Now or Never; Are We to Live or Perish Forever?* Pamphlet published in Cambridge, U.K., January 23, 1933. http://www.columbia.edu/itc/mealac/pritchett /00islamlinks/txt_rahmatali_1933.html.

Ali, Tariq. *The Clash of Fundamentalisms: Crusades, Jihads and Modernity*. London: Verso, 2003.

Allawi, Ali A. *The Crisis of Islamic Civilization*. New Haven: Yale University Press, 2009.

Alvarez, David. *Spies in the Vatican: Espionage and Intrigue from Napoleon to the Holocaust*. Lawrence: University Press of Kansas, 2002.

Amir-Aslani, Ardavan. *La guerre des Dieux: Géopolitique de la spiritualité*. Paris: Nouveau Monde, 2011.

An-Na'im, Abdullahi Ahmed. "Political Islam in National Politics and International Relations." In *The Desecularization of the World: Resurgent Religion and World Politics*. Edited by Peter Berger, 103–22. Grand Rapids, Mich.: Eerdmans, 1999.

Aubert, Roger. "Le demi-siècle qui a préparé Vatican II." In *Nouvelle histoire de l'église*. Vol. 5: *L'Église dans le monde moderne*. Edited by Ludovicus Jacobus Rogier, Roger Aubert, and David Knowles, 583–689. Paris: Seuil, 1975.

Axworthy, Michael. *Iran: Empire of the Mind: A History from Zoroaster to the Present Day*. New York: Basic Books, 2008.

Badur, Zehir-Ed-Din Muhammed. *Memoirs of Zehir-Ed-Din Muhammed Badur, Emperor of Hindustan*. Translated by John Leyden and William Erskine. London: Oxford University Press, 1921.

Barber, Tony. "Fortress Europe: Immigration." *Financial Times*, June 14, 2011.

Bartholomeusz, Tessa J. *In Defense of Dharma: Just-War Ideology in Buddhist Sri Lanka.* London: Routledge, 2002.

Beinin, Joel. *Workers and Peasants in the Modern Middle East.* Cambridge: Cambridge University Press, 2001.

Bellan, Marie. "Immigration: Quel enjeu pour l'économie française?" *Les Échos*, April 26, 2011.

Benedict XVI. "Pope's Speech to Lutheran Leaders." *Catholic Herald*, September 23, 2011.

Berger, Peter. "The Desecularization of the World: A Global Overview." In *The Desecularization of the World: Resurgent Religion and World Politics* Edited by Peter Berger, 1–18. Grand Rapids, Mich.: Eerdmans, 1999.

——. *The Sacred Canopy: Elements of a Sociological Theory of Religion.* Garden City, N.Y.: Doubleday, 1967.

Bhalla, Nita. "India Advances, but Many Women Still Trapped in Dark Ages." *Reuters*, June 13, 2012.

Biffi, Giacomo. *Risorgimento, Stato laico e identità nazionale.* Casale Monferrato: Edizioni Piemme, 1999.

Blum, William. *Killing Hope: U.S. Military and CIA Interventions Since World War II.* Montreal: Black Rose, 1998.

Bombay, Alex Perry. "India's Great Divide." *Time*, August 11, 2003.

Bovkalovski de Souza, Etiane Caloy, and Marionilde Dias Brepohl de Magalhães. "Os pentecostais: Entre a fé e a política." *Revista Brasileira de História* 22, no. 43 (2002): 85–103.

Boyle, Peter G., ed. *The Churchill-Eisenhower Correspondence, 1953–1955.* Chapel Hill: University of North Carolina Press, 1990.

Braudel, Fernand. *A History of Civilization.* Translated and edited by Richard Mayne. New York: Penguin, 1994.

——. *La Méditerranée: L'espace et l'histoire.* Paris: Groupe Flammarion, 1985.

Breitman, Richard, and Norman Goda. *Hitler's Shadow: Nazi War Criminals, U.S. Intelligence and the Cold War.* Washington, D.C.: National Archives, 2011.

Brown, Peter. *The World of Late Antiquity: AD 150–750.* London: Times & Hudson, 1971.

Bruckner, Pascal. "Invidia del Ramadan." *Il Sole 24 Ore*, August 29, 2009.

Buller, Cornelius A. *The Unity of Nature and History in Pannenberg's Theology.* Lanham, Md.: Rowman & Littlefield, 1996.

Bulliet, Richard W. *The Case for Islamo-Christian Civilization.* New York: Columbia University Press, 2004.

Bumiller, Elisabeth. "Remembering Afghanistan's Golden Age." *New York Times*, October 18, 2009.

Burleigh, Michael. *Sacred Causes: The Clash of Religion and Politics, from the Great War to the War on Terror.* New York: HarperCollins, 2006.

Caracciolo, Alberto. *Roma capitale: Dal Risorgimento alla crisi dello Stato liberale.* Rome: Edizioni Riuniti, 1956.

Carré, Olivier, and Gérard Michaud. *Les frères musulmans (1928–1982).* Paris: Gallimard, 1983.

Casanova, José. *Public Religions in the Modern World.* Chicago: University of Chicago Press, 1994.

Casaroli, Agostino. *Il martirio della pazienza: La Santa Sede e i paesi comunisti (1963-1989).* Turin: Einaudi, 2000.

Central Intelligence Agency. *The World Factbook.* Continually updated. https://www.cia.gov/library/publications/the-world-factbook/.

Chadwick, Owen. *The Secularization of the European Mind in the Nineteenth Century.* Cambridge: Cambridge University Press, 1975.

Chesnais, Jean-Claude. *La démographie.* Paris: Presses Universitaires de France, 2002.

Chojnicki, Xavier, Cécily Defoort, Carine Drapier, and Lionel Ragot. *Migrations et protection sociale: Étude sur les liens et les impacts de court et long terme.* Lille: Université Lille II, July 2010.

Chowdhury, Renuka. "India Tackles Domestic Violence," *BBC News,* October 26, 2006. http://news.bbc.co.uk/2/hi/south_asia/6086334.stm.

Chrysostom, John. "Homilies Against the Jews [Adversus Judeaus]." *Preterist Archive.* http://www.preteristarchive.com/ChurchHistory/0386_chrysostom_adversus-judeaus.html.

CNN. "Soldiers of God." *Cold War,* season 1, episode 20. Produced by Jody Gottlieb. Aired April 11, 1998.

Cohen, Daniel. "Y a-t-il une malédiction économique islamique?" *Le Monde,* December 2, 2001.

Cohen, Stephen S., and J. Bradford DeLong. *The End of Influence: What Happens When Other Countries Have the Money.* New York: Basic Books, 2010.

Connelly, John. *From Enemy to Brother: The Revolution in Catholic Teaching on the Jews, 1933-1965.* Cambridge, Mass.: Harvard University Press, 2012.

Coomaraswamy, Ananda K. *Hinduism and Buddhism.* New York: Philosophical Library, 1943.

Coontz, Stephanie. *Marriage, a History: From Obedience to Intimacy, or How Love Conquered Marriage.* New York: Viking Penguin, 2005.

Cooper, Robert. "The New Liberal Imperialism." *Guardian,* April 7, 2002.

Coquin, René-Georges. "Écueils 'théologiques' éventuels, dans le passage, pour les chrétiens d'Égypte, du copte à l'arabe." *L'École pratique des hautes études, Section des sciences religieuses Annuaire,* vol. 103, no. 99 (1990): 17-28.

Cordovez, Diego, and Selig S. Harrison. *Out of Afghanistan: The Inside Story of the Soviet Withdrawal.* New York: Oxford University Press, 1995.

Crews, Robert D. *For Prophet and Tsar: Islam and Empire in Russia and Central Asia.* Cambridge, Mass.: Harvard University Press, 2006.

Croce, Benedetto. *History of Europe in the Nineteenth Century.* Translated by Henry Furst. New York: Harcourt, Brace & World, 1933.

Cullather, Nick. "Damming Afghanistan: Modernization in a Buffer State." *Journal of American History* 89, no. 2 (September 2002): 512-37.

Curtis, Mark. *Secret Affairs: Britain's Collusion with Radical Islam.* London: Serpent's Tail, 2010.

Danino, Michel. "Sri Aurobindo and the Gita: The Problem of Non-Violence vs. Dharmic Action." In *Holy War, Violence and Bhagavad Gita.* Edited by Steven J. Rosen, 43-58. Hampton, Va.: A Deepak, 2004.

Dasgupta, Debarshi, and Pranay Sharma. "Buddha Mortified." *Outlook*, July 22, 2013.

Davidson, Paul. "Making Dollars and Sense of the U.S. Government Debt." *Journal of Post Keynesian Economics* 32, no. 4 (Summer 2010): 661–66.

de Boulainvilliers, Henri. *La vie de Mahomed: Avec des réflexions sur le religion mahometane et les coutumes des Musulmans*. Amsterdam: Chez Francois Changuion, 1731.

de Groot, Jan Jakob Maria. "Militant Spirit of the Buddhist Clergy in China." *T'oung Pao*, vol. 2, no. 2 (1891): 127–39.

Desprez, Hyppolite. *"L'Église d'orient."* In *Revue des Deux Mondes: Tome IV*. Paris: Bureau de la Revue des Deux Mondes, 1853.

Dickerson, Brian. "Adultery Could Mean Life, Court Finds." *Detroit Free Press*, January 15, 2007.

Dolcini, Emilio. "Omosessualità, omofobia, diritto penale." *Stato, Chiese e pluralismo confessionale*, no. 16 (2012): 1–10.

Doniger O'Flaherty, Wendy. *The Origins of Evil in Hindu Mythology*. Berkeley: University of California Press, 1976.

Dousse, Michel. *Dieu en guerre: La violence au cœur des trois monothéismes*. Paris: Albin Michel, 2002.

Dreyfuss, Robert. *Devil's Game: How the United States Helped Unleash Fundamentalist Islam*. New York: Henry Holt, 2006.

Dufays, Nicolas. "Les Relations de l'Union européenne avec la République islamique d'Iran: Une tradition de dialogue." *Émulations*, no. 7 (2010): 421–35.

Economist. "Anyone for Schadenfreude?" August 7, 2008.

——. "The High Price of Togetherness." August 7, 2008.

——. "Huntington's Clash." December 30, 2008.

——. "Sri Lanka's Moral Policing: Young Lovers and Naked Women Had Better Watch Out." October 28, 2010.

——. "United We Fall." August 7, 2008.

Elson, John. "Is God Dead?" *Time*, April 8, 1966.

"L'émergence de l'enseignement musulman." *Al-Kanz*, October 11, 2014.

Encyclopaedia Iranica. *Encyclopaedia Iranica*, vol. 1, no. 5. London: Routledge & Kegan Paul, 1985.

Energy Information Administration. "International Energy Statistics." https://www.eia .gov/beta/international/data/browser/#?ord=CR&cy=2014&v=H&vo=0&so=0&io=0& start=1980&end=2014.

Enseignement Catholique. "Les chiffres clés de l'enseignement catholique—no. 347 février-mars 2012." http://www.enseignement-catholique.fr/ec/images/stories/hs /eca347-chiffres-cles-2011–2012.pdf.

Esposito, John L. *Unholy Wars: Terror in the Name of Islam*. New York: Oxford University Press, 2002.

Esposito, John L., and Dalia Mogahed, *Who Speaks For Islam? What a Billion Muslims Really Think*. New York: Gallup Press, 2007.

Farrell, Stephen. "Baghdad Jews Have Become a Fearful Few." *New York Times*, June 1, 2008.

Feldman, Noah. "Does Shariah Mean the Rule of Law?" *New York Times*, March 16, 2008.

——. *The Fall and Rise of the Islamic State*. Princeton: Princeton University Press, 2008.

Feliciani, Giorgio. "La codificazione del diritto canonico e la riforma della curia romana." In *Elio Guerriero*. Edited by Annibale Zambarbieri, 293–315. Cinisello Balsamo: Edizioni Paoline, 1990.

Ferguson, Niall. *Civilization: The West and the Rest*. London: Penguin, 2011.

——. *The War of the World: History's Age of Hatred*. London: Penguin, 2006.

Ferraresi, Mattia. "Prof. ebreo spiega che il nemico del dialogo in Egitto è la secolarizzazione." *Il Foglio*, January 5, 2011.

Firstpost. "Is SC Verdict on Section 377 a War Between Gay Rights, Humanity?" *Firstpost*, December 12, 2013.

Flori, Jean. *Guerre sainte, jihad, croisade*. Paris: Seuil, 2002.

Fontana, Jacques. *Les catholiques français pendant la Grande Guerre*. Paris: Les éditions du Cerf, 1990.

Franco, Massimo. "Dietro il sacrificio estremo di un intellettuale le ombre di un 'rapporto segreto' choc." *Corriere della Sera*, February 12, 2013.

Freeman, Charles. *The Closing of the Western Mind: The Rise of Faith and the Fall of Reason*. New York: Vintage, 2002.

Frémont, Armand. "La terre." In *Les Lieux de mémoire*, vol. 3. Edited by Pierre Nora. Paris: Gallimard, 1997.

Friedlander, Dov. "Fertility in Israel: Is the Transition to Replacement Level in Sight?" In *United Nations Secretariat, Division of Economic and Social Affairs, Population Division, Expert Group Meeting in Completing the Fertility Transition*, 440–47. New York, 2002.

Fuller, Graham. *A World Without Islam*. New York: Little, Brown, 2010.

Fullerton, Howard N., Jr. "Labor Force Participation: 75 Years of Change, 1950–98 and 1998–2025." *Monthly Labor Review* (December 1999): 3–12.

Gabaude, Louis. "Approche du bouddhisme thaï." In *Thaïlande contemporaine*. Edited by Stéphane Dovert, 40–48. Paris: L'Harmattan, 2001.

Gagarin, Ivan-Xavier. *La Russie sera-t-elle catholique?* Paris: Charles Douniol Libraire, 1856.

Gallup. "Religion Provides Emotional Boost to World's Poor." March 6, 2009.

——. "State of the States: Importance of Religion." January 28, 2009.

Gandhi, Mohandas. *Complete Works*. Vol. 14. New Delhi: Publications Division, Ministry of Information and Broadcasting, 1965.

——. "To Every Briton." In *The Gandhi Reader: A Sourcebook of His Life and Writings*. Edited by Homer A. Jack. Bloomington: Indiana University Press, 1956.

Gellately, Robert, and Ben Kiernan, eds. *The Specter of Genocide: Mass Murder in Historical Perspective*. Cambridge: Cambridge University Press, 2003.

Gellner, Ernest. *Nations and Nationalism*. Ithaca: Cornell University Press, 1983.

Georgetown University Center for Applied Research in the Apostolate. "Frequently Requested Church Statistics." http://cara.georgetown.edu/frequently-requested -church-statistics/.

Gibbon, Edward. *The History of the Decline and Fall of the Roman Empire*. Vol. 6. Philadelphia: William Y. Birch & Abraham Small, 1805.

Giblin, Béatrice. *Géographie des conflits.* Paris: La Documentation française, 2012.

Godsell, Geoffrey. "1980s: Ayatollah, Pope Embody Rise of Religion." *Christian Science Monitor,* January 2, 1980.

Goodwin, Marshall, and Simms Hodgson. *The Venture of Islam: Conscience and History in a World Civilization.* Chicago: University of Chicago Press, 1974.

Gramsci, Antonio. *Prison Notebooks.* Vol. 2. New York: Columbia University Press, 1996.

Graziano, Manlio. *Il secolo cattolico: La strategia geopolitica della Chiesa.* Rome: Laterza, 2011.

Greenfeld, Liah. "Nationalism and Terrorism." *Project Syndicate,* September 10, 2012.

Gresh, Alain. "Il y a charia et charia." *Le Monde diplomatique,* August 20, 2012.

Grygiel, Jakub. "The Power of Statelessness," *Policy Review,* no. 154 (April/May 2009): 35–50.

Guardian. "Afghanistan Worst Place in the World for Women, but India in Top Five." June 15, 2011.

——. "The Beauty Obsession Feeding Iran's Voracious Cosmetic Surgery Industry." March 1, 2013.

Guerri, Giordano Bruno. *Gli italiani sotto la Chiesa: Da san Pietro a Mussolini.* Milan: Mondadori, 1995.

Haass, Richard. *The Reluctant Sheriff: The United States After the Cold War.* New York: Council on Foreign Relations, 1997.

Haenni, Patrick. *L'islam de marché: L'autre révolution conservatrice.* Paris: Seuil, 2005.

Halliday, Fred. "Tough Choices for Afghanistan's Regime and Its Opponents." *New York Times,* May 18, 1979.

Hanson, Eric O. *The Catholic Church in World Politics.* Princeton: Princeton University Press, 1987.

Haqqani, Husain. *Pakistan: Between Mosque and Military.* Washington, D.C.: Carnegie Endowment for International Peace, 2005.

Hegel, Georg Wilhelm Friedrich. *The Philosophy of Right.* Translated by S. W. Dale. Kitchener, Ont.: Batoche Books, 2001.

Hesterman, Jennifer. *Soft Target Hardening: Protecting People from Attack.* Boca Raton, Fla.: CRC Press, 2015.

Heuzé, Djallal G. "Évolutions socioreligieuses en Inde." *Revue Tiers Monde,* no. 204 (2010): 147–63.

Hiro, Dilip. *Apocalyptic Realm: Jihadists in South Asia.* New Haven: Yale University Press, 2012.

Holmes, Dave, and Norm Dixon. *Behind the US War on Afghanistan.* Chippendale, New South Wales: Resistance Books, 2001.

Huntington, Samuel. *The Clash of Civilizations and the Remaking of World Order.* New York: Simon & Schuster, 1996.

Ikenberry, John. "The Political Origins of Bretton Woods." In *A Retrospective on the Bretton Woods System: Lessons for International Monetary Reform.* Edited by Michael D. Bordo and Barry Eichengreen, 155–98. Chicago: University of Chicago Press, 1993.

Ilan, Shahar. "Reconciling Conscription." *Haaretz,* April 21, 2008.

Indian Ministry of Home Affairs, National Crime Records Bureau. "Crime in India 2013." http://ncrb.nic.in/.

Interfax. "Eastern Christian Countries Capable of Altering Humankind in 10 Years—Archpriest Chaplin." May 14, 2012.

——. "Religious Factor in International Relations." October 24, 2013.

Jaulmes, Adrien. "Et si la Torah se substituait à la loi israélienne." *Le Figaro*, December 10, 2009.

Jean, Carlo. "Ragione e oscurantismo," *Aspenia*, no. 42 (August 2008): 32–44.

Jemolo, Arturo Carlo. *Chiesa e Stato in Italia negli ultimi cento anni.* Turin: Einaudi, 1948.

Jerryson, Michael K., and Mark Juergensmeyer. *Buddhist Warfare.* New York: Oxford University Press, 2010.

Jewish Federation of North America. "Berman Jewish Databank." http://www.jewishdatabank.org.

Jiao, Wu. "Religious Believers Thrice the Estimate." *China Daily*, February 7, 2007.

John Paul II. *Memory and Identity: Personal Reflections.* London: Orion, 2005.

Jones, Jeffrey M. "In U.S., 3 in 10 Say They Take Bible Literally." *Gallup Poll*, July 8, 2011.

Jordan, Hamilton. *Crisis: The Last Year of the Carter Presidency.* New York: Putnam, 1982.

Kadri, Sadakat. *Heaven on Earth: A Journey Through Shari'a Law from the Deserts of Ancient Arabia to the Streets of the Modern Muslim World.* New York: Farrar, Straus and Giroux, 2012.

Kaplan, Robert D. *The Revenge of Geography: What the Map Tells Us About Coming Conflicts and the Battle Against Fate.* New York: Random House, 2012.

Kennedy, Paul. *The Rise and Fall of the Great Powers: Economic Change and Military Conflict from 1500 to 2000.* New York: Random House, 1987.

Kent, James. *Commentaries on American Law.* Vol. 2. New York: O. Halsted, 1832.

Kent, Peter C., and John F. Pollard. "A Diplomacy Unlike Any Other: Papal Diplomacy in the Nineteenth and Twentieth Centuries." In *Papal Diplomacy in the Modern Age.* Edited by Peter C. Kent and John F. Pollard, 11–22. Westport, Conn.: Praeger, 1994.

Kepel, Gilles. *Jihad: The Trail of Political Islam.* London: I. B. Tauris, 2006.

——. *Muslim Extremism in Egypt: The Prophet and Pharaoh.* Berkeley: University of California Press, 1985.

——. *The Revenge of God: The Resurgence of Islam, Christianity, and Judaism in the Modern World.* Cambridge, Mass.: Polity Press, 1994.

Kertzer, David I. *Prisoner of the Vatican, The Pope's Secret Plot to Capture Rome from the New Italian State.* Boston: Houghton Mifflin, 2004.

Khaldun, Abd Ar Rahman bin Muhammed ibn. *The Muqaddimah.* Translated by Franz Rosenthal. Princeton: Princeton University Press, 2015.

Khan, Inamullah. *Islam in the Contemporary World.* Karachi: Umma, 1967.

Khan, Mirza Abu Taleb. *Travels of Mirza Abu Taleb Khan in Asia, Africa, and Europe, During the Years 1799, 1800, 1801, 1802, and 1803.* Translated by Charles Stewart. London: Broxbourne, Watts, Herst, 1814.

Khosrokhavar, Farhad. "Les paysans dépaysannés et la Révolution iranienne." *Cahiers d'Études sur la Méditerranée Orientale et le Monde Turco-Iranien*, no. 27 (1999): 159–79.

King, Stephen D. *When the Money Runs Out: The End of Western Affluence.* New Haven: Yale University Press, 2013.

Kirill I (Vladimir Michajlovi Gundjaev). "Norme di fede come norme di vita." *L'Osservatore Romano*, May 17, 2010.

Kjellén, Rudolf. *Der Staat als Lebensform*. Berlin: K. Vowinckel, 1924.

Kramer, Andrew E. "Russia Gas Pipeline Heightens East Europe's Fears." *New York Times*, October 12, 2009.

Laurens, Henri. "Le Vatican et la question de la Palestine." In *Nations et Saint-Siège au XXe siècle*. Edited by Hélène Carrère d'Encausse and Philippe Levillain, 303–42. Paris: Fayard, 2000.

Le Bovier de Fontenelle, Bernard. *A Week's Conversation on the Plurality of the Worlds*. Translated by William Gardiner. London: E. Crull in the Strand, 1728.

Le Gendre, Olivier. *Confession d'un cardinal*. Paris: JC Lattès, 2007.

Lelong, Michel. *Les papes et l'islam*. Monaco: Éditions Alphée, 2009.

Lelord, Fraçois. *Hector and the Search for Happiness*. London: Gallic Books, 2010.

Le Monde. "Un collège musulman 'sous le choc' après le refus de l'État de le prendre sous contrat." June 13, 2014.

Le Nouvel Observateur. "Brzezinski: Oui, la CIA est entrée en Afghanistan avant les Russes." *Le Nouvel Observateur*, January 15, 1998.

Lewis, Bernard. *From Babel to Dragomans: Interpreting the Middle East*. Oxford: Oxford University Press, 2004.

——. *Islam and the West*. New York: Oxford University Press, 1993.

——. "Middle Eastern Reaction to Soviet Pressures." *Middle East Journal*, no. 10 (Spring 1956): 125–37.

——. "The Roots of Muslim Rage." *Atlantic Monthly*, vol. 266, no. 3 (September 1990): 47–60.

——. "Targeted by a History of Hatred." *Washington Post*, September 10, 2002.

——. *What Went Wrong? The Clash Between Islam and Modernity in the Middle East*. New York: Oxford University Press, 2002.

Liogier, Raphaël. *Le mythe de l'islamisation: Essai sur une obsession collective*. Paris: Seuil, 2012.

——. *Souci de soi, conscience du monde: Vers une religion globale?* Paris: Armand Colin, 2012.

Looney, Robert E. "The Role of Military Expenditures in Pre-Revolutionary Iran's Economic Decline." *Iranian Studies* 12, no. 3–4 (1988): 52–83.

Luxmoore, Jonathan, and Jolanta Babiuch. *The Vatican and the Red Flag: The Struggle for the Soul of Eastern Europe*. London: Geoffrey Chapman, 1999.

Maalouf, Amin. *Les Croisades vues par les Arabes: La barbarie franque en Terre Sainte*. Paris: Editions Jean-Claude Lattès, 1983.

Mackinder, Halford J. *Democratic Ideals and Reality: A Study in the Politics of Reconstruction*. Washington, D.C.: National Defense University, 1942.

Magister, Sandro. "Tra Roma e Mosca è nata una santa alleanza." March 24, 2010. http://chiesa.espresso.repubblica.it/articolo/1343399.

Mahan, Alfred. *The Influence of Sea Power Upon History*. Cambridge: Cambridge University Press, 2010.

Mahanama-sthavira, Thera. *Mahavamsa: The Great Chronicle of Sri Lanka*. Fremont, Calif.: Asian Humanities Press, 1999.

Mamdani, Mahmood. *Good Muslim, Bad Muslim: America, the Cold War, and the Roots of Terror.* New York: Doubleday, 2004.

Marx, Karl. *Critique of Hegel's Philosophy of Right.* Cambridge: Cambridge University Press, 1970.

——. *Manifesto of the Communist Party.* Rockville, Md.: Manor Thrift, 1980.

Mead, Walter Russell. *God and Gold: Britain, America and the Making of the Modern World.* New York: Knopf, 2007.

Melloni, Alberto. *Chiesa madre, chiesa matrigna: Un discorso storico sul cristianesimo che cambia.* Turin: Einaudi, 2004.

Meotti, Giulio. "Il cantico del prof. Nazir-Ali." *Il Foglio*, September 28, 2008.

Michael, Robert. *A Concise History of American Antisemitism.* Lanham, Md.: Rowman and Littlefield, 2005.

Michas, Takis. *Unholy Alliance: Greece and Milosevic's Serbia.* College Station: Texas A&M University Press, 2002.

Michon, Jean-Hippolyte. *La Papauté à Jérusalem.* Paris: Chez E. Dentu Libraire, 1856.

Micklethwait, John, and Adrian Wooldridge. *God Is Back: How the Global Revival of Faith Is Changing the World.* New York: Penguin, 2009.

Millet, Richard. *Fatigue du sens.* Paris: Pierre-Guillaume de Roux, 2011.

Moe, Kyaw Zwa. "A Radically Different Dhamma." *Irrawaddy*, June 22, 2013.

Moin, Baqer. *Khomeini: Life of the Ayatollah.* London: I. B. Tauris, 1999.

Montes, Luis Francisco Martínez. "The Catholic Origins of Globalization." *Globalist*, June 1, 2012.

Montlake, Simon. "Tiny Bhutan Aims to Become First Smoke-Free Nation." *Christian Science Monitor*, November 24, 2003.

Mottahedeh, Roy. *The Mantle of the Prophet: Religion and Politics in Iran.* Boston: Oneworld, 2000.

Museum of Jewish History. "Databases." http://www.jewishgen.org/databases/.

Muslim Religious Leaders. "Open Letter to His Holiness Pope Benedict XVI." *Islamica Magazine*, October 12, 2006.

Myntti, Cynthia. *Paris Along the Nile: Architecture in Cairo from the Belle Epoque.* Cairo: American University in Cairo Press, 1999.

Nahshoni, Kobi. "Islamization of Europe a Good Thing." *Jewish World*, November 11, 2012.

Nanda, Meera. *The God Market: How Globalization Is Making India More Hindu.* New York: Random House, 2010.

Nardin, Terry. "Review: Terror in the Mind of God, by Mark Juergensmeyer." *Journal of Politics* 63, no. 2 (May 2001): 683–85.

Nasr, Vali. *The Rise of Islamic Capitalism: Why the New Middle Class Is Key to Defeating Extremism.* New York: Free Press, 2009.

National Security Agency. "Special National Intelligence Estimate: Prospects for Further Proliferation of Nuclear Weapons." Last modified August 23, 1974. http://nsarchive.gwu.edu/NSAEBB/NSAEBB240/snie.pdf.

Nazir-Ali, Michael. *Triple Jeopardy for the West: Aggressive Secularism, Radical Islamism and Multiculturalism.* London: Bloomsbury, 2012.

Neau-Dufour, Frédérique, and Ernest Psichari. *L'ordre et l'errance*. Paris: Éditions du Cerf, 2001.

Nebel, Johannes. "Dopo il Concilio fui troppo timoroso." *Corriere della Sera*, October 19, 2007.

New York Times. "Excerpts from Pentagon's Plan: 'Prevent the Re-Emergence of a New Rival.'" *New York Times*, March 8, 1992.

Nietzsche, Friedrich. *The Anti-Christ, Ecce Homo, Twilight of the Idols, and Other Writings*. Cambridge: Cambridge University Press, 2005.

Norris, Pippa, and Ronald Inglehart. *Sacred and Secular: Religion and Politics Worldwide*. New York: Columbia University Press, 2004.

Oddie, William. "Cardinal Conway Was Wrong to Send a Terrorist Priest to Another Parish." *Catholic Herald*, August 25, 2010.

O'Lemmon, Matthew. "Buddhist Identity and the 1973 Cambodian Buddhist Holy War." *Asian Anthropology* 10, no. 1 (2011): 121–38.

Onishi, Norimitsu. "In Indonesia, Islamists Lost Political Ground." *New York Times*, April 24, 2009.

Oren, Michael B. *Six Days of War: June 1967 and the Making of the Modern Middle East*. New York: Presidio Press, 2002.

Pacelli, Eugenio. "Circa la situazione della Santa Sede in Italia." *Limes Rivista italiana di geopolitica*, no. 3 (1993): 109–22.

Pape, Robert. *Dying to Win: The Strategic Logic of Suicide Terrorism*. New York: Random House, 2005.

Partner, Peter. *God of Battles: Holy Wars or Christianity and Islam*. Princeton: Princeton University Press, 1998.

Patelos, Constantin G. *Vatican I et les évêques uniates: Une étape éclairante de la politique romaine à l'égard des orientaux, 1867-1870*. Turnhout, Belgium: Bibliothèque de la Revue d'histoire ecclésiastique, 1981.

Pedahzur, Ami, and Arie Perliger. *Jewish Terrorism in Israel*. New York: Columbia University Press, 2009.

Pew Research Center. "Countries with the Largest Muslim Populations." http://www .pewforum.org/2015/04/02/muslims/pf_15-04-02_projectionstables74/.

Picciotto, Liliana. "The Vatican and the Anti-Jewish Persecution." *Centro Primo Levi Online Monthly*, March 26, 2012. http://primolevicenter.org/printed-matter/the-vatican-and -the-anti-jewish-persecution/.

Pipes, Richard. "Muslims of Soviet Central Asia: Trends and Prospects." *Middle East Journal* 9, nos. 2–3 (Spring–Summer 1955): 147–62.

Pirenne, Henri. *Mohammed and Charlemagne*. New York: Routledge, 2008.

Poliakov, Léon. *De Moscou à Beyrouth: Essai sur la désinformation*. Paris: Calmann-Lévy, 1983.

Pollard, John F. *Money and the Rise of the Modern Papacy: Financing the Vatican, 1850-1950*. Cambridge: Cambridge University Press, 2005.

Psichari, Ernest. *Le voyage du centurion*. Paris: L'Harmattan, 1994.

Qayoumi, Mohammad. "Once Upon a Time in Afghanistan." *Foreign Policy*, May 29, 2010.

Quaroni, Pietro. *Il mondo di un ambasciatore*. Milan: Ferro, 1965.

Rabkin, Yakov M. *Au nom de la Torah: Une histoire de l'opposition juive au sionisme.* Québec: Presses de l'Université Laval, 2004.

Ramaswamy, Sumathi. *The Goddess and the Nation: Mapping Mother India.* Durham: Duke University Press, 2010.

Ratzinger, Joseph. *Europe: Today and Tomorrow.* San Francisco: Ignatius Press, 2007.

——. *Salt of the Earth: Christianity and the Catholic Church at the End of the Millennium. An Interview with Peter Seewald.* San Francisco: Ignatius Pres, 1997.

Ratzinger, Joseph, and Marcello Pera. *Without Roots: Europe, Relativism, Christianity, Islam.* New York: Basic Books, 2006.

Reardon, Patrick J. "JFK and the Cafeteria Bishops: 50 Years After Kennedy Asserted Independence from the Pope, the Tide Has Turned." *National Catholic Reporter,* August 10, 2010.

Reisman, Michael W. "The Resistance in Afghanistan Is Engaged in a War of National Liberation." *American Journal of International Law* 81, no. 4 (October 1987): 906–9.

Rémond, René. *Religion et société en Europe: Essai sur la sécularisation des sociétés européennes aux XIXe et XXe siècles (1789-2000).* Paris: Seuil, 1998.

Revue des Deux Mondes. "La Papauté et la question romaine au point de vue de Saint-Petersbourg." In *Revue des Deux Mondes: Tome V,* 265–82. Paris: Bureau de la Revue des Deux Mondes, 1850.

Rheault, Magali, and Dalia Mogahed. "Majorities See Religion and Democracy as Compatible." *Gallup News Service,* October 3, 2007.

Riccardi, Andrea. "In te, Domine, speravi; non confundar in æternum." *Giorni nella Chiesa e nel mondo,* no. 5 (May 2005): 20–24.

——. "La potenza profonda." *Limes Rivista italiana di geopolitica,* no. 1 (August 2009): 1–12.

Robinson, Geoffrey. "The Post-Coup Massacre in Bali." In *Making Indonesia.* Edited by Daniel S. Lev and Ruth McVey, 118–43. Ithaca: Cornell Southeast Asia Program Publications, 1996.

Rodari, Paolo. "Alle prese con la zona grigia: Perché sui temi bioetici c'è più sintonia con anglicani e ortodossi che con i progressisti." *Il Foglio,* May 26, 2010.

Rodinson, Maxime. *Muhammad.* London: I. B. Tauris, 2002.

Rossi, Joseph S. *Uncharted Territory: The American Catholic Church at the United Nations, 1946-1972.* Washington, D.C.: Catholic University of America Press, 2006.

Roy, Olivier. *The Failure of Political Islam.* London: I. B. Tauris, 1994.

——. *Globalized Islam: The Search for a New Ummah.* New York: Columbia University Press, 2004.

——. *Holy Ignorance: When Religion and Culture Part Ways.* Oxford: Oxford University Press, 2013.

——. *Islam and Resistance in Afghanistan.* Cambridge: Cambridge University Press, 1990.

——. *L'islam mondalisé.* Paris: Seuil, 2002.

Ryan, Alan. *John Stuart Mill.* London: Routledge and Kegan Paul, 1974.

Sacks, Jonathan. "Religion in Twenty-First Century Britain." Annual Theos Lecture, November 4, 2009.

Samuelson, Robert J. "The Shutdown Heralds a New Economic Norm." *Washington Post,* October 14, 2013.

Sand, Shlomo. *The Invention of the Jewish People*. London: Verso, 2009.

Sartre, Jean-Paul. *Anti-Semite and Jew*. New York: Schocken, 1948.

Scalfari, Eugenio. "Papa Francesco a Scalfari: Così cambierò la Chiesa." *La Repubblica*, October 1, 2013.

Schmitt, Carl. *The Concept of the Political*. Translated by George Schwab. New Brunswick: Rutgers University Press, 1996.

——. *Roman Catholicism and Political Form*. Westport, Conn.: Greenwood Press, 1996.

——. *The Tyranny of Values*. Edited and translated by Simona Draghici. Washington, D.C.: Plutarch Press, 1996.

Schwartz, Regina M. *The Curse of Cain: The Violent Legacy of Monotheism*. Chicago: University of Chicago Press, 1997.

Schweig, Graham M. "Foreword." In *Holy War: Violence and Bhagavad Gītā*. Edited by Steven J. Rosen. Hampton, Va.: A Deepak, 2004.

Schweitzer, Yoram. "Suicide Terrorism: Development and Characteristics." *International Institute for Counter-Terrorism*, April 21, 2000.

Sciences Humaines. "Qui sont les fondamentalistes chrétiens?" *Sciences Humaines*, June 15, 2011.

Selengut, Charles. *Sacred Fury: Understanding Religious Violence*. Lanham, Md.: Rowman & Littlefield, 2008.

Sen, Amartya. *Identity and Violence: The Illusion of Destiny*. London: Penguin, 2007.

Shahi, Afshin. "Erotic Republic: Iran Is in the Throes of an Unprecedented Sexual Revolution. Could It Eventually Shake the Regime?" *Foreign Policy*, May 29, 2013.

Sheehan, Michael A. "Terrorism: The Current Threat." Lecture at the Brookings Institution, February 10, 2000.

Sheikh, Zafar Mahmood. "Normalization of Indo-Pak Ties Hurts Kashmir Cause: Salahuddin." *Arab News*, May 30, 2012.

Shorto, Russell. *Saints and Madmen: Psychiatry Opens Its Doors to Religion*. New York: Henry Holt, 1999.

Siavoshani, Zohreh Salehi. "The Role of the Clerics and the Religious Forces in the Iranian Movement of the Nationalization of Oil Industry." *Historia Actual Online*, no. 26 (Fall 2011): 7–19.

Simon, Marcel. *Verus Israel: Les relations entre juifs et chrétiens dans l'empire romain (135–425)*. Paris: E. de Boccard, 1948.

Simpson, William. "The Ten Points of Seelisberg: A Significant Anniversary." *Revue SIDIC*, no. 1 (1977): 21–25.

Smidt, Corwin, Kevin den Dulk, Bryan Froehle, James Penning, Stephen Monsma, and Douglas Koopman. *The Disappearing God Gap? Religion in the 2008 Presidential Election*. New York: Oxford University Press, 2010.

Sowell, Thomas. *Black Rednecks and White Liberals*. New York: Encounter Books, 2005.

Spinelli, Barbara. "Le occasioni perdute dell'euro." *La Stampa*, December 15, 1997.

Spykman, Nicholas. "Geography and Foreign Policy." *American Political Science Review* 32, no. 1 (February 1938): 213–36.

State of Israel. *Israel, the State and the Nation*. Government Yearbook, 5716/1955.

Stehlin, Stewart. "The Emergence of a New Vatican Diplomacy During the Great War and Its Aftermath, 1914–1929." In *Papal Diplomacy in the Modern Age*. Edited by Peter C. Kent and John F. Pollard, 68–84. Westport, Conn.: Praeger, 1994.

Stehly, Ralph. "Le concile de Vatican II (1962–1964) et l'islam." *Orient*. http://stehly.chez -alice.fr/vatican.htm.

Stransky, Thomas. "The Genesis of Nostra Aetate." *America Magazine: The National Catholic Weekly*, October 24, 2005.

Tabarani, Gabriel G. *Jihad's New Heartlands: Why the West Has Failed to Contain Islamic Fundamentalism*. Bloomington, Ind.: AuthorHouse, 2011.

Tchapline, Vsevolod. "Ces dames sont priées d'aller se rhabiller." *Courrier International*, January 27, 2011.

Thompson, Lyric. "The Worst Place to Be a Woman in the G20." *Amnesty International*, June 19, 2012.

Todorov, Tzvetan. *The Fear of Barbarians: Beyond the Clash of Civilizations*. Chicago: University of Chicago Press, 2010.

Trading Economics. "Inflation Rate." http://www.tradingeconomics.com/country-list /inflation-rate.

—. "Military Expenditure (% of GDP) in Egypt." http://www.tradingeconomics.com /egypt/military-expenditure-percent-of-gdp-wb-data.html.

Uberoi, Patricia. "Family, Kinship and Marriage in India." In *Students' Britannica India: Select Essays*. Edited by Dale Hoiberg, 145–56. New Delhi: Encyclopædia Britannica India, 2000.

United Nations Population Division. *World Population Prospects, the 2011 Revision*. http:// esa.un.org/unpd/wpp/publications/Files/WPP2011_HIGHLIGHTS.pdf.

Vahed, Goolam. "Gandhi, Indian Opinion, and the Making of Indo–South African Identity, 1903–14." *Comparative Studies of South Asia, Africa and the Middle East* 35, no. 2 (August 2015): 354–60.

Victoria, Brian. *Zen War Stories*. Abingdon, N.Y.: RoutledgeCurzon, 2003.

Vittachi, Tarzie. *The Fall of Sukarno*. London: Andre Deutsch, 1967.

Walberg, Eric. *Postmodern Imperialism: Geopolitics and the Great Games*. Atlanta: Clarity Press, 2011.

Walker, Martin. *The Cold War and the Making of the Modern World*. London: Fourth Estate, 1993.

Weber, Max. *From Max Weber: Essays in Sociology*. Translated and edited by Hans Heinrich Gerth and Charles Wright Mills. New York: Oxford University Press, 1946.

Webman, Esther. "Adoption of the Protocols in the Arab Discourse on the Arab-Israeli Conflict, Zionism, and the Jews." In *The Global Impact of the Protocols of the Elders of Zion: A Century-Old Myth*. Edited by Esther Webman, 175–95. Abington, N.Y.: Routledge, 2011.

Wells, Steve. *Drunk with Blood: God's Killings in the Bible*. Moscow, Id.: SAB Books, 2010.

Wikipedia. "List of Terrorist Incidents in India." Last modified September 21, 2015. https:// en.wikipedia.org/wiki/List_of_terrorist_incidents_in_India.

Wilson, Nancy L. "Is the Pope Catholic?" *Huffington Post*, February 2, 2013.

Wirsing, Robert G. *Pakistan's Security Under Zia, 1977–1988: The Policy Imperatives of a Peripheral Asian State*. New York: St. Martin's Press, 1991.

World Bank. "Central Government Debt (% of GDP)." data.worldbank.org/indicator/GC.DOD.TOTL.GD.ZS.

——. "Urban Population (% of Total)." http://data.worldbank.org/indicator/SP.URB.TOTL.IN.ZS.

World Council of Churches. "Now We Are Fearless: Facts About Dalit Women." http://www.overcomingviolence.org/en/resources/campaigns/women-against-violence/now-we-are-fearless/dalit-fact-sheet.html.

World Economic Forum. *The Global Gender Gap Report 2013*. http://www3.weforum.org/docs/WEF_GenderGap_Report_2013.pdf.

World Public Forum. "About Us." http://wpfdc.org/about-us/about.

Wynne-Jones, Jonathan. "Britain Has Become a Catholic Country." *Telegraph*, December 23, 2007.

——. "Churches Halt Decline, New Research Shows." *Telegraph*, December 19, 2010.

Yann, Richard. "Ayatollah Kashani: Precursor of the Islamic Republic?" In *Religion and Politics in Iran: Shiism from Quietism to Revolution*. Edited by Nikki R. Keddie, 91–117. New Haven: Yale University Press, 1983.

Zakaria, Fareed. "Culture Is Destiny: A Conversation with Lee Kuan Yew." *Foreign Affairs* 73, no. 2 (March–April 1994): 109–26.

——. *The Post-American World*. New York: Norton, 2008.

Zenit. "La Chiesa cattolica in Russia non segue alcuna strategia di proselitismo." September 8, 2004.

INDEX

RELIGION, CULTURE, AND PUBLIC LIFE

SERIES EDITOR: KATHERINE PRATT EWING

GPSR Authorized Representative: Easy Access System Europe, Mustamäe tee
50, 10621 Tallinn, Estonia, gpsr.requests@easproject.com